Between the Sacred
and the Worldly

Between the Sacred and the Worldly

The Institutional and Cultural Practice
of *Recogimiento* in Colonial Lima

Nancy E. van Deusen

STANFORD UNIVERSITY PRESS, CALIFORNIA   2001

Stanford University Press
Stanford, California
© 2001 by the Board of Trustees of the
Leland Stanford Junior University
Printed in the United States of America

Library of Congress Cataloging-in-Publication Data

van Deusen, Nancy E.
    Between the sacred and the worldly : the institutional and cultural practice of
recogimiento in colonial Lima / Nancy E. van Deusen.
        p.   cm.
    Includes bibliographical references and index.
    ISBN 0-8047-4319-3 (alk. paper)
    1. Women—Institutional care—Peru—Lima—History.   2. Women—
Peru—Lima—Social conditions.   3. Catholic women—Religious life—Peru—
Lima—History.   I. Title.

HV1448.P42 L568   2001
305.42'0985—dc21   2001042865

This book is printed on acid-free, archival-quality paper.

Original printing 2001

Last figure below indicates year of this printing:
10   09   08   07   06   05   04   03   02   01

Typeset at Stanford University Press in 10/12.5 Minion

Publication of this work has been supported by a grant from the Oliver M. Dickerson
Fund. The Fund was established by Mr. Dickerson (Ph.D., Illinois, 1906) to enable the
publication of selected works in American history, designated by the executive
committee of the Department of History of the University of Illinois at Urbana–
Champaign.

FOR NANCY G. AND EDWIN H. VAN DEUSEN

Acknowledgments

I wish to begin by offering special thanks to the archivists and librarians whose careful guidance and vigilance over the materials housed in repositories makes research more pleasurable. In Spain, they include: the staff of the Archivo General de Indias (Seville), the Archivo Histórico Nacional (Madrid), the Biblioteca Nacional (Madrid), the Biblioteca de Zabálburu (Madrid), the Archivo General de Simancas (Simancas); in Lima, Peru, the Archivo General de la Nación, Archivo de la Beneficencia Pública, Archivo Arzobispal, Archivo Franciscano, and Biblioteca Nacional; and in the United States, the hardworking staff at the John Carter Brown Library (Providence), the Lilly Library (Bloomington), the Nettie Lee Benson Latin American Collection (Austin), and the Newberry Library (Chicago). Of these librarians and archivists, I would like to extend my particular gratitude to Laura Gutiérrez and Melecio Tineo Morón at the Archivo Arzobispal, to Ana María Vega at the Archivo Franciscano, to Donald Gibbs at the Benson Latin American Collection, and to Norman Fiering at the John Carter Brown Library.

This project would not have come to fruition without the support of numerous grants. A National Endowment for the Humanities grant in 1995 at the John Carter Brown Library meant that I could cull the marvelous resources of that collection. At Western Washington University, the Bureau for Faculty Research provided ample support in 1996 and 1997, and subvention funds to publish the manuscript. A 1997 American Philosophical Society summer grant enabled me to expand my database of *recogidas*. Finally, I thank the Center for Latin American and Caribbean Studies at my alma mater, the University of Illinois at Urbana-Champaign, for providing summer research money in 1996 that enabled me to use the wonderful library facilities, and the History Department for allocating subvention money from the Oliver M. Dickerson Fund to help defray publication costs. George Mariz, chair of the Department of History at Western Washington University, enthusiastically supported a leave that enabled me to revise the manuscript.

Numerous colleagues offered their insights. Susan Deans-Smith pressed for clarification of the principal arguments, and the book is much stronger as a result. Geoffrey Parker provided unstinting assistance by critiquing numerous drafts over the years. Ken Andrien, who has supported my work since I began my master's program at The Ohio State University in 1978, provided important insights on the book's structure and style. As ever, Nils Jacobsen's incisive comments proved enormously helpful. In addition, critiques offered by David Cahill, Richard Kagan, and his graduate seminar at Johns Hopkins, and my long-time friend and colleague Karen Vieira Powers, also proved essential.

A number of individuals helped turn the manuscript into a book. At Western Washington University, I would like to thank undergraduate assistants Kelly Arnold, Jennifer Gossett, Josh Hayes, and Corrine Winter. At Stanford University Press, I express my gratitude to Norris Pope (sponsoring editor) for his faith in the project; John Feneron (production editor) for his alacrity, clarity, and meticulousness; and Martin Hanft (copy-editor) for his careful editing.

Friends, the staff of life, were bastions in other ways. Those include Clara García Ayluardo, Elisabeth Barnett, Cecilia Danysk, Irene Hickman, Kathleen Kennedy, Stephanie Miller, Preston Schiller, Margarita Suárez, Nathan Snyder, Rafael Varón, and the members of Dance Gallery.

The best is always last. My parents, Nancy G. and Edwin H. van Deusen, have offered me their unconditional love, unwavering support, and champion editorial skills since I first formulated this project in the mid-1980s. It is to them, with all my heart and soul, that I dedicate this book.

Contents

Map and Tables

Preface

Throughout the early modern period, the inhabitants of Spain, Spanish Italy, and colonial Latin American cities knew all about *recogimiento*. Individuals commonly deployed the noun, adjective, and verb in private and public settings and in determining the realms of the sacred and the worldly. This seminal concept formed part of common parlance: it flowed from the pens of ecclesiastical and secular authorities, and was uttered by lovers, mothers, husbands, and daughters.

The term was ubiquitous, its connotations diverse—yet, thus far no one has attempted to study its cultural and linguistic complexities over time. Good reasons explain this neglect. Recogimiento appears in a plethora of convent and hospital records, behavioral and theological tracts, the correspondence of viceroys and archbishops, divorce cases, slave disputes, and beatification papers, making it difficult to gain a clear sense of its precise meanings and varied applications. After years of pursuing the historical development of recogimiento in such a daunting array of data, I determined that its significations fall under three distinct rubrics: a theological concept, a virtue, and an institutional practice. Each one has a different history.

The spiritual praxis or method of recogimiento developed among late-fifteenth- and early-sixteenth-century Castilian mystics and entailed physical isolation or enclosure, a series of stages of meditation on "nothing," and a total denial of one's self to achieve union with God. Francisco de Osuna (1492?–1540?) is credited with developing the mystical tenets of recogimiento; subsequent visionaries, including Teresa de Avila (1515–82) and Luis de Granada (1504–88), also advocated Osuna's theological praxis. Granada's *Libro de la oración*, first published in 1554 and intended for a general audience, was cited in etymological dictionaries as the source of the standard theological definition of recogimiento as a "separation or interior abstraction of all that is earthly in order to meditate or contemplate."[1]

Recogimiento also became a fundamental virtue employed throughout the early modern Hispanic world to denote modest, controlled behavior, enclosure in an institution or the home, and a retiring or quiescent nature. Like the notion of *vergüenza* ("shame," or "modesty"), recogimiento applied more to women than to men and assumed that women's bodies, sexuality, and social freedoms should be controlled.

The word "recogimiento" appeared frequently in behavioral treatises after 1540: beginning with the drastically altered Castilian translation of Françesc Eiximenis's *Lo Llibre de les dones*, as . . . *Carro de las donas.* . . . Other important works included Pedro de Luján, *Coloquios matrimoniales* (1563); Diego Pérez de Valdivia, *Aviso de gente recogida* (1585); Fray Luis de León, *La perfecta casada* (1583); Cristóbal Acosta Africano, *Tratado en loor de las mugeres y de la castidad, onestidad, constancia, silencio y justicia . . .* (1592); and Juan de la Cerda, *Libro intítulado vida política de todos los estados de mugeres* (1599). These authors incorporated recogimiento into their discussions of ideal female conduct and included well-elaborated nuances of the behavioral code while addressing the distinct estates—the *doncella* (virgin), married woman, nun, *beata*, widow, or servant—in separate chapters.[2]

As an institutional practice, recogimiento involved substantial numbers of women and girls called recogidas living voluntarily or involuntarily in convents, in lay pious houses called *beaterios*, in hospitals, or schools.[3] Founded throughout Spain and Latin America, recogimientos served a myriad of functions as schools, asylums, or centers of legal deposit (*depósito*) supported by the Spanish state but often under the guardianship of a religious order. They housed women and girls of different social conditions, from orphans to creole schoolgirls, from prostitutes to mestiza daughters of the conquerors, from destitute to reformed women. They operated as depositories for women called *divorciadas* seeking an annulment or divorce (a permanent separation, with neither party able to remarry). They also served as a temporary residence during a husband's absence, or as prisons or correctional houses. Some functioned as schools. Between 1525 and 1550, recogimientos housed and educated the daughters of the Nahua nobility in Mexico; one hundred years later, they operated as centers of learning exclusively for Spanish and creole elite girls in Lima and Mexico. Finally, recogimientos served as rudimentary religious houses aspiring to become beaterios or convents following receipt of the necessary license (see Appendix A).

The three rubrics of recogimiento as a mystical precept, behavioral norm, and institutional practice developed in significant ways in colonial Lima. For one, Granada's and Avila's work had a tremendous impact upon the interpretations of recogimiento by Lima's lay pious women (beatas) and by nuns during the seventeenth century. Moreover, the torrent of prescriptive literature inspired colonial authorities, married couples, and holy women in Lima to employ recogimiento enunciated in these texts to describe themselves and explain their conduct. Thirty institutions, including all known recogimientos (this book studies each one), housed recogidas, thus demonstrating the diverse institutional applications of the term. Women inclined to live in, seek asylum in, be imprisoned in, be deposited in, be educated in, or to devote themselves to spiritual practices in recogimientos represented a large percentage of Lima's female population, and comprised an entire array of categories of women and girls designated as recogidas.[4]

This monograph examines the development of the gendered discourse of recogimiento in those three interrelated ways during the sixteenth and seventeenth centuries. Its meanings and forms of expression are explored not only in colonial Lima, the principal focus, but also in other sociopolitical landscapes. The book begins in Renaissance Spain and follows the confluences of recogimiento to New Spain once Franciscan friars arrived in 1524. The greater part of the monograph concentrates on Lima between 1535 and 1713, but it also provides a comparative dimension with glimpses of the elaboration of recogimiento in Mexico, Spain, and Spanish Italy.

The Introduction presents major methodological issues to be addressed in the book: the relationship between gender and cultural codes; the significance of institutional practices for urban, colonial history; popular manifestations of Catholicism; and, the process of transculturation, or the adaptation and alteration of cultural practices to local contingencies.

Chapter 1 considers the transculturation of recogimiento—as a spiritual method, as a cultural norm related to females, and as an institutional practice—from Spain to New Spain between 1500 and 1550. The evidence suggests that dissimilar and contentious interpretations of recogimiento held by Spanish friars, beatas, and Nahua parents produced the emergence of a new, distinctly colonial practice of recogimiento. During this period, the theological significations of recogimiento became linked with its expression as a gendered norm of physical enclosure and virtue based upon misogynist assumptions that women were vulnerable, incomplete beings. The humanist advancement of female education and the prevailing influence of beatas in Spain also influenced Franciscan friars responsible for determining educational policies for Nahua children between 1524 and 1550. The semantic contest in New Spain set the stage for future manifestations of recogimiento in Peru as educational centers, as a mystical praxis, and as a behavioral norm.

After midcentury, interpretations of recogimiento continued to adapt to local contingencies as the Peruvian focus shifted to the new generation of mestizos, examined in Chapter 2. Although contact between Spaniards and Andean peoples developed in the 1530s, colonial subjects in Lima (ca. 1535) did not begin to interpret and re-create the ideals and practices of recogimiento until the 1550s.[5] At that time, colonial administrators shifted their attention from native American subjects to focus on *doncellas mestizas*: the second-generation female daughters of Spanish men and Andean women. An exploration of the foundation history of the recogimiento of San Juan de la Penitencia (founded 1553) in Lima, a school for mestizas, illustrates the desire to found institutions that would situate mixed racial groups within the sociopolitical order, a dilemma faced by many colonial societies.[6] Unfortunately, the voices of the doncellas mestizas and their Andean mothers remain silent in undiscovered texts.

Chapter 3 considers the foundation histories of the Casa de Divorciadas (founded 1589) and the Recogimiento de María Magdalena (founded 1592). Both served the divorciadas of Lima—women whose divorce or annulment cases were pending in the ecclesiastical tribunal—as well as those designated as sexually deviant. The chapter denotes a shift in the functional applications of recogimiento after 1580, when Lima officials targeted women considered a threat to the republic as transgressors of appropriate moral and sexual conduct. Mirroring developments in Spain and Italy, recogimiento in Peru acquired a disciplinary dimension that subsumed racial and class differences into socially constructed categories related to sexual purity, deviance, and enclosure. Voluntary and involuntary seclusion served in a variety of instances, ranging from abandonment of the household to the flight of slaves from their master's home, and from parental disputes with their daughters over the choice of a spouse to cases of bigamy, concubinage, and adultery.

Chapter 4 examines the discourse of recogimiento among women involved in divorce and annulment litigation between 1580 and 1650. Required by law to be placed in depósito in recogimientos such as the Casa de las Divorciadas, the testimony of divorciadas raises important issues for gender history. Only rarely do we get the chance to hear the voices of ordinary women and their interpretations of honor, gender, race, and class. Their histories also demonstrate the constant interplay between prescriptive and operative norms of recogimiento. Chapter 5 focuses upon the foundation of a number of schools, including the Recogimiento or Colegio del Carmen (founded 1619), established for daughters of Lima's rapidly growing elite to enhance their social status and marriageability in a competitive market. The patronage of observant convents in the 1640s provided additional social and religious spaces for daughters of the elite. As the cultural dialogue between Spain and Lima matured over the course of the seventeenth century, Lima's Spanish and *criollo* (American-born Spaniard) nouveaux riches reconfigured recogimiento as a spiritual practice and behavioral norm in ways that advanced their interests, but also echoed developments in Spain.

Chapter 6 examines the history of the Recogimiento or Beaterio de las Amparadas (founded 1670), which served a colorful constituency of "made up women": the *penitenciada,* or penitent woman; the *refugiada,* or woman seeking asylum; the wayward or *distraída* female; as well as pious women wishing to "retire from the world."[7] The foundation of the Casa de las Amparadas in 1670 constituted a futile effort to control what was considered an increasingly unruly and uncontrollable "marginal" element of the population, which, in fact, represented a substantial percentage of the female population. The fact that women of all socioeconomic backgrounds considered recogimiento a virtue essential to their self-identity highlights its ubiquity in colonial urban society.

The Conclusion revisits the continuities and diversions in the interpretation of recogimiento among women in Lima between the first and second half of the seventeenth century. It also shows how recogimiento continued to evolve and expand in other Latin American urban centers during the eighteenth century. Ultimately, it considers ways that the study of recogimiento may advance subsequent research on other cultural codes, gender relations, colonialism, and the process of transculturation in the early modern world.

Methodologically, a reconstruction of the cultural and institutional practices of recogimiento has been arduous and lengthy. Extensive trips to six archival repositories in Spain (in Seville, Madrid, and Simancas), six in Lima, and four libraries in the United States convinced me that my principal purpose was to understand recogimiento as an early modern precept in Spain, Italy, and Latin America. My first task, therefore, was to comprehend the innumerable facets and nuances of the word itself.

As I unraveled the semantic threads of recogimiento, I realized that I was touching upon a number of important dimensions of colonial Catholicism. After perusing mystical treatises, hagiographies, spiritual biographies, Inquisition documents, and beatification records, I gained a sense of the shifting renderings of recogimiento as a mystical precept.[8] I also came to two other realizations: first, that many of the topics considered by female mystics—enclosure, the body, and self-containment—mirrored discussions in behavioral manuals for lay women. Second, that the frequent literary, familial, and physical contact between secular and religious women fostered more permeable boundaries between "sacred" and "secular" realms.

Armed with a better sense of the linguistic and cultural complexities of recogimiento, I discovered the linkage between definitions of recogimiento in theological tracts and prescriptive literature. Moral treatises, in particular, disclose social ideals and norms: however, scholars often rely too heavily upon such sources to understand the standards that informed gender relations and patriarchal discourse. They extrapolate ahistorical, synchronic definitions of social ideals (such as honor, virginity, and vergüenza) in these texts, contrasting them against social practices found in ecclesiastical litigation records. This creates a false dichotomy between social ideals and prescriptive norms, on the one hand, and social practices, or "reality," on the other. By considering the same type of source over time, one can detect subtle yet perceptible shifts in the meanings of cultural codes. After examining treatises, sermons, and other prescriptive literature covering a 150-year period, I realized that the "ideal" meanings of recogimiento found in this genre shifted significantly.

This discovery gained further significance when measured against the discourse of secular and ecclesiastical authorities, and the language of ordinary couples found in ecclesiastical litigation records over an equally long period of time. The juxtaposition of sources highlighted the interplay and negotiation between "ideal" and "real" significations in social and cultural practices and how exchanges of meaning occurred among and within different sectors of society.

However, the most difficult task still remained. How might I explain why authorities advocated, and Lima's female population chose, temporary or permanent residence in institutions? How might I understand the thoughts and motivations of the women housed as recogidas in schools, hospitals, convents, beaterios, and recogimientos? The 568 testimonies of individual women that contributed to the final narrative on recogimiento (individual stories, and the sum of their parts) derive from divorce and annulment suits, concubinage records, criminal marriage suits, slave disputes (*causas de negros*), and betrothal cases (see Appendix F for an explanation of my statistical methodology). From the histories of the women and men appearing before the ecclesiastical tribunal I gained a more nuanced understanding of distinct gendered, racial, and class perceptions of recogimiento that could then be compared with other perspectives.

Honing my investigative approach to follow obscure but interesting clues, I then tackled the institutional dimension of recogimiento. I have not yet found a series containing the institutional histories of any of the recogimientos examined in this monograph: the Recogimiento de San Juan de la Penitencia, the Casa de las Divorciadas, the Casa de las Amparadas, and so on. Instead, I consulted an extensive array of proxy documents in three different countries. That proved fortunate, because the qualitative differences between distinct sources enriched and expanded my interpretation of the institutional practices of recogimiento. The discovery that women and girls were recogida—whether legally deposited, seeking asylum, educated, or enclosed for spiritual purposes—in schools, convents, beaterios, and hospitals clarified the functional and ideological connections between secular and religious houses.

As I learned that a recogimiento was both an institution and an institutional practice (for instance, that recogidas lived in hospitals), the universe of the "R word" expanded even further. Clues found in the institutional foundation histories of convents, hospitals, and beaterios in the Archivo de Indias helped me to decipher the motivations and interests of donors and authorities. The correspondence of secular and ecclesiastical officials elucidated what authorities perceived to be problematic, and how they sought to resolve it. At that juncture, other, larger patterns began to emerge. I understood that San Juan de la Penitencia for doncellas mestizas had far more in common with the Casa de las Amparadas than the fact that both were called recogimientos. I began to see why, at a given moment, certain recogimientos targeted specific population sectors. After more analysis I also discovered similar foundation patterns in Quito, Mexico City, Spain, and Spanish Italy. Once the linkage between the three rubrics emerged, I was able to situate recogimiento squarely within the history of the City of Kings, as Lima was usually termed in the colonial period.

An examination of censuses, chronicles, published correspondence, and municipal council records provided an additional reservoir of information to demonstrate sociodemographic shifts. They also afforded subjective renderings of events by authorities, priests, and casual observers and distinguished aspects of recogimiento that remained unique to Lima, and those that replicated larger Latin American and European social and cultural practices.

With research complete, and writing under way, I chanced upon an irksome but heartwarming quotation from Lewis Carroll's *Through the Looking Glass.* With the substitution of "recogimiento" for "glory," the dialogue might summarize how many individuals in colonial society utilized words:

"There's 'glory' for you!" "I don't know what you mean by 'glory,'" Alice said. "I meant, there's a nice knock-down argument for you!" "But 'glory' doesn't mean 'a nice knock-down argument,'" Alice objected. "When *I* use a word," Humpty Dumpty said in a rather scornful tone, "it means just what I choose it to mean—neither more nor less."[9]

Like Alice, I became confused when someone described recogimiento as "religious contemplation" and another related it to a sense of "personal honor." But as I persisted in my quest, I came to realize that—as Humpty Dumpty pedantically observed—words such as *recogimiento* do mean just what people choose them to mean—neither more nor less. It is my hope that this monograph demonstrates the complexities of recogimiento—particularly its significance to women—as well as its overreaching contribution to the history of Hispanic society in general and colonial Lima in particular.

a.   Nra. Sra. del Prado
b.   El Carmen (1643)
c.   Sta. Clara
d.   Hospital de Sta. Ana
e.   Hospital de S. Andrés
f.   Colegio de la Caridad
g.   Hospital de la Caridad
h.   Santa Catalina
i.   Colegio de S. Martín
j.   Las Amparadas (1670)
      Santa Rosa (1708)
k.   La Concepción
l.   S. Joseph
m.   S. Francisco
n.   Cathedral
o.   Viceroy's Palace
p.   Beaterio de Santa Rosa (1669)
      Las Amparadas (1708)
q.   Las Divorciadas (until 1665)
r.   Beaterio de Jesús, María y
      José, Las Capuchinas (1713)
s.   La Encarnación
t.   La Trinidad
u.   Nra. Sra. de Atocha
v.   Carmelitas Descalzas, (1686)
w.   Beaterio de Viterbo
x.   Beaterio de Nerias
      (Trinitarias Descalzas, 1682)
y   Beaterio de Mercedarias
z   San Pedro de Alcantará
1   Beaterio de Copacabana
2   Beaterio de Nazarenas

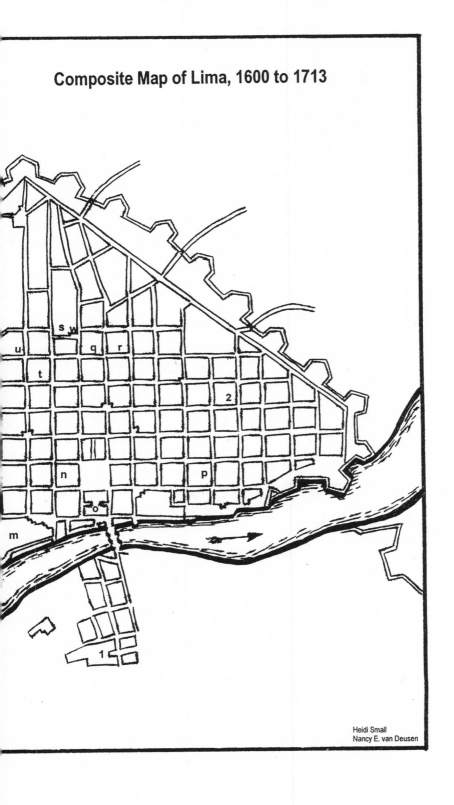

Composite Map of Lima, 1600 to 1713

Heidi Small
Nancy E. van Deusen

Between the Sacred
and the Worldly

Introduction

Recoger. v. 1. To separate oneself or abstract the spirit from all that is earthly or from that which might impede meditation or contemplation. 2. To separate oneself from excessive communication and contact with people. 3. To retire to a specific location. 4. To bring together or congregate things or people who are dispersed. 5. To provide asylum. 6. To place oneself in retreat. 7. To withdraw from the world.

Recogerse. v. 1. To still the senses or the "self." 2. To gather within the self in an act of mental prayer.

Recogimiento. n. 1. A house of spiritual retreat. 2. A house of women called recogidas. 3. A covered shelter extending from a wall, a house or barn for beggars or mendicants. 4. A house for women founded for a specific purpose, and to house them on either a voluntary or involuntary basis. 5. A school. 6. Quiescent conduct. 7. A practice of contemplation.

Recogida. n. 1. A woman who retires to a particular house, on a voluntary or involuntary basis. 2. A divorciada, or woman in the process of getting a divorce. 3. A beata, or lay pious woman.

Recogida/o. adj. 1. Virtuous. 2. Self-contained. 3. Enclosed. 4. Moral.[1]

The twenty-three early modern dictionary definitions and popular renderings listed above reflect the inexactitude of any precise one-word English translation for the word "recogimiento."[2] Linguistic elusiveness stems, in part, from the fact that the term developed distinct usages over time and, like two other key cultural concepts commonly employed in the early modern Spanish colonies—honor and *vergüenza* (modesty or shame)—it acquired a variety of new meanings alongside the old.[3] It is precisely the richness and diversity of connotations evidenced by the definitions above and echoed in the Hispanic world that makes the study of recogimiento so rewarding and so necessary.

By examining the cultural and institutional manifestations of a central Hispanic notion over a broad expanse of time and space, it is possible to trace how all three rubrics of recogimiento—a theological concept, a virtue, and an institutional practice—were redefined and reconstituted as they moved from one historical moment and location to another. It is also possible to add to our knowledge of four essential but undeveloped aspects of Latin American social and cultural history: the fundamental relationship between language and cultural practices; how gender is constituted through language and social relations; the importance of institutions and institutional practices in the lives of colonial subjects; and how to detect changes in the cultural relationship both among the inhabitants of a particular urban milieu, and between Spain and her colonies.

Language and Culture

To elucidate the spatial and temporal changes in the concept of recogimiento, I have charted an etymological-historical course, inspired by German scholar Reinhart Koselleck's concept of *begriffsgeschichte*—the analysis of the changing meanings of concepts over time.[4] Koselleck's method considers how concepts form a subsidiary part of social life, and concludes that a survey of the "space of meaning" of a given concept forms an essential aspect of historical analysis.[5] I have extended Koselleck's methodology to include linguistic, institutional, and cultural forms of expression within my examination of the "space of meaning" of recogimiento. In particular, my work emphasizes the dialogue between ideal, normative, and individual interpretations of recogimiento inherent in official discourse and conjugal politics. For instance, Spanish behavioral treatises recommended that married women remain indoors as much as possible. Ecclesiastical authorities in Lima reconfigured that axiom as a normative practice that applied to women seeking divorces, who were required to remain enclosed throughout the litigation. Depending upon the circumstances, the recogidas themselves might see enclosure as restoring, destroying, or protecting their honor and sense of well-being.

The ideas of Raymond Williams have also proved particularly useful. Williams argued that language and meanings (both neologisms and residual forms), and the process of creating and re-creating interactive discourse, are integral to larger processes, which he defined as residual, dominant, and emergent historical "phases" or epochs. A residual practice or concept is one formed in the past that remains active in the present culture; a dominant practice pervades present reality; and an emerging practice is in the process of becoming.[6] Like Koselleck, Williams examined how cultural expressions change according to time and place, but he also emphasized the interaction among his three stages. Following Williams, I argue that the etymological evolution of recogimiento was nonlinear, and that the conceptual interpretations and practices of recogimiento often retained atavistic characteristics. Residual meanings of recogimiento combined with emergent and dominant applications, and clear epochs, or shifts in meaning and discourse occurred.

The ideas of Koselleck and Williams thus help to map the relationship between language and cultural change over time. However, in order to transcend a strictly etymological study of recogimiento it is important to construct the links between gendered moral ideals and social practices—and, to demonstrate how ideal behavioral models translated into institutional practices and vice versa—as well as how the foundation of institutions for women reflected and reified particular cultural standards. I seek to trace the dialectical relationship between ideals and practices in institutional foundations, in forms of religious expression, and in social interactions between men and women. An analysis of the concept of recogimiento is particularly useful in that regard, because it embodied all three rubrics and is evident in a wide variety of texts.

Social ideals as expressed in language and institutional "practices" also form part of the larger discourses of power and knowledge discerned by Michel Foucault.[7] Foucault's vision is useful to explore the dynamics of different discourses at play in institutional policies, conjugal relations, and women's relationships to themselves and others, and how they change over time. Practices can be defined as modes of expression that evidence logic, strategy, evidence, and reason, and might include institutions such as the law, brick-and-mortar edifices, the political system, and the family. Each practice is located within a particular discursive field, or the intersection between language, social institutions, subjectivity, and power. Discourses are expressions of those discursive fields; they reproduce and sustain dominant forms of power through language and social practices.[8]

Like Foucault, I seek to chart the course of institutional foundations, practices, and discourses that had multiple points of origin and remained complex, often dissonant. In addition, my work strives to locate the heterogeneous chorus of female voices and their experiences submerged "a little beneath history."[9] It explores changes in the expression of their subjectivity—neither unified nor fixed—through language, and examines how they relate to dominant discourses about gender and recogimiento, also surprisingly mutable and cacophonous.

Like much of recent scholarship, the methodology utilized in this monograph attempts to bridge cultural history and social history. It is a social history, in that it focuses upon a particular group—women—in a specific setting—the viceregal capital of Lima; and it employs poststructural methods to show how meanings are constituted through language and social practices. This approach, I hope, sheds important, new light on the dynamics of colonial gender history and on cultural history in general.

Gender Relations and Cultural Codes

Studies of cultural codes have blossomed in the past fifteen years. Scholars have examined sociolinguistic changes of concepts such as honor, *hidalguía* ("nobility"), or even *calidad* ("social worth," or "status"), over time, both in the Mediterranean and in Latin America.[10] For instance, the important works of Ann Twinam and María Emma Mannarelli consider illegitimacy in relation to sexuality, honor, and gender.[11] Nevertheless, although they have demonstrated the existence of female notions of honor, we need further studies that explore how the meanings and interpretations of gendered cultural codes evolved, changed, and were negotiated in various contexts.[12] Twinam's work demonstrates that cultural concepts such as honor should not be transplanted casually from their Mediterranean setting to colonial Latin America, nor should differences of gender, race, and class be ignored.[13] The same is true of recogimiento.

Like honor, recogimiento lay at the heart of interpersonal relationships. When women in colonial Lima, the entry point for metropolitan values for the viceroyalty, described themselves in their testimonies, they often linked the adjective "recogida" with the terms "honor" or "virtue." In doing this, they maintained their own sense of moral self-preservation. For instance, in 1680, Doña Theresa Gutiérres requested an ecclesiastical divorce from her husband. In her own defense, she described herself as "always living in perpetual enclosure, recogimiento and virtue."[14] In the case of Theresa and many other women, female interpretations of honor and recogimiento did not derive solely from public scrutiny and the lover's or husband's patriarchal assumptions of the need to control women's sexuality and disorderly conduct.[15] Through dialogue, men and women constituted and reconstituted gender codes, and in doing so, created new possibilities of expression.[16] Both men and women framed and expressed moral ideals in terms of self-identification and in relation to their partner.[17] In their testimonies in ecclesiastical litigation records—the core archival source used in this book—women claimed recogimiento as integral to their public (nonenclosed), familial, and internal identities. Language, for both men and women, served as a weapon: as both a subjugating device and a tool of empowerment.[18]

In Latin American Studies it is often difficult to distinguish gendered practices from those related to race and class—and indeed from the nature of colonialism itself.[19] Yet it must be done. As Irene Silverblatt has pointed out, "[G]ender itself is fractured by social dimensions—of class and colony, of race and ethnicity."[20] As a moral term to judge oneself or others, recogimiento encoded various distributions of power and prestige as well as different sociolegal distinctions. Yet it also served as a cultural value shared by *limeña* women of various racial classifications and economic backgrounds. Contrary to current orthodoxy, women of nonelite status living in urban environments perceived themselves as honorable, recogida, and virtuous, just like the daughters and granddaughters of the conquerors.[21] Precisely because women and men employed the term so often, it provides an important tool with which to decipher cultural representations of inequality and difference.

An exploration of the various gendered expressions of recogimiento among women and men, rich and poor, enslaved and free, Spanish and mulatta, serves to highlight racial and class distinctions without resorting to preconceived categorical interpretations of the meaning of race, *casta*, or class. The slippery use of racial terminology should alert colonial Latin Americanists to the historically specific nature of the construction of racial terminology and, particularly, of "mestizo" and "*mestizaje*." Understanding colonial racial constructs involves utilizing contemporary conceptualizations, instead of accepting—as many do—a teleological, nineteenth-century rendering of racial terminology.[22] Concerns with moral and sexual "identities" were also contextual and plural: because a woman could be simultaneously recogida, widowed, a mestiza, a food-seller, *de calidad*, well-dressed, and literate. Racial and class constructs remained relational to other cultural codes and expressions of power.[23]

Subjectivity presents another irksome problem. Some feminist scholars have questioned Foucault's notions of power and knowledge, which, he argued, shaped a "subject" from the top down. Instead, they emphasize subjectivity and examine where resistance and the expression of distinct identities can occur.[24] Jana Sawicki postulates that social interactions are "a dynamic, multidimensional set of relationships containing possibilities for liberation as well as domination," and that resistance and struggle can occur between and within subjects.[25] More specifically, Steve Stern's study of violence in eighteenth-century Mexico shows that women's responses seldom fell within the conformity/deviance paradigm that pervades contemporary gender analysis.[26] This monograph confirms Stern's model and also demonstrates that Lima's ecclesiastical and secular authorities served as interlocutors in shaping often incongruous and ambivalent colonial policies; and that women and their spouses, as well as daughters and their fathers and mothers, fashioned their own gendered codes within accessible cultural and institutional spaces.[27]

Above all, early modern women were more likely than men to be targeted as socially deviant, because the dominant discourses of the time considered females as aberrant or defective by nature. They were thought to have more of a "natural" proclivity toward piety, and to be too weak to withstand evil. Julia Fitzmaurice Kelly's pioneering work examined sixteenth-century behavioral treatises to determine attitudes toward women. She quotes Cristóbal Acosta Africano's disparaging sentiments from a 1592 popular tract:

Weak for good and potent for evil, credulous, inconstant and timorous, vehement in her desires whether for good or ill, insatiable in her craving for admiration, addicted to idle talk, of limited capabilities and lacking in judgment, impatient of advice and unable to keep counsel.[28]

Whether women inherently possessed such negative characteristics remained a matter of considerable debate among moralists and secular and ecclesiastical authorities. However, such assumptions did influence the accepted principle of patriarchal authority, based upon the "natural" authority of the male over children and wives expressed in legal precepts.[29]

Admittedly, contemporaries' disapproving notions of the "feminine" influenced conceptualizations of recogimiento. On the one hand, the term maintained strong negative gender connotations related to perceptions of women and femaleness; on the other, its linguistic ambiguities also served to emancipate women.[30] Both religious and secular women reacted to the disparate gendered discourses of recogimiento by creating their own meanings and applications of the concept based upon their own realities and the realities inscribed upon them. In turn, the encounters between couples could reflect the disjunctures between their own experiences and the categories of power and knowledge with which they were familiar.[31]

Often, women internalized the generally held assumption of female inferiority, but found a whole skein of forms by which to express their submissiveness.[32] The complexities of both negative and positive gender constructions enabled women to find "spaces" to question and negotiate meanings.[33] In the context of conjugal disputes debated in the ecclesiastical courtroom, women used the ambiguous, richly textured concept of recogimiento to their advantage. They questioned the acceptability of abuse in their marriages and, in doing so, redetermined the meanings of virtue. The discursive practices of recogimiento revealed the heterogeneous ways in which women, whether from an elite or poor background, constituted their identities.[34] Moreover, their interpretations of cultural codes did not represent deviant conduct: they reflected ordinary attitudes of ordinary people.

Institutional Practices

Although "space" should be seen as discursive and linguistic, and constituted through gendered struggles over power and knowledge, it is also "important to consider the ways in which different epistemological claims about women's identity produce different interpretations about 'physical' space itself."[35] The construct of recogimiento—as a racial marker, as an indicator of sexual deviance or purity, and as an attribute of quiescence and virtue—applied to women who strove for self-respect and power. What operated on a daily, informal level carried over into formal institutional applications. A mestiza, literate, or widowed woman assimilated recogimiento, whether outside or inside an institutional setting.

I accept Foucault's emphasis on the critical importance of understanding that dividing practices or discourses classify, stigmatize, "normalize," and discipline individuals through institutional confinement.[36] However, this book stresses the conjunction between informal (noninstitutional, but replicating dividing practices) and formal institutional practices. The logic that espoused informal female enclosure in the home and self-control often translated into a rationale for founding institutions to house women on a formal, legal basis. Both informal and formal practices of recogimiento formed the crucible, the vessel of tension and transformation in colonial life. Moreover, the interpretations of individual women and institutions formed part of a continuum of shifting meanings and practices of recogimiento.[37] Institutions selected and channeled women by identifying them as sexually and socially marginal: labeling them as wayward, repentant, or lost. Such public, institutional categories were neither arbitrary nor spurious: they reflected social and cultural tensions in evidence throughout the urban setting of colonial Lima.

The noun "recogimiento" refers to enclosure and institutional practices, but it had another related meaning. This monograph studies all existing institutions called recogimientos in colonial Lima, and in doing so attempts to illustrate that recogimientos and other types of secular and religious institutions for women and girls—namely, convents, beaterios, hospitals, and schools—shared similar functional and ideal characteristics.[38] Connections can be seen in the categories of women and girls who inhabited these institutional spaces, and by the fact that transferal from one institution to another became a common practice. Consider, for example, the case of Inés de la Rosa in 1707. Raised from childhood in the Monasterio de Santa Catalina, Inés sought refuge in the Hospital de Santa Ana because her husband had beaten her when she accused him of adultery. After she left him, the ecclesiastical court then deposited her in the Casa de las Amparadas.[39]

Most important, all institutions for women—whether secular or religious—reproduced the shifting norms that reinforced racial, economic, and sexual hierarchies of difference in colonial society. For example, convents determined three ranks of female religious based upon criteria of race and economic status. Nuns of the black veil (generally Spanish) held the most prestigious rank; those of the white veil were either creoles or mestizas; and the *donadas*, who worked as religious servants, were all casta, black or Indian women. Those recogimientos operating as schools distinguished female entrants by race; others, such as the Casa de Divorciadas, accepted women according to the kind of sexual indiscretion or crime committed, and whether they had experienced abuse, abandonment, or economic deprivation. The Hospital de la Caridad (founded 1569) also served as a legal depository for women and girls, and treated wealthy Spanish women differently from the women of color who generally served as laborers.

What occurred within institutions often reproduced patterns in secular society. Asunción Lavrin, a pioneer scholar studying female religious, emphasizes the socioeconomic and political connections between the "world behind the walls" and society at large.[40] Other works examine the connections between convents and the colonial economies in Spain and Brazil, and Kathryn Burns's recent monograph examines various dimensions of the "spiritual economy" in colonial Cuzco.[41] Her careful study documents—among other things—the credit networks and capital investments made by nuns and lay persons. Such contributions certainly contextualize convents within larger social, cultural, and economic matrices, but it is im-

portant to go beyond this material paradigm and explore the linkages between
spiritual and secular practices inside and outside secular and religious institutional
settings.

It is also important to provide an in-depth exploration of the cultural values that
informed the spiritual economy prevailing in early modern Latin America. Unrav-
eling the tapestry of investments—in the form of loans, legacies, or endowments—
and examining exactly who lived *dentro del cerco de los muros,* or within the circle of
walls, provides only a partial understanding of post-Tridentine Catholicism. What
cultural codes influenced individuals investing their capital and their lives? What
spiritual notions of God, charity, recogimiento, the afterlife, and individual or collective piety informed their decisions? It is my hope that an examination of one
such cultural code—recogimiento—in one colonial capital, Lima, may enhance
our understanding of the sacred within the worldly, and vice versa.

A consideration of six recogimientos founded in Lima and the hundreds of
women and girls who passed through them validates three hypotheses about secular and religious institutions. First, it contributes to the debate on whether recogimientos shared many of the sacred and worldly qualities evident in more formal
religious houses. Studies of Latin American institutions for women generally consider convents, beaterios, or recogimientos as distinct institutional phenomena.[42]
In fact, they were often linked both demographically and functionally. European
scholars, by contrast, have argued that pre-Tridentine convents were multifunctional and served as a prototype from which other secular institutions, such as asylums and correctional houses, evolved after the Council of Trent ended in 1563. A
study of Italian institutions argues that one of the oldest forms of institutional life,
the convent, served a wide variety of functions, and, at the same time, engendered
other institutional offshoots for women, such as schools, asylums, correctional facilities, and lay pious houses.[43] Evidence suggests that many secular and religious
houses in Lima (including recogimientos) were multifunctional. Their adaptable
and versatile nature reflected the changing needs of the viceregal capital's female
populace, and, in many ways, replicated pre-Tridentine institutional practices.

Second, the study of recogimientos offers a methodology with which to chart
the various attempts by colonial authorities to create a social order and define, at
given historical moments, what was viewed as aberrant and disorderly conduct
based upon ideals of the sacred (pure, holy) and the worldly (impure, sinful).[44] Recent studies of prisons and asylums in early modern Europe have examined
changes in punishment and discipline within a larger historical context.[45] In post-
Tridentine Italy, an entire range of institutions founded to manage deviant and
potentially deviant females formed part of a general Counter-Reformation campaign aimed at controlling and reforming corrupt and needy women.[46] A study of
recogimientos in Lima shows that perceptions of "aberrant" female conduct

changed dramatically between 1535 and 1713 and often shifted in tandem with current discourses in Europe.

Third, Latin American scholars have so far viewed recogimientos as serving either protective or correctional purposes, but not both. According to Josefina Muriel de la Torre, an expert on Mexican religious institutions and culture:

> Recogimientos can be classified into two types: those that protected and helped women, and those that imprisoned them. The first type was voluntary, and the second received women who were punished because they had been sentenced by diverse tribunals throughout New Spain.[47]

Evidence from Lima suggests that this is incorrect: most recogimientos served simultaneously to punish and discipline, and to protect or provide an atmosphere propitious to spiritual development.[48] In spite of the increased attempt to distinguish the boundaries of the sacred and worldly in institutional spaces, and to differentiate among the holy and wanton women who inhabited them, an obfuscation in the functional differences between religious and secular houses for women gradually occurred. By 1700, beatas lived with prostitutes in recogimientos; and nuns, schoolgirls, and abandoned women coexisted in convents.

In examining institutional practices over time in Lima, it is possible to plot changes in perceptions of social deviance and in attempts to control and promote ideals of social order. But institutions such as recogimientos did not serve only as a means to control the lives of individuals. Other motivations—piety, the search for a peaceful life, or the possibility of an escape valve—also determined the interplay of social dynamics in the colonial, Catholic limeño world. Institutions served as separate religious spheres, or as an antidote to a destructive family situation. They presented an option, a spatial alternative; a woman dissatisfied with her marriage knew that she could enter that space as a protective haven.

Sociologist Anthony Giddens has argued that most individuals conceive of themselves in relation both to real and ideal spaciotemporal settings. His ideas can be applied to colonial Lima, where each day most individuals followed routine pathways. Once a woman's life path altered—whether from marital discord, abandonment, death, or poverty—temporary or permanent residence in an institution became an option to consider. A woman's understanding of what constituted her physical and emotional habitat thus expanded. By the end of the seventeenth century the "institutional possibility" had become a normal choice within the realm of a woman's understanding of her spaciotemporal world.[49]

Colonial Catholicism

Recognizing the roles that secular and religious institutions played in the lives of individuals also involves a comprehension of different perceptions of the sacred and the worldly within the backdrop of the early modern Catholic Church and the reforms of the Council of Trent (1545–63). A number of studies of colonial Peru attempt to situate its history within that broad structural framework. For instance, the work of Rubén Vargas Ugarte provides an overview of the formation of a post-Tridentine Church in Peru.[50] Other scholars explore the role the diocesan clergy, the Inquisition, and idolatry campaigns played in eradicating unorthodox practices, and, more recently, how the veneration of particular local saints, such as Santa Rosa and San Martín de Porras, fostered the growth of popular Catholicism in Lima.[51] Still, we are just beginning to understand popular interpretations of prescriptive norms and theology and how individual women and church authorities in Peru responded to Tridentine mandates that attempted to regulate sexuality, sin, and morality.[52]

This study of recogimiento aims to increase our knowledge of how colonial subjects interpreted their visions of the sacred and the worldly in sixteenth- and seventeenth-century Lima. In its examination of the worldly realm, the book details distinct perceptions of behavioral norms and, particularly, of recogimiento as a virtue. It shows why "worldly" women thought they were moral, or why they deserved to reside in sacred spaces such as convents. Conversely, the book shows how convents fought to keep "worldly" women out. It argues for a range of expressions of Catholic piety in both religious and lay sectors of society—even among ecclesiastical and secular authorities—that could compete or coexist.[53] It also situates the expressions of spirituality and recogimiento in Lima within the context of pre- and post-Tridentine Catholicism in other Latin American cities, as well as in Spain and its Italian possessions.

A study of recogimiento also enhances our understanding of how popular interpretations of the sacred changed. As a theological practice, recogimiento emerged as a method of contemplative prayer and direct union with God in pre-Tridentine Spain, where such mystical practices received tremendous support. As the parameters of spiritual expression narrowed after 1540, however, many holy women in the peninsula suffered in the climate of suspicion and censorship that eventuated. In Mexico, too, between 1524 and 1550, beatas were caught in the crossfire, as interpretations of orthodox forms of female sanctity shifted and affected their role in the education of Nahua girls. Eventually the post-Tridentine repression of mystical doctrine in Spain led to an epochal shift in Peru. By the 1620s, holy women interested in founding observant convents in Lima reinterpreted recogimiento as institutional enclosure, withdrawal from the worldly, oral prayer, and physical discipline. Concurrent with the now dominant, more conservative expression of recogimiento in Spain and Lima, others continued to define and encode their mystical experiences of recogimiento or union with God within acceptable, nonthreatening parameters. Holy women tended to emphasize more tangible aspects of their mystical experiences, and to express their divine experiences within religious houses. Even in Spain and its Italian possessions, authorities eventually had to acknowledge that mysticism had found a "natural" place within Catholicism.[54]

The Colonial Context

Another central premise of this book is that the cultural and institutional practices of recogimiento epitomize the colonial relationship between Lima and Spain. The City of Kings, although a colonial capital, faced the same problems confronting most settler colonial cities: high mortality rates, miscegenation, and intense migration.[55] In addition, Spanish women in colonial Lima also shared some of the same problems of female colonizers in other colonial settings.[56] Native Andean women faced similar circumstances of physical violence, confrontation, and adaptation as indigenous women experiencing conquest and colonization elsewhere.[57] Furthermore, most Latin American colonial cities tended to develop similar cultural values and ideologies despite their isolation from Spain and from each other, while urban inhabitants throughout the continent, particularly nonelites, developed their own internal dynamic sense of class relations.[58]

By virtue of being a viceregal capital, Lima served as a crucible for intercultural contact, and embodied Spanish elite culture and government. Therefore, it displayed some unique characteristics. Nevertheless, like other Latin American cities, it constituted a major magnet for migrants, employed large numbers of enslaved Africans, and attracted Spanish businessmen and members of ecclesiastical corporations interested in their own commercial fortunes.[59] The distance from Spain meant that elites in Lima developed their own agenda.[60] Gender relations and opportunities for women in Lima both emulated and diverged from Iberian patterns.[61] Until the seventeenth century, males outnumbered females, but after the 1630s, the balance began to shift dramatically.[62] By 1700, Spanish and mestiza women outnumbered their male counterparts by 16 percent; and Lima had three mulattas and black women for every mulatto and black man.

TABLE 1

Composition of Different Ethnic Groups according to the 1700 Census

	Men	%	Women	%
Spanish & Mestizo	4,588	42.0	6,288	57.9
Indian	1,277	45.8	1,506	54.1
Mulatto	367	21.7	1,323	78.1
Black	169	26.0	428	74.3

SOURCE: Pérez Cantó, *Lima en el siglo XVIII*, 54. Pérez Cantó's analysis is based upon a sample of 15,970 inhabitants from the 1700 *Numeración general*.

By the advent of the eighteenth century, the City of Kings had become a city of women!

Because of the specific cultural and demographic configuration of Lima, colonial administrators faced a number of internal tensions in their policy-making decisions, some of which involved determining gendered policies and practices of recogimiento toward women that differed significantly from those of Spain. For one, institutional enclosure in Peru involved a broader constituency of females. Several distinguished among particular racial groups (mestizos) or elites (creoles); others were multifunctional, accepting girls involved in betrothal disputes and divorciadas, criminals, and the needy. A study of recogimiento provides an important vantage point from which to analyze the role of ordinary women in the construction of Lima's social history: a history that changed remarkably between 1535 and 1713. It also helps to clarify our understanding of the historical transformations of the cultural relationship between Lima and the metropolis.

Transculturation and Recogimiento

Finally, the study of recogimiento, like that of any other important cultural concept, offers a precise scale by which to measure the process of transculturation. Cuban scholar Fernando Ortíz coined the neologism "transculturation" in *Contrapunteo cubano del tabaco y el azúcar* (1940) as a response to then current anthropological attempts to explain cross-cultural interactions, and as a substitute for the term "acculturation," which he found inadequate.[63] Ortíz disagreed with the idea that one culture passively adapts (acculturates) the tenets of another. Rather, he believed that "the result of every union of cultures is similar to that of the reproductive process between individuals: the offspring always has something of both parents but is always different from each of them."[64] To him, transculturation was an historical *process* that affirmed the reciprocal influences between cultures and the ongoing, dynamic interactions between complex systems that constantly reconfigured meanings and relations of power through social relations.[65]

I have refined and incorporated Ortiz's term "transculturation" into my own arguments about the colonial experiences of women in colonial Lima. Throughout the monograph, the term "transculturation" will be used to signify the process of reshaping the tenets of one culture according to local contingencies. In this instance, it involves studying the transformation of one Iberian cultural code. Understanding this process is complicated by the fact that it does not involve the interaction between cultural "wholes," such as "Iberian," "American," and "African" values. Each culture maintained discordant, ambiguous, and sometimes contentious interpretations of distinct cultural codes and practices. In the case of Spain—the colonizing power—official discourse often differed radically from what church authorities and individual men and women thought. Such discrete articulations of recogimiento formed an integral aspect of the historical convergence that occurred once different cultures began to interact and give their own interpretations of theology, the meaning of virtue, or the purposes of institutions. Thus, the introduction of the complex Spanish concept of recogimiento to American peoples did not mean that a particular peninsular value crystallized into a single ethic with clearly established parameters that dispersed uniformly throughout the continent. The cultural conquest involved American, African, *and* Spanish individuals questioning, probing, and reformulating this Iberian concept within a variety of contexts.

This initial contact had important consequences for recogimiento. For one, colonial subjects adapted the concept to specific local contingencies. On the one hand, an archbishop or viceroy serving in Lima might reconfigure the application of recogimiento in deciding only to allow particular women in an institution. For instance, in 1604, Viceroy Velasco specified that the Recogimiento de la Magdalena should incarcerate "pernicious and insolent women" (see page 70 below). On the other hand, an anguished mulatta appearing before the ecclesiastical tribunal might identify herself as virtuous (recogida), while expressing her desire to live apart from her husband. Both practices of recogimiento were unique to the colonial urban context of Lima, given its demographic configuration and financial constraints. On another level, colonial authorities and limeñas of all social ranks generated new renderings and nuances of recogimiento—in language, behavior, and prescriptive ideals—that might lead to broader changes within the viceregal capital, or elsewhere. Accordingly, understanding the process of transculturation illuminates the colonial relationship because it delineates the complexities of cultural "exchanges" on a variety of levels.[66]

It also resonates in another way. Transculturation continued throughout the colonial period and involved a close transatlantic cultural dialogue between Spain's European and American subjects as the meanings and practices of recogimiento shifted over time and place. Thus, a model of transculturation as a cultural dialogue resembles that of a DNA molecule—a double helix—in which two spirals intersect at a number of discrete points and yet retain their own identity. The bond that unites the two spirals is a shared cultural tradition, and yet includes within that structure the residual, dominant, and emergent practices discerned by Raymond Williams.[67]

Another hypothesis postulates transculturation as a nonlinear temporal and spatial historical process. The nuances of cultural codes like recogimiento are most often actualized in an interactive social context. Language adapts and is modified as emergent, dominant, and residual manifestations of a term coincide. For instance, theological renderings of recogimiento dominant in the 1520s in Spain and New Spain did not emerge again in Peru until 1600; moreover, at a given historical moment in Lima, women of different *calidades* and stages in their life cycle simultaneously manifested the practice of recogimiento as a behavioral norm in distinct, and sometimes incongruous, ways.

No cultural code should be considered in isolation from the transculturation process of other precepts and practices. Renderings of other cultural norms that interacted with and influenced interpretations of recogimiento were not static. The meanings of recogimiento shifted relative to the prevalence or dominance of other cultural constructs at a given historical moment. During the first half of the sixteenth century, concerns over native religious and moral practices were later supplanted by a preoccupation with racial markers (such as defining the mestizo or mulatto), connotations of class associated with illegitimacy, "vagabondage" or poverty, and later still (in the wake of the Tridentine reforms), sexual behavior. These epochal shifts in discourse impacted upon the reconfiguration of recogimiento in official policies and conjugal politics.

In sum, an exploration of the transculturation process of recogimiento affords the scholar a means to understand how conceptual notions changed in new contexts while maintaining an interactive dialogue between colony and colonizing power. A sixteenth-century literary example may help to illustrate this point further. In 1555 a Spanish priest named Pedro de Quiroga composed four dialogues based upon his experiences in the viceroyalty of Peru. His *Coloquios de la verdad* (*Colloquies of Truth*) provided a bitter denunciation of the conquest and forced evangelization that had occurred throughout the previous two decades. The two main characters in Quiroga's work, Justino and Barchilon, attempted in their dialogue to come to terms with the difficulties of living on the margins of Iberian and Andean society. The worldly-wise Barchilon cautioned the more quixotic Justino about his desire to stay in the new, strange land: "[If] you are to stay," he warned Justino, "you must forget everything you thought you knew at home." "Just open your eyes," he added, "everything is the reverse of what it is in Castile. . . . Here there can be no exchange, no direct substitution." After reflecting upon the matter, Justino agreed and replied, "[C]ertainly this land weakens the judgment, disturbs the spirit, harms and corrupts good customs, engenders unfamiliar conditions, and creates in men effects contrary to those which they previously had."[68]

Like the imaginary literary characters of Justino and Barchilon, most Spaniards found it impossible to shed the conceptual notions that had always ordered their cognitive and social worlds when they migrated to America. Those who crossed the Atlantic dreaming of wealth and happiness were sad to find that nothing ever arrived in the same condition as it departed. It was precisely in order to learn a different cultural language in America that Iberian peoples adapted their ways of conceiving cultural norms in this foreign context, and thus formulated a new, dynamic colonial identity. The twenty-three definitions of recogimiento that emerged during the early modern period formed part of a transculturation process that originated in the parched land of Castile around 1500, and departed to New Spain in 1524 with twelve Franciscan friars.

CHAPTER ONE

Negotiating Enclosure

Recogimiento for Women and Girls in Spain, New Spain, and Peru, 1500 to 1550

> In the city of Texcoco, there is an impressive house surrounded by a large wall. . . . [T]he Franciscan friars are the guardians and custodians of the house, dedicated to enclosure and *recogimiento* like a convent, where a great number of women, unmarried girls (daughters of important personages), and widows live along with other women who voluntarily wish to enter and who are inclined to learn the Christian doctrine.[1]

IN 1529, Juan de Zumárraga (1468–1548), the newly appointed Franciscan bishop of New Spain, wrote to Emperor Charles V informing him of the ongoing Franciscan project to build recogimientos that operated as schools for daughters of the Nahua nobility and asylums for other women and girls. He requested that five Spanish beatas (lay pious women) considered to be *muy recogida* (spiritually and morally virtuous) be sent to New Spain to instruct them.

Interest in educating Nahua girls had begun in 1523 with the arrival of the Franciscan Flemish missionary Pedro de Gante, and it gained momentum when twelve friars initiated Christianizing efforts the following year. By 1529, with Bishop Zumárraga's active support, at least ten schools dotted central New Spain. Within seven years, however, misgivings about the project developed. The ecclesiastical authorities, the beatas, and the parents of the Nahua girls harbored conflicting opinions over the choice of cloistered nuns or uncloistered beatas as the girls' primary educators. As a consequence, formal, institutional efforts to educate Nahua girls were discontinued by 1550.

Analyses of Zumárraga's attempts to promote female and male education and the abandonment of the project by midcentury attribute the change to difficulties facing the postinvasion generation of Nahuas and Spaniards. Some studies assert that preconquest Nahua educational and marital practices

clashed with Franciscan attitudes. Others ascribe declining educational interest to Spanish racist policies, or indifference on the part of the indigenous nobility. Some blame the beatas' own lack of moral virtue, or recogimiento,
which led to the Crown's refusal to send nuns. Still others focus on the epidemic of 1544–45, which decimated a large portion of the indigenous population of New Spain.[2]

All these factors are relevant in explaining the demise of the early postinvasion educational project to establish schools for daughters of the indigenous
nobility in New Spain. However, the ideological concerns and expectations of
the Franciscans also contributed to the failure of the program.[3] As in so many
other areas, the Spaniards sought to impose their own metropolitan values
intact upon their king's conquered subjects. In this instance, however, they
succeeded: various connotations of recogimiento were inculcated. The transculturation of dissimilar and contentious gendered interpretations of recogimiento held by friars, beatas, and Nahua parents produced new, distinctly
colonial practices of recogimiento that adapted to local contingencies, first in
New Spain, and after midcentury, in Peru.

In order to understand the theological, behavioral, and institutional practices of recogimiento that inspired Zumárraga and other Franciscans to found
and operate schools in the principal Nahua-populated areas, the chapter will
begin with an examination of the mystical precept of recogimiento that
emerged during a period of spiritual experimentation in early sixteenth-century Spain.[4]

Recogimiento as a Mystical Precept

Francisco de Osuna, the Franciscan originator of the theological concept of
recogimiento, found the seeds of *interioridad*, or deep spiritual contemplation, in the writings of several of his contemporaries and expounded upon
them in a more profound and systematic fashion.[5] While contemplating his
own brand of theology, Osuna talked to men steeped in the eremitic Franciscan tradition who had "lived apart from the world" in the parched terrain of
Extremadura and other isolated regions of Castile.[6] Until 1502, when the first
official recogimientos were founded, pious individuals gathered together in
recollectio, or physical reclusion, living in rudimentary conditions and ab-
staining from any earthly pleasure.[7]

In 1528, the year before Zumárraga wrote to Charles V about the Nahua
project, Osuna elaborated his conception of recogimiento as a spiritual path
toward God in his masterpiece, the *Tercer abecedario espiritual* (*Third Spiritual
Primer*), which became the basis of Spanish mysticism during the *siglo de oro*,
the Golden Century.[8] Osuna's major point about recogimiento was simple, yet

profound: "The intention of humility is to lose oneself, and recogimiento is nothing but an emptying of ourselves so that God can expand more into the heart."[9] Those who advocated Osuna's methods and chose a path of contemplative seclusion were called recogidos. They rejected medieval religious precepts that focused upon the means to perfection through external dogma, exegesis, and formal assertions of faith, seeking rather an internal path to harmony, perfection, and order. As a mystical praxis, the Franciscan mystics like Osuna perceived recogimiento as an effort to control one's self, in effect to shelter one's heart and senses from worldly temptation.[10] Internal order, they claimed, could be achieved through contemplation and communion with the self and with Christ through silent and spoken prayer in a series of graduated stages toward union or total fusion with God. The flesh (in this context), the external self, was weak, and men and women—especially women—easily corrupted or swayed by evil. Control over the "internal mechanisms" of thought, and direct communication with God, by contrast, would create harmony and order. To achieve self-control, Osuna recommended living in seclusion. Once the self was sublimated, one could live without fear and apply that order within the world.

Such notions implied a separation between the sacred (cosmos) and worldly (chaos), but Osuna argued that God could be found within the self while actively living in the world. One's dialogue with God was a private, personal manifestation that could best be achieved by renouncing the public, worldly sphere. Spiritual retreat was not an end in itself, however. Osuna advised that one could be closeted in a private room and accomplish nothing in such a fortress of silence. Recogimiento and the intimate dialogue of the soul with God required continual inward exploration, not a formulaic attempt at introspection.

Osuna's ideas of deep spiritual renewal occurred within a favorable climate of reform initiated by Cardinal Francisco Jiménez de Cisneros (1436?–1517), the primate of Castile and chief advisor to the Crown.[11] Cisneros patronized religious reformers, including a group of Franciscan mystics at La Salceda, near Guadalajara, whose community formed a crucial locus of recogimiento. By the 1520s, houses of religious retreat called casas de recogimiento had proliferated throughout the entire peninsula, and slowly Osuna's philosophy of recogimiento spread.[12] In addition, two main groups in Spain now emphasized mental prayer: the recogidos (those who followed Osuna's principles) and the *alumbrados* (illuminists), who rejected any mediation of Church officials, meditation on the Passion, fasting, or penance, and focused instead on abandonment of the will (*dejamiento*) toward God in a direct, interior manner.[13]

Osuna's work inspired another reformer, the recently elected prior general of the Franciscan order, Francisco de Quiñones, who instructed some of the first friars embarking for New Spain. Quiñones incorporated notions of recogimiento in the revised Franciscan constitution of 1523 for *casas de recogimiento*:

> Silence is the key to all Religion and virtue and if the more rigorously observant Religions are known to be well cloistered [*guardada*], even stricter enclosure should occur in these houses of Recogimiento: [They should] be far from distraction and be dedicated and entirely attendant to prayer and the spiritual life because it is written, "He who holds his tongue, guards his spirit. Perfect is he, whose words do not offend, and vain is the faith that does not hold back its tongue."[14]

Before the twelve friars embarked for New Spain, the prior general gave them his personal benediction and presented an *Instrucción* that advised them to divide their time between indoctrination and isolated introspection.[15]

Osuna influenced members of the reformed Franciscan order, but he did not limit his writings to clerics. Like other theologians, he strove to bridge the gap between the sacred and secular worlds. The contemplative life of a recogido was not for the weak of will, Osuna argued, and he conceived his *Abecedario* as a series of exercises for achieving graduated stages of recogimiento, from the exterior to the most interior, according to one's spiritual potential. Like other mystics, he wished those individuals living in the world to practice contemplative prayer. He did not distinguish between secular men and women but felt that clerics and male recogidos should serve as spiritual guides on the lay person's internal path of communion with God.[16] In that sense, Osuna's theological works bridged the sacred and secular worlds by linking the mystical notion of recogimiento with its moral and practical—institutional—application in the secular sphere, particularly as it related to women.

The Development of Recogimiento as a Gendered Moral Virtue

Francisco de Osuna's next book, *Norte de los estados* (*The Compass of Social Conditions*, 1531) was perhaps the first treatise to employ and engender the term "recogimiento" as a moral virtue and behavioral norm for females. Osuna linked the theological notion of recogimiento with the term's widening interpretation as an important virtue, like honor, particularly toward woman. Many moralists of the time believed that recogimiento—a demure, modest demeanor—was best preserved in an enclosed, recogido setting. The publication and distribution of Osuna's treatise occurred as behavioral manuals of conduct, written by both priests and laymen, began to reach a larger lay audience.[17]

Osuna's *Norte de los estados* was also timely because it attempted to ameliorate the misogynist portrayal of women of different social classes or conditions (*estados*) representative of medieval and early-sixteenth-century tracts.[18] Until Osuna, many moralists advocated physical enclosure (recogimiento) as a means to contain female imperfections. Advocacy of female seclusion had ancient and medieval antecedents in Catholic and Islamic Spain and formed part of discussions in early modern European intellectual circles. For instance, many Renaissance authors agreed with Aristotle's proposition that women were defective males and that sexual differences were preordained by the will of heaven. To Aristotle, these distinctions were naturally reflected in the organization of social life and in the division of labor within the public (male) and private, enclosed (female) spheres.[19]

The idea that women should be enclosed also had Greek antecedents. Citing the classical author Xenophon, Renaissance scholar Leon Battista Alberti advised wives to remain locked up at home: their participation in the "public" sphere should remain restricted to attending Mass and limited social events.[20] Other tracts based their arguments upon Scriptural authority and the patristic fathers. Saint Augustine (ca. 400) was one of the first Church patriarchs to develop the notion of women's corporeality. To him, a female body was a mirror image of the male, only denser and more introverted, therefore more suspect and more corruptible. Man's task was to guard over a woman; he alone offered her salvation from the dangers emanating from within her own body.

By the sixteenth century, some Spanish intellectuals abandoned the extremist view that females were, by nature, corrupt and should leave the house only three times during their lifetime: for baptism, marriage, and death.[21] More moderate positions, like Osuna's, generally prevailed. Debates over woman as the embodiment of evil and good subsided in favor of an awakened interest in establishing models of perfect or appropriate behavior for nuns, doncellas (unmarried virgins), wives, and widows.[22] It seems likely, however, that the more overtly misogynist readings of the "feminine position" became more diffuse and graduated. In their authoritative instructions, men, including friars and secular priests, still attempted to define and prescribe ideal feminine conduct. While many extolled female virtues, they also included a list of their vices and deficiencies and depicted women as childlike, inconstant, perverse, and vain.[23]

Before 1530, recogimiento, unlike honor and vergüenza, was not commonly recommended as an ideal moral virtue.[24] Subsequently, however, moral treatises began to refer to the concept as an internal, moral quality, and as external, corporal, and behavioral control. It was also applied more generally to describe the female body and the need to seclude or enclose it as a preventive measure. These new applications of recogimiento subsumed older misogynist assumptions about the need to control woman's disorderly tendencies within the private sphere. Recogimiento as enclosure thus offered a practical, moral solution to the perceived need for both internal and external control.

While previously, the female body was viewed as dense and corrupt, authors now discussed a woman's body as an analogy for a type of residence or *casa*, an enclosure of private life.[25] Hence, women were encouraged to remain locked up inside the house to guard their bodies from others. Recogimiento likewise implied surrounding the body with garments: immuring its visibility, so it would not attract a lustful gaze.[26] Appropriate, modest clothing covered any eroticism or showiness; dress should reflect the pure spirituality beneath.[27] Long and flowing hair, for instance, was thought to contain sensual powers.

Recogimiento also came to mean a restriction or sheltering of the senses: a policing of the different parts of the body. Moralists urged that "posterns" such as the mouth, eyes, ears, and nostrils, through which the sensuality of the world could enter, should be watched with particular vigilance, since sin and corruption could enter through them. They also advised women to walk with their eyes cast downward in modesty and recogimiento. The "look" had dangerous potency and was considered to be a means by which women could gain control over men with their sexuality. By averting women's eyes from the gaze of others—because the eyes were considered one avenue by which outside stimuli could invade the body—unmarried girls could guard their chaste "treasures" and deny their supposed eroticism. The mouth also epitomized danger. Treatises encouraged women to emulate Saint Susanna, who vanquished her enemies through silence—recogimiento—and *echar a su boca el freno* (to keep their mouths shut). Too much conversation obstructed one's internal dialogue with God, which should take precedence, and thus women were instructed to be *quieta* ("silent") within. By closing off external stimuli, they could achieve peace and stillness, or recogimiento within their hearts and souls.[28] To control fanciful thoughts it was best to seek a secret place within their home to find solace with God.[29]

In his discussions of recogimiento, Osuna distinguished between women of the different estates. To virginal doncellas, he recommended separation from those who might endanger their chastity.[30] To widows, he cited exemplary women, married and recogida, and advised them to emulate the cloistered Hester.[31] Some moralists advocated a more moderate policy toward married women and widows but were adamant in insisting that unmarried virgins between twelve and twenty remain under strict lock and key.[32]

Osuna's major works thus considered recogimiento for distinct purposes. His *Tercer Abecedario* counseled recogidos to enclose themselves physically and spiritually to draw nearer to God, and his *Norte de los estados*, advised lay women and girls of all estates—whether unmarried, married, or widowed—to remain enclosed, recogida, as much as possible. Unlike previous thinkers, he wished to impress upon women his belief that enclosure promoted moral and spiritual *recogimiento*, but he did not subscribe to the "residual" notion that women should be enclosed because they were defective.

Humanism and Female Education

The debate over seclusion coincided with a general humanist consideration of female education.[33] In Renaissance Italy, the Italian humanist educator Guarino rejected the brilliant and talented Isotta de Nogarola (1418–66) as a pupil, consigning her to a life of scholarly seclusion. In late-fifteenth-century Spain, by contrast, female royalty and members of the nobility received encouragement to pursue an education and even to publish their own writings. Castile boasted several educated women, such as Antonio de Nebrija's daughter, Queen Isabel the Catholic, and her daughter, Catherine of Aragon.[34] According to Antonio de Guevara's influential treatise *Reloj de príncipes* (*Dial of Princes*, 1529): "Princesses and noble ladies should not refrain from teaching all that they can to their children, nor should they be deceived by the saying that by virtue of being female, they are unfit for the sciences. This is not a general rule."[35]

Some credit the beginning of humanism in Spain to the Catalan bishop Françesc de Eiximenis (1340?–1409?), who derived his notions about woman, education, and seclusion from Scripture and St. Augustine. Eiximenis was one of the first moralists to devote a separate discussion to the different conditions (*estados*) of infants, *doncellas*, married women, widows, and nuns; and he advocated female education in his book *Lo Llibre de les dones*.[36]

Eiximenis influenced the Spanish humanist Juan Luis Vives (1492–1540), whose work exemplified some of the inherent contradictions in attitudes toward woman in the early sixteenth century. Vives's discourse contained thinly disguised misogynist attitudes, and he, like many contemporaries, believed that women were the source of all evil or good—"sick animals," as the expression went—but he agreed that a good Christian education could induce a woman to develop virtuous qualities. Vives felt that women had an aptitude for learning but should limit their choice of reading to devotional works, and, more important, should study within closed walls (*recogimiento*) in submissive silence.[37] Finally, Vives warned, an educated woman should not demonstrate her knowledge, let alone become a teacher.[38]

Desiderius Erasmus (1466?–1536), the most influential humanist of all, especially in Spain, went one step further than Eiximenis and Vives, ascribing an equal capacity for learning to men and women, and he praised their accomplishments within the religious sphere.[39] In spite of his popularity and Cisneros's support for female education, the practice in Spain remained lim-

ited to economically privileged girls who could hire a private tutor or study in
a convent. A few recogimientos or schools for girls (called *colegios* or recogimientos) existed before the sixteenth century, and Cisneros made a con-
certed effort to found more of them for daughters of the Castilian nobility.
The Colegio de las Doncellas of Santa Isabel, for instance, indoctrinated girls
in "all manner of tasks" (*todo género de labores*) for six years, providing an institutional imprimatur that guaranteed their honor, virtue, and recogimiento
to enter a convent or find a suitable husband.[40] However, such schools remained rare in pre-Tridentine Spain.

Indeed, female literacy could prove a double-edged sword. A holy woman
like María de Cazalla, raised not far from La Salceda, was criticized for her ex-
pertise in reading, writing, and teaching.[41] She transgressed a socially accepted
boundary because she held open spiritual gatherings with other women and
relied on the writings and stories of well-known religious and secular women
for her own education.[42] Although unable to read Erasmus in Latin, she became familiar with many of his ideas and admired him so much that in the
1520s she allegedly suggested he should be canonized (although he did not die
until 1536).[43]

Beatas and the Via Media

Although women were considered excessively weak of will, with a propen-
sity for evil and temptations of the flesh, they were also regarded as possessing
a greater capacity for spiritual understanding and devotion.[44] The belief in
women's "natural" predilection toward piety meant that beaterios and beatas
became extremely popular in Spain, and showed a tremendous heterogeneity
according to region and time period.[45] They either followed the eremitic tradition, took third order vows and became tertiaries affiliated with a particular
convent, lived quietly alone, or congregated with other women in their own
homes.[46] Lay pious houses for women dotted the Spanish kingdoms by the
mid-fifteenth century and by 1500 were quite numerous.[47] Until the papal bull
Circa pastoralis was issued immediately following the Council of Trent, beatas
remained uncloistered.[48] They had more opportunities than nuns to be teachers, writers, preachers, alms collectors, shrine-keepers, prophetesses, nurses,
and prayer leaders at funerals. However, because beatas were women of the via
media (the middle path), neither strictly lay nor religious, the boundaries of
their avocation were fraught with ambiguity.

In early-sixteenth-century Spain beatas were venerated by commoner and
wealthy Spaniard alike. Pious and powerful secular and ecclesiastical authorities held beatas' spirituality in high regard. Cisneros himself consulted with
holy women for their prophecies, and his vocal and literary support for formal

and informal female piety remains one of his most durable achievements.[49] Instrumental in spreading the cult of St. Catherine of Siena, he proposed the canonization of a number of female religious and published their writings.

In addition, he protected and promoted the virtues of Spanish beatas.[50] Early in the sixteenth century, María de Santo Domingo, popularly known as the Beata de Piedrahita, not only received widespread local attention at her Inquisition trial because of the miracles attributed to her but also enjoyed the intervention of pope, king and Cisneros in her behalf.[51] Wealthy individuals often patronized these holy women. The Duke of Alba financed a beaterio for María and more than two hundred other women.[52] Isabel, Queen of Castile, patronized beaterios and beatas; and her favorite lady-in-waiting, Doña Leonor de Mascarenhas, had a predilection for beatas at court.[53] Vitoria, a beata known to collect alms for abandoned children in church doorways, was on the royal household payroll for years.[54]

Like many women of ambiguous social standing, however, beatas were also often subject to attack. They abided by the principles of interior recogimiento while actively performing social services, thus questioning the common assumption that women should remain enclosed. In addition, their work as educators contradicted accepted principles of female inferiority. In one instance, the provincial of the Dominican order, Tomás de Matienzo, prohibited the beata María de Santo Domingo from entering convents and establishing contact with other holy women.[55] Like María de Cazalla, she met with criticism for imparting her knowledge to other women, and her authority and influence disquieted concerned male ecclesiastical authorities.

In general, beatas were viewed as both pious and suspicious, neither sacred nor worldly, thus reinforcing the ambiguous middle ground upon which most women trod. María de Cazalla exemplified those women who, whether married or single, were aware of the potential advantages in promoting unenclosed spiritual expression over the cloistered life. In line with the northern European humanists, Cazalla claimed that one could still reach communion with God (recogimiento) even if one were married and had given birth.[56] She criticized the laxity of conventual life and the lack of true spirituality among most female religious, thus questioning the accepted division between the sacred and the worldly. Renowned for her forthright character, she was quoted in 1529 as saying: "Villagers often say that if someone considered recogido and virtuous marries: 'Look, my goodness, so-and-so is a saint and is getting married, trust these saints'; 'so-and-so is a saint and gives birth!' "[57]

Because some holy women conflated the mystical foundations of recogimiento and illuminism, they were subject to attack by Inquisition authorities. María de Santo Domingo's *Libro de la Oración* may have influenced theologians such as Francisco de Osuna, but her writings also served as a point

of departure for other beatas, including the "mother of illuminism," Isabel de
la Cruz.[58] By the 1520s, de la Cruz argued that the praxis of dejamiento, or
abandonment of the will, served as the principal mystical path toward God
and could be practiced anywhere, not necessarily in a church. She preached
the doctrine of pure love (not based upon good works) in spiritual gatherings
held in her home, at Franciscan monasteries, and at the nearby Convent of
Santa Clara. Such a call for Scripture as the basis for direct knowledge of God
came dangerously close to Lutheranism and was thus deemed questionable by
Inquisition officials.[59] The trial of Isabel de la Cruz that resulted in 1524 and
ended five years later in her condemnation served as a warning to some
women who dabbled in heretical practices. Yet the spiritual conventicles held
by Isabel, her disciples, and María de Cazalla also provided a venue where
beatas, some of whom became the first teachers in America, developed their
own impressions about the various mystical precepts circulating at the time.[60]

The Establishment of Recogimientos (Schools/Houses of Enclosure) for Nahua Girls in Mexico, 1524–1550

Gendered attitudes toward recogimiento, education, and informal lay piety
were challenged in distinct ways in early-sixteenth-century Spain. They were
also negotiated by the friars and beatas in new ways between 1524 and 1550 in
New Spain. The exchange between "old" (Nahua) and "new" (Spanish) cultural practices did not consist of a confrontation between bipolar, homogene-
ous values, but involved the Spaniards' transculturation and rearticulation of
ambiguous gendered social and theological ideals in a "new world."[61]

Gender biases in imperial educational policies were evident long before the
friars landed at Veracruz in 1523. Since 1492, Ferdinand and Isabella had pursued a policy of Christian indoctrination through education in Granada and
were anxious to apply similar measures in the Indies.[62] Acutely aware of the
"exigencies of evangelization," in 1503 they ordered Nicolás de Ovando, governor of Hispaniola, to build a school as an annex to each church.[63] This interest in educating and evangelizing the Indians remained a top priority after
Charles V became king of Spain in 1516.

Martín de Valencia, head of the Franciscan mission to New Spain, had been
strongly influenced by Friar Juan de Guadalupe, a reformer and educator who
had participated in the massive forced conversion of the *moriscos* of Granada
around 1500.[64] Between 1505 and 1516 Valencia became the central figure in the
training of the observant Franciscans in the Province of San Gabriel in Extremadura, the locus of intense preparatory missionary activity. Their approach
emphasized conversion based upon Scriptural law, and the millenarian belief

in the impending Apocalypse made it imperative that they should swiftly save the souls of the native Americans.[65]

Missionary policies toward female education in Granada and the Canary Islands, were, at best, lukewarm,[66] but Franciscan friars in New Spain pursued a different course.[67] Pedro de Gante, a Flemish Franciscan lay brother and illegitimate relative of Charles V, reached New Spain in 1523. Educated in Louvain, he was perhaps the first to implement the humanist ideal of education in the Americas. Two major European sources influenced Gante's ideas of education for and by women: the philosophy of the Brethren of the Common Life, and the writings of Erasmus.[68] Moreover, he strongly favored girls' education, having witnessed the beguinage mixed schools of northern Europe.[69]

In addition, both Gante and the "twelve Franciscan apostles" who landed on Mexico's shore in 1524 were deeply impressed and influenced by the dedication to education among the Nahua.[70] Gante observed that both boys and girls attended particular schools according to their social status, and some were assigned at birth to a particular temple.[71] Depending upon their rank and class, some girls were secluded and taught to be priestesses (*cihuaquacuiltin* or *cihuatlamacazque*) in the major temples.[72]

From the outset, the Franciscan friars actively pursued a policy of enclosing and educating Nahua elite children to inculcate Spanish, Catholic values into the younger generation, and to keep them from being tainted by their parents' cultural influences.[73] Hence, between 1525 and 1529, at least ten schools called recogimientos were established in Mexico City and other principal Nahua towns.[74] Cloistered and carefully guarded, daughters of the indigenous elite were educated for ten years, after which time they would either marry or dedicate their lives to teaching other girls who gathered in the church patios.[75] Initially, Catalina de Bustamante, a virtuous lady who had been in the Indies since 1514, was entrusted with the education of at least three hundred Indian girls in the recogimiento of Texcoco.[76] From her they learned the rudiments of Christian doctrine, were instructed in Spanish behavioral mores of modesty (vergüenza) and recogimiento, and trained in "womanly arts" like embroidery, which, Zumárraga believed, would serve as an example for the next generation and support the teachers' salaries.[77] In addition, selected converted Nahua "spiritual mothers," many of whom had once occupied prominent religious positions in the villages surrounding Tenochtitlán, began tutoring the girls.[78] Because of their experiences with other lay pious women in Spain, Spanish beatas imparted their gendered knowledge of humanist education toward their young protégés and invited Nahua female teachers to continue their traditional practices within a Christian framework.

Zumárraga and the Politics of Recogimiento

Spanish secular authorities also supported such a venture. After his return to Spain in 1529, Hernán Cortés negotiated with Empress Isabel to send additional beatas of an "honest lifestyle" and "proper recogimiento" to serve as teachers in the nascent recogimientos.[79] During 1529 and 1530 the Empress therefore ordered the provincial of the Franciscan order to recruit five beatas from Salamanca and Seville, including a woman named Catalina Hernández.[80] Hernández had been a neighbor and friend in Salamanca of Francisca Hernández, a famous alumbrada tried by the Inquisition only the year before.[81] Soon after Catalina's arrival at New Spain, it became apparent to Bishop Zumárraga that she possessed some illuminist tendencies (*algún alumbramiento*). His suspicions were confirmed by her relationship with her spiritual consort, a Portuguese mystic named Calixto da Sá, who had slipped on board ship as a servant in Seville. At first Zumárraga tried separating the peculiar pair, primarily because he feared the influence their "heretical" notions might have upon their conversion work among the native girls, but eventually he opted to ship them back to Spain.

Meanwhile, beatas in New Spain zealously continued their missionary work, and select indigenous converts also helped in the ministry of the early Church.[82] However, the brush with *alumbrismo* may have precipitated tensions between the beatas and Franciscan authorities. The beata Juana Velázquez expressed her concern to a sympathetic empress that, because the holy women were not formally subject to any given order, they should not be required to have visitations by the Franciscans, a point with which Isabel agreed.[83] Nor, Juana argued, should they have to remain physically enclosed, because it was necessary to ask for alms in the city and surrounding provinces.[84] Her misgivings not only demonstrate the growing strain between beatas and friars but also illuminate distinct gendered interpretations of spiritual and moral recogimiento that had transculturated from Spain to New Spain.

In spite of his negative experiences with Catalina Hernández, Zumárraga requested another reinforcement of Spanish lay pious women; and the veteran Catalina de Bustamante, who had by this time spent more than twenty years in America, returned to Spain to recruit more beatas. They arrived in 1534, and, once situated in their respective schools, the beatas learned Nahuatl and taught their female charges how to read and write.[85]

By 1536, however, in spite of the fact that between eight and ten recogimientos educated nearly four thousand young girls, Zumárraga's enthusiasm began to flag.[86] Convinced that New Spain needed strictly cloistered convents, not recogimientos, he stressed that only nuns should teach the girls:

In order that they have the daughters of these Indians [*naturales*] under their care to indoctrinate and keep them in complete recogimiento and enclosure, because in this way they would be completely Christian and they would take up the model of honesty and recogimiento of the said nuns and their parents would give [their daughters up] more willingly than they had done in these [other] convents, where there was no vigilance or enclosure nor high walls, nor could there be in the way that they exist now.[87]

Zumárraga attributed the beatas' lack of integrity to the fact that they wandered "in the streets from house to house," hence could not fulfill the requirements of moral and physical enclosure necessary to instruct the young pupils. Their lack of recogimiento also meant they succumbed more easily to the (supposed) demands of the native girls.[88]

Zumárraga's ambiguous position in the 1530s underscores the longstanding, inherently contradictory attitudes toward holy women, secular women educators, and female education in general. He was, above all, a humanist in his "struggle for justice in the conquest of America."[89] Highly supportive of the spiritual and social work of lay pious women, he gave financial support to beatas both in his native Vizcaya and in New Spain.[90] Yet his experiences in Durango and Pamplona with false beatas accused of witchcraft contributed to his deep suspicion of any doctrine vaguely connected to Lutheranism.[91]

His contradictory position was not unique. Throughout the 1520s and 1530s the politics of Inquisition authorities did not coincide with imperial policies. A wave of arrests of beatas accused of illuminism in Toledo coincided with the arrival of the Franciscan missionaries in New Spain and the call by Pedro de Gante, Cortés, Valencia, and Zumárraga for beatas to teach the neophyte Nahua girls.[92] Empress Isabel patronized the first voyage of beatas in 1530, just when María de Cazalla suffered imprisonment and interrogation at the hands of the Spanish Inquisition. Spanish beata Francisca Hernández influenced the unfortunate beata Catalina Hernández, who clashed with Zumárraga in New Spain. Francisca also courted several influential Franciscans, including Prior General Francisco de Quiñones, who praised her spirituality and consulted with her not long before her trial proceedings began in 1529.[93]

Initially, Zumárraga found inspiration in Erasmus's call for male and female education, and accepted beatas' role in the early educational mission of the Church. By 1536, however, he wanted only women who were *bien recogida*: physically, morally, and spiritually.[94] His attitude changed as the political current shifted, and, in the end, Zumárraga chose a more restrictive interpretation of woman's position relative to recogimiento as enclosure. His change of heart also reflected the shifting moral tide in Spain itself, because as practices of mysticism and interior recollection came under increasing scrutiny by the Inquisition, beatas were labeled as dangerous and heretical. By 1538, Charles V even refused to support Zumárraga's desire to found a convent of Santa Clara in Mexico City.[95]

Zumárraga also faced ambiguous responses from the Nahua. An accurate rendering of pre- and postinvasion gendered Nahua notions of enclosure and modest conduct is extremely difficult, because both Zumárraga and early Spanish religious chroniclers described the Nahua girls and women dedicated to religious service in temples within the framework of their own interpretative codes of recogimiento.[96] Chroniclers often characterized *cihuaquacuiltin*, Nahua institutional accommodations for girls, as houses of enclosure (*encerramientos*) or cloistered houses (*lugares de clausura*) on the Iberian model.[97] Friar Toribio de Benavente, known as Motolinía (1499?–1569), described the girls as walking in religious processions "in such silence and recogimiento that neither did they lift their eyes from the ground nor speak a word."[98] Women serving the temple, he added, "were enclosed or recogida without doors." This implied that Nahua practices of enclosure did not necessarily mean that girls should be placed under strict lock and key. Rather, they *held* the virtue within themselves.[99]

Recent work on Nahua sources permits a better understanding of male Nahua gendered moral precepts toward enclosure and morality. On one level the *caciques* accepted the idea that boys and girls could be taken from their household at a tender age to be educated in special schools. Nevertheless, they maintained a concept of recogimiento and family honor distinct from that of the Franciscans, and many actively resisted efforts to remove their daughters forcibly from their homes for placement in a Christian institution.[100] We now know that in a customary ritual, a father would speak to his daughter when she reached the age of six or seven and advise her to live a balanced life, to pursue a "middle good," and to work hard at designated tasks within the home.[101] Prepubescent children were counseled to remain sexually and morally pure and not to "throw dust and rubbish" on their parents, "or scatter filth on their history."[102] Emphasis on premarital sex varied according to class: boys and girls involved in temple service were trained to have "pure living," or *chipahuacanemiliztli*.[103] The ideal of virginity, or being "still jade," for girls was esteemed among the Nahua, but "was not an essential feature of a person's character."[104]

These Nahua concepts of moderation, control, and pollution conflicted with the friars' Christian notions of purity and sin. They also contrasted with their obsession with stigmatizing sensuality.[105] Contrary to Nahua beliefs, Spanish friars taught girls that they were polluted and inferior creatures by nature of their gender.[106] Although the Franciscans were convinced by humanist thinkers such as Erasmus to champion female education and kept the works of the recogido Francisco de Osuna in the library of Santa Cruz de Tlatelolco, they also taught that women were "sick animals" and the embodiment of evil.[107] As objects of sexual desire, women were equated with sin.[108] Girls were counseled to model themselves after Santa Clara, who pursued an austere, rigorous life with few material comforts, an absolute dedication to a life of chastity, and, above all, enclosure.[109]

Such a consuming "cultural conquest" impacted negatively on concerned Nahua parents.[110] For one, they balked at the fact that their daughters were forcibly dislocated from their homes without their permission.[111] In addition, caciques foresaw a loss of control to the friars in their ability to choose husbands for their daughters and protect patri- and matrilinear inheritance interests.[112] They feared that the deliberate imposition by the friars as arbiters in selecting marriage partners for the pupils in the recogimientos might eventually destroy deeply embedded Nahua cultural practices.[113] Don Carlos Ometochtzin, a noble from Texcoco who was tried by the Inquisition (directed by Zumárraga) in 1539, reproached the Franciscans, who knew "nothing of the world," for interfering in the affairs of *pipiltin* ("with lineage") women, without respecting their customs.[114]

Additionally, hispanized Nahua women were disregarded by eligible native noblemen who remained free from the friars' influence; they considered them to be morally and culturally tainted. Ironically, Nahua men educated in monasteries often refused to marry the *indias recogidas* selected for them by the friars because, they claimed, the doncellas were lazy and "not willing to serve them according to their custom."[115] Friars like Motolinia were frustrated by the lack of interest and blamed the failure of the recogimiento project on the fact that the girls were educated only to be married and not enclosed for life. Zumárraga expressed outrage that many parents bestowed their daughters as gifts or tribute payment to caciques who already had many wives.[116] Zumárraga also felt disillusioned with the boys educated in Santa Cruz de Tlatelolco, whom he felt reverted to polygamy once they left the school in order to gain additional wealth through their wives' labor.[117] By the 1540s, therefore, few saw a bright future for institutionalized native education.

Between 1536 and 1543, Zumárraga shifted gears and concentrated instead on implementing the Inquisition and constructing a hospital for natives. His grand educational programs for indigenous children (particularly the project of Santa Cruz de Tlatelolco) stagnated, and, in 1544 he wrote a letter to Prince Philip, regent of Spain, requesting that the building that once served as the main recogimiento of Texcoco be converted into a hospital.[118] Demography played a role as well. A series of epidemics from 1545 to 1547 killed the few remaining recogidas.[119] By then the second generation of Spanish laymen, even less enthusiastic about converting the diminishing number of "noble savages," turned their attention toward founding schools for the fastest growing element of the population: the mestizas.

Recogimiento in Peru

As Zumárraga struggled with the dilemma in New Spain, native Andeans and Spaniards in Peru faced other concerns. Just as disease took its toll in Mexico, much of the native population near Lima (founded in 1535) had already been decimated by 1540. However, other factors delayed the transfer from Mexico and Spain to Lima of recogimiento as an educational practice, theological tenet, and moral standard. Unlike Mexico, where native resistance and strife among the conquerors remained sporadic, civil unrest rocked the viceroyalty of Peru between 1532 and 1554, thus delaying the cultural conquest until midcentury.

In the wake of the military and cultural invasion in 1532, religious and secular authorities did little to foster interest in educational centers for daughters of the Inca nobility. Vicious feuds between supporters of Francisco Pizarro and Diego de Almagro and the widespread resistance and the siege of Cuzco by Manco Inca's troops (1536–37) produced a series of uprisings, political murders, and general instability within the new viceroyalty between 1536 and 1554.[120]

As early as 1534, the *curaca* (native lord) Taulischusco, a representative of the Lima valley coastal elite (considered vassals of the Incas), curried favor with the Pizarros in negotiations for the site of the city of Lima, which fell within his *cacicazgo*, or political jurisdiction.[121] Because Taulichusco and his son, Don Gonzalo, were not the only principal leaders of the valley, they maneuvered for advantageous positions with the Pizarro family to prevail over other ethnic groups, particularly the lord of Pachacamac. Throughout the civil war period, Don Gonzalo and his people remained loyal to the Pizarrist faction, and offered troops for the various revolts.[122]

Kinship strategies between Pizarro's supporters and, among others, the Lima valley native elite proved crucial to the success of the conquest.[123] Accordingly, in order to promote education and foster favorable marriage alliances between Spanish and local Andean nobility, Don Gonzalo and other curacas might have adapted the institution of the *acllahuasi*, or houses for chosen women.[124] Like the Nahua temples, the Inca acllahuasi included temporary and permanent practices of enclosure and religious instruction; therefore, from the Spanish point of view, acllahuasi could be supplanted with recogimientos just as Nahua institutions had been subsumed in New Spain. All the preconditions were in place, but the establishment of educational houses for Andean girls did not occur until much later. Why?

Located throughout the Inca Empire, acllahuasi enclosed and trained girls from Cuzco and provincial centers designated according to age, class, beauty, and rank to serve various deities in the Inca pantheon, or to produce goods such as textiles and corn beer.[125] Irene Silverblatt maintains that the establishment of such institutions served as a linchpin of Inca imperial policy.[126] An elite girl destined to be an aclla would ensure that her "procreative potential would be determined by the rulers of the empire," precisely because enclosure and marriage among the Inca served as a means of forming political alliances and, once selected, the girl forfeited her community ties.[127]

South of Lima, in Pachacamac, Hernando Pizarro had observed a magnificent acllahuasi, where only the highest class of acllas remained virgins to the sun for life: the rest were free to leave the house during the day.[128] Other acllas lived near Lima in Huarco, Lunahuaná, and Chincha.[129] Although he made no mention of these houses, surely Don Gonzalo was aware of their presence. As a curaca seeking to placate the Pizarros, Don Gonzalo regarded Christian marriage negotiations of the coastal elite as an essential feature of his office, and the acllahuasi might prove beneficial in that regard. However, this institution also represented an Incaic form of cultural dominance, and Don Gonzalo probably sought to escape hegemony of the Incas and the neighboring lords of Pachacamac. This may partially explain why Don Gonzalo did not advocate founding acllahuasi in Lima.

Three other complications affected the delayed transculturation of recogimiento as an institutional practice to Lima. Unlike Nahua parents in New Spain, the coastal nobility in Peru did not have a well-organized missionary church to contend with until the civil wars had ended. Members of the regular clergy, more particularly the Franciscans, found it difficult to articulate a clear-cut policy in the midst of the political turmoil. At the time, letters composed by ecclesiastic authorities revealed frustration with both the conversion of the natives, and in establishing permanent structures. Only the Mercedarians and Dominicans ensconced themselves in the city; the Franciscans did not settle in significant numbers in Lima until the end of the rebellion of Gonzalo Pizarro in 1548.[130] In the end, Franciscan-inspired recogimientos were not established in Lima until midcentury because the lack of a strong physical presence prevented authorities from emulating the spiritual conquest policies implemented in New Spain.

Second, Spaniards in Peru faced other concerns. Strong resistance to the New Laws of 1542 that curtailed the inheritance rights of *encomenderos* exacerbated an already divisive situation.[131] Political bickering over the New Laws and the military skirmishes of the civil wars impeded the development of an effective, nonpartisan municipal government in Lima, which in turn affected relations with the native elite. The city council, responsible for promulgating municipal regulations and establishing cohesion in Lima—crucial to the Spanish sense of order—maintained only minimal control until the Marquis de Cañete, viceroy between 1556 and 1560, arrived.[132]

Third, Zumárraga's negative reports to Charles V in the 1530s may have deterred any royal intentions to support analogous institutions for natives in Peru. By the time the introduction of recogimientos for Andean girls seemed feasible, the idea had fallen out of fashion. Given the political exigencies, it seems the coastal native elite and Spanish encomenderos favored direct marriage negotiations over institutional practices.

The particular constraints facing local Spanish and Andean authorities before midcentury thus prevented the transculturation of schools for native daughters from New Spain to Peru. By 1549, imperial aims gained precedence; Charles V strongly advocated recogimientos for mestizas, now designated as "lost and distracted in between two worlds," in the main centers of the Spanish empire.[133] In New Spain, Viceroy Antonio de Mendoza (viceroy between 1535 and 1549) took a serious interest in the *mozas mestizas*, said to be wandering throughout the countryside, and was instrumental in founding the Colegio de la Caridad—the first institution for mestizas in America—in Mexico City around 1548.[134] Selected to be Viceroy of Peru (1551–1552), he fostered the first imperial personnel link between the two viceroyalties and, while living in Lima, endorsed the foundation of a sister institution. Although he died before implementing his plans, he nevertheless established an important precedent to create uniform policies in the two viceregal capitals. Mendoza's presence in both centers of government would ensure the transculturation of recogimiento as an educational practice to Lima.

Conclusions

By the end of the sixteenth century, hundreds of schools for boys dotted the Spanish landscape, largely due to the Jesuits and the reforms of the Council of Trent.[135] Philip II, following Cisneros's policies, sponsored schools for girls in Zaragoza, Salamanca, and Guadalajara.[136] However, in spite of the humanists' call for equal education for girls, schools or colegios/recogimientos in Spain were exceptional, and conventual or home education remained, for many, the only option.[137] In the Americas, female education endured, but in a racialized and exclusionary manner. Schools specifically for native girls virtually disappeared after midcentury.[138] A number of recogimientos for mestizas emerged between 1548 and 1580, but those founded in the seventeenth century catered exclusively to daughters of the Spanish and creole elite.

Viceroy Mendoza personally carried one manifestation of recogimiento from Mexico to Peru, but its other significations arrived in other ways. The mystical notion of recogimiento first found its way to New Spain via Spanish beatas and Franciscan friars. The ambiguous policies toward beatas in New Spain did not dissuade holy women from their teaching and spiritual practices. On the contrary, beatas remained absorbed in charitable enterprises in public, nonenclosed settings.[139] They fused Nahua and Spanish traditions by instructing young girls who would have once served in the temples (*ichpochtlayacanqui*); by living according to the principles of interior recollection espoused by Francisco de Osuna; and by practicing Christianity in the worldly realm, as their pre-Tridentine counterparts in Spain had done.[140] This occurred in spite of the fact that in Spain, Church authorities actively campaigned to inhibit beatas' independence throughout the remainder of the sixteenth century. In fact, by 1620 the Inquisition had effectively eliminated their collective presence.[141]

In Lima, however, beatas played a role in imparting Christian doctrine to mestiza girls, and their function in the transculturation process of the mystical tenets of recogimiento remained key. By the beginning of the seventeenth century beatas in Lima focused less upon their role as educators and more upon reading and interpreting the writings of Spanish religious reformers who were known to subscribe to Osuna's doctrine.[142] Two such mystics, Teresa de Avila and Luis de Granada, had tremendous appeal to holy women in Peru (see ch. 5, below).

Francisco Osuna linked the spiritual and worldly realms in his consideration of recogimiento as an internalized search for God among holy men and women, and as a moral virtue of self-containment and quiescence among women in the secular sphere. Recogimiento now offered a concept to bridge idealized differences between the sacred and the worldly in colonial Peru. On the one hand, priests trained after the Council of Trent received high praise for their virtuous conduct and pious ways (recogimiento) and they certainly carried this to Peru.[143] On the other hand, after 1540, secular tracts disseminated in Peru included the term "recogimiento" as an important virtue for women and girls, along with modesty, and honor. Whereas at the beginning of the sixteenth century recogimiento's usage was more restricted, the concept had evolved, by midcentury, into a standard gendered ideal for religious and secular women. The appearance of recogimiento in a number of widely published and widely distributed treatises meant that the concept would become the sine qua non in the life of many Spanish women migrating to Peru by 1600, and ubiquitous to the general female limeña population by 1650.

In the process of transculturation of recogimiento to the landscape of New Spain, Francisco de Osuna, Antonio Guevara, María Cazalla, Pedro de Gante, the beatas, and the fathers of the Nahua girls helped fashion a historical convergence in which various interpretations, nuances, and practices of this precept developed in a new cultural setting. The meshing of the complex manifestations of recogimiento also symbolized the nature of the early colonial endeavor. The years 1524 to 1550 in New Spain were significant historically, not because that period represented the origins of particular cultural practices, or the failure of an educational project, but because it created a "space" in which the confluence of different nonlinear positions relative to recogimiento could develop. These nascent, hybrid expressions of recogimiento would have important repercussions in other landscapes throughout the colonial period.[144] Zumárraga's attempts to interpret recogimiento, and others that followed, centered upon specific social concerns of the moment, yet always remained within the parameters of a transatlantic colonial cultural dialogue. By mid-century, the emerging notions of recogimiento in post–civil war Lima were "novel, pregnant with the future."[145]

CHAPTER TWO

Lost Between Two Worlds

Doncellas Mestizas in Lima, 1550 to 1580

I N 1572, Garcilaso de la Vega lamented the permanent exile of his mestizo childhood friends from Peru who were now scattered throughout the empire.[1] Proud of his mixed parentage, son of the Spanish conqueror Sebastián Garcilaso de la Vega and Incaic princess Chimpu Ocllo, the great chronicler viewed himself as a symbol and spokesman for the new race of mestizos: a blend of the best of two cultures.[2] Yet he was never legitimized by his father and experienced the humiliation of his mother's forced marriage to a commoner, thus enabling his father to wed a fourteen-year-old Spanish girl.[3]

Garcilaso's *Comentarios reales* mourned the loss of the mestizos' privileged status and protested their consequent characterization as troublesome and untrustworthy to Spaniards and Indians alike.[4] His account attested to the demise of the social project, popular in previous decades, that supported the formation of a second-generation Peruvian mestizo female and male elite. By 1580, Spanish authorities no longer considered such a vision viable, and Garcilaso bitterly resented the fact that attitudes toward the mestizo had changed so radically.

In order to understand the changes in racial politics to which Garcilaso referred, this chapter will focus upon the specific historical development of the gendered and racialized category of the doncella mestiza—an unmarried, virginal girl of Andean and Spanish descent. Although many doncellas mestizas were, in fact, illegitimate and poor, state officials throughout Latin America thought they deserved a distinct future.[5] Like the Franciscans before them in New Spain, secular authorities in the 1550s hoped to promote recogimiento as a norm that involved demure, modest behavior, and as an institutional setting in which that prescriptive conduct might be inculcated. The question then arises: did the transculturation from New Spain to Peru of recogimiento as a behavioral norm and institutional practice simply involve a shift in referents from Nahua girls to Andean mestizas? On a demographic level, the answer is "yes"; however, new and distinct colonial manifestations of recogimiento emerged in Lima between 1549 and 1580 that facilitated this process.

Indeed, discrete ideological strategies distinguished one generation from the next, and on one level, recogimiento evolved from an inclusionary into an exclusionary institutional practice throughout Latin America. In the 1520s and 1530s, Franciscan friars in New Spain attempted to transmit Iberian values to their female Nahua subjects in the hope that subsequent generations would embody Hispanic cultural norms. Even at midcentury, Viceroy Mendoza and his successors in Peru continued to view recogimientos as a space in which to hispanize orphaned mestizas; but they also hoped to sever them permanently from their Andean roots, and marry them off to interested Spanish grooms. This shift coincided with the emergent elaboration of the verb *recoger* as a means of physically separating marginalized individuals—particularly mestizos—from others, in order that they not contaminate or be contaminated by other groups, including native Andeans.

Subtle changes in Spanish cultural politics engendered new educational centers called recogimientos in numerous densely populated zones of Latin America between 1548 and 1580. All housed mestizas, and one in particular, San Juan de la Penitencia (founded in 1553) in Lima, educated orphaned and abandoned doncellas mestizas with the intention of imparting Christian values, including the virtue of recogimiento, and enclosing them until they reached adulthood. At that point, the owners of the recogimiento would choose a suitable husband or religious vocation for them. In addition to their utility as educational centers, recogimientos acquired a new functional dimension present in other types of institutional foundations in Spain and Italy after 1540. Recogimientos henceforth served as locales of social beneficence for orphaned or abandoned children, and operated in loco parentis in determining the recogidas' development and future.

No cultural code functions in a vacuum. Considering the analogy of a wheel, recogimiento, at the hub, evolved relative to its interaction with other cultural norms, which served as the spokes. The first section of Chapter 2 will consider the transculturation from Spain to Peru between 1532 and 1548 of the cultural notions of illegitimacy, poverty, "the mestizo," gendered notions of education, and the idea that some institutions should serve as centers of social welfare. Next, the chapter will examine how and why these attitudes shifted, thus inspiring the subsequent foundation after 1548 of numerous recogimientos whose functions—and indeed survival—depended upon adapting to local contingencies. A case study of the Recogimiento de San Juan de la Penitencia will elucidate why this was the case. Finally, the chapter will consider the period after 1570, when the emphasis shifted toward inhibiting male mestizos, thus eclipsing any sustained interest in recogimientos for mestizas.

Between 1532 and 1548: Changing Sociocultural
Practices in Spain and Peru

At least until midcentury, illegitimacy was not viewed as a major social impediment in Spain, in part because bastard children were common.[6] Those who "enjoyed the warmth of the hearth" in a given household included the nuclear family, relatives, servants, illegitimate offspring, orphans, and foundlings.[7] Those children born out of wedlock—many men had children before they married—were often later incorporated into the household in a more servile or secondary position. Legitimacy and illegitimacy were not polar opposites: what mattered most in determining one's status was whether the child was recognized as an heir and allowed to enjoy the warmth of the hearth. The possibility of *reconocimiento* (legal recognition of a child) made it possible for bastards to become fully integrated members of the family and inherit property, thus creating marked differences of status among illegitimate children.[8]

The conquerors, some of them bastard commoners themselves, transported notions of illegitimacy to Peru. As the first settlers, they gained new quasi-noble status and the attendant privileges. Moreover, most of the first inhabitants who settled in the newly founded city of Lima traveled without their wives and established informal relationships with indigenous women once on American soil. The conquerors certainly adapted quickly to the well-established Spanish and Incaic conventions of encouraging politically arranged marriages to expand and maintain kinship networks with provincial families; hence, postconquest alliances and arrangements between Spaniards and the curacas (hereditary governors) of their would-be Incaic consorts became standard practice.[9] Whether to marry remained an eristic issue; and in the immediate postconquest years secular and ecclesiastical officials expressed mixed opinions about inter-racial unions. Some opposed concubinage and actively promoted mixed marriages to forge political and economic alliances between Spaniards and members of the Incaic nobility; others preferred more informal conjugal relations.[10]

The embittered Garcilaso commented upon the fact that most Spanish conquerors in Peru did not marry the indigenous women with whom they had children, regardless of their status.[11] His father consorted with two Incaic women: Garcilaso's mother and María Pilcosisa Palla, neither of whom he married.[12] Some conquerors were brutal toward Andean women; many considered casual liaisons their inherent right. Still others treated their mistresses as possessions or persons of servile status, calling them *su india* (their Indian), but would still seize any opportunity to marry a Spanish woman, particularly of noble lineage.[13]

Admittedly, not all Spaniards (particularly plebeians) were thus inclined:

midcentury marriage records for the Sagrario parish of Lima show Spanish-Andean unions.[14] When male honor and prestige became issues, however, most men opted to take the more socially acceptable route, viewing indigenous women as part of the spoils of the conquest, of unequal status, and thus not really marriageable.[15] Given the Spaniards' strong cultural biases, the vast majority of mestizo children born of these unions were considered illegitimate.[16] The asymmetrical nature of gender relations between Spanish men and Andean women (and indeed, between Spanish men and women), established a clear paradigm for future generations and influenced patterns of illegitimacy. It may also have contributed to the proliferation of matrifocal household units in Lima.[17]

Because most mestizos were illegitimate, and their numbers increased significantly before 1550, conceptions of the mestizo also shifted during the formative colonial years.[18] Two scholars interested in popular culture, Stuart Hall and Richard Boyer, have argued (in different ways) that individual identities are multiply constructed and always in flux.[19] Their approaches toward identity formation prove useful in tracing the changes in the meanings of "mestizo" as a social identifier and racial category. Differences in the treatment of mestizo children, both before and after 1549, depended on their geographical and social context, lineage and legitimacy, the parents' social and economic position—for example, whether they came from an encomendero or artisan class—and their gender.[20]

Between 1532 and 1548, colonial authorities in New Spain and Lima attempted to define the mestizo with criteria that transcended mere physical appearance.[21] Some first-generation mestizos were categorized as Spaniards and formed part of an aristocratic conqueror or encomendero class to which Garcilaso referred in his chronicle. These *hijos de españoles* were distinguished socially and legally from indigenous children. Many fathers encouraged their children to remain in *pueblos de cristianos*, adopt Spanish cultural norms, or to return with them to be educated in Spain.[22] In the rural Andes, many mestizos were considered culturally Spanish. Another group comprised the ever-increasing number of orphaned and abandoned mestizo children. In many instances, the terms "mestizo," "illegitimate" (*hijo ilegítimo, hijo natural*), "orphan" (*huérfano*), and "abandoned children" (*expósitos*) were synonymous.[23] Orphaned mestizos were considered poor, not only because they had no money but also because they had no family connections. Even the Quechua term *huaccha* meant both orphan and poor: a person without money or family.

Thus, during this period, legitimacy, abandonment, and orphan status became commensurate with the "racial" construct: "the mestizo." Because so many mestizos lacked economic or familial resources, Spanish authorities began to argue that "poor" mestizos were marginalized and in need of state or secular guardianship. However, that notion did not develop out of the blue; the idea of equating the poor with marginalized individuals matured gradually in pre-Tridentine Spain.

Until the 1520s, someone was considered poor if incapable of meeting monetary obligations, such as paying rent or taxes. Indeed, in the Middle Ages, the destitute and homeless often held a privileged position by virtue of their association with Christ, who identified with the meek and impoverished. The prevailing attitude in Spain gradually shifted. Following the *comunero* revolt—a popular movement to maintain traditional privileges in Castile (1520–21)—vagrants in many areas were perceived as a threat to the social order and were labeled as marginal.[24] Those who could barely eke out a living were viewed as a source of shame and criticized for maintaining themselves by the sweat of others.

Determining what constituted the "poor" in Catholic Spain involved serious controversy. Intellectuals debated the meaning of "the worthy poor" and how they should be treated. The influential Juan Luís Vives, for instance, argued in *On the Relief of the Poor* (1526) that poverty was not a natural and privileged condition and that only work could prevent its development.[25] The Catholic Church opposed state intrusion into their traditional control of charity and social beneficence; thus their defensive stance formed part of a larger battle. Concerns over changing attitudes toward the poor formed one aspect of an ideological "containment policy" against the rampant spread of the Protestant faith. On the one hand, throughout the rapidly growing cities of Europe, magistrates, influenced by Protestant reformers, reconsidered and revamped poor-relief policies. On the other hand, the Dominican theologian Domingo de Soto, aware of the change, balked at the idea that the poor should be socially reformed or shut away from society and opposed the increasingly interventionist role of municipal authorities in "welfare" activities after 1540.[26]

During this period one of the applications of the verb "recoger"—to unite or congregate people or animals that are separate or dispersed—probably became more customary.[27] The noun "recogimiento" could describe a covered area extending from a wall, a house or a barn in a village that offered shelter to beggars or mendicants.[28] The connotation of physical segregation or shelter also began to be linked with the notion that the marginal or poor should be separated from the rest of society—a meaning derived from the contemporary theological signification associated with Francisco de Osuna: to separate or abstract the soul and the body from that which is worldly.[29] Just as the body should withdraw from distractions in order for the soul to achieve harmony or union with God, the inverse held true for those within the secular realm. Some authorities saw promise in the formation of congregations or villages in rural areas in which vagrants or marginalized individuals (*personas ociosas y vaga-bundos*) would be forced to live and cultivate the land.[30] The verb "recoger" now involved physical enclosure, as well as intentional separation from "others."

In spite of Soto's admonitions in Spain, state and municipal authorities increasingly patronized public works.[31] Vives recommended founding *casas de misericordia*, or asylums where the poor, according to their age, condition, and gender could be trained to work under the direction of state officials. Concentrating his attention on abandoned children, the humanist promoted the foundation of hospitals or hospices where they could be recogido, or gathered together, housed, fed, and educated.[32] His proposals reflected a growing interest in secular intervention into matters of public welfare, and an increasing tendency to create vested, more permanent loci of social control in institutions. Asylums were perceived as spaces that could shelter society from wayward individuals: or conversely, spaces in which to protect the innocent from societal harm. A similar phenomenon developed in Italy, where *conservatorios* educated poor disadvantaged girls, "conserved" their honor, and provided them with asylum.[33] The idea that state-sponsored institutions such as casas de misericordia and conservatorios could provide refuge for the poor and needy served as an incentive to found recogimientos for mestizas in Latin American cities.

Just as attitudes toward poor relief and the socially marginal shifted course during the first half of the sixteenth century in Spain, beliefs concerning children and the importance of their moral education (including imparting the virtue of recogimiento) also changed. Prescriptive literature advised children to strive for the virtues of obedience, modesty or vergüenza, recogimiento, and sobriety. In principle, their education required that they read spiritual texts and gain some familiarity with classical literature.[34] Following the humanists' initiative to promote education for all children, many manuals appropriated gendered standards when offering pedagogical advice: boys, considered to have more reason, were encouraged to pursue a vocation "within the world"; girls, on the other hand, were taught that they were less rational beings, should cultivate attributes of long-suffering and passivity, and should distance themselves from the worldly.[35] Girls were advised to guard their chaste treasures and separate themselves (recogerse) from anyone who endangered their virginity. Reclusion or recogimiento offered them the best guarantee against corruption in the physical, moral, and spiritual senses of the word.[36]

Considered her offspring's sacred refuge, mothers provided the child's first education through love and the physical contact given by breast-feeding. Together with fathers, they maintained a protective environment within which children would later receive formal tutoring.[37] Some scholars have argued that Antonio de Guevara, Juan Luis Vives, and others only appeared to advocate female accountability for children's education. But in reality their interest in public control over education, soon reinforced by the Council of Trent (1545–63), promoted the foundation of educational institutions that alienated and excluded mothers from their responsibility as the primary educators.[38] Whether inadvertent or intentional, recogimientos and casas de misericordia shifted the authority for educating children from the mother to the state.

Debate among Spanish academics over this issue remains inconclusive, but there is no doubt that in Peru, male colonial authorities attempted to exert control over educational policies and female enclosure of mestizas at the expense of maternal participation. Historian María Emma Mannarelli cites examples of extreme physical and psychological violence against Andean women, but this brutal treatment also involved emotional separation of mothers from their children.[39] Even in those families in which the maternal side proclaimed Incaic nobility, many Spanish fathers did not consider the mother as the daughters' sacred refuge, but rather, because of her apparent racial inferiority, an obstacle to the girls' cultural purity. Therefore some Andean women suffered the degradation and multiple stigmas of "not being quite human" by virtue of their gender, and because they were not of Iberian descent.[40] But how were their mestiza daughters treated?

Proper recogimiento or seclusion and education, based upon Spanish cultural notions of childhood and girlhood innocence, guaranteed that an unmarried virgin or doncella in the Hispanic world would remain insulated from the dangers of male society—thus preserving her chastity—and any contact with *comadronas,* or lost women, an image made popular by the novel *La Celestina.*[41] In the Andean world, some indigenous mothers were equated with this negative image. Many Spanish fathers insisted that their children—illegitimate or legitimate—be raised in their household: to be educated and nurtured properly, or *remediada* (cleansed of any aberrant tendencies).[42] In the case of Garcilaso's siblings, both his full sister Leonor and half-sister Francisca probably resided with their father.[43] From the Spanish perspective, the inclusion of mestizos into the recently designated legal realm of the Republic of Spaniards—developed at midcentury—would preclude their becoming one more among the masses of Indians.

If the sexual and moral purity of the doncella remained an esteemed Hispanic ideal, it was also essential for a proper and honorable marriage.[44] In Peru, issues of honor were crucial to many Spanish fathers, but matters of inheritance were equally pressing. Fathers exercised the inherent right of *patria potestas* over the daughter until she turned twenty-five or married, but after that point, the husband had legal jurisdiction over her property, with the exception of her dowry. Spanish law stated that both legitimate and illegitimate girls could inherit property or an encomienda from their fathers, if no other male children were eligible.[45] In fact, a number of mestizo sons and daughters of the Incaic nobility became encomenderos.[46] As a consequence, many young mestizas became objects of intense marriage negotiations, and possessive Spanish fathers attempted to maintain strict control over their daughters' marital choices. To them, enclosure until they reached a marriageable age could ensure that their wealth would be protected.

Thus during the period from 1532 to 1548 the first generation of Spaniards transported cultural norms associated with racial superiority, a recognition of illegitimacy and flexibility toward inheritance rights, the espousal of casual relations with women, and the notion that doncella daughters, by virtue of their gender, should be carefully supervised and recogida. During this period the offspring of the unions between Spanish men and Andean women—the mestizos—were accepted, albeit unequally, in the Spanish world, whether legitimized or not. Conversely, many children in Peru (as, somewhat earlier, in Mexico) were either abandoned or orphaned, because of war, disease, or conditions of poverty, thus creating a new social dilemma.

After 1548, attitudes and policies toward illegitimate mestizo boys and girls, and those designated as marginalized, shifted dramatically. Legislation and policies of institutional control toward a new "class" of *marginados*, already common in Spain, began to be implemented throughout the empire. Eristic debates and attitudes surrounding illegitimacy, concubinage, poverty, gendered notions of childhood, and education in evidence before 1550 also contributed to the endorsement by the Spanish Crown of state-sponsored recogimientos throughout Latin America. Founded between 1548 and 1570, they served as educational centers, asylums, and surrogate parents for illegitimate, poor, and abandoned mestizas. In Lima, these centers were also intended to exclude mestizas from their Andean maternal and cultural environment and to *remediar,* or purify, any aberrant tendencies. Nevertheless, however much Spanish legislation attempted to homogenize mestizos and render them synonymous with marginalized individuals, differences in status and class still held sway. Local needs also dictated their function, and Spanish fathers considered sending their daughters to recogimientos for a variety of reasons. Such institutions could impress an elite imprimatur upon their young daughters, protect them from suitors interested in gaining the father's fortune, serve as a depository while fathers traveled on business, and operate as surrogate homes for those unwilling to accept the girls fully into their hearth and home. The changing political climate in Lima also served as an impetus to develop new social welfare policies to care for marginalized individuals, especially mestizas.

Between 1549 and 1570: Experimentation
in Social Control

Because the strife among Spanish colonists persisted for nearly twenty years, only minimal effort had been made to construct a viable municipal government in Lima. Yet early settlers contributed to the growth of a bustling metropolis. In his path-breaking social history of early colonial Peru, James Lockhart ably demonstrated that the city's inhabitants engaged in intensive agricultural production, commerce, and artisanal activities throughout the civil war period.[47] At the same time, encomenderos conformed to the "seigniorial ideal" by living in magnificent homes surrounding the central square. By the mid–1550s, Lima's central core featured several monasteries and hospitals, and distinctive commercial and bureaucratic networks that represented the growing colonial nexus.

Two contemporary chroniclers, Agustín de Zárate and Pedro Cieza de León, commented upon the sumptuous and spacious residences of the five hundred homes of *vecinos*, or elite city residents.[48] The grid plan defined a clear center, with the principal symbols of the Castilian state—the cathedral, viceregal palace, and city council offices—located around the main square. From the plaza, streets spread out, each one representing a different trade: *Mantas* for textiles or clothing and imported Castilian cloth, *Mercaderes* for merchants, *Ropavejeros* for new and used clothing, *Plateros* for silver-workers, *Pescadería* for fish, *Carnicería* for meat, and so forth.[49] The market, or *Tianguez* (from Nahuatl), dominated the city's activities, both spatially and economically.[50]

As interest grew in consolidating Spanish authority in the viceregal capital, Crown officials began to encourage Spanish couples to immigrate. Still, in the early 1550s, Spanish men outnumbered Spanish women in Lima by a ratio of eight to one, but following the end of the civil wars, greater stability and security meant that women began to arrive en masse.[51] Crown authorities insisted that no male should travel to America without his wife and actively began promoting legal marital unions between Spaniards.[52]

State-sponsored colonization efforts and the subsequent demographic upsurge in the Spanish population in Lima had various effects; for one, many first-generation Spaniards felt threatened by the arrival of ne'er-do-wells, or "men who bring nothing but the cloak on their shoulder."[53] Reacting to the increase in tensions, colonial authorities began referring in their letters to marginados, marginalized individuals, and vagabundos, vagabonds: those unmarried Spaniards without home or hearth.[54] Increasing requests for financial assistance and the foundation of confraternities dedicated to poor relief served as signals to Crown and Church officials to develop a more coherent policy of social control over "marginalized" individuals throughout the colonies: whether Spanish, mestizo, mulatto, or Indian; or in Peru, Alto Peru, Guatemala, or Mexico.

At the same time, Crown authorities grew increasingly concerned with the widespread practice of concubinage, or *pecados públicos*, public sins. Some also feared that Spanish-native formal unions would only foster the growth of a mestizo elite, thus endangering Spanish inheritance rights or access to encomiendas.[55] In 1549, the president of the Audiencia Pedro de la Gasca (sent to pacify the unruly viceroyalty) encouraged intermarriage to improve fortunes: thus men like Garcilaso's father married their Inca concubines off to lower-ranking Spaniards they knew in order to manifest some influence over the couples' goods and inheritance.[56] Unlike earlier decades, the encomendero class of the 1550s felt that increasing legal restrictions threatened the conservation of their status and wealth—particularly in light of the implementation of the New Laws of 1542—and therefore supported the change in policy.

To complicate matters further, a law passed in 1549 stated that no mestizo born out of wedlock could inherit an encomienda.[57] This marked a critical shift in reconstituting the meaning of "mestizo" among policy-makers, because inheritance laws now limited the possibilities for these illegitimate children.[58] This effectively forced Spanish fathers to recognize those children whom they wished to adopt as legal heirs and resulted in documents called "reconocimientos."[59] In some cases, fathers recognized some of their mestizo children, but not others.[60] Thus, after the death of the nobleman Sebastián de Torres, his mestiza daughter Isabel continued living with his Spanish widow (not her biological mother) in a servile position.[61] Those children not legitimized were now considered both economically and socially marginalized, thus exacerbating tensions between Spaniards and mestizos in Peru on familial, social, and political levels.

In reality, however, most mestizo children were abandoned or orphaned and thus not fortunate enough to have a home where they could receive a proper upbringing. Some orphans lost their fathers in the civil wars.[62] For whatever reasons, this subgroup of unrecognized mestizos presented a dilemma to colonial officials who felt responsible, as representatives of the Castilian state, for their welfare.[63] In Lima, after 1550, official discourse replicating descriptions used in Spain called for young, so-called vulnerable children to be separated from older delinquents and wayward women, as the Crown asserted its authority as moral arbiter in matters of public welfare.[64] Emulating a medieval precedent established in Spain, an official "Father of Orphans," was appointed "to supervise the increasing number of abandoned and orphaned children" and give them legal counsel.[65] Perhaps influenced by Vives's ideas, Lima's officials debated whether to found asylums for children, particularly for girls, to shelter and guide them toward appropriate Christian behavior before becoming irretrievably lost in the jaws of society. But hidden within the general discussion surrounding care for abandoned children lay the seeds of racial overtones that differentiated mestizos from "others." Royal decrees specifically labeled the new generation of mestizo children (lumping them all together) as *marginados*.[66]

In the transculturation process of the term "recoger"—to provide shelter or designate a separate space for poor, marginal individuals—from Spain to Peru, the referents changed. In Spain the verb's class connotation applied to poor, unemployed individuals; after 1550 in Peru, it also developed a racial component and pertained to castas, and mestizos in particular. Correspondents expressed an interest in gathering mestizos together, or *recogiéndolos*, to Christianize and hispanize them. Domingo de Santo Tomás's Spanish/Quechua *Lexicon* (1560) translated "recoger" as *tantani*, or to gather or congregate people together.[67] Alonso de Molina's Spanish/Nahuatl dictionary (1571), defined "recogido" in terms of the early colonial administrative practice of *reducciones*. Those "recogidos" had come from different villages and lands to be gathered together in a village or neighborhood (barrio).[68] Garcilaso also referred to the term in the same sense but added that to re-coger, or gather together *again*, usually implied for a new purpose. While originally applied to native peoples, the notion of separating the wheat from the chaff, or to isolate the socially marginal from the *gente de razón* (decent or socially acceptable people), now began to be applied toward mestizos.

These semantic changes were then translated more directly into restrictive social policies toward mestizos. The outcome of the debate between Bartolomé de las Casas and Juan Ginés de Sepúlveda in 1551 proved crucial because the presiding judges determined that Aristotle's definition of slavery did not apply to Indians.[69] With the Indians' status as "natural man" now clearly defined, the Crown felt it necessary to protect the Indians by creating (at least in theory) a separate legal and social republic for them. Once accomplished, this meant defining other groups relative to the Indians. Hence, officials turned their attention toward redetermining the social and legislative position of mestizos, now considered not quite Spanish.

Rather than totally exclude them from the Republic of Spaniards however, they reconfigured mestizos as a subcategory within that privileged realm. Their inclusion within the Republic of Spaniards remained tenuous and rested more upon racial suspicion than affinity: officials feared that discontented mestizo and Indian groups might unite against the still outnumbered Spaniards. Their trepidation did not lack foundation. Mestizo revolts had already erupted in New Spain in the 1550s, as the first generation reached maturity. Because New Spain often proved, at least in the sixteenth century, to be a test case for Crown officials in developing imperial policies elsewhere, they were particularly concerned with the future of the majority of young Peruvian mestizos about to come of age. Accordingly, even those mestizos like Garcilaso who enjoyed a privileged status as sons and daughters of the conquerors gradually began to be viewed as racially marginal and socially untrustworthy.[70] Nevertheless, differences in status and calidad still held sway. For the time being, a privileged few remained immune to these negative cultural attitudes, particularly in areas where Spaniards remained in the minority.[71]

Just as on past occasions, authorities saw advantages in implementing a strategy of institutionalized education throughout the colonies, with the intention of segregating mestizos from Indians and assimilating or culturally absorbing elite children into the Republic of Spaniards. Hence they created a policy predicated upon racial differences, but with the understanding that mestizos of a higher status (by virtue of their Spanish or Inca parentage) should serve as a model of Iberian values for other mestizos. Throughout Peru, elite mestizo boys were encouraged to assimilate the Spanish cultural value of recogimiento, which for them did not necessarily imply enclosure but rather the maintenance of self-control and abstinence from excessive contact with the worldly, or with that which was considered immoral. Recogimiento for doncellas mestizas involved learning to speak, read, and write Spanish; as well as to sew, cook, and prepare themselves for marriage in an enclosed setting.[72] Advocates of enclosure for girls suggested that they could become more easily "distracted" and "lost" than boys. Both female seclusion and separation of the children from one another were considered imperative not only for their mutual protection but also because of the desire to implement distinctive gendered educational programs.

Ensuring a Christian education was not always the prime motivating factor, however. In many instances, to recoger or deposit a daughter safely in an institution away from a suitor who, through abduction and rape, could possibly claim the right to marry her—and gain access to the father's encomienda rights or inheritance—seemed the most politic decision. Some fathers had died in the civil wars but had provided benefactors to see that their daughters would marry properly or receive their inheritance. Many children were minors when such arrangements were made, and abuses were rampant. Designated by her father as his heir, Elvira de Coca had received only part of her inheritance after his death in battle, and she found it necessary in 1560 to file a civil suit in the Audiencia against her tutor and the executor of the estate.[73] Fortunately, she regained some of her endowment, but many mestizas were orphaned, abandoned, and left without any means of support.[74] Still, there were exceptions. In 1551, Diego de Ovando legally recognized his daughter

Beatríz as his sole living heir and provided an "honorable provision" for her before returning to Spain.[75]

Not surprisingly, some fathers took their illegitimate daughters back to a conventual life in Spain because, if they chose that course, very few institutional options existed in Peru in the 1550s.[76] Convent admission policies for elite mestizas varied according to demographic configurations of the city and the specific policies of the religious order sponsoring the foundation.[77] In Lima, the dominant peninsular and creole contingent did not readily approve of mestizas taking religious vows or studying in convents. The Augustinian convent La Encarnación (founded 1561) only provided dowries for Spanish girls, and housed them in separate quarters from the nuns, called the *seglarado*.[78] So strict were their policies that the two mestiza daughters of the *Mariscal* Alonso de Alvarado, one of the most colorful military figures in the history of the conquest of Peru, were denied access to the convent. Only when their father agreed to pay a dowry price of twenty thousand pesos to the financially needy institution were Doña Inés and Doña Isabel Alvarado even considered as candidates. A public scandal resulted, but the Augustinian prior general eventually agreed to accept the girls.[79]

Convents in other cities were not so blatantly exclusionary.[80] At this stage in Cuzco, the Convent of Santa Clara accepted indigenous, mestiza, and Spanish nuns: a representative sample of the demographic distribution of the city.[81] Although initially the convent expressed a preference for Spanish women, the patrons were unable to find enough candidates to fill the thirty-three black veil positions, the most prestigious rank in the convent. Almost immediately the convent revised its ordinances and eliminated the distinction between the white and black veil in order to accommodate mestizas who wished to become nuns of equal standing. The ratio of Spaniards to mestizas also affected policies elsewhere: in La Plata, another city in the viceroyalty with a small Spanish population, one-third of the nuns were mestizas.[82]

Precisely because convent admission policies were inconsistent and unreliable, recogimientos represented an intermediate, immured setting—one between the convent and the home—that suited individual needs and reinforced social control policies favored by colonial authorities.[83] They appeared to be the panacea to ease tensions resulting from conflicting attitudes toward mestizas on all levels of Spanish society.

The impulse to establish such institutions clearly derived from a Crown interested in developing more systematic imperial policies, but the success of recogimientos would not have been possible without the sanction of local Spanish secular and ecclesiastical authorities. In Lima, authorities could refer to the institutional precedent already established in New Spain. But the request to found a recogimiento in Lima also formed part of a greater initiative. Not only did the Crown approve their establishment in Mexico (the Recogimiento de la Caridad [1548]) but also in the Audiencia of Guatemala; in Cuzco (the Recogimiento of San Juan Letrán [founded 1551]); in Quito (Santa Marta [founded 1564]); and in Chuquisaca or Sucre, [Santa Isabel]). All of them served poor doncellas mestizas and Spanish daughters of the conquerors.[84]

The various recogimientos served different functions designed to meet immediate sociopolitical needs. In Cuzco for instance, the recogimiento of San Juan Letrán—in 1560 it would become the Monasterio de Santa Clara—served as a convenient and safe repository for daughters whose fathers resided in Chile, Potosí, Huánuco, La Paz, and so forth.[85] Fear for their daughters' safety was warranted by the many abductions reported around Cuzco during this period and its reputation as a "city of wolves" full of lascivious friars.[86] The recogimiento/convent operated, in effect, as a temporary boarding school, protecting and providing a Christian education for the girls during their fathers' absence: but it did not instruct the majority of the doncellas for an extended period.[87] The institution represented a broad spectrum of Spanish society: for instance, the fathers of the girls ranged from encomenderos to artisans.[88] It also served as an employment center where elite women could select servants—usually orphaned mestizas of humble backgrounds—who had the institutional stamp of being bien recogida, thus morally sound.[89]

In addition to their service as temporary asylums and boarding schools, the guardians of the recogimientos sometimes assumed the responsibility of choosing husbands for the orphan and foundling girls. For many Spanish fathers, recogimientos eased their guilt-ridden consciences by finding a way of indirectly providing for their illegitimate daughters while, at the same time, allowing them to remain within the grace of God because of their acts of Christian beneficence. In fact, the desire to care for orphans and abandoned mestizas served as motivating factors in the establishment of two recogimientos in Lima: Nuestra Señora del Socorro and San Juan de la Penitencia.

The Foundation of the Recogimiento de San Juan de la Penitencia

On Christmas Day of 1551, not long after Antonio de Mendoza became viceroy in Peru, Charles V suggested that he extend the policy he began in New Spain and found a shelter for orphan girls in Lima.[90] Although the viceroy died in 1552, before the project came to fruition, he fervently supported the foundation of the Colegio de Nuestra Señora del Socorro—also referred to as a recogimiento—constructed as an annex to the Hospital de la Caridad (founded 1559) for Spanish women.[91] The school began operation in 1562, ten years after his death.[92] Like its counterpart in New Spain, the recogimiento accepted truly poor girls and orphans with no family connections. Founded before any convent in Lima, and situated in one of the most prestigious areas of the city, it educated Spanish girls and mestizas. The hospital's confraternity provided dowries to marry or take religious vows: doncellas mestizas received three hundred pesos if they worked as servants or helped the infirm women, while Spanish doncellas were provided with four hundred pesos and were considered *educandas,* or schoolgirls.[93] This *recogimiento cum colegio* embodied mestizas within a privileged Spanish realm, but distinguished them from Spanish girls through the type of education (vocational versus preparation for marriage) and dowry they received.

In the same Christmas letter, the emperor also suggested founding another asylum in the form of an annex to the Franciscan Monastery of San Francisco.[94] Charles V hoped the recogidas would be properly cared for, instilled with Spanish values and Christian virtues, and prepared for marriage.[95] As a result, in 1553 three pious individuals—Sebastián Bernal, Catalina de Castañeda, and her husband, Antonio Ramos—donated prime real estate in the heart of the city to found the Recogimiento of San Juan de la Penitencia, whose patron saint was Nuestra Señora de los Remedios.[96] (The institution derived its name from a school operated by Franciscan terciaries in Alcalá de Henares in Spain.)[97] Three years later Viceroy Cañete (1556–61) gave fifteen hundred pesos, and an additional one thousand pesos in annual rent from the *repartimiento* of Surco to aid in the completion of the house.

Nine girls resided in Catalina de Castañeda's home until the recogimiento opened in 1559, at which time it began housing and educating orphaned and foundling doncellas who had little or no chance of inheriting their fathers' wealth, and who were not the daughters of well-known conquerors. Founders Sebastián Bernal and Antonio Ramos (Ramos represented Catalina Castañeda's vote) maintained the right to determine the entry of other candidates who would meet the same requirements.[98] Once recogida, the girls remained institutionalized until marriage.[99]

Sebastián Bernal, the father of an illegitimate child himself, testified before the Audiencia in 1560 on behalf of the institution. His account provides a touching illustration of his interest in the future welfare of his four-year-old daughter Juana. Should he die before she was fully grown and could marry, he wanted the recogimiento to provide for her needs and to see that she would be suitably married, allowing him to die in peace.[100] Unlike many fathers of illegitimate children, he assumed full responsibility for raising the child; but by entrusting the recogimiento to serve in loco parentis in case of his untimely death, he could also satisfy his Christian conscience. In another unusual statement, Bernal expressed concern that "when I bring my daughter to the recogimiento, [the founders] should also receive Angelina, her mother."[101]

Six Franciscan beatas taught the children, a process that normally lasted ten years, after which they were prepared for marriage or a religious vocation. (Some girls were deposited at a tender age, because they were assumed to be ready to leave by age twelve.) Assisted by their teachers, they learned to weave, read, sing hymns and psalms, and recite the Our Father, the Hail Mary, the Nicene Creed, the Ten Commandments, and other fundamental Catholic texts.[102] Friars said Mass for the children in a small chapel in the recogimiento, where family members and employees could also attend, while remaining separated by an iron grill.[103]

Their characterization as doncellas is significant. In Spain, the title "doncella" symbolized Christian purity, or *limpieza de sangre,* as well as chastity, youth, and an unmarried status. Medieval literature portrayed them in courtly ceremonies and activities, thus associating them with members of the nobility.[104] In Lima and elsewhere in the 1550s, these particular mestizas doncellas, now enclosed and virtuous, enjoyed a privileged status relative to other mestizas in spite of their illegitimacy and mixed parentage. An institutional setting redeemed them (from the verb *remediar*) and cleansed one-half of their blood. San Juan de la Penitencia sheltered girls who were probably not daughters of well-known conquistadors or Indian nobility, as reflected by the surnames listed; yet an institutional education and the exercise of social control served as a reasonable guarantee of the physical and cultural purity of the doncella orphan, and increased her chances of marrying well.

The founders of San Juan de la Penitencia took great care in preparing them for a suitable marriage, because they considered this to be the recogimiento's most crucial function. Bernal and Ramos exercised *patria potestas* over the girls, and thus had the right to choose their husbands once they reached a marriageable age. They felt themselves better suited to judge the qualifications of the potential suitor than their spiritual guardians, the Franciscan friars, because of their familiarity with worldly affairs. They claimed that the many years dedicated to the teaching of the Christian principles of recogimiento would be wasted if a proper husband were not chosen. Indeed, unscrupulous and opportunistic men might lead the innocent girls astray, and the honor of the institution would then be tainted.[105]

Bernal, Castañeda, and Ramos appointed Catalina de Argüelles, the widow of the Audiencia judge, Licentiate Cepeda, administrator of the institution, and named the Franciscans as guardians, giving them the right to administer the house and its properties. Ultimate patronage was vested in the viceroy in the name of the king, and the 1553 ordinances specified that no bishop or other ecclesiastical official could visit or intervene in the institution's internal affairs.[106]

The founders' good intentions received a great deal of support from Charles V and two consecutive viceroys, but rivalries and selfish interests prohibited the recogimiento from functioning properly and, in the long run, contributed to its financial ruin. The patrons did not realize that their right to limit authorities from visiting the recogimiento would spawn major conflicts between the Dominican archbishop Gerónimo de Loaysa and the Franciscans; between the archbishop and various members of the Audiencia; and among the Audiencia, Viceroy Cañete, and his interim successor, Licentiate Castro. Ultimately, the survival of the recogimiento did not depend upon spiritual goodwill or consideration of the doncellas' well-being, but upon determining the boundaries of political authority and allocation of state resources.

Archbishop Loaysa, who according to the historian Riva-Agüero "shared the government" with the president of the Audiencia from 1549 to 1550, Pedro de la Gasca, had no interest in whether the institution provided a satisfactory Christian upbringing for orphan girls. Known for his shrewd politics, Loaysa obtained the approval of the dean of the cathedral to visit the recogimiento. This act, although declared illegal in the 1553 ordinances, would give him effective control over the administration of the tribute from the Indians of the repartimiento of Surco, assigned by Viceroy Cañete in 1556 to the recogimiento.[107] A trial in the Audiencia resulted. The treasurer of the Audiencia, a friend of Loaysa's, insisted that because patronage was vested in the king's name, the archbishop had the right to intervene in its internal affairs by virtue of royal patronage. But many of the Audiencia judges, wishing to curb the archbishop's abuse of power, ruled in favor of the founders and the Franciscans, and prohibited Loaysa's visitation rights.[108] Shortly thereafter, Viceroy Cañete appointed Franciscan Juan de la Palencía guardian and patron of the house, and in 1562, King Philip conferred the patronage upon the Franciscans.[109]

The recogimiento survived these political intrigues but was soon plagued by litigation over repartimiento rights in Surco. In 1562, Antonio Navarro asserted his claim by right of inheritance from his father. Licentiate Santillán, a powerful member of the Audiencia and also a friend of Archbishop Loaysa, was Navarro's father-in-law and part of a faction within the Audiencia opposed to the politics of Viceroy Cañete and later Licentiate Castro, interim governor from 1564 until Toledo arrived in 1569.[110] Castro argued in support of the "monastery of mestizas" and against Navarro, whom he said was "living well from the tributes of another repartimiento."[111] Nevertheless, the case went before the Council of the Indies, which ruled in favor of Antonio Navarro in

1571: he regained the rights to the repartimiento, and San Juan de la Penitencia was left with no income.[112]

Viceroy Toledo was aware of the plight of the recogimiento when he wrote to the king in March of 1571, requesting financial support for the mestizas. He explained that the house functioned as a place of enclosure, or *encerramiento*, and not as a recogimiento or educational center as was its original intention. He argued that a proper recogimiento in Lima did not exist and that instead, San Juan de la Penitencia served as a depository for women involved in marital disputes.[113] One year later, a friar commented that the house had fallen into disrepair, and the lack of proper supervision enabled "many blacks and Indians to scale the walls and enter the recogimiento."[114] In spite of its dire state, some ecclesiastical and secular officials hoped to gain the necessary license to convert the recogimiento into a Franciscan convent of the Poor Clares, thus replicating what had just occurred in Cuzco. However, they also recognized that the chances of raising the funds were remote.[115]

In spite of his tacit support, Toledo had ulterior motives. He coveted the centrally located spacious building for the newly expanding University of San Marcos.[116] Writing to the king in 1572, he expressed regret that funds were unavailable to convert the recogimiento into a convent and to pay the necessary dowries for the "nuns, mestizas of the recogimiento, and other women." He wondered if funds were being misappropriated, because the remaining income from tribute payments still did not suffice to repair the wall of the house.[117] Four years later the city council approved the transfer of the University of San Marcos (founded in 1554) to the enormous building that had housed the doncellas mestizas.[118] Juana Escalante, a woman dedicated to social causes, was named governess of San Juan de la Penitencia, and after its relocation next to the city jail the institution received little further attention.[119]

San Juan de la Penitencia operated for less than twenty years. The initial financial and moral impetus given by Spanish colonial officials and a few pious individuals led to its establishment, but because the recogimiento was located in a viceregal capital, still in turmoil over the repartition of encomienda rights and rife with political corruption, the initial priority given to matters of public welfare and Spanish colonial measures of social reform were absorbed by more immediate political concerns. Its failure to survive was in part due to powerful individual economic interests, which in the end proved weightier than any spiritual ideals of Christian social welfare toward illegitimate, abandoned, poor, and marginalized girls of racially mixed backgrounds.

Toledo's decisions also indicated a strong gender bias toward male mestizos because he requested that the University of San Marcos educate them as well as Spaniards.[120] He did, in fact, have legitimate political reasons to be more concerned with their welfare: in 1567, two years before his arrival, a handful of the mestizo sons of some of the principal conquerors of Cuzco had planned an attack on government officials in Lima. Proud of their heritage, they proclaimed that "the worst mestizo from Peru was better than the best Spaniard."[121] Calling themselves *montañeses*, they were concerned that mestizos were being dispossessed of their legitimate "rights" by opportunistic Spaniards fresh off the boat.[122] Toledo and ecclesiastical officials therefore took more of an interest in mestizos, whose education until that point, according to a preceding viceroy, had been limited to learning "how to ride a horse and shoot an arquebus."[123]

Beyond his immediate political concerns, Toledo also represented the new generation of post-Tridentine Spaniards emigrating to Peru with a different set of expectations.[124] The conquerors were linked to the mestizos by blood; most of the Spaniards arriving in the 1570s were not. By the 1570s mestizos, not mestizas, had become the targets of social control policies that carried a new set of expectations, and clear, racist overtones. Toledo thought mestizos should integrate into Spanish society ("trayéndolos y tratándolos con la gente española") and learn a vocation.[125] Schools, he argued, should be established in urban and rural areas for indigenous, mestizo, and Spanish boys.[126]

Colonial authorities remained concerned about all beggars or vagabonds— whether Spanish, mestizo, or mulatto—wandering through the countryside and sought a coherent strategy to segregate miscreants (*errantes*) from innocent Indians to prevent their moral contamination.[127] Indeed, Toledo's abstract vision of separate, social republics also involved classifying colonial subjects according to race, class, gender, age, and status. But, to Toledo and future Spanish administrators, establishing and maintaining recogimientos as exclusionary educational centers and asylums for mestizas within the Spanish realm no longer seemed worth the investment of spiritual and economic capital.

Conclusions

Toledo's policies provoked Garcilaso's lament for the permanent exile of his mestizo childhood friends from their beautiful, rugged land with which this chapter began. The sons of the conquerors and the Inca nobility had formed bonds now severed. The majority of less privileged mestizos, first designated as "lost" and then "forcibly relocated" because of the redefinition of both race and class by Spanish authorities, were now scattered throughout the diverse population composing the Viceroyalty of Peru.

Between 1532 and 1548, the term "mestizo" incorporated gender and class connotations associated with legal recognition, status (orphaned), and economic stability that reflected existing cultural ideals in Spain. Incongruities in imperial legislation and colonial policies contributed to the ways in which mestizo children were incorporated into the Andean and Spanish worlds. After 1549, changes in legislation and the creation of socially and legally bifurcated republics engendered racial distinctions intended to differentiate mestizos from "others," to ascribe negative characteristics associated with marginalized individuals, and to include them within the Republic of Spaniards as a subcategory. More clearly articulated, conscious notions of gender and class differences also influenced the racialization process and the creation of the "recogida, doncella mestiza" by Spanish authorities.

In Peru, recogimiento meant far more than it had in Spain. On the one hand, several usages of the precept that had developed in the Iberian peninsula at the beginning of the sixteenth century remained constant. For instance, recogimiento's importance as a virtue and essential component of a moral upbringing continued to grow and influence a new generation of mestizas. And many colonial authorities and fathers continued to believe that reclusion (recogimiento) to preserve sexual purity could also lead to a fortunate marriage. On the other hand, other, distinct nuances and practices also spread. Many thought that mestizas living in recogimientos, and purposefully separated (excluded) from native Andeans, could be reformed (remediada) and purified in order to sustain a new colonial order. This notion stemmed from the emerging assumption that institutions—and recogimientos in particular—could serve as more permanent loci of social control. In the transculturation process of these new applications of the concept, recogimientos began serving myriad functions: they could just as easily promote an elite, hispanized class of mestizas destined to marry hand-picked Spaniards as provide refuge for orphaned and destitute girls. They might also simultaneously protect daughters from unwanted suitors, guarantee a moral upbringing while training young charges to be future servants, act as a depository while fathers traveled on business, and operate as surrogate homes for those unwilling to raise their female offspring. Perhaps the utilitarian, adaptable peculiarity of recogimientos—characteristics that would persist throughout the colonial period—enlivened perceptions that recogimientos were transient and incidental, and that they served primarily as temporary, extreme solutions for various social quandaries.

Certainly, the plethora of legislation on mestizos, and subsequent interest in creating recogimientos for them, subsided when—demographically and socially—they were no longer considered a pressing political or social problem. Not until the 1620s did the association between elite status and female education revive among a new constituency: the growing Lima creole aristocracy. As a consequence, numerous convents established separate areas in the cloister to educate girls, and newly founded recogimientos trained young elite girls of

Spanish descent. Mestizos did not receive serious legal and political attention until the Bourbon reforms, when authorities required them to pay tribute and perform labor obligations.

Moreover, by the beginning of the seventeenth century, the conquistador class no longer constituted the principal political force. Conquerors or their offspring often vied with newly arriving Spaniards for the same shrinking resources. But a nostalgic postconquest spirit survived, and the conquerors still exemplified the glorified past. Well into the seventeenth century, women continued to solicit the Crown for support by identifying themselves as daughters of the conquerors who deserved charity.[128] Curiously, status as the descendant of a conqueror could still prevail upon racial criteria. In 1585 the abbess of an elitist convent, La Encarnación, referred to the two mestizas, Doña Inés and Doña Isabel Alvarado, both residents, as two of the most noteworthy examples of daughters and granddaughters of the first conquerors of Peru (see page 49 above).[129] She did not mention the difficulties the young women faced in being accepted into the convent. Instead, the abbess asserted a lineal nexus with the "glorious past" in which mestizos had played an integral role, and attempted to revivify the older, "residual" meaning of "mestizo" to which Garcilaso had proudly referred.[130]

Select mestizas continued to be accepted as boarders or schoolgirls in the Hospital de la Caridad or the Colegio (Recogimiento) de Nuestra Señora del Socorro, but by 1600, several convents admitted young women as nuns of the white veil, because by then the Church had become more tolerant in its admission of mestizas.[131] More lenient ecclesiastical policies may well have resulted from apathy toward founding a recogimiento for doncellas mestizas after 1585, or from lessening pressure to resolve the "problem" of mestizaje.

Mestizas, unlike mestizos, were considered more socially mobile and able to assimilate Spanish or Andean cultural values through marriage or family ties. The more economically fortunate doncellas in Lima married Spaniards or native nobles. Yet in contrast with ideal Spanish patriarchal norms, many girls probably resided with and were educated by their mothers—their sacred refuge—and in appropriating Andean cultural norms, also enforced matrifocal kinship patterns.[132] Long before 1608, when Diego Gonçalez Holguín published his *Vocabulario* of the Quechua language, Andean women imparted various meanings of recogimiento to their daughters. They understood the scope of the concept to mean reserved conduct, denial of the senses, a place for the poor, a religious house, or a modest life.[133] This implies that recogimiento as a virtue, mystical practice or place of enclosure and asylum had been disseminated throughout the Andean world in other, more discrete ways.

After 1580, colonial officials became engaged in dealing with the increasing numbers of Spanish women arriving at Peru, some of whom were considered to be "wayward and unstable."[134] Some came in search of a wealthy husband; others sought their own fortune and fame. In certain contexts, male officials responded to the introduction of Spanish women to the colony by taking measures designed to limit female contact with natives who might contaminate their "race."[135] In the case of Peru, however, authorities shifted their attention toward "white" women, but this did not involve an increase in racist concerns to protect European women from contaminating races. On the contrary, Spanish institutional policies targeted all "wayward" women—including Spaniards—and considered *them* to be contaminating factors. Their growing presence presented a new threat to the colonial order, and the meaning and application of the term "recogimiento" shifted once again to include and define a new group of sexually and morally deviant women.

CHAPTER THREE

Transgressing Moral Boundaries

Sanctioning Recogimiento for Fallen Women, 1580 to 1620

B ETWEEN 1550 AND 1580, authorities implemented racial and institutional policies separating mestizas from the world of Indians, and
schools such as San Juan de la Penitencia enclosed and educated orphaned
mestizas to assimilate the Spanish value of recogimiento. After 1580, secular
and ecclesiastical officials focused upon those women considered a threat to
the republic as transgressors of appropriate moral and sexual conduct. Mirroring developments in Spain and Italy, the transculturation of emergent
manifestations of recogimiento from Europe to Peru subsumed racial and
class differences into amorphous, socially constructed categories related to
sexual purity and deviance. Authorities hoped that immoral and wayward
women could be physically enclosed in recogimientos that now acquired a
punitive dimension. It was believed that penitential discipline could ameliorate sexual misconduct and that reformed women could either re-enter society or remain enclosed and serve as a deterrent for vulnerable girls or unman-
ageable adults.

Officials intent on implementing Tridentine reforms in Lima also began
distinguishing between sacred and worldly spheres based upon gendered sexual and moral prescriptive ideals established by the mid–sixteenth century.
Many authors, including Francisco de Osuna, discussed the importance of
self-control and enclosure for females occupying different estates in both the
secular and religious realms, but they barely mentioned those women who fell
outside this model. As a consequence, new linguistic and cultural paradigms
and institutional spaces distinguished among different types of "made-up"
women who imperiled these norms, including divorciadas (women involved
in divorce litigation); single mothers; *arrepentidas,* or repentant women; distraídas, or wayward women; women *de mal vivir* (prostitutes); and *mujeres
perdidas,* or lost women, among others.[1]

Changing claims about women's identities also produced different inter-pretations of the functions of institutional spaces.[2] Recogimientos began to serve as loci for involuntary deposit and moral redemption, and enclosure be-came a standard procedure for curtailing sexual and moral transgressions in-cluding divorce or abandonment of the household and crimes such as bigamy, concubinage, clandestine marriage, and adultery. Slave-owners and slaves also utilized the institutional practice of recogimiento for purposes of protection and punishment. The foundation of two specific recogimientos in Lima—the Recogimiento de las Divorciadas (founded 1589) and the Recogimiento de María Magdalena (founded 1592)—reinforced the notion that worldly, sexu-ally and socially marginal women and vulnerable girls should be placed in sanctioned institutional spaces and segregated from secular society, and fe-male religious in convents.

In order to understand the transculturation of emergent interpretations of recogimiento from Europe to Peru, the chapter will begin by focusing upon how Tridentine reforms influenced gendered interpretations of enclosure and sexual morality in Spain and Italy. The chapter will then explain the socio-political changes that occurred in Lima between 1580 and 1620, and how the Recogimiento de las Divorciadas and the Recogimiento de María Magdalena adapted to these local contingencies while replicating patterns current in Europe.

European Precedents

Following the Council of Trent, providing shelter for female vagabonds, disreputable or fallen women, or those wishing or needing to be morally redeemed (remediada) became a high priority in Spain and Italy. Documents and treatises described the proliferation of "fallen," "wayward," or "lost" women—novel descriptive categorizations—as the inevitable consequence of poverty and vagrancy. They thought that secular institutions could contain, remedy (remediar), and reintegrate them into society.

Gendered notions of immoral conduct were linked to ideals of the sacred and the worldly in the symbolic representation of two significant Christian figures—the Virgin Mary and Mary Magdalene. Each embodied conflicting attitudes toward women and sexuality. Holy virgin and worldly whore: the two symbols competed for prominence in the early modern Catholic world, and provided pivotal role models for women to espouse or eschew. By 1600, Mary Magdalene personified the moral regeneration of the Counter-Reforma-tion Church.[3] An embodiment of the sacrament of penance, the converted prostitute became a symbol of the duality of sensuality and spirituality.[4] She surpassed all others by virtue of her magnanimous behavior, and rose above the tide of moral contamination.[5] Because Mary Magdalene had tasted corruption and rejected it, Spanish writer Pedro Malón de Chaide (1530–80) saw her as the union of body with soul and the perfection of divine love.[6] Married women might choose Saint Catherine or Saint Isabel as their guides, but "fallen" women could emulate Mary Magdalene, Woman of Joy and Sorrow.[7] On her feast day, priests delivered sermons to wayward women.[8]

While popular during the late medieval period, the Virgin Mary gained even greater eminence by 1600.[9] Ever distant, women could never achieve her perfection, only venerate and emulate her. As one writer stated in an *abecedario* (primer) dedicated to her, her qualities included: M—mercy; A—abstinence; R—religiosity; I—innocence; and A—abundance.[10] The heavens stood at her beck and call; she represented the sun and the moon and was associated with fertility and reproduction. The omniscient Mother could spread her cloak to shelter all who sought her protection.[11]

Before 1563, religious houses dedicated to the Virgin in Italy and Spain could extend their institutional cloak by providing asylum and correcting their wayward, fallen sisters.[12] After Trent, officials in the various states of the Italian peninsula sought a compromise solution that resulted in the creation of separate institutions, unique from convents, for repentant women who would be required to pay a dowry and remain enclosed for life.[13] Founded at the end of the sixteenth century, the Florentine Casa delle Malmaritate (House of the Unhappily Married Women) provided an answer for those concerned that the Convent of Converted Prostitutes, another institution, was inappropriate for women who wished to become nuns or live separately from their husbands. The founders recognized the need to provide an additional institutional space for women not guilty of any "sexual crime," and to reconcile troubled couples.[14] In Naples, conservatories sheltered poor, legally separated, violated, and repentant women, and the Recogimiento or Convent of Las Arrepentidas (founded 1634) housed Spanish prostitutes (*mugeres pecadoras públicas*).[15]

In Seville, Augustinian nuns of the Convent of the Sweet Name of Jesus (founded 1540) dedicated their lives "to the recogimiento ['gathering together'] and reformation" of repentant women. Unlike the Casa delle Malmaritate, they quartered divorciadas not guilty of any sexual crime with repentant women—whether prostitutes or destitute—to remedy (remediar) them in more godly ways.[16] After 1563, institutional enclosure became more stringently enforced in convents and beaterios: holy women were shut in and worldly women locked out. No longer permitted to reform repentant recogidas within their "circle of walls," many female religious vehemently resisted the radical differentiation between secular and religious spheres.[17] Even though the number of convents and nuns increased dramatically, many nuns continued to protest the strict interpretation of the principle of enclosure.[18]

As a response to the institutional separation of sacred and worldly women, two distinct but related models of recogimiento appeared in Europe around midcentury.[19] From 1540 onward, the Jesuits actively promoted social welfare programs for marginalized women. Their founder, Ignatius de Loyola, considered it the order's mission to found *casas pías o públicas*, or pious houses (also called recogimientos), throughout Spain that emphasized spiritual exercises and moral reform. By the end of the century, Jesuit-run recogimientos operated in Granada, Seville, and Málaga.[20]

The Spanish Crown also expressed interest in founding recogimientos called Casas de Arrepentidas, or Magdalene houses, named after the woman who embodied sin and redemption. One example dates to 1566 in a papal brief authorizing a house for repentant women with the express purpose of reforming them through prayer and contact with holy women.[21] Other foundations soon followed: a royal order in 1582 provided wood for a "recogimiento of repentant women," newly founded in the town of Ocaña, and in the same year, a royal order protested that a casa de mujeres recogidas, being erected in the town of Tafila, blocked the view from the royal residence there.[22]

The Jesuits and the Spanish Crown saw recogimientos as places where moral redemption would occur. Their convictions predated later reformers who began to champion vicious corporal punishment common in prisons. Cristóbal Pérez de Herrera, the "Protomédico de las galeras de España" and councilor of Philip II, best illustrated this viewpoint. In 1598, Pérez de Herrera wrote a treatise advocating the codification of laws toward mendicants and the poor to abbreviate the significant increase in delinquency and mendacity in an economically depressed Spain.[23] He considered asylums and correctional institutions for impoverished females in danger of moral contamination a viable option and thought secular institutions such as recogimientos should replace convents as centers of reform.[24] He felt that vagabond women should not be killed or physically harmed but forced to work weaving and spinning in self-financing correctional houses, or *galeras*.[25] Emphasizing a strict regimen of work and prayer, sullied women would enter voluntarily on a temporary basis with the intention of later "re-entering society." Outside, beatas prayed for their souls.

The Casa de Santa María Magdalena de la Penitencia, which opened at the beginning of the seventeenth century in Madrid, epitomized Pérez de Herrera's ideals. The foundress, Magdalena de San Jerónimo, resorted to severe disciplinary measures to reform "wayward" internees.[26] She considered it her divine mission to eliminate "the lineage of women who have no fear of God and contaminate the Republic," and her recorded volume of prescriptive measures for recogimientos served as a model for future institutions.[27]

This and other recogimientos founded in Spain served as moral reminders and brick-and-mortar saviors at a time when state and church vied for increasing intervention into the private domain of individuals' lives. Similarly, recogimientos founded in America after 1570 were also defined as preventive and fell under the rubric of "custodial institutions."[28] Officials determined that they should protect, provide asylum for, and incarcerate women.[29] They were emblematic of the Catholic Church's Counter-Reformation role as arbiter in social matters through penance, sanction, and deterrence, and of its avocation of "penitential discipline" instead of punishment.[30] In effect, they served as a link between correctional houses and places where inner conversion might take place.

The transculturation of these values from Spain to Latin America became evident in the foundation of "custodial houses" (recogimientos) in Mexico City, Quito, and Lima between 1570 and 1600.[31] All recogimientos served different constituencies, from repentant prostitutes to orphaned schoolgirls; and all emphasized controlling aberrant conduct. The creation of two hybrid institutions in the City of Kings—the Recogimiento or Casa de las Divorciadas, and the Recogimiento de María Magdalena (La Magdalena)—also adopted European values according to local contingencies. In Lima, however, the explicit correlation between the institutional ideal of recogimiento and control of sexuality also resulted from a number of other immediate concerns. The tremendous growth of the city's African, Spanish, and casta population, the constant migration of men and women to and from the viceregal capital, and evidence of discord in gender relations—including lengthy or frequent separations, concubinage, and abandonment of the household—as well as the increase in political stability in the City of Kings influenced changing interpretations and decisions relative to the practice of recogimiento as a moral or physical safeguard or deterrent, and as a disciplinary measure.

Lima 1580 to 1620: Balancing the Sacred and the Worldly

There is no doubt that the 1580s tested the will of Lima's populace. The earthquake of 1586 so devastated the viceregal capital that the viceroy, Fernando de Torres y Portugal, count of Villar (1585–89), purchased hundreds of African slaves to help rebuild the city's infrastructure.[32] A series of epidemics struck Lima, and Sir Francis Drake and other buccaneers menaced the port of Callao. Despite natural disasters and foreign threats to the "well-being of the Republic," the bedrock of the viceregal administration remained firmly intact as a result of Francisco de Toledo's reforms. Archbishop Toribio de Mogrovejo (1581–1605), who arrived immediately after Toledo's term as viceroy had expired, strove to consolidate ecclesiastical hegemony.[33] Called the "Supreme Organizer" of the Church (as Toledo had been for the viceregal government) and defender of clerical immunity, Mogrovejo was considered to be a saint in his own time by Lima's inhabitants, who later promoted his canonization. Like the Franciscan friars who had landed on New Spain's shore, Mogrovejo concerned himself with the spiritual well-being of the entire viceroyalty, and allegedly baptized thousands of Andeans single-handedly while traversing thousands of kilometers on foot.[34] He oversaw a provincial council, implemented Tridentine reforms, and reinforced the power of the secular clergy.[35] His formal entrance into the city to take up his charge as archbishop was celebrated with the pomp and circumstance usually reserved for viceroys, and signaled the commencement of an era of more centralized Church authority throughout the viceroyalty.

By the beginning of the seventeenth century Lima had become a key center of commercial, ecclesiastical, and secular government activity. It boasted three convents for women (owning one-fifth of the city's territory), six monasteries, six hospitals, an Inquisition tribunal, and a university. (In fact, the area encompassed by religious houses exceeded the territory occupied by the general populace.)[36] In 1614, some 25,500 people inhabited the four parishes of Lima.[37] Indians, Africans, and (after 1591) Spaniards gravitated to the neighborhood (barrio) of San Lázaro, across the Rímac River, and a newly established, well-populated Indian barrio of El Cercado. Highly productive estates surrounded the city, some of them owned and operated by Spanish *beneméritos*, or descendants of the original conquerors and encomenderos, and ecclesiastical corporations.[38] Spatial aggrandizement accompanied two distinct demographic developments during this period: intense migration to and from the city, denoting a peculiar transience lasting into the twentieth century; and an increasing number of individuals electing to spend their lives in religious and secular institutions that supported a permanent population.

By 1630 the city had grown to twice its size in 1600, expanding toward the south and east. (The four parochial jurisdictions were expanded in 1626 to encompass outlying territories and parishioners.)[39] A bridge now traversed the Rímac River, connecting San Lázaro to the rest of the city. Lima maintained the largest market and commercial network in South America, with millions of ducats passing through the hands of Lima's merchants and businessmen.[40] More than four thousand residences, from the most ornate homes to shacks hugging the riverbank in a neighborhood called el Baratillo, composed the urban core.

Increased social problems coincided with the rapidly growing population: crime, delinquency, and poverty, problems since the 1570s, became more prevalent during the early seventeenth century.[41] Viceroys complained about the perceived rampant immorality and increase in marital discord throughout the territory. Although authorities in most places and at most times have voiced such laments, not all of it was imagined. Constant migration and extended business ventures left many wives stranded and isolated in Lima or provincial areas where they were required to "mind the hacienda." Married couples separated for lengthy periods often maintained separate residences: this fostered abandonment, concubinage, adultery, illegitimacy, and more indiscriminate conjugal relations in Lima. Matrilocal households proliferated, and women came to the city from diverse areas of the viceroyalty; they migrated frequently, and held only temporary jobs.[42] Officials complained about the increasing number of women unable to marry "well" (in spite of the fact that Spanish men outnumbered women in 1614; see Appendix C), and about the many Spaniards who arrived with insufficient family wealth to sustain themselves.

In the hope that specific social control measures would prevent or abbreviate conjugal discord, colonial authorities passed ordinances to regulate untoward behavior in public. Anxious to curtail the seductive power of the "one-eyed gaze," ordinances prohibited *tapadas* (women who wore a shawl covering everything except one eye) from going to the Alameda (the meeting place of lovers); participating in processions; walking in the streets; or from hanging over the balconies or out of windows, because of the "scandals and inconveniences arising from such a social custom."[43] Legislation attempted to segregate women and men in the theater ("que en las comedias no entren los hombres en los aposentos de mugeres") and during processions.[44] Women of mal vivir (prostitutes) were denied access to the popular taverns (*pulperías*).

Authorities also hoped that institutions would preserve a strict separation of the sacred and the worldly, the pure and the corrupt. Convents served as a repository for some daughters of the elite conquerors; excluding mestizas, by 1614, no less than 16 percent of the Spanish female population—one out of every six women—lived in religious houses (see Appendix C). Ideally, convents served as a means to maintain a racially pristine population of nuns, and to provide a space for religious expression. Convents also provided a temporary alternative for Spanish or mestizas not wishing to marry, for those with no family support, or for young women in need of asylum. Because post-Tridentine entrance requirements expressly excluded sexually contaminated "wayward" women, authorities felt the need to establish recogimientos specifically geared toward sexually aberrant, abandoned, divorced, and poor women. In principle, they formulated their institutional ideals based upon their understanding of sacred and worldly notions current in Italy and Spain. In practice, transculturation modified them.

Lima's Institutional Foundations: The Recogimiento
de las Divorciadas

For several decades three convents and two hospitals (La Caridad for Spanish women and Santa Ana for indigenous women) served as depositories for the few divorciadas or abandoned women in need of temporary shelter in Lima.[45] In provincial cities like Huánuco, divorciadas went to the homes of "principal" women of the local elite who provided shelter and enclosure for the recogidas and established a small hermitage for them to hear Mass.[46] However, in 1589 the Casa or Recogimiento de Divorciadas in Lima began operation, the same year as the Recogimiento de Santa Monica in Mexico City.[47] Structurally, it resembled a convent on a smaller, less opulent scale, in part because of its proximate location to the future Convent of Santa Clara.

The motivation to finance the recogimiento came from a wealthy Portuguese landowner named Francisco de Saldaña, who took pity on María de Torres, an upstanding lady ("una muger principal") from Ica (a town south of Lima). After being abandoned by her husband in the early 1580s, she was shuffled from one home to another over a ten-year period while her divorce proceedings endured. Her case served as an incentive for Saldaña to gain the support of Archbishop Mogrovejo for a recogimiento. They finally agreed that the institution would house a broad array of females: "divorciadas or women whose cases are pending, doncellas, daughters of poor individuals, and [it would also] serve as a depository for women whose husbands were traveling."[48] Saldaña and Mogrovejo sought to create a spatial setting that encompassed both the sacred (moral) and the worldly (immoral) and thus accommodated Lima's growing spectrum of "fallen" women.

Saldaña's donation specified a generous sum of money for the recogimiento and also for a Convent of Santa Clara. Both he and Mogrovejo understood that the Council of Trent specifically prohibited lay women from living in convents unless their lives were in danger. They also knew that Counter-Reformation policy makers insisted upon the creation of separate institutional spaces for holy and secular women. However, Mogrovejo still saw convents as the answer to numerous social problems and as a means to shelter the many daughters of the conquerors who could not find adequate "refuge" elsewhere.[49] In order to adapt to local needs and meet imperial concerns, the archbishop found a compromise solution. He and Saldaña agreed that the Recogimiento de las Divorciadas should be adjacent to the future Convent of Santa Clara (founded 1605), but Mogrovejo felt it necessary to underscore the physical separation between the (as yet unoccupied) convent and the recogimiento in a report sent to King Philip in 1598:

The Church is finished, very sumptuous with two choirs, high and low and with very sturdy iron grills. There are high adobe walls, and a large room, with a wall in the middle for women who are requesting divorces, so that they can be recogida while their cause is being deliberated and after the sentence has been declared . . . [and] so that they do not walk freely about; also to gather together (recoger) young women and daughters of those who travel to distant parts and do not know where to leave their wives and daughters . . . and for the women who have had a bad life and who would like to seclude themselves (recogerse) and live well there is an iron grill where they can hear Mass every day.[50]

Even after the Casa de Divorciadas had been founded, the archbishop wrote a letter to the pope in 1590 requesting permission to allow some divorciadas to be housed in convents, because in their contact with religious women, divorciadas would repent of their "misdeeds" and return to their husbands.[51]

The recogimiento operated for sixteen years as an asylum, home for young girls, and reformatory for "lost" women.[52] During that time, the construction of the convent continued, but its inauguration was delayed fourteen years because of overspending. On the one hand, in 1592, Philip II granted *repartimiento* Indians to build the convent and declared that patronage lay exclusively within the jurisdiction of the archbishop and that no viceroy or member of the Audiencia could intervene in its internal affairs.[53] In addition, Mogrovejo personally helped finance the foundation.[54] On the other hand, although Saldaña donated fourteen thousand pesos, nine slaves, and houses in the plaza of María de Escobar to this cause, the construction costs of Santa Clara had exceeded twenty thousand pesos by 1594.[55] A skeptical Viceroy García Hurtado de Mendoza, marquis of Cañete (1589–96), argued to King Philip that expenditures far exceeded the original estimates.[56] In spite of these setbacks, the convent opened in 1605, and by that time the nuns had acquired extensive wheat-producing lands in Lurigancho, a valley close to Lima, to help sustain them.[57]

Aside from budgetary problems, an uncomfortable tension pervaded the Casa de Divorciadas and Santa Clara for the four years (1605–9) of their spatial coexistence. A wall separated the sacred space from the secular world of "lost women," as the nuns called them. In principle, the barrier restricted communication between the two worlds, but in reality the recogimiento constituted a perpetual thorn in the convent's side, and the nuns tried repeatedly to have the institution moved elsewhere. The wall, they claimed, "disfigured the perfection of their cloistered state."[58] They complained that the Casa de Divorciadas hoarded water from the aqueduct of the mill of Santa Ana, which they claimed as theirs. They remonstrated that the ecclesiastical council favored the Casa de Divorciadas in determining ownership and access to various properties, and claimed that certain authorities maintained "very close friendships" with the governess and some of the recogidas or "lost women."[59] For four years the clarisas continually petitioned for the recogimiento's removal from "their space." Finally, in 1609, Archbishop Bartolomé Lobo Guerrero (1609–22) approved the transfer of the Recogimiento de Divorciadas to a location "far removed from the convent" (the current location of the Beneficencia Pública), where it remained until its demise in 1665. In turn, the convent agreed to reimburse the recogimiento for the vacated space and moving costs. Ten years later, however, they still had not met those expenses.[60]

The agreement specified that Santa Clara should pay the governess's salary and reparations to the Casa, but this too they often failed to do, resulting in fresh legal suits.[61] The nuns rationalized that the Casa did not concern them because it was a "house of *legas,* or lay sisters, where matters of sin, not spirituality, prevail."[62] Nevertheless, between 1589 and 1665, the Casa de Divorciadas remained the preferred choice for women petitioning for annulments or divorces, and a place of involuntary deposit for those accused of concubinage or other sexual crimes (see map). A lack of separate recogimientos to distinguish between sexually deviant and abused women, which did exist in Mexico City and some Italian cities, meant that Mogrovejo's intention to redeem divorciadas by placing them in a sacred setting came to naught.

The nuns of Santa Clara clearly distinguished the "worldly" recogimiento from their convent for holy women, but colonial authorities continued to maintain ambivalent attitudes toward the function and ideal purpose of the new structures. Like his religious contemporaries elsewhere in Latin America, Archbishop Mogrovejo emphasized the importance of the institutional role of prevention, "penitential discipline," and reform.[63] Bishop Luis López de Solís of Quito echoed his sentiments when in 1600 he requested Crown support for the newly founded Recogimiento de Santa Marta in the city. He called divorciadas "prejudicial to the Republic" and emphasized the need to reform them:

> I am trying to put an end to the many divorce cases pending or being requested because of the many women who only wish to separate from their husbands [in order] to live with greater freedom. . . . When they are put in the recogimiento they come to terms with their condition and regain a sense of peace and marital accord with their husband so that the disharmony ceases.[64]

Whether or not the actual number of divorces presented a serious problem in Quito, there is no doubt that Mogrovejo felt that even the minute number of instances in Lima (only three divorce cases survive for the sixteenth century) required attention.[65]

The transculturation of dissimilar interpretations of the disciplinary, punitive, or protective dimensions of recogimientos from Spain to Lima led Mogrovejo to respond to local contingencies by combining pre-Tridentine functions of convents as centers of reform with the Jesuit idea that recogimientos should "redeem" lost women in the company of holy women who would serve as their guides. However, he did not subscribe to the emerging view, advocated by Pérez de Herrera, that recogimientos should serve as prisons. The history of another institution, the Recogimiento de María Magdalena, serves as a second example of a controversy that arose over determining the functional boundaries denoting sacred and worldly spaces.

Lima's Institutional Foundations: The Recogimiento de María Magdalena

In Lima, divorce, marital disputes, and travel arrangements may have become formidable problems after 1580, but women de mal vivir had presented a dilemma to colonial authorities as early as the Caribbean phase of the Spanish invasion. The first New World recogimiento—in Santo Domingo (founded 1526)—was constructed strategically near a brothel to "serve as an example to curtail excesses and scandals."[66] In 1572, nearly a half-century later, Viceroy Luis de Velasco enthusiastically provided financial support for the first house of "repentant" (arrepentida) Spanish prostitutes and "sinners" in Mexico.[67] It was initially conceived as a convent for converts similar to some pre-Tridentine houses in Europe, and the nearly one hundred recogidas remained permanently enclosed with their religious superiors and exemplified how other young, vulnerable women might save their souls.[68] In Lima, a separate ward in the city jail (founded 1584) imprisoned female criminals accused of indebtedness and sexual transgressions such as prostitution (some were labeled as mujeres públicas, mujeres de mal vivir, or mujeres perdidas), concubinage, or adultery.[69]

The establishment of the Recogimiento de Santa María Magdalena (founded 1592) was meant to house women of "ill repute," but like its sister institution, the Recogimiento de las Divorciadas, it was founded in pari passu with another institution, in this case the Hospital of San Diego (founded 1586) for convalescing males. Financial support for both institutions came from the pious María de Esquivel and her husband, Cristóbal Sánchez de Bilbao, both of whom donated their fortunes for the hospital. At the same time, Esquivel expressed her desire to build a recogimiento for women "who wished to live apart from the world."[70] Once completed, the Recogimiento de María Magdalena remained contiguous to the Hospital of San Diego. Ordinances strictly prohibited any women except the foundress and her female attendants from entering the male hospital; the recogidas were carefully guarded, and hospital administrators hired workers to reinforce and heighten the wall separating the two institutions.[71]

Now serving in Peru, Viceroy Velasco (1596–1604) shared Archbishop Mogrovejo's opinion that recogimientos should rehabilitate "wayward" divorciadas; but, like Pérez de Herrera, Velasco now stressed punishment over persuasion.[72] The viceroy sponsored the already-established Recogimiento de la Magdalena, which he viewed as an institutional hybrid between a prison and a house of spiritual reform. Unlike Mogrovejo, he included divorciadas under the rubric of "fallen women," along with concubines, prostitutes, and other "pernicious and insolent women":

> In view of the increasing offenses against Our Lord in this Republic, related to matters of sensuality resulting from hatred and licentiousness, and from not having a house to provide asylum for and to incarcerate some of the pernicious and insolent women, it seemed fitting to establish one which would serve this purpose, on the one hand, to punish them by locking them up and, on the other, to serve as a deterrent for the rest.[73]

During its brief existence (1592–1610), the recogimiento served a variety of functions. It operated as a depository for divorciadas, even though the ordinances prohibited this.[74] The statute allowing only Spanish recogidas was also ignored.[75] In addition, La Magdalena incarcerated criminal, abandoned, pernicious, and "wayward" women (distraídas), and hospital board members referred to the institution as a "recogimiento for rameras (prostitutes)."[76] Apparently, the *provisor* (the ecclesiastical judge responsible for marital litigation cases) did not discriminate among women of different racial or economic backgrounds when depositing them in La Magdalena, but some evidence suggests that women carrying the title "doña" preferred the Casa de Divorciadas (Santa Clara) because, in their opinion, it was a more appropriate location.[77] If either the husband or wife lacked the resources to pay the required monthly board in the Casa de Divorciadas, the recogida would be transferred to La Magdalena.[78] This suggests that both authorities and limeños considered the latter to be for women of a "lower" moral, economic, or racial status. Apparently, calidad, race, and differences in sexual comportment distinguished the two recogimientos.

The foundress, María de Esquivel, had long hoped that the recogidas could hear Mass through the bars that separated the sacristy of San Diego from the chapel of the recogimiento.[79] In 1607, hospital administrators reluctantly agreed to build a chapel and sacristy specifically for the repentant recogidas. Once completed, however, the addition came "dangerously" close to the prestigious and powerful convent, La Encarnación. Because the chapel bells' "constant ringing" disturbed the nuns' sense of "recogimiento" or silence, La Encarnación sued La Magdalena and won; the tower was destroyed.[80] Already plagued by financial and legal problems, the recogimiento ceased to function shortly after the settlement of the suit with La Encarnación, and the income from its properties was transferred to the Casa de Divorciadas in its new location.[81]

Viceroy Juan de Mendoza y Luna, marquis of Montesclaros (1608–15), regretted this decision:

[I would like the King] to decree that Ministers of Justice obey what I saw practiced in Spain. . . . I send [this request] to your Majesty so that you can put an end to and remedy the vices and public sins rampant in this Great Republic. . . . [The king] should decree that an *emparedamiento* which Viceroy Velasco had begun be established with new enclosure ordinances so that one exists for women who lead scandalous lives.[82]

The Casa de Divorciadas managed to survive spatial incursions from nuns inhabiting a proximate sacred realm; La Magdalena did not. The recogimientos existed because colonial authorities saw them as essential to the well-being of the republic. Viceroy Velasco and Archbishop Mogrovejo thought divorciadas-cum-recogidas presented a danger to the republic, but Velasco subsumed them into the broader category of "fallen women" defined by sexual indiscretion. Velasco also emphasized the punitive nature of reform, while Mogrovejo considered recogimientos as a space for moral redemption. Both adopted distinct post-Tridentine European notions of enclosure, penance, and reform to treat local, immediate problems, which in turn structured institutional possibilities and choices for limeñas.[83] At the same time, the institutional practice of recogimiento—providing spaces to incarcerate, protect, and redeem women—began to adapt to the exigencies facing the Lima populace. The placement of women and girls in secular and religious institutions—temporarily or permanently—increased dramatically as parents, couples, and colonial authorities wrestled with the potential applications and consequences of voluntary and involuntary seclusion.

Voluntary or Involuntary Recogimiento?

Those unwilling to risk the legal entanglements of a divorce or annulment might seek temporary refuge, counsel, and employment outside the home.[84] Many filed a formal complaint (*querella*) against their partner, but did not pursue further legal action. Marital litigation records show that many women sought physical refuge because of their husband's or partner's absence. Their testimonies also address issues of abandonment, long absences, or separate households established by their partner with another woman, either in another town or in Lima itself.[85] Since divorce and annulment suits were infrequent before 1640 (see Chapter 4), temporary separation or immediate asylum (some women referred to it as *la fuga*, or flight) remained a modus vivendi.

Before resorting to an institution for protection, many women fled to a female friend or family member's home that they claimed were places of "honor."[86] Some abused or repentant women (in the sense that they regretted an action they had taken) from Lima or the provinces sought the security of the sacred space of convents or recogimientos like La Magdalena.[87] Many feared for their physical safety; others desired psychological protection.[88] Still others felt they would receive institutional support and sanction for their actions, and indeed they did. In 1609, Alonso Pérez petitioned the governess of the Recogimiento of Divorciadas to release his wife, Catalina, whom he knew had been hiding there for three months (and the Corregidor of San Pedro de Mama had confirmed it). After a delayed response the governess finally complied with the law (because Catalina had not actually petitioned for a divorce), but in stalling, provided Alonso's wife with a temporary safe haven.[89]

Women seeking to escape an intolerable situation commonly used the phrase *estaría mi vida en conocido peligro* (my life would be in evident danger) to describe the urgency of their need for asylum. "Conocido" implied notorious knowledge, and public verification of abuse or neglect lent further credence to women trying to make the painful decision to temporarily desert their household.[90] The home was considered the center of a woman's world, and when a woman "abandoned" the casa she crossed a moral boundary: the notion of recogimiento as enclosure, and the home as integral to her identity.

Leaving the home, or the enclosed, protective space, still had to be justified, whatever a woman's social rank. In 1639, Doña Cathalina de Uceda requested a divorce and explained to the judge that she ran a bakery (*panadería*) and employed five slaves; she also supported her illegitimate daughter and nieces. Her husband had abandoned her more than eleven years ago and they had been "separated" for four. During the divorce proceeding, she requested deposit in her own home and emphasized that she would comply with all regulations. She then added: "As the petition states, I am a woman of such standing that makes it necessary to reside in my home, because otherwise I would lose my bakery business and be ruined."[91] Cathalina felt the need to justify her choice of deposit by explaining her husband's prolonged absence, the number of people she supported, and her reliance upon the bakery for survival. Moral qualifications were simply not enough.

Her case also illustrates the importance of "place" in colonial society. In colonial gender relations, couples "played" with spatio/temporal moral codes in determining the right of enclosure or recogimiento as a type of physical and moral (self)-possession. The same logic that abandoned women used to justify voluntary recogimiento or enclosure (protection) also applied to women forced into involuntary enclosure (incarceration). Male interpretations of honor also formed an important element in the equation.

For instance, even though a husband, whether Spanish or enslaved, had abandoned the household long ago, he could still express a sense of possession toward his wife. This was particularly true if, in his absence, "his" wife had engaged in sexual relations with another man. Such "perfidious" behavior could provoke a violent reaction even in a long-absent husband. In 1617, Juan de Dios, a creole slave, who had been gone for six years, claimed that his honor had been offended by the infidelity of his wife, Rosa de Orellana. Rosa, in a matter-of-fact manner, stated that because Juan had been away too long, she had tired of waiting and became involved with another man with whom she had a son. Because Rosa comprehended her husband's logic in "seeking revenge to save his honor" (she had internalized this "norm"), she requested that her owners support her request to seek refuge in a convent where she might redeem her virtue. She understood that, even in his absence, her husband's control of her physical presence in a location of which he approved could restore his self-esteem and perhaps hers as well.[92]

This case also reveals the gender bias of institutional vigilance. An absent or negligent husband rarely faced incarceration for charges of abandonment. Men were jailed in cases of extreme violence toward their wives, indebtedness, flagrant concubinage, or, in the case of slaves, escape.[93] But women were involuntarily incarcerated for reasons ranging from abandonment of the household to immoral indiscretions, or simply because their husband traveled.

More often, husbands asked the ecclesiastical judge to deposit their wives in institutions "on account of their naturally jealous and hostile ways" and abandonment of the household.[94] Diego Velásquez, a mestizo shoemaker, requested that his wife, Petronila de Escobar, be deposited in an honorable (recogida) home because she had stained his honor through her association with a group of women *de mal vivir* in Callao.[95] In another case, Pedro López Gallego, a free mulatto, paid six hundred pesos to free his wife, Martha Hernández, from slavery. When she disappeared, he expressed his rage:

> She only brings ruin upon herself not knowing the good I have done for her. While I was in prison, she robbed me of all my possessions and now there is an order out for her arrest. She has the reputation of a sinful woman and she greatly offends Our heavenly Father and me.

For him, her deposit in the Hospital de la Caridad would serve both to punish her and to help restore his honor.[96]

The same sense of honor in instances of abandonment applied when the wife was free and the husband enslaved. In 1633, Bartolomé López, a mulatto slave, petitioned the judge to deposit his wife, Juana María, a free mestiza, in the Recogimiento (Hospital) de la Caridad because she had abandoned him more than two years before: "She could serve the poor of the Recogimiento: there they would pardon her bad deeds, because walking around free as she does is not just and I would then receive justice and favor."[97]

Husbands of the elite about to embark on extended business trips to the provinces or to Spain also deposited their wives in an institution or home for safekeeping, thus constituting another form of involuntary enclosure.[98] They may have taken what moralists recommended literally: that women, if left to manage the household alone, should maintain an orderly appearance of rec- ogimiento (enclosure and a moral posture) and honesty to their servants, relatives, and neighbors by remaining secluded as much as possible.[99] Many husbands arrived from more remote provincial areas of the viceroyalty to cloister their spouses temporarily in Lima while they traveled elsewhere. Gen- erally such recogidas were wealthy Spaniards living on isolated estates. In some instances, however, women reinterpreted this practice of enclosure to their own advantage. Some volunteered to live in recogimiento because they did not want to relocate to a remote estate where their husbands worked as overseers or field hands.[100]

Still, many husbands abused their right to deposit their wives while they traveled. In one particularly revealing instance in 1622, Doña Catalina Bravo complained bitterly to the ecclesiastical judge that she had remained in de- posit against her will for over a year in the Hospital de la Caridad in Lima while her husband went to Potosí to work as an official "in the service of His Maj- esty." She knew, however, that he had returned to Lima without releasing her from her internment. She asked the judge:

> Why should my husband force me to live here, when I am a free person and cannot be pressed either by him or by anyone else to be shut up and locked away against my will, or denied the right to live with my husband? I have not committed any crime to warrant my being locked up. Moreover, I know he is in this city enjoying himself and just does not want to live with me.[101]

A few years later, Benito Pereyra forced his wife, María de San Pedro, to be recogida in La Caridad, allegedly because she refused to accompany him on his "travels" to the mines of Caylloma. The truth, however, was that he wanted to escape to a safer location, because he had been accused of murdering someone in Callao, and María no longer wished to follow a "criminal." Benito might have succeeded in escaping had he not taken advantage of María's con- finement in La Caridad by trying to abscond with nearly five thousand pesos from her dowry.[102]

Not all expressions of recogimiento involved litigious married couples: slaves and slave-owners also used it as a form of legal deposit. In 1648, Gracia Caçanga protested the unjust treatment of her daughter, Luisa Criolla, a slave, who had been ordered "against her will to the cloister and recogimiento" of the Monasterio de la Concepción. When she tried to escape, her owner, Fran- cisca de la Cruz, a nun of the white veil, had her incarcerated in a panadería (bakery) and tried to send her to another city. Gracia pointed out the illegality of the involuntary recogimiento because Luisa had been sold to another owner and should not have had to face imprisonment in either the convent or the bakery.[103]

The Third Council of Lima (1583) reiterated the right of married slaves to remain together: "Slaves and morenos who wish to marry should not be prohibited from doing so; their owners should not impede them, nor should they forcibly prohibit their slaves from exercising their conjugal rights."[104] In spite of this law, many slaves appeared before the ecclesiastical judge to request the return of their absent spouses, forced to another location by their owners.[105] Many owners feared that the desire to be with a distant partner served as a justification to escape and, thus, ecclesiastical officials charged with the care of slaves felt pressured to deposit them while they deliberated their case. A safe and appropriate place for a female might be a panadería, or the ecclesiastical or city jail; men most often went to jail.[106]

The interference of an owner could also complicate conjugal disputes among married slaves. In 1618, Joan Ramos claimed that when he allegedly beat his wife, Ysabel Bañon, her owner had him thrown in jail for six months.[107] In another case, Juana Criolla's owner put her in jail as a recogida to protect her against supposed mistreatment by her husband, who complained bitterly to the judge that the assertions were false.[108] In both cases, owners used enclosure/imprisonment as a means to protect and prohibit contact between married slaves.

During the negotiation for a slave's resale, which might reunite a married couple, the judge usually deposited the woman for her protection. After Jacinta de Horosco, a mulatta slave, married Pedro Rico, her owner brought her to Lima. Her husband, also a slave, remained in Quito. She was subsequently sold to a second owner, who, she argued, badly mistreated her. Willing to pay her personal earnings to her owner, she requested deposit while the judge negotiated her sale to a new owner:

> I have not tried to flee or hide, only to procure protection from the arm of the church and its power in order to live with my husband. . . . [The church] should protect and place me in deposit or send me to one of the public jails in the city where I will receive more protection because in my owner's house I fear that something disgraceful will occur, not only to my body, but also to my soul for being almost deprived of hope because of the mistreatment I have received.[109]

Women, like Jacinta de Horosco, who went to court consciously demonstrated their need for physical and moral protection (that something disgraceful could occur to their souls); they also represented themselves as morally "recogida," honorable, and deserving to have their husbands with them. The control of slaves' sexuality and forms of self-identification (as men and women and as husbands and wives) was not viewed as the exclusive domain of owners: these couples knew they had legal recourse for protection.[110] To foster and maintain family ties, slaves took advantage of recogimiento as a form of legal deposit and expressed it as a moral quality.

The practice of recogimiento also served when dissension arose among family members. Convents and recogimientos operated as incarcerating institutions in betrothal disputes, especially when parents were unwilling to accept their daughter's spousal choice;[111] if the couple failed to comply with the preliminary procedures to gain the necessary marriage license;[112] and to protect a young girl's right of marital choice.[113] In 1618, Pasqual de Navamuel, a slave, wished to marry Ursula de Vergara, a free mulatta, but her mother strongly disapproved of such an "unequal match." The judge ordered Ursula's deposit in a private residence, where undisturbed, she could calmly make up her mind.[114] In an annulment case waged against him by his in-laws, Diego de la Cruz persuaded the judge that his wife, Rufina, although under twelve years of age, needed to be recogida in a convent and not in her parents' home until mature enough to decide whether to return to the marriage, which he claimed had already been consummated.[115] Diego's persistence resulted from his awareness that Tridentine law supported couples' free will to choose their spouse. Diego de Castillo was also aware of his rights even before the couple married. He petitioned to have his fiancée, Francisca Bazan, removed from the Monasterio de la Concepción where, he affirmed, she was being held captive, to an honorable home where she would not be under duress from the nuns whom she served in the convent.[116]

In order to restore the honor of a young woman who had engaged in sexual relations with her betrothed and was then rejected, parents often decided to deposit their daughter and then sue the intended groom for breach of contract.[117] In such instances, the character of the young woman and her sense of recogimiento and honor came under heavy scrutiny, and numerous witnesses were required to attest to her proper upbringing and strength of character.[118] The doncella Doña Gerónima de Allioza had received a verbal marriage promise (palabra de casamiento) from Diego de Loarte. When he reneged upon his responsibilities, she protested and sought legal retribution. In the interim, she was deposited twice, once in the Monasterio de la Encarnación and later in the Casa de Divorciadas, while both judge and parents tried to persuade the reluctant groom to keep his word.[119]

Some elite Spanish or creole parents were heartless in forcing daughters into convents for an extended period of time until the "danger" of wanting to marry an unacceptable suitor or pursuing a different future had passed.[120] One man in Lima complained that he and Inés, his wife, were unable to consummate their marriage because her father had forced her to enter La Concepción, "in spite of all the warnings of the Council of Trent against women entering convents against their will."[121] Here the right of patria potestas, or patriarchal will, on the part of fathers was most explicitly exercised. Some parents even forced their daughters to take formal vows, thus remaining involuntarily cloistered for life. Young women like Doña Hierónima Bravo de Sotomayor protested that they were continually threatened, beaten, and locked (*encarce-lada*) in a room without access to siblings until "persuaded" to take religious vows. Hierónima described herself as being "in the condition (estado) of don-cella, beneath the dominion, subjection, and power of her father," and for those reasons, acquiesced to his will.[122]

Clandestine marriages were a continual source of embarrassment to eccle-siastical officials who felt that irresponsible couples had broken God's sacred law of matrimony.[123] Retribution included imprisonment for either or both parties, heavy fines, excommunication, the *tablilla* (a public listing of those individuals who had committed an immoral or criminal action and faced ex-communication), and possible exile. Sentences toward women were generally more lenient, although detention in a recogimiento could last several years.[124]

Even convents could punish intractable religious women or servants with enclosure in a cell designated for transgressors, or "recoger" them in another institution. In 1627, the Convent of Bernardas sentenced María de Ayala, an Indian professed servant (*donada*) to two years of labor, daily prayer, and fasting in the Casa de Divorciadas because she had left the convent dressed in her religious garments on the pretext of running errands in order to flirt with a tailor.[125]

Sexual transgressions, the main source of concern to various colonial authorities, also served as a major source of involuntary incarceration. Licen-tiousness was not considered socially or morally hopeless, and being labeled as *penitenciadas* or arrepentidas implied that, although like Mary Magdalene they had "fallen" into sin, they could be saved if willing to repent and do pen-ance. Bigamy and *amancebamiento* (concubinage, or living in a separate household with a married partner) were considered more serious crimes, and violators were often imprisoned, excommunicated, or exiled.[126] Concubinage had to be a publicly acknowledged fact, with ample evidence to prove that the couple had been seen leaving one another's home, had eaten together, shared the same bed, or had been sighted riding the same mule.[127] Incarceration served both to punish and physically separate the couple until one or both parties acknowledged their "sins."[128] Involvement with a married woman (who would remain nameless in the documents) carried a stiffer penalty.[129] In one case, Juan de Quiroga and his wife, Petrona Flores, accused one another of amancebamiento: she tried to have him exiled to Chile, and he insisted that she be deposited in La Caridad.[130]

Concubinage cases for the first half of the seventeenth century reflected the

entire social spectrum, although the popular classes appeared more frequently.[131] Gender, race, and class distinctions affected the judge's choice of incarcerating institutions. Men went to jail, and women were sent to the Casa de
Divorciadas, jail, an *obraje* (textile factory), or a convent according to her or
her husband's social status. Admission of guilt or confession remained a crucial aspect of those individuals incarcerated for concubinage, and many were
released once they admitted their "sins."[132] In principle, slaves and Indian
women accused of concubinage went to the city jail or a panadería. Most married women accused of concubinage went to the Casa de Divorciadas, which
did not discriminate against admitting casta women.[133] An *amancebada* about
to give birth, or who feigned pregnancy (and some did), went to La Caridad.[134]

Another sexual transgression—adultery—was considered a capital crime,
and a woman, whether a wealthy Spaniard or a poor slave, faced deep humiliation.[135] Since medieval times, preachers had invoked tales of wanton
adulteresses and contrasted them with the image of the Virgin Mary, or divine
grace herself.[136] Cheated and embittered husbands were apt to wreak brutal revenge upon their unfaithful wives; some wanted their wives to suffer *la muerte
en la Rebeldía* (death in Defiance).[137] Simón Román from Arica would not give
his wife, Francisca, the "privilege" of seeking a divorce because she had had
sexual relations with another man. When Román discovered the identity of
her lover, he killed him.[138] Fearing for her life as well, Francisca escaped to
Lima, but her husband followed her there in his boat. Once in Lima, he threatened to press criminal charges unless she agreed to live perpetually as a
donada in the Monasterio de la Trinidad. Fifteen years later, after the death of
her husband, she appealed her case, stating that she had taken religious vows
because she feared he would kill her, but the court denied her permission to
leave or to nullify her vows.[139] In this instance, the convent served as a locus of
punishment and humiliation and also helped foster a patriarchal double standard of intolerance for a female adulteress that would enable a cheated male
partner to restore his sense of honor.

Conclusions

Between 1580 and 1620, authorities in Lima transformed their perceptions
of casas de recogimiento and gender relations partly in response to three major developments in Europe. First, the increased concern with sexual and social mores in Spain and Italy led to a proliferation of new categories of women
who did not conform to those ideals. Moralists linked "dominant" norms that
women should contain themselves morally and physically with the "emergent" practice that advocated redemption for sexually aberrant women through
penitential discipline in institutions. Behavioral treatises also emphasized the

separation of the sacred from the secular, and the moral from the immoral. Second, once the Council of Trent declared that troubled women could no longer be housed in convents, authorities began promoting the foundation of secular institutions for women in need of asylum and moral reform. An emphasis upon the separation of the sacred and the worldly led to the proliferation of houses for "malmaritate" or "repentant" women and girls throughout Italy and Spain.

Third, evidence suggests that the increased moral monitoring by church and state authorities in Italy and Spain, and the foundation of new institutions to house unethical women or vulnerable girls, led to a marked acceleration in the voluntary enclosure and forced incarceration of females. These three developments in Europe contributed significantly to changes in the practice of recogimiento in Lima. But local concerns also altered the application of European models.

In Lima, rapid demographic and political changes served as a backdrop against the plethora of city ordinances and public outcry against rampant immorality and licentiousness. Archbishop Mogrovejo and Viceroy Velasco assiduously sought to inculcate Counter-Reformation values into the minds of their colonial subjects, but the tremendous influx of various ethnic and racial groups and the development of gender issues characteristic of Lima required adopting in situ control measures. Authorities faced problems similar to those of their European counterparts—illegitimacy, marital discord, and informal unions—but the combination of these factors with the constant migratory flux and large permanent female religious population gave the meaning and application of categories such as "wayward," "repentant," and "lost" a different cast. In fact, these categories persisted throughout the seventeenth century and bolstered convictions held by authorities about gendered codes of femininity (see Chapter 6).

Archbishop Mogrovejo knew that the few religious houses in Lima would have to minister to a diverse population because of limited resources and short-term interest in recogimientos. Convents continued to serve the "lost" daughters of conquerors, the growing creole elite, and occasionally provided refuge to divorciadas and women seeking asylum away from the "world." The Casa de Divorciadas and La Madgalena provided an acceptable, intermediary social outlet and an avenue for grievances to be settled in an institutional realm. But they also housed an entire array of women and girls, including prostitutes, repentant women, divorciadas, and women in need of temporary employment.

The increase in the institutionalization of women in Lima between 1580 and 1620 was symptomatic of the attempt by ecclesiastical and secular authorities to intervene in the lives of all colonial subjects, and particularly women.

On the one hand, Tridentine decrees, reinforced in both the Second and Third Provincial Councils in Lima, offered protection for individuals with dissimilar concerns. They upheld the sanctity of marriage and freedom of marital choice of all colonial subjects. Church laws served both frightened couples intent on carrying out their will and angry parents determined to thwart them. A slave suffering from forced separation from her partner, or recalcitrant wives who refused to reside with their husbands, had the right to use recogimiento to avoid further victimization. On the other hand, institutions could also incarcerate women who transgressed post-Tridentine interpretations of moral and sexual boundaries. Officials took allegations of sexual misconduct, including amancebamiento, clandestine marriage, adultery, and bigamy very seriously and felt justified in advocating involuntary recogimiento and rigorous punishment. Institutions served a greater variety of social functions than their European counterparts because of the diverse, free and enslaved, racially mixed, and culturally distinct population in Lima.

Authorities throughout Latin America attributed the "problem" of sexual misconduct to "aberrant" female desires; in no instances were men earmarked as abusive and in need of reform. But if women were seen as defective, they were also viewed as needing protection and moral and physical asylum, because ideally, they could not be trusted on their own. This contradictory "defective victim" paradigm continued to predominate in official discourse throughout the seventeenth century.

Aware of this misogynist norm, women sought to articulate institutional and moral recogimiento in ways that explained and justified their own conduct. Women and girls spent time in private homes or institutions while they filed a formal complaint against husbands, owners, or parents. However, the vast majority of ecclesiastical litigation suits in Lima resulted from divorce and annulment petitions. No less than 95 percent of divorce requests between 1580 and 1650 were initiated by women arguing before the ecclesiastical judge that their husbands had broken the conjugal contract.[140] Divorciadas faced judges who exemplified prevailing gendered codes, and adapted to the exigencies of the moment by articulating their narrative histories in ways that would maintain the status quo without compromising their own sense of moral order. In Lima, voluntary and involuntary enclosure increased throughout the seventeenth century, not only because officials sanctioned such practices but also because both husbands and wives quickly learned the rules of the game and began to use recogimiento to their advantage.

CHAPTER FOUR

Breaking the Conjugal Contract

The Voices of Recogidas Seeking a Divorce, 1580 to 1650

I N 1594, Hierónima de San Miguel appeared before the *provisor eclesiástico* (chief ecclesiastical judge) in Lima seeking a divorce. Her plea stated: "Without cause or reason but out of hatred and contempt my husband has treated me and treats me cruelly, both physically and verbally." She described an instance of extreme violence:

While I was bedridden and pregnant, he shut the doors of the house upon me and whipped me with an iron-studded belt, leaving serious wounds over my entire body and scandalizing me among the neighbors because the said incident was public and notorious.

After establishing the life-threatening nature of her husband's actions, significant in divorce litigation, Hierónima defended her own moral character as follows:

I am an honorable woman of high regard and very "recogida," having lived here for a long time. I have supported my husband with the labor of my own hands for years as a silk weaver and yet he spends over seven thousand pesos on a mistress in Chile. He has defamed me publicly.

Her husband responded:

She lives on her own in a house near the city gate on the plaza with a great deal of freedom and in such a way as to cause scandal throughout the entire neighborhood, and even though she has requested a divorce she has still been able to live freely; but until this case is resolved she should live with the necessary recogimiento and honest lifestyle appropriate to my honor. She should be deposited in the Hospital de la Caridad or in Martín de Ocampo's home (an honest and recogida home), where I am willing to support her financially. This means she will not be dishonored in front of her customers who buy her silk handiwork. I have dominion over her.[1]

Utilizing her own interpretation of recogimiento, Hierónima successfully refuted her husband's argument. She described herself as already "living honestly and recogidamente," not in a publicly scandalous manner. She portrayed herself as a moral individual (*de buena fama y recogida*), and argued that she could be trusted to live "openly" (*sin recogimiento*) in a home near her place of employment to provide for her three children (one of them from her husband's previous relationship), two servants, and a slave with a small child. She felt justified in requesting depósito (legal deposit required during divorce proceedings) in a private home because, like many women, she supported her husband financially and felt she had the right to remain free and unenclosed.[2]

Inherent in the confrontation between Hierónima and her husband is the issue of how individuals infuse cultural codes with meaning. Some historians exploring honor have emphasized the relationship between self, individuals, and "public" scrutiny, while others suggest that a sense of honor among elites was not internalized and "did not describe a code of personal integrity, honesty or virtue."[3] As an important component of honor, women such as Hierónima assimilated recogimiento both as a set of self-defining characteristics and as identifying features relative to others, particularly their male partners. In colonial Lima, the preservation of recogimiento was not always a matter of appearances or externalization. Women believed they *held* honor, *were* recogida, and drew strength to challenge others from an experiential sense of self-as-virtuous.

Like many women in colonial Lima, Hierónima knew that her (re)-definition of recogimiento would involve challenging established norms of appropriate "private" and "public" conduct.[4] She, like other women, knew she might face individual and collective scrutiny if seen frequently outside the home; but reality often obliged women to spend time in social or economic activities in communal settings. Women discovered that the cultural code of recogimiento served as a means to situate themselves within the interstices of imposed ideals that specified appropriate female public and private spheres.[5]

Evidence found in female legal testimony undermines twenty-first-century oppositional assumptions that distinguish between inside=private and outside=public spheres; apparently, the bifurcation seemed less magnified and discernible to early modern colonial subjects.[6] In fact, the feminine use of recogimiento "blended" these spheres. The courtroom setting made "public" the "private" internalized aspects of recogimiento as judges heard and witnesses testified about the plaintiff's conduct. Conversely, husbands and wives disclosed "private" meanings of recogimiento, drawn from generalized (public) understandings, but contextualized within their individual (private, subjective) history as a couple.

Hierónima ultimately achieved a small victory defending her sense of honor and recogimiento by being able to choose her place of deposit. She represented all women who negotiated recogimiento according to moral princi-

ples of self-identification (a private, internalized space) that transcended the
spatial limits of the home (casa) to include the world (beyond the home).
Hierónima personified a gendered position relative to established patriarchal
norms of appropriate private (recogimiento as a virtue) and public (recogimiento as nonenclosed but self-contained) by simultaneously conforming to
and subverting them.[7]

Women reinterpreted the cultural codes of recogimiento at a time when
divorces in Lima were more easily obstructed.[8] In 1563 the Council of Trent
confirmed the sacrament of marriage and the need to take vows before a
priest; but the Catholic position on divorce remained unresolved.[9] Although
considered inviolable, marriages could be terminated when extreme cruelty,
abandonment, adultery, or a lack of economic support could be clearly demonstrated. A divorce in the early modern period signified a permanent separation of the two parties, and prohibited remarriage. While more difficult to
prove, an annulment was granted when a party could demonstrate they had
married against their will or the matrimony had never been consummated
(other reasons were also considered).

The previous chapter investigated the transculturation from Europe to
Lima of post-Tridentine gendered attitudes toward sexual and moral deviance
and how institutions came to be considered as disciplinary and redemptory
centers. The practice of recogimiento or enclosure was also meant to separate
sexually remiss or vulnerable women from others. Ecclesiastical and secular
authorities in Lima appropriated and adopted these attitudes and normalizing
practices in creating recogimientos that would respond to local contingencies.
In that transculturation process, officials infused the concept of recogimiento
with their own interpretations of what constituted sexual misconduct and
how to handle it. As moral arbiters, they attempted to control the "public"
and "private" conduct of their colonial subjects. In turn, parents, slave owners, single women, and married couples responded and adapted these cultural
codes and institutional normative practices to their own concerns. In the cases
of dozens of divorciadas to be considered in this chapter, recogimientos continued to serve as redemptive centers, but by midcentury, they also reproduced the ambiance of the casa as a locus of patria potestas where male, female, or family honor could be preserved, regained, or reinterpreted. Ultimately, they evolved into centers where married women could challenge and
negotiate recogimiento.

By 1650, the Spanish precept of recogimiento had become a ubiquitous,
colonial virtue shared and utilized by urban women of all social classes and
races in Lima. Its pervasiveness appears in the intricacies of divorce and annulment proceedings: their prevalence, the social groups represented, and the
different strategies women employed to subvert and/or conform to accepted

norms of recogimiento as a practice of enclosure and a moral virtue. In order to unravel the complexities of conjugal politics in divorce proceedings, the chapter will consider strategies about deposit, female and male interpretations of recogimiento after women entered the institution, and economic and racial influences in adjusting to life in a recogimiento.

Breaking the Conjugal Contract

Generally, death remained the only legal way to terminate a marriage, and the majority of women believed it was God's will to obey their husbands, even under the most disagreeable circumstances. Misogynist arguments, many of them based upon Iberian cultural "norms," militated against a legal separation. One Spanish example dates from 1548 in Valladolid when Antonia del Aguilar sought to divorce Juan Vázquez de Molina, one of the secretaries of state of Emperor Charles V. The prosecuting attorney argued in his carefully crafted protest that her divorce petition should not be heard because the plaintiff expressed only her "sensible soul" of irascibility and concupiscence and, like children or beasts, women possessed less "intellectual" reason. Vázquez argued:

Although [women] have some gifts of understanding, they do not comprehend the reason [for actions] . . . which, as we have shown, is what distinguishes men of understanding from children, idiots and animals. I conclude that we have proved the lack of judgment and perspicacity of this lady, which prevents her from knowing what "marriage" means.[10]

Breaking God's law and human law were almost indistinguishable in late-sixteenth-century Catholic society, and the difference between crime and sin was minimal. Divorciadas might not be criminals, but they had broken God's law. Like other women defined as marginal, they had experienced some sort of slippage in status relative to their sexual identity. In that sense they were associated with prostitutes or fallen women because they had lost or were in danger of losing their honor or social reputation. At a time when "the criminalization of sin" formed a key component of Church discipline, ecclesiastical authorities felt it was necessary to institutionalize divorciadas for "correction."[11] Well aware that Protestant reformers sanctioned divorce with the ability to remarry in cases of adultery or abandonment, Catholic theologians saw institutions as a means to deal with unsuccessful marriages without openly sanctioning divorce. Authorities throughout the viceroyalty echoed European sentiments: they ascribed blame to women who wished to separate from their husbands, calling them "scandalous." In Quito as well as Lima, some authorities considered divorciadas a "threat to the Republic," and a bad example for Indians and other residents of the city.[12]

This disparaging discourse also resonated with many husbands who complained that the legal right to divorce only encouraged their wives' "desire for freedom and falsehoods" (*falsedades*).[13] In 1601, the attorney representing one litigant in Lima, Gregório Arias, argued:

Each day married women ... proceed with their bad customs [*sus malas condiciones*] ... walking about in liberty and freedom because it is a well-known and public fact that those husbands [against whom the women seek a divorce] work honestly to support their wives. They [the women] should be reprehended and remain at home to uphold their [the husbands'] honor. This is not the reason why the said woman wants to acquire freedom and this case should not proceed further.[14]

Given the biases against, and pressures placed upon, women, it is incredible that any woman could initiate divorce proceedings. Yet, as time passed, more women became dissatisfied with their plight and considered the nuptial agreement breached.

The marriage contract obliged husbands to be faithful and provide economic support in the form of money, clothing, food, and proper shelter; women promised fidelity and the maintenance of honor toward the male. An imbalance could occur after a transgression of legal and socially acceptable boundaries transpired. A husband might indulge in physical brutality, concubinage, or adultery, but such violations of the marital pact, although denounced as la mala vida, were usually tolerated up to a certain point.[15] Moralists discouraged jealous husbands from resorting to extreme violence, but saw no harm in locking up their wives if they were in dangerous company.[16] Spouses like Cristóbal de Barrera, in 1609, could argue that wife-beating served as a disciplinary measure and fell within the rights of patria potestas:

[If] there have been occasions when I beat or struck her, it is not because that is part of my nature.... I am not a man who is accustomed to such horrible behavior ... but if I placed my hands upon her it was in moderation and with the idea of correcting some imperfection in her behavior and to straighten her out, which is permitted a husband according to his rights.[17]

More often the catalyst for a legal separation came once the husband abandoned the household, physically or economically. In a society in which migration and transitory occupations were common, it is not surprising that female litigants complained most frequently of long-term absences and financial insecurity.[18] In spite of other grievances, most women—whether poor Spanish or wealthy indias—sought legal action against their partners when they considered the demand on them to support the household to be excessive and a stain on *their* sense of honor. Allegations of abuse or infidelity were often voiced in conjunction with clear economic negligence. No single reason—such as brutality, infidelity, or lack of economic support—predominated; instead, a combination of such factors usually inspired a woman to initiate legal proceedings.[19]

The divorce process began when the *procurador* (defender of the legal rights and privileges of individuals, councils, and religious orders) of the ecclesiastical court presented a "demand for divorce" (*demanda de divorcio*) in the plaintiff's name before the ecclesiastical judge (provisor). In the pleading, women could state, in their own words, the reasons for their request: they might cite extreme physical violence or mistreatment (*sevicia*), economic neglect, adultery, or drunkenness on the part of their husbands.[20] The judge would then decide whether to hear the case, and the defendant would be served with a copy of the complaint to which he was required to respond within a specified period of time. At that point, the ecclesiastical judge ordered the female plaintiff to be deposited in a private home or an institution until the case was dismissed, discontinued, or a sentence pronounced.[21] Many cases, however, did not proceed beyond the initial demand because either the defendant would not answer the plea or the couple lacked sufficient funds. Each party paid its own legal costs, but the husband was obliged to pay the bed and board for the deposit. If the case did continue, witnesses were called upon to attest to the moral, physical, and economic reasons motivating the plaintiff to seek a divorce. While the case was pending, the divorciada's lawyer would request the devolution of *bienes gananciales,* or property held in common, and the dowry. Eventually the judge pronounced a sentence, either to return to the marriage (*hacer vida maridable*) or to divorce.

Although a divorce sentence permitted the legal restitution of the dowry (and for many women this was a principal motive) as well as half of the communal property and the children, it was an arduous and cumbersome process, requiring tremendous courage and fortitude. If the husband protested, separate legal suits had to be filed for child custody, living expenses, and the restitution of the dowry.[22] Women were subject to humiliation and intimidating legal complexities. The process often required an inordinate amount of time and money, not to mention the public scrutiny of intimate details of their lives and the likelihood that—whatever the verdict—they would lose their standing as "respectable women." Once divorced, they could never remarry, and they found it necessary either to remain in seclusion in a relative's home or continue living as an institutionalized recogida.[23] In spite of their limited options, many complained that they lived like slaves in the marriage and preferred the humiliation of a divorce to the harshness of marital life.[24]

The divorce case of Marí Pérez, initiated in 1569, is significant because very few women sought divorces in this period. Marí persevered because, she argued, her much older husband was impotent and unable to impregnate her. She had resorted to witchcraft—putting herbs in his food and taking pieces of his beard and hair to two sorceresses—but to no avail. Her mother, who did not approve of her marrying an older man, testified that no blood could be found on the sheets the day after their wedding, even though Marí had provided a three hundred–peso guarantee (*arras*) of her virginity. The disconcerted husband, Pedro Sánchez, asserted: "I should not be denied my marriage," and he added that, not only had he "provided" his previous wife with children, but he had had frequent carnal relations with Marí. "She would be better recogida in my company," he argued, "than in the private home where she is currently deposited."[25] According to Pedro (and many other men), proper enclosure could be achieved only in his presence. And, in the end, Marí's attempt to expose his lack of sexual virility was not deemed a sufficient reason to sever the union. The judge ordered that Marí return to the marriage and that Pedro treat her with more "respect."[26]

During the sixteenth and early seventeenth centuries, ecclesiastical officials in Europe and Peru actively encouraged women to return to their marriages.[27] With this purpose in mind, the conventual-like regimen in recogimientos such as the Casa de Divorciadas divided each day into specific times for prayer, singing, and acts of penance to facilitate self-improvement and provide an atmosphere of seclusion to examine one's conscience.[28] Beatas or terciaries serving as administrators or teachers in recogimientos often dedicated their lives to the spiritual development of the hapless recogidas. The most notable example is Doña Isabel Porras y Marmolejo, a Franciscan terciary of noble Sevillian lineage, who served as abbess in the Recogimiento de Divorciadas for eight years (1606–14?).[29] Considered one of the most influential directors the institution ever had, Isabel was exemplary in "illustrating God's will to the enclosed divorciadas who obeyed her out of love."[30] Her dedication to a life of piety was apparent in her daily actions: she prayed continually, and took communion as frequently as possible.[31] Teresa of Avila served as her spiritual guide, and Isabel de Porras followed her recommendations on meditative prayer and advice on achieving a state of mystical union, or recogimiento, with God.[32] Having Isabel de Porras as her role model, it is understandable why the divorciada Elvira de Toro returned to her marriage in 1608 because of her "intervention."[33]

But persuasive tactics were not always successful. In 1600, Ana de Torres, filing for divorce against her husband, told the ecclesiastical court that she had been severely reproached and goaded by "principal religious persons" to return to the marriage; but when she did, her husband took such violent revenge upon her and her parents that she reinstated divorce proceedings.[34]

In spite of the active intervention of family members and ecclesiastical personages to hinder legal separations, women of all social and economic backgrounds requested divorces and annulments until both became more com-

TABLE 2

Total Number of Divorce Cases by Decade, 1569–1650, Lima

1569–1600	3	1621–30	52
1601–10	35	1631–40	83
1611–20	40	1641–50	186

SOURCE: AAL, Divorcios, Leg. 1–29.

mon and more readily secured in America than in Spain.[35] Divorce petitions increased steadily throughout the first half of the seventeenth century, reaching a total of 186 cases between 1641 and 1650.

Women of all calidades—defined by one's station in life and family affinities—filed complaints and, with the exception of Indians, most racial groups were fairly evenly represented in divorce suits. Using qualitative information to conduct statistical analyses is very difficult, because the shorter, incomplete cases, of which there are many, often lack racial data. Of eighty-one divorce cases analyzed for the period between 1569 and 1650, 60 percent yielded no racial data. Only five cases of "yndias" were found, but 17 percent of the divorciadas in the sample were slaves. Women classified as "doña" represented 62 percent of cases, but a note of caution is warranted because women of the popular classes could have used the title, especially given the need to demonstrate their status and impeccable moral conduct. Some wealthy women held significant amounts of property and were married to prominent male figures; other husbands held positions in the military.[36] Plebeian Spanish or casta women married to men of the same economic class worked as artisans and operated their own businesses as seamstresses or vendors.[37] Even a few destitute couples lacking legal funds initiated divorce proceedings. Most, however, did not pursue them for long.[38] Litigants in annulment petitions, on the other hand, represented a higher social status: couples here often used the title "don" or "doña" and held substantial dowries.[39]

Indians may have been underrepresented in litigation records until around midcentury because they had to answer to the *corregidor* (political administrator of a district) in El Cercado as well as to the ecclesiastical judge. They were assigned special attorneys called *procuradores de indios*, many of whom did not have their clients' interests at heart. Most of the cases initiated in Lima never progressed beyond a formal complaint because prosecuting attorneys would utilize racist arguments to hinder divorce suits among Indians. They reasoned that if one Indian were permitted to divorce, everyone would follow suit, because Indians were violent and untrustworthy by nature. One procurador recommended imprisonment, beatings, and fines to deter or punish recalcitrant husbands and wives.[40]

The divorce rate increased slowly until 1640, when in one decade petitions more than doubled. This occurred for several reasons: women no longer accepted misogynist arguments that their "sensible soul" was irascible and corrupt; they objected more vociferously to unwanted marriages forced upon them by family members; and they were more willing to face possible public scrutiny and humiliation of their moral character. Above all, they saw courtrooms as a space where they could vocalize that they were overworked, that their husbands were lazy and abusive, and that their honor and their family's honor were at risk because their spouses did not support them properly.

Increasingly, female plaintiffs expressed the sentiment that they had not broken God's law: their husbands had. Once willing to conform, and internalize a set of practices to maintain the conjugal contract, the divorciada living in a recogimiento "outside" the realm of marriage began to question her willingness to accommodate an unreasonable relationship. Recogimientos no longer served as a moral deterrent to uphold the marriage bond: women saw them as a space in which to develop emancipatory strategies. They subverted the established order (the idea of recogimiento as a brick-and-mortar moral savior) by providing a space where women could negotiate a different future.

Negotiating Recogimiento in Conjugal Politics

Once a woman decided to petition for a divorce or annulment before the ecclesiastical court, she entered a "public" arena and questioned her husband's legal and moral authority over her before a tribunal. Her testimony lacked the weight of a male's, but women found means to circumvent their supposed lack of credibility. The act of speech in divorce and annulment litigation gave women the power to reconstruct their reality in a public forum.[41] By portraying themselves as recogida, women showed keen awareness of the fact that their reputation relied upon public sanction and that what was "well-known and public" held tremendous value in colonial society. Because a "triangular dialogue" existed between husband, wife, and the ecclesiastical council, external witnesses (adding a fourth dimension) also played an important role in the ways divorciadas developed narrative strategies.[42]

A female plaintiff placed herself in an ambivalent moral position vis-à-vis the public, her husband or lover, and the ecclesiastical court. But in producing herself as a recogida she exploited and recoded particular interpretations of recogimiento that would benefit her in the public setting. This does not mean, however, that negotiating the significations of recogimiento—as a virtue and practice of enclosure—served as mere strategic and rhetorical tropes or theatrical posturing: on the contrary, the meanings often formed a component of a woman's identities.[43]

During testimony, women frequently asserted that men were superior, mirroring the accepted principle of patriarchal authority, predicated upon the "natural" authority of the male over children and wives as expressed in legal and economic relations.[44] Women claimed that they had treated their husbands with proper "submissiveness and honesty," had served them as punctually as slaves, and had given their spouses no occasion to doubt their fidelity and devotion.[45] Women of all socioeconomic groups in Lima described themselves as recogida and "living honestly and recogidamente," and denied that they had stained their husbands' honor.[46] In the 1646 dispute between Juan de Quiroga, a free mulatto master carpenter, and Petrona Flores, a mulatta, her lawyer said she had "behaved with the required honesty and chastity" and "served him in everything," but that Juan had blemished her honor by sleeping and eating with his mistress and allowing her to ride on the back of his horse.[47]

Even those women who had married men of unequal status found it important to express their submission and service to their husbands. María Flores, a Spaniard, reported that she married Bernardo Simón, an enslaved *quarterón de mulato*, who eventually gained his freedom. She claimed to have "behaved with all the respect a married woman owes her husband in spite of who I am, because I am his wife, even though he is of the said species/type (*especies*)."[48] Women like María Flores did not express specific "elite" or "plebeian" understandings of recogimiento; rather, social, racial, and economic considerations informed their perceptions of what they were expected to contribute to the marriage.[49]

In general, a man's accusation that his wife was immoral and "without recogimiento" because she lived outside the casa, or home, was compelling. A husband could claim that his "reputation and honor" were at risk and that he had moral dominion over her. It was as though the woman served as a "negative elaboration" of the man, and that her illicit behavior tarnished his honor because her recogimiento or honor was indistinguishable from his.[50] It also indicates that men and women understood that a moral "space" existed where their collective identity as a couple could be verbalized and contested.

If the wife claimed moral and economic abandonment, the husband might attempt to defame his wife's character. Accusations and counteraccusations evoked an invective dialogue usually involving defamation against a woman's sexual comportment, and slanderous accusations that she was a "whore," "licentious," "fallen," or morally unfit for the matrimonial state.[51] Thus in 1590, when Marta Hernández, a *morena* slave, sought to divorce Pedro López, a Spaniard, he called her a sorceress who relied upon her wicked customs to survive. He, like a number of other men, conflated female sexuality, power, and morality when attacking their integrity.[52]

Historian Bernard Lavallé has shown that couples resorted to racial slurs when attempting to justify an annulment because they claimed they had been duped into marrying a partner of unequal status. Ana Criolla, a free *morena* married to Juan Cortés, a black creole slave, maintained that her honor had been discredited because, since her marriage, she had provided the economic support for Juan and their five children. Juan claimed that the judge should not believe her just because she was "free" while he was not, and asserted that in spite of being enslaved he supported the household with his earnings as a day laborer.[53] In courtroom exchanges, many males also used defamatory racist language to associate the physically and morally unrestrained behavior of their wives with the conduct of inferior races. In 1638, Ana de Ayala, a free mulatta, not only suffered the indignity of being labeled as "nothing but a freed, black slave (*una negra horra*)" but also endured deposit in four separate locations within several months.[54]

Even though women had to face private and public scrutiny of their character, many felt that gaining seclusion offered an attractive alternative to a psychologically or economically difficult family situation. Nevertheless, the practice of recogimiento had a negative corollary: spurned males enjoyed the privilege of determining whether their wives would be placed in recogimiento or depósito (similar to the legal notion of escrow) in a home or an institution throughout the course of the divorce or annulment proceedings.[55]

The case of Pedro Sánchez and Marí Pérez in 1569 (see page 87 above) exemplifies patriarchal cultural assumptions about the domain of patria potestas which, for many men, included physical containment. When Pedro Sánchez protested his wife's petition for an annulment in 1569, he asserted the commonly held male notion that proper enclosure or recogimiento could occur only in his company. To him, an institution or private home could not possibly serve as a male spousal surrogate. He defined female recogimiento as enclosure within the casa, a male-dominated sphere.

However, unlike Pedro Sánchez, some men thought that a woman's lack of recogimiento (virtue and seclusion) constituted a direct offense to male honor, and "deposit" or institutionalization could help them regain it. As one unhappy husband testified, not only was his "free" wife damaging his honor, but her behavior served as a "model of dishonor" for the infinite number of other married women who might "choose to act in such a brazen and shameful manner."[56]

Institutional enclosure or recogimiento did not just serve the purpose of reinforcing male authority, however. Some women rejected the notion that something had been "lost" and that through institutionalization they could regain their honor and make a dignified re-entry into society.[57] In the verbal exchanges, a woman could argue that her moral superiority, or *buen recogimiento,* was affirmed simply by the fact that she put the food on the table. Her husband's failure to fulfill his economic obligation carried far more weight than her lack of seclusion or virtue. By accusing the husband of abandonment, a woman could argue that her husband had created a lack of institutional rec-ogimiento in the casa, a gendered space that to her symbolized the couple's union. In the end, the absence of reciprocity provided the most formidable weapon for women trying to negotiate their own terms of institutionalization.

In divorce and annulment litigation, the ecclesiastical judge was the ulti-mate authority in deciding where a woman would reside, but the husband's choice, by virtue of patria potestas, carried legal weight.[58] In cases involving a sexual transgression—concubinage, adultery, or prostitution—the judge's in-stitutional preference prevailed. In divorce cases, by contrast, women had more say in the choice of recogimiento, type of accommodations (whether a woman could bring her own bed and sheets with her), and company (chil-dren, friends, relatives), although conditions within the institution clearly re-flected differences in social and economic status.

Men and women interpreted the meanings of honor and recogimiento in distinct ways while negotiating the politics of enclosure or "location."[59] For many women, recogimiento symbolized protection. They realized before leaving the home that their honor had been tarnished and sought an alterna-tive that would reduce the risk of further scandal, exclude intrusive family members, and preserve their reputation. Husbands expressed concern over physical control to ensure that their wives, outside their purview (the domain of the casa and themselves), would not go astray and experience too much freedom of movement; and that communication with impartial individuals (both familiar and unfamiliar) should be restricted.

Life in a Recogimiento

In spite of numerous constraints, almost two-thirds of divorciadas were granted requests to be placed in the location of their choice, often a "house of honor" with a well-known married couple (see Appendix E).[60] Enclosure in the home of a single woman or a female relative could provide a sense of secu-rity and camaraderie for distressed women.[61] When considering institutional options, most women saw the Casa de Divorciadas as the most appropriate, legitimate location. The Hospital de la Caridad remained the second institu-tional choice, and its infrastructure provided legal support (lawyers, solici-tors) as well as protection and comfort from the governess assigned to look after the women.[62] La Caridad served as a hospital only in the sense that it cured divorciadas who had been physically abused or were ill. Following re-covery, they were usually transferred to the Casa de Divorciadas. Some reco-gidas who voluntarily chose La Caridad or a particular convent as their asylum were later involuntarily transferred to the Casa de Divorciadas because the court considered that location more appropriate.[63] In unusual circumstances, however, women of high social position (with the title "doña") were deposited in convents.[64]

Class differences within the marriage served as an important factor in determining the place of deposit. A wife who was moderately wealthy, with more money than her husband (by means of a dowry, inheritance, or own earnings), and who provided the main income for the household, was more likely to negotiate the terms of deposit to her advantage. In cases where women found it necessary to be recogida near their place of employment, the judge usually honored their request if they could demonstrate economic control of the household and the ability to care for their offspring. As early as 1608, Ysabel Franca requested and was granted deposit in a private home near her place of employment in order to support her five children. She demonstrated that her husband, a mulatto artisan, would not be able to provide economic assistance because he faced imprisonment for two years.[65]

Slavery also circumscribed institutional choices. In one case previously mentioned, Jacinta de Horosco, a mulatta slave married to Pedro Rico, a black slave in Quito, requested that the ecclesiastical judge administer her sale to an owner who would not mistreat her and who would safeguard her return to Quito. Rather than emphasize her virtuous character, she emphasized her "self-control" in not trying to "flee or hide."[66] She requested deposit in a public jail, either because she was unaware of the existence of recogimientos or because she felt herself only worthy of going to a jail. The judge decided in her favor, and she soon traveled with her new owner to Riobamba, closer to her husband still in Quito.

Many women preferred deposit in a home to facilitate care for their children.[67] Even poor and unemployed wives expressed the need to attend to their children's needs, and many offspring accompanied their mothers to the Casa de Divorciadas.[68] Some mothers even removed their daughters from convents to reside with them in their place of enclosure, to protect the girls from threats of "abduction" by the father.[69] This expanding practice of institutional recogimiento—as a protective space that could reproduce the casa—enabled young girls to learn the rudiments of recogimiento within a new setting (outside the home), and impart their understanding to the next generation.

Many husbands preferred their wives to be deposited in institutions rather than private homes, and if dissatisfied with the place of deposit, petitioned for the wife's transfer to another location. The most common arguments included the potential freedom of movement private recogimiento would allow and the influence that caretakers might have over their wives, particularly if they were family members.[70] In addition, men saw control over their wives' communication with family members or others as a male prerogative. In 1599, Domingo Hernández expressed concern that his wife, María, might "fall into the hands of his enemies": "Maria de Torres should not speak with men nor leave her cell, as we suspect has occurred, [in order to] spread rumors. The governess of the recogimiento should not permit this upon pain of excommunication."[71]

While unable to prove a lack of proper enclosure, he insisted that María only wanted her freedom (*libertad*), and to communicate openly with "other" women of "ill repute."[72] In 1646, Francisco de Valladares, married to María Magdalena, a criolla, wanted his wife transferred from the Casa de Divorciadas to La Caridad because she conversed with "suspicious individuals."[73] A few years earlier, Don Francisco de Urbina y Flores expressed his horror at the fact that his wife, Doña Francisca de Quiros, had developed an "excessively close" friendship with a woman in La Caridad while he traveled on business to Quito. When she initiated a divorce suit against him, he protested that she lived in the recogimiento "with the greatest dissolution and insolence in the world, which is well known throughout the city."[74]

Complaints of "public exposure" were more common when a woman resided in a private home. In 1599, one husband remonstrated that while his wife, Ana, was deposited in a private home, an elderly man harassed her (*poniendo su mal intento en execución*), by trying to convince her to leave her marriage.[75] Ana assured the judge that this was not so and that she wished to remain there so her husband could not put his *mal intento* into effect. In another case, one husband argued that his wife could be seen all day long "hanging over the balcony."[76] In 1640, another husband, Antonio de la Mota, pleaded for his wife to be removed from her current deposit in her mother's home to another location because:

although it proved advantageous to deposit Blasa [his wife] in the house of my mother-in-law Ana de Guzmán, it is with little fear of God, our Lord, that she breaks the solemn pledge to keep her in deposit, giving in to her will, taking her to the theater on Sundays and allowing her to go out at all hours of the night in bad company, bringing dishonor upon me and causing much scandal in the city.[77]

Control over communication proved to be a major source of friction among many couples, but for many women, seclusion and separation from family members who could offer psychological and economic support proved unbearable.[78] For husbands, families could provide both support and interference.[79] Often the judge would side with the husband if he could argue convincingly that his wife's guardians in a private home were biased against him (unless clear evidence of spousal abuse existed), and she would usually be transferred to a more "neutral" residence.[80] From the judge's point of view, the location of deposit had to provide a suitable, impartial environment where the woman could weigh her conscience in peace and recogimiento, or internal silence.

Solitude and peace of mind were important considerations, but in the strategic game of "deposit," surprisingly, almost half of all women who had initially chosen to be deposited in a private home asked to be relocated to an institution because, in principle, it could provide them with better protection (they had thicker walls, barred windows, and guardians at the exits).[81] Two or three transferals in the course of the litigation were fairly common in spite of the fact that it was "inconvenient and risky for an honorable woman to go from house to house."[82] In one extreme instance in 1608, Ana Colón faced five changes of "residence": once in the home of Elvira de Coca; later to the Recogimiento de Divorciadas; a third time to another private home; again, back with Elvira de Coca; and finally, to stay with Isabel Mejía.[83]

The choice to go to a private home could have negative repercussions. Many feared physical and psychological abuse because the numerous entrances to a home provided easier access for an enraged husband.[84] Several recogidas were admitted to the Hospital de la Caridad after severe beatings once husbands gained access to them while they resided in a home.[85] Still others feared for their safety even while deposited in an institution. In 1608, Ysabel Franca was so terrified of physical retaliation that she petitioned for her husband to be denied access to a four-block radius surrounding the recogimiento. If the wife could provide physical evidence of beatings by her husband, establish the life-threatening nature of his conduct, and find witnesses to testify on her behalf once she had been deposited, the husband would usually be sentenced to jail.[86]

Elite recogidas often preferred deposit in a home to an institution. Those who went to recogimientos cited three main reasons why they should be transferred to a private home: they maintained that their honor would be tainted by the inappropriateness of the location; they complained about the lack of proper accommodations; and they disdained the idea of coming into contact with "dangerous" women of lower status. Many tried to elicit a transfer to another location by emphasizing their state of destitution within the recogimiento, where they lacked a proper bed and clothing and were exposed to contagious diseases.[87] In 1599, María Torres, appalled at the bad condition of the institution ("es un páramo": it's a wasteland), felt the need to have her material possessions with her to comfort her "in such a jail."[88] In another instance twenty years later, Doña Francisca Renxifo's lawyer requested her transfer to a private home from the Casa de Divorciadas, because the institution lacked medicine and other comforts "that place my client's life at risk."[89]

Several divorciadas in La Magdalena and the Casa de Divorciadas complained that being housed together indiscriminately with other recogidas—

with little concern for status and class differences—was the most humiliating aspect of their internment.[90] A terrified Doña Magdalena de Roxas y Sandoval, about to be moved in 1604 from a private home to the Casa de Divorciadas, expressed her concern:

At the moment I am in a private home where I receive the comfort necessary to recover from a serious fall I have suffered, but my husband asks the judge to deposit me in the Casa de Divorciadas where "lost" women repeatedly go for different reasons.[91]

She contended that she was being forced to live below her economic means and social status, and felt her sense of honor had been tarnished.

Male assertions about the camaraderie among recogidas in institutions was not always mistaken.[92] Support could range from sharing food or bedding to plotting an escape. Once enclosed, the governess, beatas, other recogidas and the *portera*, or concierge, also served as invaluable witnesses.[93] Sebastiana Delgado provided a mattress for Lorenza de la Cruz in 1629 and testified on her behalf, saying that her husband did not support her and she had "holes in her clothes." The governess of the Casa de Divorciadas and two other recogidas also testified on her behalf to refute the charge of adultery her husband had made against her. As witnesses they bolstered her argument that a moral breach and lack of reciprocity had occurred in the marriage.[94]

Women also conspired to find ingenious means—hatching escape plots or feigning illness—to be released or transferred from their internment. One *comadre* provided a recogida feigning labor pains with pastries and money to escape and consort with her lover.[95] Other recogidas complained of shortness of breath, fever, as well as pregnancy and labor contractions, malnutrition, general discomfort, and aches and pains: doctor's certificates were required to leave the recogimiento, but forgeries were common.[96] In 1620, Doña Francisca de Rojas embellished her list of ailments in order to change locations: she complained of pains in her legs, continual fever, that her life was in danger, and that she had a contagious disease. But her efforts paid off. The judge issued her transfer from the Casa de Divorciadas to the Monasterio de la Encarnación, where the abbess welcomed her.[97]

Genuine illness or pregnancy did not deter some husbands from ordering their wives' redeposit once they had recuperated. In 1623, Ysabel Galindo left the Casa de Divorciadas to give birth (she had been married only six months), but her husband then ordered her return: "If the little infant girl survives and after Ysabel cares for her [during] the allotted time necessary, she must return to her deposit in the Casa de Divorcio where I will provide four reales each day for her."[98] Once she had given birth, Ysabel apparently decided that rather than face imprisonment in yet another location, her best option would be to escape to Chile. And that is exactly what she did.

The foyer of any institution—be it convent, recogimiento, or hospital—

was of crucial importance, because business transactions, conversations, whispered rumors, disguises, excuses, lies, and violent confrontations could take place in this small but crucial space.[99] Servants came and went with money, goods, and messages for the recogidas housed within. In spite of the fact that La Magdalena and Las Divorciadas maintained female guardians, an assistant, a doorkeeper, a domestic servant, and a salaried male employee to watch the rooms near the door to the street, the security of each recogimiento was flawed. Although the recogidas remained separated by lock and key from visitors, lawyers, or solicitors, who could see them only in the vestibule, still walls could be scaled and secret entrances or exits found. In 1639, Francisco de Carvaxal climbed over the wall of the Casa de Divorciadas to see his wife, Doña Ana de Mendoza, much to the chagrin of the inhabitants, and "causing tremendous discord and great scandal within." The governess, Doña Inés de Castro, pressed criminal charges against him for "breaking the cloister's rules."[100] In spite of the lawsuit, the couple were reconciled as a result of Francisco's "heroic" efforts to see Doña Ana, his "beloved wife" whom he did not wish to lose.

Husbands were obliged to pay monthly board for their institutionalized wives, but some wives still had to pay for their bed and keep with their own earnings.[101] Because some women were rushed to the recogimiento at inconvenient times (one litigant went at one o'clock in the morning with nothing but the clothes she was wearing), they literally found it necessary to negotiate the terms of their "bed" and their "board."[102] Donations from charitable funds sustained a few fortunate individuals, including Juana de Sandoval, whose survival for four months in the Recogimiento de las Divorciadas depended upon the governess.[103] In one exceptional instance, the founder of the Casa de Divorciadas, Francisco de Saldaña, donated four hundred pesos to enable María de Torres to pay the monthly twelve pesos necessary for food (which her husband refused to provide) and an additional six pesos for her slave, who would also serve the recogimiento.[104]

In general, however, most women did not have wealthy benefactors, and the cost of upkeep ranged from twelve to twenty-four pesos monthly (twelve to fifteen pesos on average).[105] The judge decided how much would be paid, but many times the woman would request an exorbitant amount out of malice, or because "that was the style in which she was accustomed to live." The husband faced excommunication or public condemnation (the tablilla) if he consistently refused to pay, and after one or two months of hardship, the judge might decide to transfer the recogida to a less costly private home.[106]

During this crucial period, recogidas had to rely upon their earnings, their sense of economic independence, and family or friends' support. How they survived within the recogimientos reflected economic and racial differences.

Women often transported material goods with them to reproduce the home environment, and often claimed that the objects they later demanded—beds, sheets, items of clothing, and jewelry—logically belonged "only to women," and should not be removed from their possession, even at the behest of angry husbands.

While recogida, women also negotiated the return of their personal property. Restitution of the dowry remained a major irritant between couples (and, in that sense, the threat of divorce constituted an economic hazard for men), and other material possessions proved to be a source of bitter contention.[107] Safeguarding slaves in the recogimiento proved to be an important concern to many women, whether creoles, mulattas, or mestizas, because they feared their husbands would sell them along with the rest of their property.[108] Propertied women like Doña Cathalina de Uceda (see page 72 above) felt compelled to protect her assets when she requested that five slaves accompany her to her place of deposit, "to ensure that nothing happens to them."[109]

Life in the recogimiento was more difficult for divorciadas whose husbands were unable to sustain the costs of bed and board. Many women, rather than ask for assistance or beg for alms, worked in the institution. The Hospital of la Caridad and several convents served as temporary places of employment for casta or poor Spanish women who worked as nurses or supportive staff to pay their board and legal costs. In 1622, Gerónima de San Francisco, a free mulatta, was deposited in the Hospital of la Caridad, on the condition that she work, because her husband, a slave, could not support her. After several months she requested a transfer to a private home: "I was two months pregnant when first deposited in La Caridad, but I was not well and very very poor and in the said hospital I had nothing to eat and was unable to earn my bread and keep because of my delicate condition."[110] Gerónima used her physical frailty (she also claimed that her arms had been severely bruised by her husband's beatings) and her status as a free mulatta to negotiate a transfer. Her husband's owner, however, pressured for her return to La Caridad, stating that he, the owner, would support her.[111] In this particular instance, patriarchal authority extended from judge to husband to her husband's owner, who served as an extension of her husband's control. By contrast, another recogida, Ana Ruíz, perceived herself to be a woman of calidad (high status) and therefore considered it beneath her dignity to work and suffer from hunger in the recogimiento.

Many women reported harrowing escapes from extreme violence in their marriages; others were not as fortunate. And yet, the majority of the cases remained unresolved. Some divorce and annulment litigants spent an inordinate time in recogimiento only to tire of the turmoil and desist. Most litigants dropped their cases and continued living apart. If the evidence was insubstantial, or the papers conveniently misplaced, the recogida was released from her enclosure. At that point, some elite women chose a religious vocation while others returned to their parents' home.[112] Others still "repented of their ways," and returned to their marriage.[113] Those who remained under the supervision of the ecclesiastical judge were usually advised to seek a *casa honrada* where they could live a decent life.[114] Others, who could no longer tolerate confinement or impingement of any sort, escaped to Chile or the provinces.[115] The myriad responses indicate that, by midcentury, women now had numerous possibilities to reconstruct social ties once divorce proceedings had ended.

Conclusions

Between 1580 and 1650, many husbands viewed recogimientos as normalizing spaces where women could reformulate and remedy themselves under strict surveillance. Colonial authorities determined the categories of women entering discipline-wielding/protective institutions: they were branded as lost, repentant, or wayward. However, in the process of enclosing women in these spaces, recogimiento—as a virtue and practice of enclosure—became the vehicle by which men and women attempted to exert control over the woman's identity, her physical location, and her material possessions.

The quality of being recogida depended upon perceptions of self, self in relation to others, and how others viewed that individual. The definition and defense of one's position toward the moral precept and practice could sometimes result in emotional combat. Husbands declared that female recogimiento involved male control over her virtue, access to resources, freedom of movement, public exposure, and personal contacts and communication outside the home. Aware of these contingencies, women petitioning for divorces or annulments attempted to demonstrate the ways in which the conjugal contract had been broken, and how their internal sense of honor had been tarnished. They argued that they had remained loyal, submissive, and morally recogida, but their husbands' economic and physical abandonment of the household forced them to work. Class differences were evident in what was considered as acceptable work and conditions of employment; nonetheless, women often expressed a sense of moral superiority even though they were no longer physically contained in the casa.

During the battle over recogimiento, women were able to subvert the idea that institutions served as spaces in which to redeem their immoral character. In protesting their unjust treatment in the courtroom setting, women gradually appropriated the moral and institutional space of recogimiento as a location where they could conceive of themselves as distinct from the conjugal (male-dominated) domain. At the turn of the seventeenth century recogimientos constituted a spatial "placement" for women experiencing a conjugal crisis; by midcentury, they had become "habitual" or "routinized" in the minds of many limeñas as a possible place where the redetermination of the meaning of casa could occur.[116] Having witnessed the physical relocation of their mothers from their home to another location, the next generation internalized these emerging gendered moral codes associated with recogimiento.

By 1650, divorce and annulment litigation had proliferated, and while women were still deposited, divorciadas were no longer seen as dangerous or a "threat to the Republic." The street in Lima called the "Calle de Divorciadas" had become a permanent locus of the viceregal capital. As a cultural code, recogimiento had become ubiquitous; the precept had experienced a cultural mestizaje or blending into the minds of women of distinct stations, racial affinities, and class backgrounds in an urban context that fostered a shared cultural vocabulary. Racial and class constraints influenced how women strategically employed recogimiento as a virtue and practice of enclosure in divorce proceedings, but the generalized belief that women could be recogida and nonenclosed (outside the home) helped transmute the imposed dichotomy of "public" and "private" ethics into a more viable reality.

Yet, at the same time that conjugal battles over the meaning of recogimiento were being fought in homes and institutions, an emerging Spanish and creole elite sought to appropriate recogimiento as a spiritual and educational practice to bolster their status and position in Lima relative to the established beneméritos, the land-based or encomendero class. During this period, elites managed to imbue recogimiento with new meanings based upon moral, theological, and educational significations still prevalent in the viceregal capital. They saw recogimiento as a cultural symbol that embodied sexual purity, physical enclosure, communion with God, and moral conduct, and promoted the foundation of institutional spaces that not only sheltered and educated elite women but also accentuated their difference from the rest of their "fallen" gender.

CHAPTER FIVE

Elite Formation and the Politics of Recogimiento, 1600 to 1650

T HE FIRST TIME Spanish chronicler Bernabé Cobo entered the city of Lima in 1599 he noticed only four or five expensive horse-drawn coaches. Thirty years later he counted more than two hundred, indicating that the fortunes of some of Lima's residents had improved considerably and the viceregal capital had entered an age of obvious prosperity. According to Cobo, an individual qualified as very wealthy, or *boca llena* (full mouth), when his annual income surpassed one hundred thousand pesos.[1] In 1630 more individuals with noble status resided in Lima than in any other Latin American metropolis, and the number of encomenderos in the City of Kings reinforced the city's "centripetal power" as a driving economic force.[2]

The beneméritos constituted the highest social echelon. As direct descendants of conquerors and war veterans, and as encomenderos and nobles (the most prestigious rank), they alone numbered some eight hundred individuals, or 2.7 percent of Lima's population.[3] Compared to their "glory days" in the sixteenth century (James Lockhart tallied some 480 encomenderos in 1555), the beneméritos had lost some economic power. Yet well into the seventeenth century, the dwindling elite still maintained tremendous social prominence and financial significance in Lima.[4] By 1630, however, "old" elites were competing with individuals who had developed distinct family networks and cultivated new avenues to wealth, power, and prestige.[5]

The nouveaux riches utilized various methods to consolidate their position vis-à-vis the beneméritos in Lima.[6] The formation of kinship ties and selection of distinctive occupations and capital ventures facilitated their ability to purchase the "costly carriages" to which Cobo referred. But the investment—in capital terms and through their sons' and daughters' professions—in church enterprises and schools called recogimientos also heightened their status and attendant privileges.[7]

Spanish and creole elites chose to cultivate recogimiento to achieve cultural and political hegemony in three ways. First, education served as the main modus operandi for increasing family status and a daughter's marriageability in a competitive market. Many elite males were functionally literate and trained in theology and law at the best schools or seminaries,[8] while a number of recogimientos or schools for daughters of the elite were founded during the first third of the seventeenth century. Convents served a similar purpose in providing an environment of enclosure and protection to educate girls *de buenas familias.* Not since the sixteenth century, when Franciscan friars founded recogimientos for Nahua girls and Charles V sponsored them for mestizas, had the educational function of recogimientos held the attention of authorities representing elite interests in Lima. Indeed, policies in Lima toward educating the Spanish elite paralleled developments in seventeenth-century Mexico City.[9] In both viceregal capitals, it was felt that Spanish and creole daughters could assimilate the behavioral characteristics of rec-ogimiento *in* recogimientos and convents that separated and protected their sexual purity from the sin and seduction that prevailed in the world.

Second, the elite appropriated recogimiento as a virtue related to quiescent conduct and enclosure, and refashioned it as an essential attribute for a good marriage. One can trace the articulation of recogimiento as a means to a felicitous matrimony in sixteenth-century Spanish behavioral tracts; the discourse that encouraged Nahuas, native Andeans, and mestizas to cultivate this Hispanic virtue; and concurrently, in the acrimonious dialogue of troubled couples involved in divorce litigation. Although hardly unique, elites in Lima consciously appropriated recogimiento as a distinguishing feature of females associated with *their* class. They asserted that elite women were sexually and morally pure, their demeanor impeccable, and their contact with the outside world limited.

The links between recogimiento, marriage, and social status remained key in seventeenth-century Lima, but a new application also emerged. Chapters 3 and 4 discussed the ways in which authorities attempted to classify females into separate sacred and worldly spheres and how couples responded to those normative criteria. By the 1620s, elites feared that the sin and corruption in secular society might pollute their daughters. They also felt that its permutation into convent culture left little recourse for those elite women wishing to pursue a life of strict recogimiento in a sacred space. While attempting to assert their influence in the secular realm, creole and Spanish men and women responded by creating alternative spiritual spaces. They promoted the foundation of several *conventos recoletos,* or observant convents, for daughters of the elite. This replicates a pattern described by historians Bernard Lavallé and David Brading: the growth of an elite creole male clergy and the demographic growth of convents for women in the seventeenth century.[10] Unlike the larger religious houses, observant convents emphasized austere material conditions. They also maintained a limited number of nuns (often thirty-three), complete physical and mental withdrawal from the world, and a dedication to a life of contemplation or spiritual recogimiento.[11] For young women these sacred spaces served as a symbolic intermediary between heaven and earth and complied with the mystical principles of recogimiento attributed to Francisco de Osuna, Teresa de Avila, and Luis de Granada. For parents and relatives, the entrance of a daughter into the sacred realm afforded greater familial contact with God and complete separation from the "worldly."

The combination of "material with spiritual profit" in religious houses and educational centers, as well as in business and charitable works, involved investment in an ideological framework.[12] To accomplish that goal, the new elite introduced symbolic representations of the sacred as integral to their identity. Lavallé has shown how creoles, in particular, endeavored to promote their noteworthy contribution to the spiritual well-being and history of Lima through *crónicas conventuales,* or conventual chronicles, and other literary mechanisms.[13] Antonio de la Calancha's (1584–1653) *Crónicas agustinianas* is a key example of a text that depicts women rejecting the "world" for a life of contemplation or recogimiento in the observant convent of Nuestra Señora del Prado (founded 1640). His work also illustrates how, by the time of its publication in Barcelona in 1653, elite notions of the sacred had permeated cultural thought and represented a norm in Lima.[14]

None of these changes occurred in an historical vacuum. Creoles and Spaniards both constructed their identities relative to the political power held by the beneméritos, but their delineation of the sacred and the worldly occurred during the peak period of popular religious expression. Lay devotion to living saints—including Rosa de Flores de Oliva, Martín de Porras, and Francisco Solano—increased, while a concomitant campaign against idolatry resulted in the destruction of thousands of older religious artifacts and the punishment of hundreds of "heretics" throughout the viceroyalty until the 1660s.[15] Colonial administrators, many of them connected to the emerging elite through kinship ties, sought to control and eradicate "aberrant" forms of religious expression and to re-educate those individuals who did not conform.[16] They sought to delineate the acceptable boundaries between the sacred and the worldly.

This chapter will begin by focusing upon the economic and political consolidation of Lima's elite, and then will examine how the nouveaux riches determined their own vision of—among other things—the various representations of recogimiento as a quality for a good marriage, as an institutional practice related to the foundation of religious and secular educational centers, and as an expression of religious contemplation in convents and newly founded observant convents.

The Consolidation of a New Elite in Lima, 1600–50

Throughout the seventeenth century, Lima served as the hub of commercial and banking activity for the entire viceregal economy. Silver production declined after 1616, but Lima's merchants and entrepreneurs were quick to diversify and restructure their investments.[17] As a result, the viceregal capital became more self-sufficient in the production of foodstuffs and artisan goods.[18] *Estancias de pan llevar* (wheat-producing estates in the fertile valleys surrounding Lima) supported the rapidly growing, self-reliant city, in part because of an increase of enslaved Africans imported to serve as laborers.[19] Until 1660, the wealthiest families and ecclesiastical corporations were able to accumulate profits from agricultural production despite the city council's counterproductive grain policies.[20] Consistent with seventeenth-century notions of public beneficence and Christian charity, merchants, bankers, and commercial agents invested simultaneously in urban real estate and religious philanthropy, patronizing hospitals, religious houses, and charitable institutions.[21]

Beneficiaries of the new wealth achieved additional status from elite family networks, initially based upon the encomendero/conqueror power base but incorporating new vocations with each succeeding generation.[22] As a result, a patrician ethos developed among merchants, bankers, and landowners investing in developing industries—including shipbuilding, textiles, and increasing agricultural production. In addition, new kinship links were forged among those involved in inter-regional trade. As shipping businesses expanded from Callao to major port cities along the western seaboard, including Santiago, Guayaquil, and Acapulco, new American family alliances followed suit.[23] Recently arrived Spanish immigrants also assimilated into Lima's commercial market and merchant guilds, and many found that the sale of public offices enhanced their opportunities to gain elite status.[24]

Families also utilized marital strategies to maintain transatlantic links and consolidate expanding provincial kinship and commercial ties with Quito, Guayaquil, Cuzco, and Potosí. How much influence young women had in the choice of a marriage partner is unclear, but certainly parents' preferences had changed. Previously, elite families encouraged economically advantageous matches with noble families, usually with a base in Spain; by 1630, young men who held public office, participated in commerce, or were well educated were considered more suitable candidates.

A tremendous increase in the number of Spanish women migrating to Peru in the latter part of the sixteenth century meant that by the 1620s, a number of families placed even greater significance upon marrying well. The fact that the number of Spanish women and mestizas increased by 65 percent between 1613 and 1636 served to heighten competition for suitable spouses.[25] Several Spanish behavioral tracts, including Luis de León's (1528–91) *La perfecta casada* (1583) and Juan de la Cerda's (1560–1643) *Libro intitulado vida política de todos los estados de mugeres* (1599), were popular among aspiring Spanish and mestiza elites. Both works stressed marriage, marriageability, and recogimiento as a virtue that could ensure individual, family, and community honor. According to de la Cerda:

Oh recogimiento for women: of inestimable value. A dowry necessary for marriage, abundant wealth which a woman can enjoy; honor for the house where she resides, an example for her neighborhood, honorable paragon of the village where she grew up; brilliant crown of her lineage, and a resplendent model for her descendants.[26]

Recogimiento, as enclosure, enhanced a woman's "marketability," ensuring virginal status, protection from unacceptable company, and separation from *lo malo*.[27] Guevara counseled women to marry their "equal in blood and status," but love and fidelity were also important elements.[28] Once married, Luis de León advised that a woman's sense of virtue and recogimiento should be applied to govern the casa: a woman's "natural" domain.[29]

Another popular writer of the time (indeed, probably the best-selling Spanish author of the century), Luis de Granada, specifically addressed the "less perfect" lay person. Women, he instructed, could be pious *and* married:

[Y]ou shall find a married woman . . . burdened with children, family, and a house to administer . . . and if with all this she manages to still her senses [recogerse] at a certain time every day and take part in this type of prayer . . . you shall see in her soul a simplicity and purity so large, a chastity so pure, a devotion so intense, a love of God so vibrant, [and] a rejection of the world.[30]

A young, marriageable woman could not expect to gain respectability solely through solid moral conduct, spirituality, and physical reclusion, however. A "good" marriage also required a substantial dowry, but many women in Lima complained that they were unable to find a suitable husband because of inflated dowry prices. A cursory review of divorce records for the seventeenth century indicates that dowry prices for elite Spanish women could range from ten thousand to forty thousand pesos. More moderate dowries ranged between two thousand and five thousand pesos.[31] This concurs with dowry prices in Mexico City.[32] Limeñas were not the only concerned parties: Crown officials, and also Philip III and Philip IV, recommended that wealthy individuals provide legacies for dowries of poor and orphaned girls and, on an institutional level, that the church should support pious works to this effect.[33] The anxiety that developed in the 1550s for the growing poor and marginalized element of the population persisted into the seventeenth century and resulted in the foundation of numerous charitable institutions for needy girls in Mexico and Peru.[34]

Because of the preoccupation with purity and recogimiento as requisites for a good marriage, dowry-granting institutions, sodalities, or confraternities (both lay pious organizations devoted to the cult of a particular saint) selected doncellas who met specific qualifications. Several catered to moderately wealthy girls. Others offered donations to those of more modest means, and still others to foundlings or orphans. Sodalities (in themselves often racially based) specified racial criteria (whether to accept only Spanish or mestiza applicants) and in what proportion (no dowry fund existed solely for mestizas, for example). The sixteenth-century Hermandad de la Caridad y Misericordia (founded 1564) served as a prototype for many seventeenth-century charitable organizations because it provided dowries and social services to females.[35] Later, the Cofradía de la O (founded 1632) and the Cofradía del Rosario (founded 1640s) began granting dowries as a response to the need for such institutions in Lima.[36] Funds from the sodalities were underwritten by the wealthiest religious corporations and merchant communities in Lima, and coincided with investments in other charitable works. The Jesuits of the College of San Pablo, for instance, administered the Cofradía de La O; its eight hundred to one thousand members included wealthy merchants, nobles, and royal officials.[37]

It is impossible to ascertain whether sodalities actually made a difference in social beneficence toward the "truly poor," but, in principle, their dowry funds served at least some "needy" girls by providing the opportunity to marry above their status.[38] Once a year, sodality members drew lots to provide money for a specified number of girls (for instance, the Franciscan Sodality of the Immaculate Conception provided twelve dowries). *Sacando la lotería*, or winning the lottery, guaranteed a brighter future for an indigent young woman. Yet many "dowry-granting agencies" maintained inconsistent policies: some, rather than helping the "poor," provided an additional means by which moderately wealthy families could care for their daughters' needs without depending upon winning the dowry lottery.[39] Dowry provisions were also contradictory: one ordinance for the Sodality of the Immaculate Conception required that dowries should serve only Spanish and mestiza orphans, but stated in a later clause that relatives of confraternity members were also eligible. Because resources were limited and competition intense, confraternities precluded girls from "enjoy[ing] the fruits" of other confraternal funds.[40]

Education and Lima's Elite

While family name, recogimiento, an upstanding moral character, and a substantial dowry were necessary ingredients for a good marriage, education served as a direct avenue to improved status. As a result, colonial administrators and individuals became more actively involved in promoting and expanding opportunities for female education during this period. Depending upon class, race, and legitimacy, instruction ranged from private tutelage in the home, through training from *amigas* or beatas, to private lay schools, orphanages, or conventual education where the girls were called *educandas*.[41] The Council of Trent allowed convents to accept secular girls as educandas, resulting in their admission into schools in Italy, France, and Mexico, but this practice remained more the exception than the rule in Lima before 1618, in part because the admission process was so time consuming.[42]

Increasing interest in female education and the desire to foster additional institutional safeguards of recogimiento created pressure on convents to admit more elite daughters. A papal bull issued in 1618 empowered the archbishop of Lima to determine the admissibility of educandas, with limitations in age between seven and twenty-five. They would remain cloistered throughout their stay, pay every six months, and maintain separate cells from the rest of the convent.[43] Entrance requirements were simplified, and either the conventual community voted to accept or reject the candidate, or the abbess presented a signed statement of approval.[44] Several convents constructed a separate seglarado, or area for lay educandas, as an annex to the convent.[45] The procedural adjustments had significant results: Archbishop Pedro de Villagómez (1641–71) calculated that a total of 117 girls were being educated in La Encarnación, La Concepción, and Santa Clara in the 1640s; a decade later, all eight convents, including the observant convents, taught a total of 250 educandas.[46]

The cost and the quality of education naturally varied from convent to convent and from one teacher to another.[47] Nuns were expected to read and write but did not always impart those skills to their female pupils.[48] Most entrants came from affluent families, evidenced by the liberal use of the title doña, but their backgrounds and circumstances differed. Some infants were deposited immediately after birth, while others were the daughters of widows or widowers, either unable to provide economic support or unwilling to accept responsibility for their daughters' upbringing. For example, Ambrosio de Arbildo y Berriz, the recently appointed corregidor of Chachapoyas in 1630, like other fathers who regularly traveled long distances, found it more convenient to deposit his "doncella" daughter in a convent for safekeeping. The petition to the nuns by his lawyer gave three reasons:

[B]ecause it is so far away, he cannot take his doncella daughter [twelve years old] with him, [because] she has no mother or other relative with whom he can leave her in the comfort and decency required of a person of her condition [*estado*] [as a doncella][49] and because there is no recogimiento here [in Chachapoyas] for girls of her status [*calidad*].[50]

A few years earlier, a girl whose mother had died petitioned La Encarnación to enter as a lay person:

[My] mother has died and my father is absent from this city without any certainty when he will return. I am alone and without a place where I might remain secure according to my social class, to be able to live honorably and recogidamente and so for this reason I request the license and permission to enter the seglarado of Nuestra Señora de la Concepción.[51]

A convent's internal hierarchy segregated girls according to class, race, and legitimacy. The status of educanda, for example, distinguished elite girls from those categorized as *seglares*, or boarders.[52] Still, girls (and women) who paid to *pisar el suelo* (literally, to step on the ground) required significant financial backing to provide the one hundred peso annual fee. Some seglares represented the elite, but many performed menial tasks to earn bread and keep and shared a cell with a nun.[53] Orphans and expósitos (abandoned children or foundlings), left on the doorstep of the convent, invariably served as a labor force for the nuns or the schoolgirls.

After 1618, the open admission policy for educandas contributed to the proliferation of other poor children in convents. This caused the archbishop, as early as 1630, to order strict compliance with the established policy that no young girls or boys other than schoolgirls and servants could reside in religious houses.[54] Still, the conservation of class distinctions in convents meant that by midcentury several generations of children of diverse backgrounds had experienced lifelong enclosure. Their "education"—above all, an awareness of their social position—would eventually enable them to foster "emergent" perceptions of the virtue and spiritual practice of recogimiento based upon their own racial and class affiliations (see Chapter 6, below).

Just as convents throughout Europe, Mexico, and Peru opened their doors to elite children, state-sponsored or private schools and asylums for poor and orphaned children flourished in seventeenth-century Italy and France.[55] In Spain, Crown authorities also favored state or individually sponsored charitable institutions that would provide educational services. Philip III had encouraged Viceroy Francisco de Borja y Aragón, count of Esquilache (1615–21), to endow and establish "public institutions" (as opposed to convents), to target the poor and orphaned young. His successor, Philip IV, reiterated this point in 1623 by decreeing that poor women and orphans should be given particular protection throughout the viceroyalty.[56] In his judgment, expósitos—

many of them female—had become a major demographic and social concern. Like their sixteenth-century predecessors, both kings felt they should be provided with proper recogimiento (enclosure and training in virtue) and shelter. Not only were the numbers of abandoned children on the rise, but María Emma Mannarelli's analysis of the parishes of El Sagrario and San Marcelo in Lima shows that 95 to 98 percent of the 332 abandoned children during the course of the seventeenth century were designated as "Spanish."[57]

Four secular institutions founded between 1603 and 1655 in Lima—the Casa de Niños Expósitos (eventually, it merged with the Colegio de Santa Cruz), Colegio de Santa Teresa, Recogimiento del Carmen, and the small-scale Recogimiento of Nuestra Señora de los Remedios—offered educational services to girls.[58] For decades the Casa de Niños Expósitos (founded 1603) provided refuge to Spanish boys and girls, many abandoned on church doorsteps, in the streets, corrals, or irrigation canals of the city.[59] Continuing financial assistance enabled the house to expand its services, and, by the 1620s, the orphanage housed more than 120 foundlings and nearly 50 other children. By the 1630s classes were available for select children; others were trained to care for the very young, to work as servants, or to solicit alms in the street.[60] In 1654, a generous endowment by Mateo Pastor to upgrade the orphanage and establish the Colegio de Santa Cruz enhanced the institution's role as a locus of public beneficence for children.[61] This timely donation concluded a period of increased support for public works such as orphanages and recogimientos for children.

Private lay institutions such as recogimientos were more likely to attend to the needs of abandoned children and orphans, but some proved as discriminatory as convents in admission practices and excluded or ranked children according to criteria of race, legitimacy, family connections, and wealth.[62] Finding an honorable space for abandoned Spanish or creole children seemed to have been a central priority. The Casa de Niños Expósitos is a case in point, since administrators classified most of the children admitted as "Spanish."[63] Somewhat less restrictive, the Colegio de la Caridad educated and housed Spanish and mestiza girls, training some as nurses' assistants while educating others in reading, writing, and "womanly arts." Even in the sixteenth century, selected girls received dowries on the lottery system. By 1610 or 1620, hospital council members, composed of prominent merchants, were eager to create a separate school to protect "[the girls] from contact with diseased women and married or single recogidas of all ages."[64] With such a show of support, the Recogimiento de Santa María del Socorro (also known as the Colegio de Santa Teresa) began operation in 1614 and provided six girls with scholarships and an additional 600 pesos for their dowry once they became nuns or married.[65] Fifty girls, all legitimate and between the ages of eight and twelve, were educated at the recogimiento. Dressed in a Carmelite habit, each schoolgirl paid 150 pesos per year for room and board.[66]

Impressed with the spiritual and administrative gifts of Doña Isabel Porras y Marmolejo, the directors of the Hospital de la Caridad selected her to run the recently constructed recogimiento of Santa María del Socorro (founded 1614), now a separate annex of the hospital.[67] While teaching, Isabel counseled her students in spiritual matters in the school's chapel and was so deeply respected that many of her students, wishing to emulate her piety, became nuns.[68] Her religious fervor and support of female enterprises so impressed many of Lima's inhabitants that three years after she died in 1631, Archbishop Arias de Ugarte sent her papers to Rome to encourage her beatification.[69]

Another exceptional woman, Catalina María Doria, and her husband, Domingo Gómez de Silva, founded, at their own expense, another school to educate girls: the Recogimiento del Carmen (founded 1619).[70] The orphaned Catalina María had been educated by one of the great Counter-Reformation leaders, Carlo Borromeo (1538–84), the archbishop of Milan, who was later canonized.[71] Catalina traveled with her mistress, Doña Brianda de Guzmán, to Spain following the expiration of Guzmán's husband's political term in Milan. Once in Spain, Catalina married Domingo Gómez de Silva and later accompanied him to Peru, where she drew upon her privileged education and status to tutor daughters of the creole elite in her home.[72]

Doria's and Gómez de Silva's request to found a school was timely, and, in their petition for royal approval and financial support of a work "so beneficial to the Republic," they stressed the "public utility" of the recogimiento. (In fact, Doria's true aim was to establish a Carmelite convent, but she could not secure the license for its foundation until 1643.) They argued that, unlike convents, the work for which they sought support was "public" and destined for orphaned girls without recourse (*sin remedio*).[73] In her petition, Doria referred to the Recogimiento de la Caridad in Mexico City, founded in 1548, as an important institutional precedent.[74] She encouraged students to read in Latin and Spanish, to write, work, pray, and sing, and she trained them to be virtuous and recogida.[75] Girls were required to be Spanish, at least twelve years old, and orphans or poor, and they lived in the recogimiento until they became nuns or married.[76]

Increasing demands for female education also led to the establishment of smaller, more modest schools, usually lacking the patronage of any religious order. The Recogimiento de Nuestra Señora de los Remedios, founded by Jorge de Andrade in 1637, required that girls dress in "decent and honest clothing" while Jesuit priests heard their confessions every two weeks, and taught them "to read and remain well occupied in useful exercises so as not to fall into pernicious habits."[77] An elected abbess supervised domestic affairs, which included operating the kitchen, infirmary, and refectory as well as keeping the offices clean. The ordinances stated that the school would accept poor, orphaned, and virtuous Spanish girls who, during their stay, were prohibited from contact with anyone but close family members. They were to remain recogida until they became nuns or married.[78] Enclosure was so rigorously enforced that the administrators requested, and were pleased to receive, permission from Philip IV for the recogidas to hear Mass through a door with access to the street.[79]

Girls emerged from these schools spiritually trained but with a limited practical education. Their virginity intact, they abided by the popular saying: "La doncella no sea salidera ni ventanera" (unmarried virgins should not go out a lot, nor tarry near windows).[80] Most opted to marry, but some pupils, who had spent most of their lives cloistered, chose to become nuns in either the *conventos grandes* (large convents) or the newly founded observant convents, also popular among the daughters of the nouveaux riches.[81] The decision to take religious vows proved mutually beneficial both to the girls' families, because they achieved additional "spiritual" status, and to the convents accepting them, because they gained additional brides of Christ.

Elite Women and Conventual Life

According to Bernabé Cobo, by 1630 the "mystical body" of the "Christian Republic" of Lima had reached a level of piety comparable with that of the best European cities:

[It] forms part of the supernatural and divine order, and [religiosity] is the soul and principal ornament of this Christian and religious city. She [Lima] can glorify herself with an excellence known only in the greatest noble Republics of Europe.[82]

Six "sumptuous" convents for females and fourteen male monasteries formed an integral part of the urban landscape, and Cobo estimated that in 1630, 3,600 individuals lived in monastic institutions, including more than 1,000 nuns, 1,000 servants, slaves, and lay women in convents; compared with 1,126 priests and 500 *donados*, servants, and slaves in male monasteries.[83] By midcentury, eight convents housed a total population of 2,444, an increase from 1,245 nuns and servants in five convents in 1614 (see Appendices B and C).[84]

Just as elite families sought politically and economically advantageous matches for their daughters, they also considered conventual life as a springboard to further prestige and wealth.[85] Kathryn Burns argues that Cuzco's "first families" donated their capital and their daughters to convents during a period of economic expansion, beginning around 1600.[86] Similarly, investment into the spiritual economy of Lima also corresponded to an increase in prosperity. Priests, friars, and nuns were linked economically and demo-

TABLE 3
Female Religious Orders in Latin America

Year	Religious order	Location	Total founded
1540	Conceptionists	México	21
1551	St. Clare	Santo Domingo	34
1571	Cistercians	Osorno	2
1576	Dominicans	Oaxaca	13
1579	Jeronimites	Guatemala	6
1598	Augustinians	México	12
1604	Discalced Carmelites	Puebla	21
1666	Capuchins	México	11
1668	Bethelemites	Guatemala	1

SOURCE: Pedro Borges, *Religiosos en Hispanoamérica* (Madrid: Ed. MAPFRE, 1992), 268.

graphically to expanding family kinship networks composed of merchants, bankers, and bureaucrats. All members inhabiting the sacred and secular realms actively contributed to Lima's dynamic economy.[87]

The desire on the part of the nouveaux riches to found convents was also based upon historical precedents established in Spain. Many of the Iberian convents—which witnessed a profound increase in numbers and population between 1550 and 1650—were founded and patronized by noble women.[88] Particular orders such as Santa Clara and the Concepcionistas proved to be extremely popular in Spain and ubiquitous in America.[89] Table 3 indicates the year of the foundation of the first convent of that order in America; the religious order; the location of the first foundation; and the total founded throughout the colonial period. After the Council of Trent determined that convents should no longer shelter economically and socially "needy" women, religious houses in Spain and Italy that had once provided such services to the poor now catered more exclusively to upper-class women.[90] And, as Spanish historian Elizabeth Lehfeldt states, "[T]he profession of nuns in the period after Trent reflected a heightened emphasis on ensuring that these women were making informed and devout decisions as they moved from the secular world to the cloister."[91]

Observant convents associated with orders such as the Discalced Carmelites, the Trinitarians, and the Reformed Augustinians also experienced a period of tremendous growth in sixteenth-century Spain and seventeenth-century America.[92] In Lima alone, six observant convents were founded between 1603 and 1713 (see map).[93] The founders often expressed an interest in providing an environment in which they might live *en mayor y estrecha recogimiento*: strict enclosure that sheltered them from the prodigality and spiritual laxity that prevailed in the world (el siglo) and in the *conventos grandes*.

Because so many convents were established by the nobility for the nobility, the internal social structure reproduced and reinforced the imbalance of power in social relations outside "los muros" (the walls).[94] All convents generally classified religious women according to different ranks of the black and white veils, and donadas, or religious servants who took informal vows. The nuns of the black veil held the most prestigious position in the convent, paid a larger dowry sum (3,195 pesos in the convent of Santa Clara), and sang the canonical hours in the high choir.[95] Primarily of Spanish descent, they usually came from notable families and were the best educated women in the city. They generally owned their own cell.[96] White-veiled nuns required a lower dowry payment, did not vote in conventual elections, could be either Spanish or mestiza, and usually did not own their own cell.[97] Over the course of the seventeenth century their numbers increased in some convents, because of limited slots for black veil candidates.[98] In Santa Clara, some poor or orphaned nuns of the white veil served nuns of the black veil.[99] Novitiates ranged between the ages of twelve and twenty and spent one or two years preparing to take formal vows, either as a nun of the black or white veil. Donadas (literally, those "given by God") took informal vows but wore a religious habit. As intermediaries between religious women and servants, they took responsibility for the more menial tasks in the convent. They were, as historian Luis Martín put it, "exalted maids."[100] Often racially designated as mestizas, mulattas, sambas, or pardas, they worked alongside the servants or *criadas* and hundreds of slaves who performed most of the menial tasks in the large convents: cooking, cleaning and running errands, or making candles and carrying the cross in processions. Many also served the nuns. In La Encarnación, there were three servants or slaves for every two nuns; other convents had an even higher ratio (see Appendix B for statistics).

Women of the nobility chose permanent enclosure for a variety of reasons. From the 1560s, the widowed wives and daughters of the conquerors had been the principal founders and inhabitants of the convents of La Encarnación, La Concepción, and La Trinidad.[101] Some entered convents as a "preventive" measure: to ensure that the number of marriages within one family would be restricted, or to limit the dowry payments parents would need to provide for sisters. Others chose a religious vocation to avoid an unwanted suitor or mitigate parental pressure; and some followed a spiritual path out of affinity with their fellow nuns. Still others treasured a life of contemplation, recogimiento, and closeness to God.[102]

On the one hand, Lima's new elites were able to insinuate themselves and enhance connections with the generation of the daughters of the conquerors and beneméritos in the large convents. On the other, the foundation of observant convents enabled the "new" generation to create a place for themselves. At the same time, they established an atmosphere propitious to higher degrees of spirituality and contemplation or silent prayer (recogimiento) vis-à-vis the older conventos grandes. Two creole daughters of the Chuquisaca (Sucre) elite established a precedent by founding the first observant convent in Lima, the Monasterio de las Descalças de San Joseph, in 1603.[103] After 1615, petitions to found observant convents increased, because of an interest among donors—many from the most prestigious family networks in Lima—to create sacred and social spaces for their daughters and widowed family members; and, because they were seen to be making wise investments.[104] For example, the founder of Nuestra Señora del Prado, Doña Angela de Zárate, descended from Spanish nobility on both her maternal and paternal sides;[105] whereas, other nuns came from families involved in recently established commercial, banking, or government enterprises.[106]

In spite of an abundance of private capital offered to support the foundation of convents, requests for new institutions met with strong opposition for several reasons. Secular authorities reasoned that Lima had too many convents and monasteries; observant convents were impractical because they housed fewer than twenty women (when in fact they could maintain thirty-three); and ecclesiastical funds should instead provide alms and refuge to poor women.[107] In an effort to curb the power of the regular clergy, petitions to found religious institutions received strict scrutiny by both the Council of the Indies and the king.[108] In this regard, Crown and local interests clashed on more than one occasion. In 1624, for example, Lima's elites circumvented the Crown's restrictions and decided to take matters into their own hands by founding the Monasterio de Santa Catalina. This incident only heightened tensions between Lima and Spain.[109]

Misunderstandings may have developed because secular and ecclesiastical authorities in Lima were unsure whether a royal decree prohibiting the foundation of religious houses excluded female convents, and viceroys and the king exchanged a number of letters during the 1620s and 1630s attempting to clarify the issue.[110] The lack of a common dialogue also indicated that transatlantic communications and cultural needs were no longer harmonious. The vision of the local elite did not coincide with Crown concerns, which increasingly focused upon political and economic strife within Spain and upon the struggle for European hegemony.[111]

Only when the archbishopric lay vacant for several years was it possible to found two new observant convents, of Nuestra Señora del Prado and El Carmen (f. 1643). The arrival of the new viceroy, Pedro de Toledo y Leiva, marquis of Mancera (1639–48), expedited this policy reversal. Unlike his predecessor, the count of Chinchón (1629–39), Mancera and his wife offered support and invested a great deal of their personal capital in secular and religious institutions, including new hospitals, schools, and convents.[112] The dream of Catalina

María Doria and her husband was realized in 1643 when the Recogimiento del Carmen, which they had founded in 1619, became the convent of Discalced Carmelites.[113] As a symbolic gesture, Catalina María became the first prioress.[114] Infirm and elderly, the foundress could no longer tolerate the strict regimen of religious observance and requested a small room adjacent to the convent where she could live out her remaining days "in peace and recogimiento."[115] Several of her protégées, including a student awarded a scholarship by the vicereine, entered as the first nuns.[116]

The Co-optation of Recogimiento as an
Elite Form of Religious Expression

Women who chose a religious vocation often believed that their pious resolve and sense of recogimiento would be viewed by society as a major triumph against the incursions of the "worldly," considered the embodiment of evil. Conversely, a life of enclosure (recogimiento) served to buttress the boundaries of the sacred. For a family, the daughter's choice of an ecclesiastical vocation was a symbolic act directly related to implicit assumptions about religiosity, honor, and prestige. A daughter linked the family to heaven: she embodied divine spirituality, true recogimiento, spiritual piety, enclosure, and the most noble path to God in the living flesh.

This predilection resonated with the Tridentine decree that ordered the strict enclosure of all professed women. However, monastic cloistering in Spain, as in Peru, was not always "enforced or accepted."[117] While carving out a new cultural space of *lo sagrado* in Lima, elites reacted against a movement of popular pious expression that endured roughly from 1580 to 1630, and involved mystical formulations of recogimiento that transcended barriers of ethnicity, class, and gender.[118] Concurrently, "idolatrous" practices of native Andeans were curtailed more systematically. Between 1620 and 1640, women accused of witchcraft or sorcery were transported from the provinces to Lima to serve their sentence (*estar recogida*) as laborers in the Hospitals of La Caridad or Santa Ana.[119] The Inquisition placed beatas and bigamists, Portuguese Jews, and Muslims on trial for their religious beliefs, marching them in solemn processions through the streets of Lima before the public's condemnatory gaze.[120]

While for some individuals the 1620s constituted a period of generalized suppression, many elites took advantage of the reformulation of spirituality occurring among ecclesiastical authorities by consolidating their vision of recogimiento in three distinct yet interrelated ways. First, the foundresses of new observant convents adapted the meanings of recogimiento found in Spanish contemplative texts to their more conservative vision of the cloistered life. Second, individual convents began appropriating images and cults to create a foundation "history" for their fledgling institutions that would elevate their status vis-à-vis other convents and elites. Finally, notions of recogimiento as enclosure and separation from the "worldly" were employed to promote qualities of spirituality and family honor among select, elite young women. Calancha's foundation history of Nuestra Señora del Prado, for example, exemplified the popular trend to write conventual chronicles that eulogized holy women rejecting the world for the "divine on earth."

The writings of mystics such as Luis de Granada, Luis de León, or Teresa de Avila, profoundly influenced by Francisco de Osuna's principles of recogimiento, proved extremely popular in early-seventeenth-century Lima.[121] Readers could assimilate their ideas relative to a particular agenda. All three were concerned with perfection of the spiritual life among the clergy and the laity but sought a wider secular audience because they believed in the connection between human and natural law and the humanity of Christ.[122] Immediately following the Council of Trent, "there was, in fact, a great gap between the books owned by secular priests and those read by lay persons"; but by the end of the sixteenth century in Spain, devotional works and theological treatises had "trickled down" in Spain and America and were read by lay and religious audiences.[123]

Luis de Granada, in particular, stressed that monastic cloistering, strict observance, and penitential acts were not sufficient to achieve the ascetic ideal without internal prayer and recogimiento or a quieting of the self. He appealed to all females—schoolgirls, nuns, and married women—and his works proved particularly popular among beatas in Lima and Mexico who manifested their spirituality and "union with God" in the world.[124] In Peru, the Dominican tertiary Isabel Flores de Oliva, later known as Santa Rosa of Lima, read Granada fervently and believed, like him, that piety was not achieved solely through external acts.[125] The director of the Colegio de Santa Teresa, Isabel de Porras, advocated Granada's vision of direct mystical union with God, as did a number of nuns who never achieved fame or recognition. Beatas testifying before the Inquisition in Lima in the 1620s also cited the *maestro de espíritu.*[126]

Writing during the height of the Counter-Reformation, when social control measures were being implemented on a multitude of levels, Teresa of Avila's interpretation of recogimiento as mystical union coincided with a shift in emphasis toward recogimiento as a form of moral and physical control in the secular and religious realms. To Teresa, recogimiento involved a gathering within of the senses in order to leave behind the world, the body, and all that was exterior.[127] She, like Osuna and Granada, emphasized contemplative prayer (recogimiento) over oral recitation.[128] Aware that Inquisition authorities could easily conflate recogimiento with dejamiento—a method of prayer associated with the alumbrados—a circumspect Teresa (denounced to the Inquisition at least six times) spilled a great deal of ink elaborating upon the differences between the two mystical traditions.[129]

Teresa of Avila included many descriptions of women's inferior character and wrote as she perceived *mujercillas* ("little women") would speak. On the other hand, she adapted accepted principles of inferiority by creating a "rhetoric of femininity" as a covert strategy of empowerment.[130] She posited that women were particularly able to reach their "internal" palace of gold because they had a greater aptitude for contemplation and mental prayer and were more willing to love and to serve.[131] But, she also understood that in post-Tridentine Spain, those women who avowed a life of mysticism, wished to cultivate an interior spirituality (recogimiento), and practice their devotion in a noncloistered setting faced increasing intolerance and persecution.[132] In fact, by the 1570s, the Inquisition began systematically attacking beatas in Seville, Extremadura, and Jaén, Spain, and by the 1640s had effectively "reduced [them] to silence and invisibility."[133] Beginning in 1598, the Mexican Inquisition also initiated charges of heresy against beatas accused of illuminism or alumbramiento.[134]

In Lima between 1600 and 1625, noncloistered beatas in Lima also advocated mystic theology based upon emotion, internal experience (*lo experimentado*), and contemplative prayer. Luisa Melgarejo de Soto, Isabel de Ormaza (or Jesús), Ana María Pérez, María de Santo Domingo, Inés de Ubitarte, and Inés Velasco gained a sense of spiritual empowerment by following the mystical tenets of Granada and Teresa de Avila. Many of these beatas saw recogimiento as an internal, individual, contemplative dialogue with God: they fomented an open sense of community; they knew each another; they shared Jesuit confessors; and they belonged to spiritual conventicles.[135]

The fact that they unabashedly advocated direct mystical experience or recogimiento and offered their own theological renderings of Scriptural or hagiographic matters meant that they transgressed the concept of "balance" in spirituality as it was then interpreted.[136] Because they transcended perceived boundaries of the sacred, all were accused by Inquisition tribunal members in the 1620s of dabbling in *cosas de los alumbrados* and of making false claims of ecstasy, visions, and other supernatural phenomena considered to be illusory.[137] Inquisition members ridiculed and summarily dismissed their behavior as "trying to avoid domestic labor and live idly."[138] They questioned their personal search for God and publicly reprimanded them in the auto-da-fé of 1625 with the broader intention of defining more carefully the boundaries of "feminine superstitions" to avoid further contagion in the viceregal capital.[139]

Before their Inquisition hearings, beatas in Lima consulted the spiritual tracts written by Luis de Granada and Teresa of Avila: works that also served as models for a widely diverse audience desiring a sense of communion with God. Like the beatas who chose Granada as their spiritual guide, readers could select passages that appealed to their moral and political needs. Teresa of Avila's efforts to redefine female religiosity attracted beatas seeking the via media, but she also inspired hundreds of cloistered nuns of various orders in the Americas, including the Reformed Carmelites, especially after her canonization in 1622.

In Spain, by that time, notions of recogimiento began to be associated more closely with formal assertions of faith, including ascetic gestures such as physical enclosure and denial of the senses. One mystical element, contemplation on "nothing," was de-emphasized: discipline, the whip, and self-flagellation served as extrapolations of what previously had been internalized.[140] Developing a sense of interior spirituality remained important, but prayer, an avenue toward this goal, was redefined as essentially vocal rather than meditative or silent. Contemplative practices remained, but most focused on a particular objective such as a saint's life, or the Passion of Christ. This sea change in Europe resonated very strongly among Peruvian female religious aspirants in the 1630s who followed the modified canons that defined contemplation and recogimiento.

For instance, the cofoundress of the Augustinian del Prado, Angela de Zárate, found inspiration in Teresa de Avila's writings about enclosure.[141] But Zárate chose to focus upon the Counter-Reformation timbre of her writings. Santa Teresa emphasized the silent, meditative, internal path to God, *and* considered enclosure and a solitary life of contemplation to be an important component in the expression of recogimiento for the devout. In contemplative texts, she and her contemporaries exalted:

[T]he blessed saints who chose a solitary and withdrawn [recogida] life: deep in humility, lofty in contemplation toward God, forgetful of the world, indifferent in their love of material things, embraced by the love of heaven; dead in the flesh and alive in spirit.[142]

The writings of the Augustinian theologian Juan de Soto also enlivened Zárate. He stressed complete separation from the world, akin to physical and emotional amnesia of an extremely painful experience.[143] Entrances and exits, or "intermediary spaces" such as doors or foyers, symbolized proximity to the precipice of hell or death where many religious persons met their end.[144] Those who entered the realm of el siglo and then returned were somehow altered, Soto claimed, as though part of their soul had been robbed. Like a disease or a sinful thought, they were advised to "beat it out of themselves."[145] Silence formed an essential practice in the more rigorously observant religious houses, enabling cloistered nuns to protect themselves from the external distractions of the world in order to direct themselves toward their inward path. Nuns in the Monasterio de Carmelitas Descalças and El Prado, founded in the 1640s, practiced recogimiento in such a manner.[146]

The two foundresses of the Monasterio del Prado, Angela and Francisca de Zárate, based their decision to found a new sacred space upon a concern for stricter recogimiento: for physical enclosure that included less contact with other convents and the outside world, and higher spiritual standards.[147] Both had spent most of their lives cloistered in La Encarnación, and now sought a life away from the "multitudes" in the large convents. Of life in La Encarnación, Doña Angela wrote:

Although the Monasterio de la Encarnación is most religious and houses nuns of great perfection, the vast majority or crowd of people, [including] nuns who have taken their vows as well as lay pious women, donadas, and servants, are so numerous as to cause much confusion that is alien to their solitude, which the religious and recogida life demands and whose perfection consists of discipline and solitude.[148]

They also sought to distinguish their convent from "inferior" religious houses. The history of the institution, included in Antonio de la Calancha's chronicle, elevated the convent to a higher spiritual level than others in the city and based its origin myth upon a miracle. According to the Augustinian friar, a Spaniard of modest background, Don Antonio Poblete, left Spain and wandered for twenty-two years throughout the viceroyalty with a small replica of the image of Nuestra Señora del Prado as his constant companion. Finally settling in Lima in 1602, he established a hermitage on the outskirts of the city, near Callao. Word quickly spread that the statue performed miracles when people prayed before her. Renowned for curing the sick and helping the lame walk, the image was alleged to have cast an eerie, resplendent light at particular moments and to have given off a pleasant fragrance.[149] For decades, the image of Nuestra Señora del Prado attracted both rich and poor, from Viceroy Chinchón to a dying enslaved man, all eager to experience a miracle. The statue provided a space of reverence where individuals could transcend the imaginary boundaries of class and caste.[150]

Calancha then claimed that Angela de Zárate, the "Arquimandrita de Preladas," and "foundation stone, garden, and meadow of the establishment," received a direct message from God to found an observant convent.[151] Soon thereafter she requested permission to found a convent on the site of the hermitage, and Antonio's widow, María Poblete, entrusted to care for the image, agreed to the terms.[152] Because of a strong friendship between Viceroy Mancera and Doña Angela's brother, she quickly acquired the license she had been trying to obtain for years. Angela donated fifty thousand pesos and received other contributions from the nuns at La Encarnación, merchants, and businessmen.[153] Once established, however, the nuns of the Monasterio del

Prado closed the popular image of Nuestra Señora del Prado to the public, and the reverent could no longer kneel before her to experience her miracles.

By appropriating the cult, by establishing the house on sacred ground, and by fostering their own interpretation of recogimiento, the nuns presented their institution as superior to other religious houses. Teresa of Avila and Jerónima de la Madre de Dios (another religious reformer in Spain) served as role models, and the nuns followed their advice on how to care for the sacristy and religious relics, including a portion of Teresa's wimple.[154] Within the convent, true recogimiento initially translated into a lower servant/nun ratio and a stricter regimen of prayer and penitential disciplines: fasting and mortification occurred three times a week; cells were small; and the beds held thin mattresses.[155] The day began at 4:00 A.M. with prayers (even earlier for the more devout nuns) and continued until 10:00 P.M.[156]

The nuns residing in observant convents were aware that their practice of recogimiento involved an exclusion of the world, the body, and all that was exterior. Some nuns, however, were averse to complete isolation from the world. As in other convents, Nuestra Señora del Prado reproduced the hierarchical society of castes evident in the external world. By 1643, the convent included thirty nuns of the black veil from very noble and respectable families; four nuns of the white veil; two donadas who had taken their vows; two Indian servants; two young donada novices; and four slaves.[157] These statistics reveal that even in the convent's incipient phase, the servant/nun ratio was one-to-three, because donadas performed communal labor. Three seglares and several divorciadas of elite status paid room and board, an indication that the "world" was more prevalent in El Prado than their ordinances would indicate.[158] By 1700, El Prado had more servants than professed nuns, a ratio that equaled that of the larger convents relative to its size (see Appendix B). In order to circumvent the population limitation of thirty-three nuns of the black veil, the convent began admitting nuns of the white veil.[159]

To what extent young nuns living in the observant convents renounced the pleasures of the world is difficult to ascertain, but a life of recogimiento under God's wing must have appealed to many daughters of the elite. They were certainly familiar with popular narratives about young women relinquishing material wealth for a life of austerity: stories that served to reinforce shifting paradigms related to female elite spiritual "conversion."[160] Calancha's chronicle, for example, served several agendas simultaneously: while elevating the status of the Augustinian order and its connection to families of noble (both Spanish and creole) origin, the author's historical/mythical narratives also appealed to the sensitivities of young, aristocratic women. His work chastised parents who prohibited daughters from following the path of religion: "Oh cruel parents, who in loving their daughter so that she [might] spend her riches on the vanities of the world, detested her because she wished to spend her years in God's service!"[161]

The chronicle related the anecdote of Doña Isabel de Astete, who had taken vows of chastity secretly; faced with her parents' insistence that she marry, she walked eighty leagues to Lima to enter the "paradise of La Encarnación."[162] Calancha also cited the example of Doña María Antonia de Ondegardo y Campuzano, of high noble lineage and raised from birth in the convent of La Encarnación. In spite of her family's pleadings, and efforts to sway her with riches and attractive suitors, her eyes were directed toward God and she would not be dissuaded from her "true" path.[163] The appeal of such a noble sacrifice might be intensified further by the ritual known as the *paseo preclaustral*, a procession through the streets of Lima that commemorated the exquisitely dressed young woman's last triumphal walk "in the world."[164]

Popular discourse on spiritual sacrifice strengthened the desire of young elite women to attain a true sense of spiritual recogimiento in convents, but not without some concessions. Several young nuns, under the supervision of their parents and "now the Wives of Christ Our Lord," preferred "to party and keep a palace for many other people." Longing for their previous sumptuous lifestyle, some attempted to nullify their vows.[165] Still others felt forced to enter the cloistered environment against their will.[166] An enclosed upbringing, whether in a convent or lay boarding school, made rejoining the secular world a difficult adjustment; young women forced into arranged marriages surely suffered; girls pressured by their families to take religious vows often bitterly regretted the decision.

Some priests were aware of the painful dilemmas facing young women. More than one hundred years earlier, the Franciscan mystic and founder of recogimiento, Francisco de Osuna, had strongly urged Spanish parents not to force their daughters into seclusion in convents, whether to elevate their status or for lack of a sufficient dowry to marry. God, he reasoned, favored only voluntary sacrifice.[167] In spite of its ostensible prestige, the imposition of enclosure, austere conditions, and sensorial deprivation upon young elite women, some of whom truly desired to follow a spiritual path of recogimiento, may have been too rigorous. And some members of the nobility found it difficult to comprehend what the contemplative life in an observant convent could offer to the "delicate and beautiful women" who would profess to bleed their noble blood for their chosen husband, Jesus Christ.[168]

Conclusions

During the period of tremendous growth and prosperity in Lima from 1600 to 1650, elite women found a variety of ways to situate themselves within the realm of the sacred, thereby relegating those of nonelite status into the "world." These confrontations, however, were not battles between "high" (or elite) and "low" (nonelite) groups, but constituted an historical moment when an emerging, powerful elite sought to realign notions of the sacred realm relative to other interpretations of lo sagrado.[169] The perception that the moral laxity "in the world" obscured the future of their daughters motivated elites to delimit and map out a politicized space that redefined the domain and practice of recogimiento in educational policies, the centrality of marriage, and in the foundation of observant convents.

Their rendering of the discourse that promoted sexual purity, quiescent and restrained conduct in preparation for marriage, or a religious vocation embraced "dominant" formulations of recogimiento that dated back to the sixteenth century. This contrasted strongly with the "emergent" notions of recogimiento-as-virtue in the testimonies of women appearing in ecclesiastical courts during the same period (see Chapter 4). In addition, the reformation of the significance of recogimiento as a theological concept also involved a rejection of those who advocated recollective mysticism in favor of safer, more moderate interpretations of recogimiento as strict enclosure, oral prayer, and more formal manifestations of religious observance.

On a larger level, the shift in the spiritual interpretations of recogimiento in Lima reflects two aspects of the transculturation dialogue at this point in the city's history: first, elites replicated Counter-Reformation religious practices in Spain that promoted more orthodox, formal manifestations of the Catholic faith and recogimiento, and de-emphasized the possibilities of direct, unmediated experiences with God. "Residual" practices of recollection and mystical contemplation continued to exist in a more muted fashion in Spain and America; however, by midcentury the emergent formal manifestation of recogimiento had become dominant.

Second, creole and Spanish elites accommodated Iberian cultural practices to meet local conditions, which in turn bolstered the capital's increasing economic self-reliance from the metropolis. Evidence of the tremendous prosperity in Lima, which so impressed Bernabé Cobo, seemed to the Franciscan, Buenaventura de Córdova y Salinas in 1651 to provide the city with a status comparable to that of some of the great European cities:

a holy Rome in its temples, ornaments, and religious cult, a proud Genoa in the style and brio of those who are born in it, a beautiful Florence for its benign climate . . . a wealthy Venice for the riches it produces for Spain and prodigally distributes to all, remaining as wealthy as ever . . . a Salamanca for its thriving university and colleges.[170]

Contemporaries observed an affluent metropolis abounding with costly carriages and sumptuous religious houses. Within this milieu, institutional, spiritual, and moral recogimiento guaranteed elite women status and "wealth," before the community and the eyes of God. Their appropriation of recogimiento not only reflected material concerns but also had a peculiar colonial cast to it, in part because of the specific articulation of status, race, and class among elites. And yet, while unique to Lima, these "dominant" notions of purity, education, and spiritual recollection still remained firmly rooted in the Iberian tradition.

Institutional practices of recogimiento continued to promote racial and class hierarchies of difference: to provide elite girls access to observant convents that fortified the newly emerging nobility, and to relegate orphans and other women to positions of servitude within the stone edifices. The "aristocratic pyramid of unequals" dates to the foundation of La Encarnación and La Concepción in the sixteenth century, but the cultivation of recogimiento as a quality and practice espoused by truly spiritual elite holy women was new.[171] Yet, at the same time, social welfare programs made available to the poor and needy *did* create avenues to safeguard the virtue of some less fortunate girls. While scrubbing convent floors, nursing the sick, and indulging the nuns, their young charges also developed a sense of recogimiento and spirituality that would come into prominence later in the century.

During the last half of the seventeenth century, many limeñas formulated an even clearer sense of their own brand of baroque spirituality, as they continued to manifest visions of the sacred and the worldly, in contradictory but coexistent ways. Insular, elite visions continued to exist, but the surge in popular piety, in combination with the increasing number of secular women entering institutions and obtaining divorces, meant that the boundaries of recogimiento—and indeed, the sacred and the worldly—would become increasingly blurred. In the transculturation and adaptation of recogimiento to local contingencies, the concept and practice took on a more "dominant" colonial cast than ever before.

CHAPTER SIX

Contesting the Boundaries of the Sacred and the Worldly, 1650 to 1713

O N M A R C H 16, 1670, Viceroy Pedro Fernández de Castro, count of Lemos (1668–73), ordered that broadsheets be distributed in every church of Lima requesting all devout Catholics of the kingdom to join him and his wife with lighted candles in a solemn procession to be held three days later. His proclamation read as follows:

In order that all know of this work and of the Casa de Amparadas, it is stated that it is [to be] dedicated to young women, who by the mercy of God have realized the dangers of their fragility and, wanting to resist all temptations, place themselves under the protection of the most Pure Queen of Angels, Mother of God and Special Mother of this House.[1]

The entourage was to proceed from the viceregal palace chapel to its final destination—the dedication ceremony at the new Casa de las Amparadas de la Puríssima Concepción.[2]

By establishing this institution, Lemos and his confessor, Jesuit Francisco del Castillo (1615–73), intended to reform women caught "in the nets of the World, the Devil and the Flesh."[3] In 1668, Castillo had convinced the viceroy of the need for such a house of piety, asserting that women in danger of losing their virtue continuously begged him for guidance and had volunteered as the first recogidas or enclosed, repentant women of the new institution.[4] After locating a plot of land and collecting donations, the construction of the house and chapel were finally completed in 1670.[5] For three days in March, the city's populace watched as the viceroy, his wife, members of the tribunals, nobility, and militia followed an image of the Immaculate Conception from the viceregal palace to the Casa de las Amparadas.[6] However, the attentive audience also observed the embarrassing absence of the most important element: not a single woman had volunteered to march publicly into institutional seclusion. Apparently, those inclined to repent their lost ways considered such a public display to be "an eternal source of infamy," and in spite of Father Castillo's insistent pleadings, the Casa de las Amparadas stood empty for almost two months.[7] According to a contemporary observer, José Buendía (1644–1727), the "voices of the city" mocked the priest's "overzealous efforts," and some argued that the house should be converted into some other, more useful enterprise.[8]

Eventually "moved by God's love" and Father Castillo's spiritual counseling, a number of "wounded souls" came, "weeping and begging on their knees to be candidates of the sainted house of retirement."[9] With sturdy resolve, nine "truly" repentant women "disregarded the malevolent reasoning of the common people and worldly opinions" who mocked their conversion efforts, and made preparations to enter the Casa de Amparadas while the cathedral choir sang "Te Deum Laudamus."[10] Buendía called the second inauguration "a triumph against [Lima's] invidious and malevolent voices," and once again the procession departed from the viceregal palace. A panoply of religious icons led the way, beginning with the image of the Immaculate Conception and followed by one of Saint Ignatius, considered by the viceroy to be the "Father of Recogimientos"; Saint Francisco de Borja (representing the Jesuits' continuing dedication to the institution); the Virgin Mary surrounded by six angels; and the Christ child. Then came important secular and ecclesiastical authorities. An image of Lima's patron saint, the recently beatified Isabel Flores de Oliva, or Santa Rosa, formed a centerpiece of the cavalcade. According to Buendía, few processions remained so vividly etched in the memory of Lima's inhabitants.[11]

Sixteen years later, in December 1686, another procession commenced when four nuns left their old convent of Santa Teresa (founded 1642) to establish the new Convent of Santa Ana of Barefoot Carmelites. In the vestibule, the four foundresses received the viceroy's wife and daughter, and together they proceeded in the royal carriage. The entourage, which included the archbishop, the viceroy, members of his council, and his family, paused at several locations before arriving at the sacristy of Santa Ana, where the archbishop placed the image of Saint Teresa. The public watched as the four nuns entered their new cloistered home: "closing the door with the keys of spirituality," said Francisco López—confessor to the new viceroy—in his sermon preached that day, served as "a whip of punishment for the Devil."[12]

In this sermon, dedicated to the nuns who had "left the World" in 1686, Francisco López invoked the popularly held notion that four imaginary concentric circles surrounded the world.[13] The outermost circle contained corrupt individuals; the next encompassed those who lived in the world without following a life of perfection; the third ring encircled those who left the world to inhabit religious institutions; and finally, observant convents, which advocated strict enclosure and disciplinary practices, occupied the smallest circumference because they embodied perfection. "The virtue which is the greatest," López said, "is that [circle] which appears to be the smallest, but it is the core of the four circles that comprise the great circle of the New World."[14]

In one sense his perception of ideal concentric spheres of spirituality reflected the attempt to reinforce the separate realms of the sacred and the worldly in the foundation of observant convents, beaterios, and recogimientos. The increasing array of inaugural ceremonies associated with institutional foundations such as the Casa de las Amparadas and the Convent of Santa Ana signaled a burgeoning interest in the promotion of distinct spaces for limeñas seeking protection, asylum, and separation from the worldly.

More than ever before in Lima's history, the foundation of institutions served to demarcate the sacred and secular in a spatial setting. By 1700, more than forty-eight monasteries, convents, schools, and hospitals existed in Lima, and the thirty-nine hundred women who lived in convents (including servants) represented 20 percent of the total female population in the city.[15] Equally significant, the foundation of ten beaterios (the Casa de las Amparadas was also referred to as a recogimiento) and three observant convents occurred between 1669 and 1713. Unquestionably, secular and religious institutions continued to retain their central importance to the cultural, social, and economic vitality of the urban colonial world.[16]

Both the Convent of Barefoot Carmelites of Santa Ana and the Casa de las Amparadas epitomized the increased concern with order (within the worldly) and extravagance (in expressions of the sacred) that mirrored the intense social and cultural changes occurring in the City of Kings. In addition, dominant notions of recogimiento served as motivating factors in delineating the functions of institutions according to ideals of the sacred and the worldly. Authorities continued to employ and refine the use of the verb "recoger" that had developed in the 1580s: to protect sacred women from the contamination of the world; or conversely, to separate those women labeled as licentious and sexually immoral from others. In that sense, the observant convent of Santa Ana and the beaterio cum recogimiento of las Amparadas represented opposite ends of an ideal spectrum. The former braced itself against the growing secular population within many convents and the need for strict enclosure (recogimiento), while the latter served as an intermediary space, or middle ground, between the world and a "sacred" institution, because it operated as a beaterio *and* a recogimiento—in other words, as a lay pious house for spiritual expression and as an asylum for secular women.

The Casa de las Amparadas characterized Lima in the last half of the seventeenth century in another way. The tentative start of the recogimiento, and the reasons the procession of 1670 created such a marked impression, reveal a great deal about different perceptions of the function of convents, beaterios, and recogimientos among secular and religious authorities, Lima's "malevolent voices," nuns and beatas, and the "repentant, wounded souls" who reluctantly chose to inhabit these spaces. The institution symbolized the increasing permeability of the boundaries distinguishing the sacred and the worldly in the late seventeenth century.

Despite the wishful thinking of colonial authorities, the majority of poor, deserted, or unemployed women did not seek the company of beatas or nuns to reform and act in a modest and penitent manner.[17] More likely, beaterios and convents offered mobility for secular women—by facilitating relocation between the home and institution—and created new channels of discourse defining "sacred" and "worldly." Dominant practices of recogimiento—as a practice of voluntary and involuntary enclosure—endured, but clearly the adage *aut murus aut maritus* ("either cloister or husband") no longer prevailed.

The imprimatur of recogimiento had particular appeal to elite girls in the 1620s, and became more commonplace among women of all walks of life by the end of the century. This may be related to the fact that the centrality of recogimiento as a self-identifying feature also increased, and women continued to challenge the "defective victim" paradigm.[18] In order to demonstrate the changes and continuities of recogimiento, this chapter will begin by exploring the transculturation of Spanish baroque spirituality to Lima from 1650 to 1713 and its reception among Lima's populace in late-seventeenth-century Lima. Next I will explore female visions of recogimiento, and explain the changing dynamics of institutional life in convents, observant convents, and beaterios. The chapter will then consider María Jacinta Montoya's vision of recogimiento for the beaterio she founded, and will also examine the foundation history of a second beaterio/recogimiento, the Casa de las Amparadas. Finally, a discussion of the strained relationship between the Casa de las Amparadas and the Beaterio de las Rosas provides an example of how institutions could challenge the understood realms of the sacred and worldly.

Shifting Notions of the Sacred

In Spain, the "formalization of mysticism" occurred between 1605 and 1650.[19] The papacy contributed actively to this process: between 1588 and 1690, twenty-seven saints—thirteen of them Spanish and fifteen subjects of the king of Spain—were canonized, including Teresa de Avila (1622).[20] In Lima, the appropriation of mystical precepts and their transformation into more formalized, ritualized practices began around 1620 as a new elite entrenched itself (see Chapter 5). By midcentury, limeños had become increasingly obsessed with appearances, in the form of pageants, processions, and the proliferation of exemplary lives of local and European saints. Authorities and individuals envisioned and upheld a normative order in public rituals, confraternity activities, the organization of cults, and the promotion of religious institutions. Festivals honoring the Virgin increased after papal confirmation of the Immaculate Conception in 1661; cults of the cross, the Christ Child, and the penitent Jesus also grew.[21] In both Peru and Spain, more formalized representations of spirituality also involved an intensification of externalized disciplinary practices: fasting, mortification of the flesh, and, for women, a life of enclosure with a bare minimum of contact with the worldly.[22]

After 1650, a number of popular saints eulogized during the first half of the century were promoted for beatification.[23] On the one hand, the beatification (1668) and canonization (1671) of Santa Rosa of Lima, patron saint of Lima and America, illustrates how ecclesiastical authorities conscientiously refashioned local spiritual figures by characterizing them with specific saintly qualities that linked them to a European hagiographic tradition.[24] (Rosa was re-created in the likeness of Saint Catherine of Siena.)[25] On the other hand, the cult of local "saints" like Martín de Porras (1579–1639) provided ample evidence of an assertion of Lima's particular brand of Catholicism and the increasing cultural and economic independence of the city and the colonies from Spain, now a declining power.[26]

Competition among the five major orders in Lima gave an added intensity to the "production" of saints in crónicas conventuales (conventual chronicles), containing accounts of pious nuns.[27] The Augustinian Antonio de la Calancha paved the way in his exaltation of the nuns of the Monasterio del Prado, and Franciscan Diego de Córdoba y Salinas followed suit in 1651 by producing brief biographies of Peruvian nuns of Santa Clara who transmitted the "fragrance of sanctity and excellent virtues."[28] By highlighting the importance of illustrative holy women, authorities hoped to provide models for lay and religious individuals alike.[29]

More formalized, conformist manifestations of piety, in evidence since the 1640s, also characterized the practices of spiritual recogimiento among some of Lima's female religious. Most were more inclined to follow rules than to advocate a praxis related to direct mystical experience. The ideas of radical Spanish mystics like Miguel de Molinos, writing in the 1670s, did not immediately gain a receptive audience among holy women in Lima. Author of a *Guía espiritual*, Molinos's doctrine of "annihilation" of the self and "quietism" in the interior path toward God was reminiscent of Francisco de Osuna's method more than 150 years before.[30] Spiritual recogimiento in late-seventeenth-century Lima required a sheltering of the self from outside distractions, mainly achieved through enclosure, disciplinary measures, and oral prayer, but it did not subscribe to the intense, internal cleansing or "annihilation" that Osuna and some of Teresa de Avila's writings avowed. María Jacinta

Montoya, founder of the Beaterio de Jesús, María y José, referred to the writings of Teresa of Avila and Ignatius of Loyola in formulating her disciplinary regimen. Others looked to "exemplary models" like Saint Catherine of Siena or Santa Rosa of Viterbo for guidance. Reliance upon more traditional figures also coincided with the trend to eulogize popular Peruvian religious figures like Santa Rosa.

The vestiges of Osuna's mystical notion of recogimiento remained visible in the spiritual practices of some seventeenth-century Spanish and Italian holy women.[31] Like their counterparts in Mexico, female mystics in Lima (the vast majority cloistered) continued to stress lo experimentado, or direct experiential contact with God, as an essential aspect of their religious expression. However, emptying oneself toward God was not the chief aim; unlike Osuna, Teresa of Avila and Luis de Granada, seventeenth-century visionary nuns and beatas, tended to place greater emphasis on contemplation, revelations, ecstatic states, visions, and physical ailments than on meditating on "nothing."[32] In general, many orthodox Catholics tolerated these aspects of mysticism because they had a social, beneficial content and did not involve fusion with the Divine. Holy women tended more often to serve as channels of charismatic messages that lost their value if not communicated and transmitted; accounts of individual experiences of the transcendent and ineffable diminished.[33]

Hence, it is important to emphasize that in spite of Counter-Reformation efforts, mystical practices of recogimiento in early modern Latin America continued to exist in a more subdued fashion. Nevertheless, within the more orthodox expressions of spirituality, important changes also occurred. Pious individuals, some of humble backgrounds, were able to emerge from relative obscurity and anonymity in unabashedly avowing their religious piety during this period. Casta women and men found fresh opportunities to transcend barriers of race and class and gained respect and honor in their contributions to popular religious expression. Attempts were made to promote particularly pious "saints" of color, including Martín de Porras, a mulatto; Nicolás de Ayllón, an indio; or the former black-slave-turned-donada, Ursula de Jesús. The mestiza beata Jacinta de Montoya openly encouraged non-Spanish women to become nuns or beatas in the Beaterio de Jesús, María y José. In 1697, she informed the king that true racial representation in religious orders (and in particular, her beaterio, which she wanted to become a convent) only underscored the strengths of colonial society:

If the Indians of this entire Kingdom received the news of such a universally approved act [the foundation of their own beaterio], having admitted them in saintly equality with the other vassals, and [learned] that their daughters could achieve the union and company with Spanish women, such an act would reflect . . . the royal piety of Your Majesty.[34]

As rituals, processions, and cults proliferated, so too did the popular participation of all sectors of urban, colonial society. Hierarchical divisions of class, caste, gender, and religious/secular status were evident in these practices, but, at the same time, certain "spaces" expanded to accommodate all people in their particular forms of devotion to God. This was remarkable, given that such multiracial creeds could not be found anywhere in Europe, least of all in Spain.

The number of powerful and effective viceroys who actively encouraged popular manifestations of pious expression and the foundation of institutions served as an indicator of the strong union of church and state. Viceroy Lemos (1668–1673), considered by some contemporaries to be excessively devout, expressed his piety in daily confession and communion, and his humility by frequently sweeping the floor of the Church of Los Desamparados, which he had helped to found. He advocated harsh, punitive measures against anyone who refused to comply with his efforts to "pietize" Lima, and demanded that all inhabitants should fall on bended knee whenever the cathedral bell rang.[35] More than five thousand limeños allegedly fled the city to avoid his repressive measures.[36] Archbishop Liñán de Cisneros, viceroy between 1678 and 1681, and less extreme in his religious dedication, oversaw the canonization of his late-sixteenth-century predecessor, Toribio de Mogrovejo, and promoted greater awareness of Christian morality, including more humane treatment of slaves. In the aftermath of the devastating earthquake of 1687, Viceroy Monclova (1689–1705) shouldered the responsibility for the reconstruction of many of Lima's heavily damaged sacred sites and also supported the foundation of new religious structures.

Shifting Notions of the "Worldly"

Piety certainly motivated secular and ecclesiastical figures to support institutionalized and ritualized expressions of the sacred, but it also emboldened them to express concern over what they perceived to be a lack of virtue or recogimiento among the worldly populace.[37] To them, the City of Kings, despite a facade of splendor in dress, art, architecture, and piety, hovered on the edge of social and moral decadence. Many interpreted the various earthquakes, epidemics, and poor wheat harvests as God's punishment for Lima's continued degeneracy.[38] Sermons implored Saints Bridgit and Roche to protect the city against plague or beseeched Our Lady of the Rosary to guard against earthquakes.[39] Yet other preachers chastised Lima's immoral population for bringing the wrath of God upon themselves. In their elaborate baroque style, priests contended that the 1687 earthquake seemed to unleash a brief moment of "hell," when even criminals managed to escape their forced enclosure.[40] They recommended antidotes such as more frequent communion, prayer, and self-reflection as remedies against the "Babylon of their guilt," and the presumed rampant immorality pervading the opulent viceregal capital.[41]

In their attacks, colonial authorities targeted women in gender specific ways. Juxtaposing the sacred with the worldly, Archbishop Liñán y Cisneros inveighed against limeñas' obsession with ornamented dress by contrasting them with devout, morally pure church-going women whose hearts had not been corrupted "by the idol of the gusseted skirt":

> Many of the pardas, whom they vulgarly call mulattas, live modestly [recogida] and honestly, showing in the exterior of their dress the interior state of recogimiento and virtue; but the common enemy does not sleep. It seems that he has induced others . . . and helps to carry souls to hell through the misuse of decorated skirts, so short, that dishonestly one discovers more than the foot.[42]

Limeñas may have served as symbols of sexual transgression and immorality in certain circles, but other domestic and foreign observers extolled their charms as a metaphor for the city's beauty and opulence.[43] To María Jacinta Montoya, founder of the Beaterio de Jesús, María y José, and the wife of one of Lima's "living saints," Nicolás de Ayllón, Lima was the wealthiest and most populous city in the kingdom: "[T]he depository of riches, treasury goods, and the storehouse of abundance."[44] Yet, she added, Lima's wealthy facade could scarcely hide the growing social and economic rifts between aristocracy and commoners.

In Lima, by the late seventeenth century, a growing gap in living standards between rich and poor corresponded to an increase in social assistance, preaching in the various plazas, or visits to the infirm and needy in the hospitals for Africans, Indians, or Spanish men and women.[45] In addition, the 1700 census indicated a three-to-one female-male ratio for blacks; a three-to-two ratio between Spanish females and males; and an impressive four-to-one ratio for mulattos (see Table 1).[46] This gender imbalance may have precipitated an increase in interracial marriages and informal, unsanctioned unions, as well as criminal and civil lawsuits.

More impressive is the fact that divorce petitions more than tripled and annulments doubled during the last half of the seventeenth century. The dramatic escalation during the last decade of the seventeenth century may be attributed to an economic depression in Lima caused by earthquakes in 1687 and 1690, the increasing importation of grains from Chile that signaled a decline in local production, the continued loss of revenue from silver, forced loans exacted by the Spanish government, and the costs incurred by the fortification of the entire city (1685–87). However, the number and variety of institutions also may have exacerbated marital discord. More plausible, however, is the idea that the increase in divorce and annulment petitions illustrates the willingness of women to express dissatisfaction with the violence that had

TABLE 4
Divorces and Annulments, 1651–1713, Lima

	1651–60	1661–70	1671–80	1681–1690	1691–1700	1701–1713
Divorces	111	190	232	233	362	143
Annulments	61	124	137	165	118	98

SOURCE: Lavallé, "Divorcio y nulidad," 430; AAL, Divorcios, Leg. 61–63; Nulidades, Leg. 46–49.

formed a tolerable aspect of conjugal relations.[47] Although difficult to quantify, divorce testimony exhibited greater outrage over the emotional and physical brutality occurring primarily against women.[48] Complaints of abandonment, long absences, or the maintenance of more than one household also demonstrate how fragile bonds had become.

Divorce statistics indicate that all racial groups, particularly Indian women from Lima and the provinces, were more likely to initiate divorce suits in the second half of the seventeenth century than before.[49] Women pressed for their right to be deposited, *in spite of* their race and *because of* their gender. Statements similar to that made by the morena Melchora de los Reyes—"[A]lthough I am a poor morena, the judge should deposit me"—became more commonplace among nonelite women of color willing to initiate divorce proceedings, even if they lacked the resources or emotional support to sustain the case.[50] A sampling of annulment cases shows that, while Spaniards still predominated, other racial groups became more numerous, especially when women claimed they had been duped or married against their will.[51]

Like Hierónima de San Miguel in the first half of the seventeenth century, many women continued to employ the concept of recogimiento as a positive self-identifying feature, while finding it necessary to defend their sexual honor and morality in both public and private settings. In 1678, Josepha Ferrer, a mulatta slave, complained to the judge that her beloved had promised to marry her in front of the statue of the Virgin in the chapel of the city jail, but had then duped her and married someone else. She claimed her sense of honor had been betrayed.[52] In 1685, María Ferrero, a mixed-blood slave, argued to the court that it was a well-known, established fact (*es notorio y público*) that she was virtuous, recogida, and also frequently took communion.[53]

More frequently, women in marital litigation suits expressed disappointment that their sense of moral well-being and recogimiento had been tarnished because economic expectations had not been met.[54] Micaela Flores testified to the ecclesiastical judge in 1674 that she never would have married her husband had she known he would force her to raise feed for his horses.[55] As in the first half of the century, wives like Valeriana Pimentel in 1691 argued they had complied with their marital duties: "always trying to meet [the] expectation to live a virtuous and *recogida* life, which the married state requires."[56] In the words of another litigant, Doña Francisca Crespo, in 1654:

[I try] not to pay attention to the fact (only to acquiesce to his will), that he [my husband] has me working in a pastry shop attending to unfamiliar tasks. I work at the counter and administer the candle making process. I have done everything possible to win [his] respect and to deserve him.[57]

Most parties seemed well aware of what engendered ideals of "good" sexual and moral conduct meant; the issue to resolve was whether to continue submitting to their husband's will (*voluntad*) when an economic breach had occurred in the marriage. Many women in the last half of the century came to feel that it was no longer worth the price in spite of the fact that they might be characterized in negative ways, or left without a home.

Thus María Jacinta Montoya noted the growing *género* (class) of poor and economically marginalized people, predominantly female, whom she passed on the streets or visited on her frequent rounds in the hospitals during the 1670s and 1680s.[58] Many of these women were older, in their thirties and forties, with few possibilities of marrying well or gaining family support. Some may have even been *divorciadas* who could no longer tolerate marital strife. The city pullulated with these women—many of them categorized as "wayward and worldly"—attempting to eke out a living in any way possible. Some became the targets of priests and beatas eager to divert them from the path of hell, but others voluntarily sought "God's handmaidens" in search of aid, advice, and spiritual council.[59]

Disenfranchised women suffered as a result of an increase in conjugal discord, illegitimacy, and the abandonment of children and households. Moreover, mounting economic pressures, as well as growing competition for jobs, contrasted starkly with the finery in dress and architectural splendor of the city.[60] Some witnessed these discordant phenomena—along with the appearance of comets, meteors, and eclipses—with growing trepidation as the century's end approached.[61] On the surface, increasing social tensions did not correspond with the unprecedented growth in popular piety and investment into spiritual culture. The two phenomena were, however, inextricably related. It is within this complex social and cultural milieu, where expressions of popular piety flourished and women increasingly questioned rigid patriarchal norms, that a sudden proliferation of religious institutions occurred.

Changing Dynamics of Institutions: Convents

In his tribute to the city of Lima, *El sol del Nuevo Mundo* (1683), Francisco Montalvo wrote that "the community of religious women who ennoble the city of Lima surpass those of Spain in their silence, recogimiento, and mortifications."⁶² The number of female religious in convents like La Encarnación, La Trinidad, Santa Teresa, and the observant convents of El Prado and San José, remained constant throughout the seventeenth century, but Santa Catalina (founded 1624) became an increasingly popular choice for women seeking a religious vocation after 1660 (see Appendix B). Santa Clara experienced a tremendous period of growth between 1637 and 1669, but, like La Concepción, witnessed a decrease in its population of nuns after 1669, the year of a major ecclesiastical visitation.

Montalvo also alleged that one convent in Lima spent more on religious festivities in one month than all the other convents of the Spanish colonies in one year. Others shared his views. Archbishop Villagómez (1641–73) recognized the need to reform convent finances, which he considered to be wildly out of control by the 1660s because of poor administration, corruption, excessive and wasteful spending, and the fact that each abbess had an ever-increasing population to administer.⁶³ But internal malfeasance only partially explained the story. Since their foundation, convents had invested dowry funds and other capital in the royal treasury in the form of *censos*, or loans, for which they received interest payments on the principal.⁶⁴ The Spanish Crown, increasingly short of money after a century of continuous warfare, poor economic policies, and growing French and Dutch power, requested that the royal treasury force ecclesiastical corporations to buy more bonds, but, at the same time lowered interest rates on them.⁶⁵ Such a change in policy had serious repercussions for religious houses. In 1655, La Trinidad complained that the convent had lost more than four thousand pesos in income because of the reduction in interest rates; they needed the money to rebuild a chapel, partially destroyed by an earthquake.⁶⁶ Nine years later, the abbesses of six convents addressed a joint letter to the king stating that they had complied with the request to lend the Crown dowry funds, but expressed concern because the Crown had delayed repayment.⁶⁷ This financial contest continued unabated throughout the rest of the century.

Other problems plagued female religious houses. Ecclesiastical authorities, including Archbishop Villagómez, were concerned that the "world" or nonreligious inhabitants of the cloister predominated and religious houses no longer functioned as "houses of God."⁶⁸ In spite of an ecclesiastical visitation in 1669, intended to place constraints on the unwieldy nonreligious population (namely, seglares—secular women and girls—and servants), their numbers continued to increase dramatically.⁶⁹ Rather than succumb to high-level pressure, convents, badly in need of additional income, responded by more readily accepting schoolgirls and female boarders willing to pay a 150 to 200 peso annual fee. In 1614, seglares (excluding servants or criadas) composed only 10 percent of the conventual population; by 1700 they formed between 15 and 17 percent of the total in the three largest convents.[70] In the convents of La Concepción and San José, the number of seglares more than doubled in ten years (from 1690 to 1700), and in other convents the rate tripled between 1660 and 1700 (see Appendix B).[71]

The need for additional entry fees contributed to the increase in the secular population, but pressures from "below" also played a role. Women elected to live in convents in growing numbers because they could not find a partner (given the serious gender imbalance), because they chose not to marry, because their marriages had failed or they became widowed, because family members were nuns, or because they needed temporary refuge or employment.[72] Girls, too, continued to be placed in convents at a tender age.[73] As convents opened their doors to lay women, divorciadas were also more readily admitted, particularly after the Casa de Divorciadas closed in 1665 (see Appendix E).[74] Once divorced, Spaniards and mestizas remained in the conventual setting as seglares or nuns.[75] And, unlike the first half of the century, women of color were now encouraged to enter if they had once worked there or had been physically abused by their husbands.[76] The "world of walls" increasingly admitted women seeking sanctuary against harsh treatment or a lack of economic support, but socioeconomic status still had a great deal to do with a woman's likely position as a servant, slave, or "retired" woman after she entered a religious house.[77]

Cultural convictions offer another explanation for the prevalence of non-religious females in convents. After 1650, most limeñas considered recogimiento as integral to their identity and viewed "proper" institutional upbringing as a status symbol and means of personal enhancement. Orphans raised in convents or colegios/recogimientos stood a better chance of marrying well or gaining a privileged position in secular society or in the convent.[78] This practice dates back to the sixteenth century in Mexico and Peru, but its demographic pervasiveness after 1650 was new. Another carryover from the sixteenth century is evidenced by the protective fathers who saw enclosure as a method of preserving the moral and physical welfare of their daughters. For instance, Mathias Polanco, a free pardo, complained to an ecclesiastical judge in 1678 that his wife, Theresa Salgado, who had left him five years before, had attempted to abduct their daughter from the Convent of Santa Clara. The girl worked "in the service" of a nun but, her father argued, had lived in recogimiento and was receiving a good education. To remove her from such an environment, he felt, would only "endanger her delicate condition."[79]

Slaves and servants reared in an enclosed setting were more likely to succeed in marriage and find gainful employment. Some slaves fled alone or with their daughters, to seek refuge or "recogerse" in a convent where they hoped for better treatment.[80] Slave-owners also placed young girls in convents for safekeeping, or buen recogimiento, they contended, to prevent flight or sale. In 1690, General Don Andrés Gutiérrez de la Torre y Rocas, recently appointed corregidor of the province of Conchucos, placed two young slave girls under the care of the abbess of the Monasterio de la Concepción (the sister of his wife, who had recently died) while he left Lima to occupy his post.[81]

Limeñas had long provided an inexpensive labor force for the nuns, and in convents such as La Encarnación and La Concepción the number of servants jumped from 20 percent in 1614 to more than half of the total convent population by 1700.[82] The increase in the number of servants relative to female religious reflects a general trend in Lima: in 1614, the free servant population in convents constituted 24 percent of the general population; by 1700, that level (including servants and donadas in convents and beaterios) had risen to 29 percent (see Table 5).[83] Most of the 1,342 servants and more than 700 slaves performed demanding, back-breaking labor for their superiors. Well aware of their place in the social hierarchy, nevertheless, those women and children raised in convents and destined to serve others defined themselves, or were described by their owners, as recogida and honorable.[84]

Three examples from the late seventeenth century illustrate the circumstances facing enslaved women of color and the distinct interpretations of recogimiento that resulted. In 1663, the mulatta Feliciana de Salinas, illegitimate daughter of Don Juan de Salinas and his slave, complained that her father had deposited her at birth in a convent to be raised in recogimiento under the care of his sister, a nun. When María de Salinas tried to sell her niece, Juan protested her judgment, stating that she entered the convent to be "educated and trained."[85] While considering whether she were free or enslaved, witnesses described her as recogida.[86] In 1673, Florentina del Sacramento, a slave in Santa Clara, recounted to an ecclesiastical judge that she had been raised in recogimiento and honesty and, being a doncella, was ignorant of the "ways of men." Unfortunately, she had been raped and forcibly abducted from the convent, and after dishonoring her, the man reneged on his promise to marry her. "Socially blemished," she felt shame that she had lost both her virginity and her sense of recogimiento, and wondered whether anyone would now want to buy her.[87] In 1694, María del Carmen Noriega, a free black, felt angry that Matias Ceballos had broken his promise to marry her after she consented to have sexual relations with him. She regretted leaving the "comfort" (*comodidad*) of the convent, where she had been raised "in recogimiento."[88] The protective space of the convent afforded these inexperienced girls a chance to be raised in virtue and seclusion; once Florentina and María del Carmen entered the siglo and learned the ways of men, they realized they had lost more than their virginity.

TABLE 5

Population of Free Women of Color in Lima, Seventeenth Century

Year	Secular population	%	In convents and beaterios	%	Total
1614	1,375	76.0	425	24.0	1,800
1700	3,311*	71.0	1,342	29.0	4,653

SOURCE: Bronner, "The Population"; *Numeración general.*
*The 1700 *Numeración* indicates indias (1,506); mulatas libres (1,323); and negras libres (482).

Convents provided sanctuary, safeguarded virtue, and also enabled some women to enhance their status within the institution. Nuns annually reviewed selected women of color for promotion from the rank of criada to donada: requiring one year as a novice, taking informal religious vows, performing labor in the kitchen or infirmary, and carrying out tasks appertaining to divine worship (see Appendix B for the number of donadas). Applicants held an intimate, familial, yet servile relationship with the nuns who sponsored their candidacy: most novices between twelve and twenty years of age had already spent much of their lives working in their service. Many were illegitimate or orphaned with few family bonds outside the convent. Nearly all donadas entering La Encarnación, Santa Clara, and La Concepción were free (a prerequisite) indias or castas.[89] Although some nuns paid a small dowry on their behalf, many donadas were admitted because of their physical strength or ability to work.[90]

The daughters of slaves who worked in the convent aspired to freedom and the position of donada by exhibiting characteristics of sanctity, receiving a minimal education, and being associated with a particular nun willing to support their cause. Fifteen-year-old Melchora del Sacramento stated that her owner had freed her:

Since I was born I have been dedicated to the service of the Holy Virgin and because of the devotion that my owner, Margarita de Jesus, has toward the Immaculate Conception she brought me to this convent, freed and raised me, and I [now] serve in the sacristy of the Monasterio de la Puríssima Concepción.[91]

Donadas held a variety of positions that granted them additional status relative to *criadas*. Some were *sacristanas*: they cleaned religious objects and washed the linen for the altar. Others monopolized specific tasks: for decades, Juana de Sejas rang the bell to specify the liturgical hours in La Encarnación (which required a great deal of strength); and the exceptional physical fitness of Teresa de Jesús ensured that she would carry the heavy cross during religious processions.[92] Some donadas exhibited a particular artisanal flair: Antonia de la Concepción's ability to fashion candles for processions, festivals, and special masses made her a welcome addition to the Convent of Santa Clara.[93] Remarkable expressions of piety were also welcome. Juana Josepha, a free black, entered La Encarnación as a donada in 1688 because of her reputation for mortifications and other acts of humility. María Josefa de Jesús and Adriana Flores y Cabrera became donadas because of their capacity for "mental prayer."[94]

Many novices expressed their desire to live a truly religious life. María de Vargas, a parda, who once had been a criada, claimed that "since childhood I have had the goal to follow my true vocation and obtain the habit I desire in the service of God."[95] Agustín de Mora described his legitimate daughter, the free parda María, as "touched by the hand of God."[96] Many girls, however, claimed that life as a donada attracted them because it guaranteed economic and social security that the dangers of the world (el siglo) could not provide.[97] While some confessed to wanting to "die in the holy house" where they had been raised, others longed to be "liberated from the sins of the world."[98] Lucia Bravo de Laguna and Catalina de la Madre de Dios, quarteronas of seventeen and sixteen years of age, respectively, feared the siglo: a world filled with the horrors of temptation and evil that they had never experienced. To them, the life of a donada "in the house of the Holy Virgin" seemed a natural recourse.[99]

Formal expressions of spirituality were thus no longer reserved for the Spanish elite of Lima, but the bounds of sanctity had their limits. Nuns also still chose donadas because they could "serve the community" and they needed laborers to stir the bread dough and stoke the fire for the organ. Still, women of color could express their spirituality and fervor toward God in a milieu that upheld clear racist and class divisions. Whether they chose temporary or permanent enclosure and recogimiento, many more women could now benefit from the imprimatur of convent life: economically, morally, and spiritually.

The climate of toleration had its limitations, however. Some religious spaces resisted allowing "worldly" women and girls within the cloister. For instance, the three observant convents founded between 1643 and 1713 (see Appendix A) did not allow donadas into the cloister. Many holy women argued that although Francisco López claimed that convents constituted the "third concentric circle" of the world, they were contaminated by the intrusion of too many lay women. To some, the obvious permeability of this sacred sphere also resulted from a combination of natural disasters, overcrowded conditions, ostentation, political infighting, a lack of financial stability, and spiritual recogimiento. Some nuns reacted against these changes by attempting to reinforce the boundaries of the "smallest circle in the world" and fleeing from the "worldly" convents to observant convents. Continuing a tradition established earlier in the century, the founders of three new observant convents (two originally beaterios) expressly justified their requests on the grounds of overpopulation and the lack of spiritual recogimiento in the large convents.[100] At the inauguration ceremony of the recollection convent of Santa Ana in 1686, four nuns retired from the "world" (which Francisco López equated with a "living death") to live a "complete" life of recogimiento in their new environment:

[T]hey enjoy the quietude of Religion. . . . Because one type of life animates the body; and the other life, which is that of quietude, is the life of this primary life. The life of the body is the life that one has; the life of contemplation is the life that one achieves. The life of the body is subject to many deaths; the life of quietude is that which is subject to one only; and this, such as it is, one embraces as a new and happy life.[101]

Observant convents fostered the "primary life" and reinforced the smallest circle; however, they also remained exclusive social spaces that excluded "inferior" individuals from becoming nuns on the basis of race or economic status. Like their forebears, Angela and Francisca de Zárate (p. 119 above), the initial entrants to the Beaterio de Nerias (which became the Monasterio de las Trinitarias Descalzas in 1682) were, more often than not, the legitimate daughters of parents de buena fama, and ranged in ages from eight to fifty-two (twenty-two was the average age).[102] Their numerous servants handled more "worldly" tasks such as baking bread and washing the linens: in 1700, thirteen servants attended nineteen nuns and two novitiates in the Monasterio de Trinitarias Descalzas; and within Santa Ana, the twenty-one nuns who enjoyed a "life of quietude" possessed nine servants to help them achieve it (see Appendix B).[103] Because the boundaries of race and class remained so firmly set in the observant convents, other religious houses, including newly founded beaterios, began to cater to a broader constituency.

Changing Dynamics of Institutions: Beaterios

Emerging nearly fifty years after their popularity in Spain had diminished, Peruvian beaterios still maintained vestiges of their Iberian roots.[104] Their historical development in America diverged over time and place. Beginning in the 1520s, Empress Isabel, Hernán Cortés, and Archbishop Zumárraga had patronized Spanish beatas to instruct the daughters of the indigenous nobility in New Spain. In Lima, the few beaterios founded between 1540 and 1669 quickly gained conventual status.[105] Individual beatas were more common: some maintained the cult of a saint or provided herbal remedies for needy patients; others chose to live in a communal setting, without official church recognition.[106] Even after beaterios were established, some holy women continued to support particularly devout women "outside" institutional confines.[107]

Beaterios became popular in Lima only during the later seventeenth century when colonial officials and wealthy limeños promoted the foundation of ten lay pious houses between 1669 and 1704, a unique phenomenon in Spanish America.[108]

Many factors explain the sudden proliferation of beaterios.[109] First, overcrowded conditions in Lima's convents resulted in demand for beaterios from religious women. Second, the gender disproportion made it necessary to furnish appropriate institutional spaces to accommodate the rising number of young and old women who did not wish to become nuns and could not find suitable husbands. Third, wealthy and pious individuals seeking to invest "spiritual capital" in religious houses saw beaterios as an attractive prospect because, whereas the likelihood of receiving a license for a convent was negligible, the required license for a beaterio was less time consuming and the capital investment in the construction of the house and chapel seemed minimal.[110] In some instances, huge investments meant that the beaterio could eventually accumulate enough funds to gain the necessary royal license to become a convent.

Creole politics also played a role because, for decades, the lower nobility donated their capital to spiritual enterprises, in part to bolster family prestige and status.[111] By financing beaterios or other charitable institutions, prominent businessmen and women could perpetuate and "immortalize" their family names.[112] Women of hidalgo (low nobility) status, with few financial possibilities, could also find satisfaction by supporting religious foundations.[113] As long as women followed prescribed guidelines in making investments, it was considered an acceptable outlet of spiritual expression. Antonia Lucía Maldonado de Quintanilla (later del Espíritu Santo) was of hidalgo status, but her father died while she was very young, forcing her mother to support her by working as a cigar-maker in Callao. Antonia did not wish to marry, but did so, her daughter later claimed, out of financial necessity.[114] Her true aim was to found the Beaterio de las Nazarenas, which she accomplished in 1672, but only by enlisting the support of royal authorities and begging for alms in secret, since patriarchal norms limited the degree to which a married woman could advocate such a cause in public.[115]

The formalization of several seventeenth-century cults further explains the beaterio phenomenon. For instance, the popularity of the cults of El Señor de los Milagros and the Passion of Christ resulted in the foundation of the Beaterio de las Nazarenas.[116] The devotion to Nuestra Señora de Copacabana, which originated among the Indians in the parish of San Lázaro, grew steadily throughout the seventeenth century; in 1633 a chapel was constructed, a confraternity founded soon after, and by 1691 enough capital had been collected to build a beaterio.[117] In a third instance, a group of devout beatas continued to imitate the extreme piety of Rosa de Santa María after her death in 1617, in an informal, noninstitutionalized setting. By the time she was beatified in 1668 and canonized in 1671, her cult had increased substantially. In 1669, the Dominican Order constructed the Beaterio de las Rosas in front of her childhood home, and shortly thereafter thirty-three beatas began their formal communal existence.[118] The strong Dominican influence in the Vatican also motivated the foundation of a fourth beaterio in 1680, dedicated to the Italian saint Rosa de Viterbo. The arrival of the Dominican Third Order, the Congregation of San Felipe Neri, propelled the foundation of the Beaterio de las Nerias (founded 1674), the Beaterio de Patrocinio (founded 1688), and the Beaterio del Corazón de Jesús (founded 1704) (see Appendix A).

If the desire of wealthy individuals to invest in works of Christian charity, the growth of particular religious cults, and the arrival of new orders influenced the foundation of the Lima beaterios, major ideological and social differences distinguished them. The Beaterio de Nuestra Señora de Copacabana had more of a vested interest in the coastal Indian nobility—in Lima, La Magdalena, Ica, and Chiclayo—which pressed for more equal representation in religious orders. Eleven of its thirty-three sisters in 1700 were the daughters of *curacas*; the remainder were of Spanish descent.[119]

Three out of the ten beaterios established during this period admitted casta or indigenous women.[120] This would suggest a range of choices for young girls that corresponded to contemporary class and racial specifications. Beatas attracted to the Casa de las Amparadas were generally casta women of the popular classes, many of whom had weathered poverty or destabilization in their lives.[121] Administrative posts, however, generally went to Spaniards, although the mestiza María Jacinta Montoya proved the exception to the rule.[122] Nonetheless, the majority of beaterios replicated racial and class divisions in convents and admitted only girls and older women de limpia sangre.[123] Nor were all beatas young neophyte doncellas: many were older and widowed, and saw beaterios as a protective haven after having experienced a moment of rupture in their lives.[124]

The desire for more equal racial representation in beaterios complemented the ambitions of several founders to create spaces distinct from the corruption, materialism, and overcrowded conditions that characterized many of the large convents in Lima.[125] However, fear and circumspection also motivated many late-seventeenth-century beatas to seek a cloistered, controlled setting within which to express their piety. The example of Peruvian beatas condemned by the Inquisition in a 1625 auto-da-fé for their open advocation of direct mystical experience may have served as a lesson (see page 117 above).

Many beaterios founded between 1669 and 1704 provided a formal institutional haven and a safe enclosure for lay pious women conforming to an institutional, conservative expression of the sacred.[126] Adhering to the Council of Trent's decrees, all beaterios, with the exception of Jesús, María y José, were placed under the direct authority of the regular clergy, thus effectively limiting the spiritual and social independence of these women.

The Ideal of Spiritual Recogimiento: The Beaterio of Jesús, María and José

Of all the beaterios, Jesús, María and José best represents the attempt to emulate the model of spiritual recogimiento popular at the time. Both María Jacinta Montoya and her husband, the *beato* Nicolás de Ayllón (1632–77), renowned for his religious virtue and nominated for beatification immediately after his death, had a specific vision for their foundling institution. Like Nicolás, Montoya had already experienced life in a cloistered setting: at twelve, she entered the novitiate of La Encarnación but soon left. After some years of marriage they decided to take informal vows of celibacy and live *como unos troncos* (like tree trunks).[127]

By 1672 they decided to gather together seven poor, dispossessed doncellas, provide them with material and spiritual guidance, and teach them notions of Christian charity based upon the principles advocated by Teresa de Avila and Pedro de Alcántara, the Spanish mystic who edited Luis de Granada's book.[128] A scribe recorded the testimony of one of their young converts, Juana de San Lorenzo, who recalled Ayllón's efforts to redeem her:

[W]hen she retired to Nicolás de Dios's home, she was so wayward [distraída] that she confessed and took communion [only] infrequently. Now she tends to do them more often, although she could still [easily] revert to [a life of] sin out of a lack of respect for God. In His holy care she is diverted from such actions.[129]

Upholding an informal vow of poverty and dedication to a life of charitable labor, the young recogidas volunteered to nurse, console, and provide gifts to infirm Spanish women in the Hospital de la Caridad on a regular basis.[130] Upon visiting the house six years later, in 1678, Viceroy Liñán y Cisneros was so impressed with the spiritual dedication of the recogidas that he gave his immediate support to found a beaterio.[131]

Contemporary observers imagined the new beaterio (founded 1685) to be a true representation of heaven on earth and to be embodied in one of the "smallest circles of the world." In his panegyric *La estrella de Lima convertida en sol* (1688), Francisco de Echave y Assu characterized the inhabitants as "angels, not women" who continually fasted, occupied themselves in prayer and penitent acts, and avoided contact with family members.[132] Well aware of the recogimiento's reputation for exemplary spirituality and interested in gaining support to convert the beaterio into a convent, Montoya employed her own literary skills in extolling the virtues of the institution. It was, she claimed:

> a nursery of abundant flowers; a beautiful fountain; an enclosed garden; a paradise of delights; a walled city; precious crown and ship full of riches; an immaculate dwelling; a tabernacle to kneel and pray; school of virtues; military station; house of saintliness; guardhouse of chastity; firmament of modesty and mirror of religion.[133]

Montoya felt called upon by God to discipline, govern, teach, and police her recogidas.[134] She purposely chose girls who had not been "tainted" by any previous experience in another religious institution and formed them through ten to fourteen years of enclosure and constant spiritual exercises.[135] Involved in long hours of silent and spoken prayer, "her" recogidas dressed in a purple tunic and veil, hair hanging down the back, with a rope tied at the throat and a crown of thorns to evoke the image of the penitent Jesus.[136]

To Montoya, recogimiento also involved a total lack of oral or written communication with the outside world. So strict were her measures that she permitted only approved visitors and expelled any recruits who rejected what they considered to be her "excessive" practices of recogimiento.[137] In order to maintain an "uncontaminated" environment of recogimiento, where things of the world remained totally absent, and to adhere to her notions of poverty, Montoya would not allow servants or slaves in the beaterio and insisted that all beatas share in household duties.[138] As in several other beaterios in Lima, secular women boarders were prohibited, no matter what their social rank (see Appendix B). And, like the abbesses of two other beaterios—Antonia Lucía del Espíritu Santo and Ana de Robles—her authoritarian command resembled some medieval beaterios where, instead of vowing obedience to a male secular or regular cleric, the beatas swore their allegiance to an older female figure.[139]

Beaterios such as Jesús, María and José offered a sacred space for women to express the purity of spiritual recogimiento. The Beaterio de las Nerias and Las Nazarenas were also renowned for the high level of spirituality of its female inhabitants. Other beaterios, however, provided a wider array of services to females: Las Mercedarias or Copacabana operated as a space for women seeking asylum from marital strife, served as a temporary shelter for economically disadvantaged women, and also functioned as educational centers. The Casa de las Amparadas fulfilled similar functions but was best known as a lay pious house for spiritual retreat and as an asylum or type of reformatory for women "caught in the nets of the World, the Devil and the Flesh."[140]

The Beaterio or Recogimiento de las Amparadas
de la Puríssima Concepción

Las Amparadas served simultaneously as a beaterio and a recogimiento and performed four primary roles: it ministered to women seeking asylum from marital strife, including divorciadas; operated as a temporary home for economically disadvantaged women; served as an educational center for at least eighty girls; and functioned as a space for pious expression based upon Jesuit prescriptions. Its foundation also prefigured a sister institution in Mexico City, the Recogimiento de San Miguel de Belem (founded 1683), which catered to an equally colorful constituency of poor married or single women "with experience," prostitutes, and innocent schoolgirls, all of whom lived like nuns.[141]

In Lima, secular and ecclesiastical authorities, the recogidas, and married couples constantly struggled to determine the precise role of the Casa de las Amparadas. The confusion and dissension that resulted may be explained in part by the lack of clarity and precision in determining the distinguishing features of the "sacred" (lo sagrado) and the "worldly" (*lo mundano*) that permeated discussions of sanctity, sin, and purity in the late seventeenth century. In addition, the assorted interpretations of recogimiento and recogida complicated matters, as did the tremendous variety of recogidas inhabiting the institution, many with distinct agendas. The discourse of secular and ecclesiastical male authorities reflected this linguistic and cultural slipperiness as they continuously interpreted the ideal functions of the Casa de las Amparadas in different manners.[142]

For instance, each viceroy directly involved with the beaterio/recogimiento expressed an opinion about its purpose. The count of Lemos believed the recogimiento could shelter "public women" inhabiting the streets: "[M]any women accustomed to living licentiously have decided to reform and act in a modest and penitent manner, something totally lacking before, with this 'type' of person."[143] Lemos hoped that women "living freely in the world," without families or marital ties, would reconcile themselves to "God's holy Law."[144] Fervent in his support of the poor, he speculated that some women, because of their advanced age and poverty, resorted to a life of sin for lack of any alternative. Whether for prostitutes or for women who had lost their sense of virtue, Lemos imagined this space as serving both correctional and educational purposes.[145] His interpretation of recogimiento echoed the sixteenth-century Jesuit model and included elements of Juan Luis Vives's humanism. It also resonated with sentiments in Mexico, where, for example, authorities expressed similar opinions about the applications of recogimientos for prostitutes and "wayward women."[146]

Lemos's successor, Archbishop-Viceroy Liñán de Cisneros, chose to focus upon the sacred nature of the recogidas and likened them to Mary Magdalene, describing the women as "leaving the World behind" to atone for moral or sexual transgressions. They could opt to take formal vows as beatas, or travel a less formal path as penitents or recogidas:

[T]he women who enter the house are Spanish. Disenchanted with their worldly blunders, and desiring to better their Life, they introduce themselves to the healthy path of penitence from which the term recogida derives; poor women in danger of losing their honor also reside there, cloistered and without communicating with anyone.[147]

The administrator of the Casa de las Amparadas, Francisco de Castillo, based the constitution he wrote upon his interpretation of Jesuit notions of spiritual exercises.[148] Strongly influenced by his teacher, the Peruvian Jesuit mystic Antonio Ruíz de Montoya, who taught him *oración de unión*, or direct communication with God through the use of conceptual images, he was also well versed in the writings of Teresa of Avila.[149] These ideas reinforced the more orthodox Jesuit interpretation of recogimiento that involved silent prayer while concentrating on a specific event like the Passion of Christ, and an attempt to order one's life according to God's will through disciplinary measures. Like other Jesuits, Castillo recognized the importance of recogimientos in reforming wayward and lost women.[150]

For some of the women, Castillo served as a model of spirituality and a pillar of paternalistic support. In an attempt to appeal to a wide-ranging female constituency, Castillo instituted the practice of hearing confessions of morena slaves and pardas on Thursdays, Spanish women on Saturdays, and indias on Sunday mornings.[151] They heard him preach and witnessed his "miracles" in a local sanctuary or poor neighborhood called El Baratillo. The beata Agustina del Christo said that Castillo's sermons in the Baratillo convinced her to "leave the world to serve God," and she soon entered the Carmelite monastery.[152] A number of beatas and recogidas from the Casa de las Amparadas testified that they were saved from their worldly ways because of Castillo's great oratorical powers. Many expressed complete devotion to him, and upon his death, advocated his beatification. The first abbess of the recogimiento, Sor Inés María de Jesús, affirmed that she once saw the Virgin Mary by his side, and after his death she sensed his presence and took solace from his spiritual counsel. Others claimed he interceded on their behalf when disagreements occurred, or when provisions were scarce and the recogimiento had little income on which to rely.[153]

Initially, the Casa de las Amparadas had few inhabitants, but between 1677 and 1680 the number of recogidas increased from twenty to forty.[154] The count of Monclova's order in 1690 for "scandalous women" (an expression he never explained) to be housed involuntarily in the recogimiento swelled its ranks considerably, so that by 1708, the Casa de las Amparadas had more than two hundred women, including "repentant women," "schoolgirls," and "recluses."[155]

In their black and white habits, the permanently cloistered recogidas (also called beatas) engaged in constant acts of penitence for their misdirected past and enjoyed the advantages of the monastic state.[156] In addition to the permanent recogidas, other women entered for eight days, quartered in a room above the other inhabitants, to partake in spiritual exercises, according to the prescribed Jesuit formula.[157]

After visiting the house in 1680, Archbishop Liñán de Cisneros reported that "the mortifications, penitence, and spiritual exercises were continual."[158] The daily regimen resembled the conventual pattern. The beatas and recogidas awakened at 5:30 A.M., participated in one-half hour of communal mental prayer, attended Mass, and dedicated themselves to particular devotions. Later in the day they performed collective tasks, ate their meals, said the rosary, conducted spiritual readings, held additional mental prayer sessions, and finally retired at 9:30 P.M. On Wednesdays, Fridays, and Saturdays they were encouraged to practice mortifications such as eating from the floor, prostrating themselves in the form of a cross, kissing the feet of their companions, and allowing others to step on them: "all humble acts which bring alive and nourish the spirit."[159] Recogidas who were mothers were permitted to see their children only two or three times a year, and all inhabitants were discouraged from forming close friendships, "except with Our Lord" (see Appendix D).[160]

Little is known about either the permanent recogidas or the eighty young schoolgirls entering the establishment to learn the "love of God," but information about the so-called "scandalous" inhabitants is available.[161] Ironically, the very women labeled by authorities as having a suspect past described themselves as having been abandoned, or fleeing conditions of forced enclosure or imprisonment in their marriages to what they considered to be a space of peace, tranquillity, and freedom in the Casa de las Amparadas.[162] In fact, the recogimiento functioned as the most popular institutional refuge for women involved in divorce suits: 40 percent of divorciadas between 1670 and 1713 were housed there at some time.[163] So were 46 percent of women involved in marital litigation suits.[164] The recogimiento served as a depository and provided asylum and temporary refuge primarily for nonelite women of all races, including Spanish women.[165]

Instances arose when elite women sent to Las Amparadas would request a transfer to their preferred choice of institution—a convent—because the recogimiento "was not to their liking."[166] Because institutional deposit continued to serve as a major source of contention among litigious couples, recogidas were often transferred to Las Amparadas from other locations because it provided rooms, spiritual consultation, camaraderie with other *divorciadas*, and an infrastructure suitable to carry out necessary legal transactions.[167]

Not all men and women saw life in a beaterio, whether temporary or permanent, as an honorable recourse. To some men, beaterios had a negative reputation of promoting, not preventing, aberrant sexual conduct.[168] Beaterios housed lay pious women of "voluntary recogimiento," not full fledged nuns, and many performed social services that might rouse suspicion. Some husbands detested the exposure of their wives to persons from vastly diverse backgrounds, and the associations formed within the institution.[169] Pedro de Cárdenas was furious not only because the ecclesiastical judge had ordered his wife's deposit in the Casa de las Amparadas in 1701 but also because her opinionated mother accompanied her there, and (he feared) might dissuade her from returning to the marriage.[170]

Even the pristine Beaterio de las Rosas could suffer from a tarnished reputation. Unhappy with her marriage, the young Doña Francisca Zambrano followed her parents' advice and went to the Beaterio de las Rosas while they traveled to their *chacra* in the valley of Guaura. Her husband found it appalling that she had lived in a beaterio where "they have no other profession than voluntary enclosure (recogimiento)," and then left the institution "of her own volition" to go to a "house of ill repute" with a mulatta girlfriend in a "questionable neighborhood."[171] He doubted the beatas' reputation for strict enclosure and piety and the fact that his wife could easily flee. Doña Francisca countered by arguing to the ecclesiastical judge that she had left the beaterio because of ill health and that the rigors of the spiritual exercises proved too much for her delicate condition. Her husband, she continued, had improperly characterized the laxity of moral recogimiento of both the institution and the home in which she subsequently resided, thus she felt it necessary to defend the "honor" of her new voluntary enclosure:

The Archbishop, with the support of my parents and doctors insisted that I be moved [from the beaterio] to the home of an illustrious woman of great virtue and good upbringing, Doña María Reynosso, to care for me ... in order to continue the exercises of virtue I had learned in the beaterio.[172]

Finding the stringency of the spiritual world too demanding, she asserted that the *lack* of enclosure and proper ecclesiastical supervision (she could easily leave) were sufficient reasons to transfer to a private home where she could still practice her "exercises of virtue." Thus, she reiterated her husband's argument that the institution lacked physical enclosure, but for different reasons, and found a way not to compromise her personal virtue, for which the institution/private home served as a metaphor.[173]

The austerity, dampness, and poor conditions in Las Amparadas often horrified women accustomed to greater degrees of comfort.[174] Nevertheless, temporary recogidas tried to reproduce their home environment by bringing beds, sheets, clothing, and other possessions that they claimed logically belonged "only to women."[175] Juana Magdalena listed the possessions she wanted her husband to send, including one Santa Rosa, one portrait of Nuestra Señora de la Soledad, another of Santa Catalina, one of Nuestra Señora de la Concepción, and a painting of Saint Joseph.[176] Some recogidas found it difficult to tolerate the conventual regimen; others found it gratifying.[177] Others still, like Luisa Sivico, a free samba deposited in the Casa de las Amparadas while seeking a divorce, felt uncomfortable because her infant daughter's screams disrupted the "praying women" and requested a transfer.[178]

Marital litigation records provide impressions of the recogidas' temporary enclosure, but it is more difficult to determine how the permanently cloistered beatas felt about their worldly housemates. Fragmentary evidence suggests, however, that angry husbands and tearful wives could prove too much for the spiritual tranquillity of the beatas, the governess, and their chaplain.[179] In spite of the strict regulations prohibiting contact among the different recogidas, disagreements arose. For example, Gertrudis de los Reyes was in charge of the room where women entered for eight days to conduct spiritual exercises in the Casa de las Amparadas. One woman, however, came unprepared:

[L]acking the instruments of penitence [necessary for the spiritual exercises] I loaned her my scourge and hair shirt but she took them with her when she left . . . and the Servant of God [Father Castillo] reproached her for having taken the discipline and hair shirt . . . but she said they were hers and were both covered with blood. Afterward I was very upset and wished to leave the recogimiento but Father Castillo consoled me.[180]

In addition, recogidas deposited during divorce proceedings often had to force their spouses to pay the required monthly fifteen pesos for bed and board, while the beatas bickered among themselves over scarce resources such as bread and oil for the lamps because the income supporting Las Amparadas remained so unpredictable.[181]

No viceroy secured any permanent source of support for the institution, and until 1673, when Father Castillo died, the Casa de las Amparadas depended upon weekly alms collections from the Commerce Tribunal members.[182] At that point, the beatas were forced to sell their handiwork to provide for basic necessities.[183] Weary of such hardship, the "Abbess and nuns of the Monastery of Recogidas," as they called themselves, appealed directly in a letter to King Charles II, expressing their concern for the permanence of their institution, which for nine years had survived in a state of destitution.[184] In spite of these and other efforts, the house lacked steady financial support until the mid–eighteenth century.[185] The building was heavily damaged by the 1687 earthquake, after which the recogidas resided in Santa Catalina for three years, but no problem equaled the crisis that ensued in 1708.

A Battle between the Sacred and the Worldly

Competition over "sacred" space remained a recurrent theme in Lima's colorful history: one only needs to recall the demise of San Juan de la Penitencia, the struggle between the Casa de Divorciadas and the nuns of Santa Clara, or the conflict between the Recogimiento de la Magdalena and the nuns of La Encarnación. History repeated itself in 1708, but with a slightly different twist, pitting the Recogimiento de las Amparadas against the powerful Beaterio de las Rosas, which venerated the city's most revered religious figure, Santa Rosa de Lima.[186]

The arrival of the first hand-crafted statue of the saint, direct from Rome, generated a huge celebration in Lima in 1670, with scores of women carrying candles in the procession leading from Callao to her sacred "temple."[187] Immediately following the establishment of the Beaterio de las Rosas de Santa Rosa (1669), popular support, particularly from the upper ranks of society, clamored for the beaterio to become a convent, in order to support "the cult of Santa Rosa, the glorious first fruit of the Divine omnipotence in all America."[188] Substantial donations poured in, amounting to more than four hundred thousand pesos, and construction of the enlarged chapel was completed by 1708.[189] The nuns, however, complained vociferously about their new location. Not only were they isolated from other convents and schools, they argued, but expansion was impossible, because the ordinances prohibited the purchase of additional property or raising capital funds for this purpose. The nuns considered their current site to be "dangerously close" to the "dreadful airs of sickness" wafting from the Hospitals of San Bartolomé, San Andrés, and Santa Ana. The widespread plagues seem to justify their concern (they were unaware that plague does not spread through the air), but their chaplain of fifteen years testified that this was only a ruse to gain public support to relocate. Of all the beaterio's inhabitants, only their founder, Doña Elena Rodríguez, had died, and not from disease, but old age.[190]

In fact, the nuns really coveted the building occupied by the recogidas of the Casa de las Amparadas which, they argued, was close to the fresh mountain air, and strategically placed near the Monasterio de la Concepción and several other schools (see map).[191] La Concepción and the neighboring Jesuit Colegio de San Martín welcomed the opportunity to replace the recogidas with nuns because they were irritated by the constant alms collection for the Recogimiento de las Amparadas, which "drained the pockets of the faithful" in the vicinity.[192] More important, the Casa de las Amparadas' property had, at one time, belonged to Gonzalo de la Maza, Santa Rosa's adoptive father, in whose home she had died. They felt that the sacrosanct site should be theirs.[193]

But why would the Colegio de San Martín, a Jesuit enterprise, not support the Casa de las Amparadas, whose recogidas followed Loyola's *Spiritual Exercises*? Apparently, the generation of Jesuits following Father Castillo was less concerned with the spiritual interests of "fallen women." Father Alonso Messía, a zealous supporter of the foundation of a convent for the beatas in Las Rosas, followed in the footsteps of Father Castillo, but nevertheless remained more closely linked to his teacher in the Colegio de San Martín, the well-known Audiencia judge, Miguel Núñez de Sanabria.[194] For some time, Messía had coveted the building of Las Amparadas for the proposed convent, and he was not alone.[195] Messía, a key figure in deciding the fate of the Casa de las Amparadas, was assisted by Núñez de Sanabria and, in turn, the Audiencia judge convinced Viceroy Marques de Castel-dos-rius (reported to be excessively "dependent" upon Núñez de Sanabria's opinions), to give the order in 1708 to evict the Amparadas and replace them with the nuns of Santa Rosa. Like the "exodus of the Israelites from Egypt," the "secret" eviction duped even Las Rosas's administrator, Francisco de Oyague, because the nuns timed the relocation to coincide with his absence, aware that he would not support such a venture.[196] Oyague was not the only one to be alarmed by such an audacious act: the "move" caused "universal sentiment and scandal throughout the city for the lack of justice and charity and the violent manner and absence of appreciation for the said Recogidas."[197] The same malevolent voices that had mocked the beaterio's first unsuccessful inauguration in 1670 now exhibited tremendous popular sympathy for the recogidas' silent exodus and institutional demise.

The day following the eviction, the mother superior of the Casa de las Amparadas, Isabel del Sacramento, and three other beatas rushed directly to the viceregal palace to protest, but their pleas fell on deaf ears. In the end, pressure from highly placed individuals who had donated substantial sums, combined with the personal interests of Castel-dos-rius and Núñez de Sanabria, both of whom wanted a secure convent for their daughters and granddaughters, overpowered the recogidas. Núñez de Sanabria upheld the eviction order when he became interim viceroy in 1710. His successor, Viceroy/Bishop Diego Ladrón de Guevara, followed suit.[198] Six years after the "tragedy," the abbess wrote:

Isabel del Sacramento and the other Sisters, the Recogidas of the city, find ourselves abandoned outside of our house without possession of it nor of our blessed Church, [and] alienated from our jewels and ornaments for the divine cult, built at the cost of our sweat and labor, because of the tyranny of D. Miguel Núñez [de] Sanabria, the senior Audiencia judge and D. Francisco Garcés, Maestreescuela of this Holy Church who usurped everything for the foundation of the Convent of the Rosas, all because Dr. Miguel Nuñez had two daughters in the convent.[199]

The legal dispute continued unabated for thirty-seven years, and in spite of two royal decrees issued in 1717 and 1721 ordering that the Casa de Amparadas,

"having been deprived of its location and income from its surrounding properties be provided another," this did not occur until 1735.[200]

The house remained in the hands of the nuns of Santa Rosa, and the Casa
de las Amparadas, now reputed to be the poorest of all the beaterios in the city,
continued to lack sufficient financial support, even after they had a new location.[201] Its turbulent history served as a deterrent to found another "house and
prison for wayward women."[202] The report issued by Archbishop Soloaga in
1736 illustrates his prejudice toward the house, which he thought trafficked in
"profane commerce":

> The said Beaterio or Recogimiento is of virtually no importance in this city, and it does
> not live up to the goals set forth by the Count of Lemos when he built it, so that re-
> pentant women would be gathered together as an example to reform other scandalous
> or badly married women that the judges should order to be enclosed for some time;
> [on the contrary] it has only served poor women who attempt to cover up their men-
> dacity with the Honest cloak of the Beata [in order] to exercise more efficient piety [to
> increase] their income from begging which sustains them; there is no example of any-
> one who has truly wished to mend her ways and change her habits; they chose this
> place knowing there are others where they can be brought up in discipline without
> shaming themselves in the company of divorcees and others of poor repute. I do not
> see any reason to provide rent for this kind of beaterio.[203]

In spite of the public outcry, support from higher authorities was at best
lukewarm and shifted with the "moral" winds over time. However, the institution continued to function throughout the course of the eighteenth century
as a house of spiritual retirement, an asylum for women involved in marital
litigation and a school for orphaned girls.

Conclusions

The foundation of the Casa de las Amparadas, on the fringes of the figura-
tive ring of the sacred world, symbolized an attempt by colonial authorities to
incorporate the sacred and the worldly in one institutional setting. The gender
imbalance, conjugal discord, and increasing disparity of wealth compelled
women to seek institutional seclusion and coexistence with holy women embarking on a life of spiritual union with God. Beaterios like the Casa de las
Amparadas brought together sacred and worldly women as recogidas, schoolgirls, and holy women resided side by side in formally approved enclosure.

The nuns of the new Monasterio de Santa Rosa, backed by a powerful faction, convinced themselves that the recogidas of Las Amparadas were be-
smirching the memory of Lima's most powerful saint by inhabiting her sacred
space, a space to which they, as "truly spiritual" and devoted women, were entitled. Because the residents of the Casa de las Amparadas embodied a series of
normative identities—ranging from the sacred to the worldly—the institution

was vulnerable to attack for not being "sacred" enough. Yet it survived nearly another century in a new location because a real need and demand for such an institution came from the city's female populace. In late-seventeenth-century Lima, secular and religious authorities attempted to create order and reinforce hierarchies through extravagance, rituals, and edifices, but in the end, their intentions showed more blatantly how arbitrary spatial and moral boundaries had become. But, why?

The foundation of institutions and institutional practices were a micro-cosm of a larger universe that included disparate expressions of gender, sexuality, race, class, and spirituality within sacred and secular domains. Contro-versial interpretations of recogimiento were representative of this tension that played out in daily interactions, church and state authorities' declarations, and among institutions that reinforced social and cultural hierarchies. On the one hand, the ten beaterios founded within a thirty-five-year period provided ad-ditional sacred spaces in which women could meet both sacred and worldly needs. On the other hand, many believed that the reinforcement of the "small-est circle of the world"—in the foundation of three observant convents—protected "truly" holy women against encroachment from the "world." But "truly" could operate coterminously as a characteristic of potential sanctity and as a coded signal for racially Spanish and pedigreed doñas. The dominant practice—developed earlier in the century—to house elite women of Spanish descent in observant convents persisted; but the nuns' association of rec-ogimiento with wishing to flee the dangers of sensuality prevalent in the "world" cast the sacred and the worldly in artificial opposition. Such charac-terizations also placed gender relations in harsher, separatist terms; they as-sumed that "danger" and the prevalence of sensuality resulted from contact with "maleness" (and men) and could engender a "depraved" nature. They also embodied assumptions about "fallen" or "wayward" women of particular racial and class affinities who might contaminate themselves, and the truly spiritual nuns.

At the same time, expressions of the sacred deeply penetrated the domain of the mundane and the everyday, and women *in* the world responded enthu-siastically. Shifting, more conservative interpretations of recogimiento pro-pelled women to consider forms of doctrinaire spirituality; for instance, nonelite women of color fashioned and "unveiled" new manifestations of re-ligious expression as beatas or donadas. Beaterios that fostered religious ex-pression and recogimiento also contributed to a more expansive feminine space of recogimiento. In fact, the inclusion of hundreds of women in a gen-dered enclosed and recogida space provided greater leeway for the expression of *lo femenino*: or the increasing variation in forms of spiritual and secular ex-pressions of the female self. Just as institutional confines accommodated new demographic and spiritual configurations, limeñas like Melchora de los Reyes, the donada Lucia Bravo de Laguna, and the recogida Doña Francisca Zambrano elaborated—on their own terms—an internalized sense of recogimiento as a "space" of morality, well-being, and resolve.

By the end of the seventeenth century the use of the adjective "recogida," as a virtue and as invented categories for women, had multiplied to such an extent that its root semantic fields were no longer apparent. Some recogidas were excluded from society, others were "redeemed" and integrated. The term served as a behavioral code to distinguish the different estates—doncella, married woman, nun, or widow. A recogida was also equivalent to a pious woman, a beata, or a young student. A woman could be called recogida either because she had repented of earlier sexual misconduct, or because she was particularly devout. She could empty her heart toward God or withdraw from the distractions of the world. Some were enclosed or imprisoned, as criminals or heretics, or by virtue of having lived in an institution. Women and girls identified themselves as recogida because they lived modestly with their families, leaving the casa only when appropriate. Divorciadas were called recogidas, and "recoger" remained synonymous with legal deposit. Finally, a woman might define herself as recogida because she was the moral and economic head of the household.

On one level, the complex changes in the meanings of "recogimiento" in Lima were masked by nominal continuity, so that the word, which many assume to have remained immutable for two hundred years, albeit with a variety of significations, had in fact come to express radically different yet almost imperceptibly distinct meanings.[204] Between 1600 and 1700, thousands of women claimed to be "recogida," but the cultural and contextual referents of *why* they thought this might vary. The transculturation and etymological expansion of recogimiento incorporated residual, dominant, and emergent meanings that also mirrored shifts in gendered, racial, and religious meanings and practices in Lima.

In the colonial Catholic world of the sixteenth and seventeenth centuries, most individuals in Lima lived within the realm of the worldly, but a surprisingly large number sought to attain internal harmony in the sacred sphere. The imagined boundaries of the sacred and the worldly were social constructions acted out in the rationale for founding institutions and in conjugal relations. Different understandings of what constituted those parameters intensified during the latter part of the seventeenth century as women sought to determine their own meanings of the concentric rings of difference between the "sacred" and the "worldly" realms. They questioned normative ideals by claiming recogimiento as a virtue held outside the home; they pushed institutional limits as they flocked in greater numbers to sacred spaces. The economic constraints of poverty, migration, and solitude, in combination with the opportunities and restrictions delimited by race and class, influenced how women determined the moral and spatial limits of virtue. These unresolved tensions formed part of the cultural landscape of Lima as the new century, the eighteenth century, was ushered in.

Conclusions

IN 1713, Amédée François Frezier recorded his impressions of Lima. Like most contemporary observers, he was delighted by the flowers and fruit trees lining every block of the city, as well as by the ornate fountains that served as gathering places for limeños to stroll about, boasting, discussing politics, flirting, or celebrating. On a more ponderous note, the French visitor postulated that the fascination with rituals, ostentation, and fanfare made a mockery of sincere piety. In reality, he argued, the absence of true religious faith revealed the city's decadent state:

> It would seem from the number of monasteries and religious houses that Lima is a city where great devotion reigns [supreme]. But it would be erroneous to believe that this beautiful illusion is sustained by the piety of its inhabitants.[1]

Frezier's remarks might suggest that Lima's inhabitants lacked any true sense of spirituality; other contemporaries, however, described Lima as "a continual temple of God."[2] The tremendous investment in baroque spirituality did not end with the advent of a new century and a new dynasty. The year that Frezier denounced Lima's state of decadence saw the inauguration of the Monasterio de Capuchinas, when Spanish nuns accompanied María Jacinta Montoya (the abbess of the former Beaterio de Jesús, María y José) in solemn procession toward their new palace of God.

Frezier's observations only partially encapsulated the tensions of midcolonial Lima. The number of monasteries and convents, the architectural grandeur, the fascination with symmetry and order, and the ritual and public fanfare *were* all valid expressions of Lima's religiosity and of the city's persona. By creating ornate religious structures and promoting elaborate ceremonies, Lima's inhabitants wished to convey the illusion of invincibility and immortality precisely because they and their forebears continually had to rebuild the city's identity in the fragile urban landscape. Earthquakes, epidemics, major

Dutch and English naval offensives, constant migration, great divisions between rich and poor, high divorce and illegitimacy rates, and informal conjugal relationships all reinforced the desire for order and stability. On the one
hand, the display of pomp exemplified Lima's brand of baroque spirituality;
on the other, it cloaked the city's inconsistency.

More than any other institutional and cultural practice, recogimiento reflected both the tensions between wealthy and destitute and distinct manifestations of the sacred and the secular.[3] On a structural level, convents constituted a centerpiece of formal religious expression and, as a result, were rebuilt
quickly whenever a major earthquake occurred. Recogimientos, by contrast,
symbolized the transitory, informal nature of Lima: once built, more often
than not, either their inhabitants were relocated or the building was abandoned. Serving as an intermediary between the desire for order and the tracta-
ble nature of social relations in colonial society, they stood as testaments to
the permeable boundaries between the realms of the sacred and the worldly.

By 1713, the year the Monasterio de Capuchinas was founded, the era of establishing secular and religious houses for women had peaked. Throughout
the remainder of the century the Crown sanctioned only a few additional convents. Shrinking investments in the spiritual economy, coupled with the most
devastating earthquake of the colonial period in 1746, hastened the end of the
baroque period in Lima. Religious and secular structures, meant to immortalize the city and its elite, now crumbled. While a certain nostalgia for the
glory of the colonial past lingered, never again did writers eulogize the splendor and opulence of Lima by comparing it with some of the great European
cities.

Amid these changes, nevertheless, the process of transculturation continued, and fresh connotations of recogimiento emerged. The recogimientos
built in the seventeenth century gradually lost their principal function as centers for "religious conversion": entrants were now evaluated for their pros-
pects of rehabilitation, or were condemned as criminals, shut away from society and forced to perform hard labor for their transgressions.[4] In Mexico, as
Josefina Muriel succinctly noted, "the idea of offending society [began] to replace the concept of offending God."[5] In Madrid, the functional link between
recogimientos and correctional facilities, or casas galeras, inspired by the work
of the sixteenth-century reformer Magdalena de San Jerónimo, developed
further.[6] Emerging theories on the role of the secular government and its relationship with society also influenced debates over whether state or church officials should administer recogimientos.[7]

In Lima, too, recogimientos increasingly became associated with the
criminal reform of women who had committed sexual transgressions within
civil society. Because Lima had fewer recogimientos than the more prosperous

Mexico City, and because requests to found a *casa galera* in Lima failed, "criminals" (recogidas) went to beaterios, including the Casa de las Amparadas.[8] Even into the Republican period, convents, beaterios, recogimientos, hospitals, and panaderías continued to recoger women: both to provide refuge and to incarcerate them.[9]

Even terminology changed. The use of the terms *reas* ("criminals"), "rameras" (prostitutes or lascivious women), and "mujeres públicas" ("public women") became more popular in Spain, New Spain, and Peru, gradually replacing the traditional "repentant" (arrepentida), "sinful," "morally lost" (*perdida* or *desviada*), or "wayward" (distraída) categories.[10] At the advent of the nineteenth century, the word "recogida" became so derogatory and pejorative in Mexico City that one viceroy reported that by virtue of entering a recogimiento, "a woman would *lose* her honor."[11]

Language and Culture

The main focus of this study has centered upon placing a cultural construct within an ever-changing historical context. An analysis of the institutional and cultural practice of recogimiento involves the study of language, gender relations, cultural codes, institutional practices, and the process of transculturation itself. It also raises important questions for future research in other areas of Latin American colonial history.

Reinhart Koselleck's notion of *begriffsgeschichte* served as a tool to survey the linguistic and cultural "spaces" of recogimiento and sketch out its historical trajectory in early modern Spain, Mexico, and Peru. Raymond Williams's ideas of "emergent," "dominant," and "residual" meanings also helped to denote shifts in meaning over time. Considering the theological rubric of recogimiento one can see how it evolved from a mystical praxis into an expression related to physical denial of the senses. Nevertheless, had the early sixteenth-century Spanish mystic Francisco de Osuna, who conceptualized recogimiento as a means of achieving "nothingness" with God, witnessed the advent of the eighteenth century, he might have recognized residual interpretations of his precept. Holy women privately sought direct union with God in their "interior gardens"; while in their homes, lay women employed the notion of enclosure and virtue espoused in Osuna's *Norte de los estados* of 1531. The continuous reprinting and dissemination in Peru of this and other mystical treatises written by Luis de Granada, Teresa de Avila, or Antonio Ruíz de Montoya, and the hagiographies of Santa Rosa helped perpetuate the mystical tenets of recogimiento.[12]

Teresa of Avila's writings, for example, inspired "a new generation of spiritual women, encouraging literary expression of themselves and their world."[13]

The ambivalent, interpretative "space" embodied in Teresa's notions of recogimiento provided room for holy women in Lima, including Isabel de Porras,
Catalina Doría, and María Jacinta Montoya to negotiate their positions of
authority and to create alternative forms of sanctity. Countless other nuns,
donadas, and beatas expressed their piety in similarly creative ways: in the preclaustral procession toward lifelong enclosure, in prostrating themselves on
the floor, in carrying the cross during religious festivities, and in visionary experiences of souls in purgatory. It seems probable that, although unique cultural and historical contingencies informed their spiritual practices, a common epistemological thread also linked holy women across time and space.
The variety of forms of expression of female sanctity therefore merits further
investigation and should be considered in relation to the spiritual climate
elsewhere—especially in early modern Spain, Italy, and Catholic France.

Gender Relations and Cultural Codes

The "spaces" that women found to express spiritual interpretations of recogimiento also applied to conjugal relations. Women stretched the semantic
range of normative practices while, at the same time, racial, class, and status
constraints informed their interpretations. The process and context within
which they expressed recogimiento also mattered, whether in a courtroom
setting, or on a larger level, within each particular historical period. For instance, Jacinta de Orosco, a mulatta slave, defined recogimiento as "self-control" because she did not try to "flee or hide" in order to negotiate her sale to a
new owner closer to her husband. In contrast, Ana Ruíz perceived herself to be
a woman of calidad (high status) and recogida, and therefore considered it beneath her dignity to work and suffer from hunger in the recogimiento where
she had been deposited.

The expression of recogimiento *toward* and *among* women also shifted
throughout the early modern period. Behavioral norms ordained that women
should be controlled and contained because they were considered aberrant,
childlike, irrational beings, and because their inherently lascivious nature
might overpower them. As a virtue that developed relative to these misogynist
assumptions, recogimiento acquired a vast range of meanings. In seventeenth-
century Lima, female renderings of recogimiento transcended a strict association with sexuality and the male-female relationship. Women gave distinct—
and sometimes contradictory—explications relative to patriarchal ideals and
notions of femaleness, in addition to their role as wives and as family members. In gendered social interactions, women expressed relationships of power
in ways that included not only coercion and conflict but also conformity and
complicity. As early as 1594, Hierónima de San Miguel attempted to demon-

strate her submissive nature as well as her unwillingness to tolerate abuse and a lack of moral and economic support from her husband.

Most women equated recogimiento with modest and moral conduct, sexual self-containment, and physical enclosure. As the demographic and economic configuration of Lima changed, however, women spent a great deal of time in a nonenclosed public setting, working to maintain the household. Many were single mothers or abandoned spouses who felt pressured to defend what their experiences dictated and to accommodate and match their notions of recogimiento with normative prescriptions of enclosure and morality. Thus they converted recogimiento into a virtue associated with an internalized sense of honor and virtue that they *held*, whether in a "public," nonenclosed setting, or quietly laboring in the casa. How they negotiated these nuances seemed more situational than systematic, and more a question of adapting prescriptive norms to the exigencies of the moment.

In the courtroom setting, women became aware of the quadrangular dialogue between plaintiff, defendant, judge, and what was "well known and public." Some scholars have argued that the ecclesiastical court provided a forum for women to construct narratives that functioned as "social acts," because their stories contained ambiguities that could prove beneficial in deciding their matrimonial fate.[14] This may be true, but it is important to remember that these same women also risked exposing intimate details of their lives within a potentially threatening public forum. An ecclesiastical judge could uphold established norms of patriarchal dominance and racial inequality just as easily as subvert or override them. A more balanced perspective would be to see women's testimonies as including the *possibilities* of both resistance and co-optation, and the formulation of alternative models of appropriate gendered conduct.[15]

Others have argued that women of color realized that because the courtroom forum provided an exceptional opportunity to speak and be heard, they manipulated cultural and racially exclusive indicators of social correctness such as honor and recogimiento to their advantage. In creating a "history" of their self-identity, such litigants produced statements that would be viewed as morally correct.[16] Once again, this forms only part of the story. It may have been true in Inquisition hearings because the accused had to defend herself and her integrity and answer an established list of questions. By contrast, in divorce suits, most of them initiated by women, they were plaintiffs, not defendants, and were free to tell their story.

Disparate courtroom procedures may thus explain differences in strategies. This assumption, however, also presupposes that women *other than* Spanish used "socially correct" values such as recogimiento as strategic and rhetorical tropes and did not internalize them as an essential part of their self-identity.

Evidence for Lima suggests precisely the opposite: that the significations of recogimiento—as a virtue and as a practice of enclosure—remained integral to women's identity throughout the seventeenth century. The ubiquity of recogimiento among women of all walks of life, facing vastly different circumstances, makes it difficult to believe that their testimonies were mere histrionics.

Let us now follow, for a moment, the "linguistic turn" in poststructural studies. Constructions of race and gender examined through the lens of cultural categories—such as honor, calidad, and shame—can illuminate the strategies employed by distinct peoples rearticulating the social categories that influenced their lives.[17] Just as the prescriptive norms that informed constructions of gender remained fluid and mutable, colonial subjects had no reductionist definitions of race, class, and status.[18] Recent scholarship has advanced our understanding in this regard, but additional research that demonstrates a sensitivity to semiotics and changing discourses would illuminate further the complexities of social and cultural relations in colonial society.[19]

Paying attention to specific sociopolitical configurations that informed the interpretation of codes related to gender, race, and class is also important.[20] A clear intersection between these three social constructs is evident in the select educational policies adopted toward the daughters of the Nahua nobility between 1524 and 1550 and the negative cultural impact upon them. The subsequent imperial construction of the doncella mestiza at midcentury illustrates that clearer, exclusionary parameters were being drawn by colonial authorities in gendered and racialized ways. Between 1580 and 1620, however, issues of gender and sexuality eclipsed "race" in the creation of specific "classes" of deviant and wayward women, while institutional practices continued to highlight racial and class characteristics in selecting how and where a woman might be accommodated. In the 1620s, elite Spaniards and creoles attempted to assert their economic and cultural pre-eminence by displaying their superior class, purity of race, and gender ideals relative to "others." During the last third of the seventeenth century, shifting patterns in gender relationships and changing notions of the sacred and the worldly also provided additional institutional and cultural spaces for single and married women of color, and the rich and the poor to express themselves.[21]

Given these changes, how then can scholars (re)conceptualize gendered cultural notions while bearing in mind contextual and historical differences?[22] Patricia Seed argues that, in the eighteenth century, cultural attitudes toward honor and love shifted when parents in New Spain became concerned with marital arrangements based upon economic or political interests rather than affection.[23] In Lima, however, marriage either for love or for the calculated pursuit of money and status remained common in all periods. In elite circles, competitive economic interests and a disproportionate number of Spanish women led to an increase in arranged marriages or forced entry into convents in the first half of the seventeenth century. This may partially explain the significant increase in divorces and annulments after 1640.[24] Why cultural discourses varied in distinct Latin American settings requires further exploration. The answers may reveal how contextual constraints, as well as human agency, informed and altered interpretations of cultural codes.

Institutional Practices

In addition to reassessing cultural practices, any notion of secular and religious institutions as distinct phenomena must be reconsidered in relation to the degree to which Catholicism permeated most aspects of life in early modern society. Convents were not only separate worlds of spirituality; they were also linked in functional, spiritual, economic, and demographic kinship with other types of institutions. In principle, life in a convent involved the renunciation of the secular world and an avowal of self-abnegation, acceptance of communal disciplinary rules, and dedication to the service of God. But they could also provide far more. This study confirms recent findings that conventual life offered a range of experiences: from the pursuit of an education to a sense of camaraderie with other religious and secular women from various social backgrounds.

It also confirms that the foundation patterns of convents and other institutions resulted from immediate and local sociopolitical concerns. In spite of the decrees of the Council of Trent, the functional nature of convents, beaterios, and recogimientos altered over the course of the colonial period and eventually encompassed the sacred *and* the worldly. Within the "world of walls," each woman carved out an internal space, according to her definition and application of sacred and secular norms. The division between the sacred and the worldly was therefore permeable and negotiable, as evidenced by the realities experienced by women, whether living inside or outside an institution. Secular women entered beaterios to practice mortification rituals for eight days; wealthy widows "retired" to convents; and donadas who never experienced the "world" scrubbed the floors of nuns' cells while devoting themselves to lives of interior contemplation.

By the late seventeenth century, secular and religious houses provided employment, shelter, asylum, and legal deposit for women who understood that the possibility of an alternative institutional "life" existed. Many would reside in institutions, on a voluntary or involuntary basis—for a variety of reasons and on more than one occasion—over the course of their lives. As noted above, the 1700 census registered an astonishing 20 percent of the total female population of Lima as residents of institutions. The percentage of those who had lived there at some point in their lives might have reached 60 or 70 percent had it included case histories of women like Inés de la Rosa, who temporarily resided in at least three institutions in the course of her life. Statistics reflect unimaginative calculations, while narratives of recogidas capture the fluid dynamics of institutional demographics.

The increasing number of institutions, and their availability to women of all socioeconomic backgrounds, explain why the concept and practice of recogimiento as enclosure became a component of colonial life in Lima. Consistencies remained between the first and second half of the seventeenth centuries: intrusion by Church officials into the moral and sexual conduct of their Catholic subjects continued, although specific concern with concubinage cases diminished.[25] Institutions continued to occupy the dual roles of incarceration and protection, and women and men could identify with either characteristic at will. Husbands continued to conflate the purpose and function of religious houses and saw them as prisons and centers where recalcitrant wives could be re-educated and forced to work like slaves.[26] In 1706, Juan de Monzón requested that his wife be "incarcerated" and subsequently "educated" by her slave and daughter within the "sturdy walls" of the Casa de las Amparadas: a combination of imprisonment, moral and physical punishment (by her "inferiors"), and redemption in a sacred setting.[27]

The practice of depositing wives or mistresses while husbands traveled abated, but extreme instances still occurred.[28] On the other hand, female migrants seeking work increasingly found institutions a practical resource. Tomasa María de Gadea, who resided and worked as a wet nurse (*ama de leche*) in the Hospital de los Niños Huérfanos of Lima for six months after traveling from Trujillo in 1681, was representative of hundreds of women seeking temporary employment in institutions.[29] Still others sought charity: Doña María de Lara y Figueroa went to the Monasterio de la Trinidad because "I find myself in dire necessity without a place to find shelter, or the means to feed myself in the world."[30]

Of all the reasons for temporary deposit, conjugal discord remained the primary motivating factor throughout the seventeenth century. Multiple transfers during divorce proceedings, in evidence since the 1580s, remained the norm after 1650 as women were shuffled between private homes and public institutions. Increasingly, women chose private homes as their place of deposit during divorce or annulment litigation; and between 1651 and 1713, private homes accepted more than 50 percent of all first-time deposits. Recogida wives selected the residences of relatives, widows, prominent officials, and beatas: slaves often chose their owner's home.[31] The popularity and accessibility of private homes for deposit supports the conclusion that women saw the casa (their own or another's) as an acceptable legal compromise, and indicates that, in spite of their proliferation, institutions could no longer accommodate the increasing number of women seeking changes in their lives.[32]

Young girls whose parents disapproved of their choice of spouse continued to face institutional deposit. In 1677, Doña Magdalena de la Cruz, a provincial governess (*governador*), traveled to Lima to oversee wedding preparations of her daughter, Doña Josepha Carrillo, raised in the convent of Santa Clara. Concerned that Doña Josepha succeed her in the governorship, Doña Magdalena encouraged her daughter to marry a Spaniard, unqualified for the position on the basis of his race (only native Andeans could become a governador). She learned that one of the nuns, in collusion with her husband, had tried to dissuade Doña Josepha from her spousal choice. The governess requested her daughter's removal from Santa Clara to a private home where, she claimed, her daughter could make up her mind of her own free will.[33] In this case, and others, free will remained a sixteenth-century abstraction when parents weighed economic or political considerations. In imposing *their* choice of son-in-law upon reluctant daughters, they employed recogimiento or involuntary deposit as a strategic device.

"Retirement" to a convent still proved a common option for well-to-do widows. In 1679, Doña Francisca Brabo de Lagunas, the widow of a military officer, requested entry into a number of different convents where she could reside comfortably with women "of high rank." She wrote:

As the brief from Clement X states: He granted me the license and faculty to enter for a period of five years, three times each year, the convents of this city accompanied by two principled ladies of my choice. The brief shall go into effect for the convents of Santa Clara, La Encarnación, La Concepción, La Trinidad, Santa Catharina, and the Descalças of San Joseph.[34]

Doña Francisca consciously used her rank and class to appeal directly to the highest authority in the Catholic world to obtain her goal. Her case not only illustrates the power that race and class could have in colonial Lima but also the accessibility for individual women to reach "the top": a phenomenon unique to the Iberian political system.[35]

As an institutional practice, recogimiento thus applied to all stages of the female life cycle—from newborn infants, to young schoolgirls, through women about to marry and battered or abandoned wives, to widows. Some willingly experienced enclosure in religious and secular houses; others were forced into seclusion. Above all, recogimientos provided a space in which women and girls could determine a different future.

The Colonial Latin American Context

How typical was recogimiento in colonial Latin America? By 1650 women of all social groups in Lima regarded recogimiento as a cardinal virtue, confirming that the viceregal capital served as the entry point for Iberian cultural notions. Furthermore, Andean provincial women—from Ica, Huáraz, and Huarochirí—also came to Lima to assert their sense of recogimiento before a judge, thus arguing that the cultural notion had a wider reception. But what about other provincial cities? Quiteñas describing their lives as recogidas in the Recogimiento de Santa Marta certainly employed the notion; it remains to be seen whether women in Cuzco or Chuquisaca did the same.[36]

They probably did, because the cultural practice permeated the lives of colonial subjects in many other Spanish American cities. By the eighteenth century, recogimientos existed in Santiago de Guatemala, Puebla, Guadalajara, Oaxaca, Ciudad Real (Chiapas), and Guanajuato, to name but a few in New Spain;[37] as well as in Arequipa;[38] Trujillo;[39] Santiago de Chile;[40] and Buenos Aires. The increased attention to the foundation of recogimientos in provincial cities in the eighteenth century may be related to their delayed demographic and economic expansion, as well as to the fact that the bulk of wealth remained concentrated within the two viceregal capitals until 1700.[41]

Can one go further? The demographic configuration of Lima as a "city of women" leads one to question whether this phenomenon existed in other colonial cities and with what ramifications. The imprecision of seventeenth-century censuses makes such analysis difficult.[42] Nevertheless, we know that in late-seventeenth-century Mexico City the chronicler Agustín de Vetancurt counted eight thousand peninsular and creole male Spaniards, and twenty thousand "women": an indication of the predominance of women in the other viceregal capital.[43] Now we need research to show how demography influenced gendered behaviors, cultural codes, and choices made by women there, as well as in other colonial cities.[44]

After all, Lima faced certain problems common to all cities of the early modern period: demographic imbalances, the effects of migration from rural areas to the city, the creation of individuals categorized as socially marginal, and the development of an "urban underclass," as well as the division of the city into segregated zones according to class, race, or profession. Furthermore, like all colonial cities, Lima developed cultural values distinct from those of the metropolis, in part because of its distant setting.

Nevertheless, the two colonial capitals differed from other colonial cities. Lima, like Mexico, served as an interlocutor of the cultural norms of the metropolis. The City of Kings served as the nexus through which all values—Iberian, Counter-Reformation, and Catholic—passed and were disseminated.

It served as the paradigm for the rest of the viceroyalty and for those European observers who came to witness and report back to Europe. Many never passed beyond: for them, Lima *was* Peru. The cultural "middle ground" created by colonial authorities to suit the distinct needs of the capital therefore seemed the norm. Given the present state of research, the case of Lima offers a model to compare with other urban and rural communities in Spanish America.

Latin American History and Transculturation

Finally, a study of recogimiento offers a precise scale by which to measure the process of transculturation: the metamorphosis of conceptual notions and cultural practices according to local contingencies. The double helix model helps us to envision the discrete points as distinct manifestations of recogimiento that reflect the colonial relationship. The cultural bonds between Spain and Peru remained secure throughout the early- and midcolonial periods, and quite often cultural developments on both sides paralleled each other: but not always simultaneously, or in exactly the same way.

In the sixteenth century, the conquest of native peoples in New Spain and Peru involved the modification of Iberian notions of recogimiento. Policymakers equated hispanization with gendered notions of enclosure, modesty, and sexual purity. Still, recogimiento survived and was transculturated to the post–civil war environment of Lima as a colonial, hybrid practice of education, enclosure, and as a behavioral norm that fostered racialized, class-conscious subjects like doncellas mestizas. By the mid–sixteenth century, the referents had shifted from Nahua girls to mestizas. Recogimiento changed from an inclusionary to an exclusionary social and educational practice that coincided with the emergent application of recoger as a means of separating marginalized individuals from "others." Replicating practices current in post-Tridentine Spain and Italy, the state also began monitoring social and cultural mores more actively, and recogimientos began serving in loco parentis for orphans and the poor.

Next, recogimiento evolved into a practice of social discipline for women categorized as sexually and morally wayward, a paradigm that closely resembled developments in Madrid, Seville, and Italian cities. The goal was to "redeem" them and inculcate the virtue of recogimiento as modest conduct, enclosure, and sexual purity. Institutions called recogimientos served this purpose, while hospitals, and convents in Lima also provided some protection, asylum, and incarceration in spite of Tridentine decrees. The adaptation to local contingencies also became evident in the ecclesiastical courtroom as women responded to the dominant discourses of recogimiento in distinct ways, thus engendering emergent articulations of the behavioral code and institutional practice that would become the norm by the end of the seventeenth century.

At the same time that women were "negotiating" the meanings of virtue, Lima's elite appropriated recogimiento sui generis as an educational practice and strict form of conventual enclosure that only vaguely mirrored patterns developing concurrently in Spain. By this time Lima was clearly shaping its own cultural identity as it aspired to a status of urban greatness comparable to that of European cities. On the one hand, the appropriation by elites of the "dominant" virtue of recogimiento was not new: it is evident in the policies that encouraged Nahua girls and mestizas to cultivate this quality, and in the acrimonious dialogues of troubled couples appearing before ecclesiastical courts. So, what had changed? Elites appropriated recogimiento as a distinguishing feature of *their* class because they feared that the sin and corruption in the world might pollute their daughters. Many also felt that the permutation of the worldly into convent culture left them little recourse but to found observant convents and advance new expressions of spiritual recogimiento and the orthodox Catholicism prevalent in Spain.

The mystical tenets of recogimiento active in the first half of the sixteenth century remained subdued (residual) until its emergence between 1600 and 1630 and systematic repression by colonial authorities. However, by midcentury, popular responses to more conservative formulations of recogimiento led to a "beaterio phenomenon" (1670–1710). This epochal shift provides a subsequent example of the further development of Lima's own brand of formal spiritual expression. By that time, beaterios had been nearly extinguished in Spain, yet more "conservative" interpretations of recogimiento and mysticism expressed by beatas in Lima replicated patterns of baroque spirituality in Spain. At the same time, many convents after 1650 increasingly allowed "worldly" women within the circle of walls, and women of all calidades experienced life in an institution at some time during their lives. In turn, this change in institutional practices influenced women's conceptions of recogimiento as an internal "space" of honor. By 1713 in Lima, renderings of the "sacred" and the "worldly" relative to recogimiento were quite different from the cultural tradition from which those practices derived.

Nevertheless, it is important to emphasize that the cultural dialogue between Spain and its colonies persisted. Moreover, some patterns of recogimiento in Lima may also be linked to a larger Catholic cultural tradition. In his book on early modern visions, Jean-Michel Sallmann argues that because the kingdoms of Spain and the viceroyalties of Naples, Mexico, and Lima held a king and many religious practices and beliefs in common, one can speak of a "southern cone" that encompassed the cultural traditions of the Mediterranean and Spanish America.[45] The study of recogimiento supports his argument that institutional practices in Spain, Italy, Mexico, and Lima often mirrored one another. Cultural exchanges were also facilitated when commoners either returned to Spain or settled elsewhere in the Spanish empire.[46] Just as Viceroys Antonio de Mendoza and Luis de Velasco served in Mexico and Peru, other colonial administrators imparted their understandings of recogimiento to Italy and other colonial outposts. Likewise, information could travel from America to Europe quickly by word of mouth or in written texts. In 1671, the year Santa Rosa was canonized, a young woman in the highlands of Elvira, Spain, had a vision that Santa Rosa transported her to a cave where she would live as a contemplative hermit and Rosa would serve as her teacher. Meanwhile, in their spiritual colloquies, nuns in Tomasi, Italy, read and discussed a biography of the saint published to commemorate the great event.[47] A number of observers noted that Catholicism served as the glue that held the Spanish empire together.[48] The historical process of transculturation perpetuated that bond.

One final point should be made. Charting particular aspects of the transculturation process accomplishes two goals. First, it helps differentiate what is peculiar to Lima and certain sectors of the populace, what is unique to the Spanish colonial context, and what is distinctly early modern. It illuminates the linkages between, and singularities of, different cultural traditions. Second, considering transculturation as an historical process provides a mechanism to survey the parameters of "culture"—that amorphous, prevalent term—and to elucidate the power that cultural practices exert on the complexities of social interaction: from everyday discourse to the broad palette of early modern thought and action.

This monograph has attempted to analyze the practices of recogimiento to show the pattern of transculturation as a fluid, nonlinear adaptive process. Its historical etymology in Peru mirrored trends in Europe, yet the cultural code also experienced significant semantic modifications as it adapted to local social, economic, and cultural contingencies. The linguistic and cultural parameters of recogimiento pervaded many aspects of society. Its meanings were embodied in institutional practices; its neologisms were found in the dialogues between couples, or in the distinct visions held by Archbishop Mogrovejo and, one hundred years later, the count of Lemos; and its mystical applications were located in the transcendent and ineffable knowledge of a beata.

Chronology of Institutions for Women in Lima, 1548–1713

1548   *Beaterio de las Dominicanas.* Founded by Mari Hernández de Pereda. Housed needy Spanish, mestiza, and indigenous women as well as mestiza and mulatto children.

1549   *Hospital de Santa Ana.* Founded by Archbishop Gerónimo de Loaysa for native men and women.

1553   *Recogimiento de San Juan de la Penitencia.* Founded by Catalina de Castañeda, her husband (Antonio Ramos) and Sebastián Bernal, under the patronage of the Franciscans. Housed and educated poor and orphaned mestiza girls. Beatas were responsible for their education. In 1572 Viceroy Toledo ordered that the house be used for the University of San Marcos. The institution ceased to exist shortly thereafter.

1559   *Hospital de la Caridad.* Also known as the Hospital of San Cosme y Damián (its patron saints). Don Pedro Alonso de Paredes founded the sodality while Doña Ana Rodríguez de Solórzano and Dr. Juan José de la Herrería y Velasco donated property to establish the hospital. Served as a hospital for ill women (Spanish and mestiza), as a school for poor young girls, as a place of refuge for divorcees and for widows who wanted to "retire from the world." The hospital's confraternity provided dowries of four hundred pesos for some forty to fifty young marriageable girls each year (begun in the time of Viceroy Velasco, 1596–1604). In 1615 the hospital's council authorized the foundation of a separate school, called the *Colegio de Santa Teresa* (see below).

1561   *Monasterio de la Encarnación.* This convent began as a beaterio, housing widows of Spanish conquerors, under the canonical rules of the Agustinians in 1556, but shortly thereafter received the necessary capital from Doña Leonor Portocarrero, the wife of Treasurer Hernando Alonso de Almaráz, and her daughter Doña Mencia de Sosa to become a convent. One of five *conventos grandes* of Lima.

1573   *Monasterio de la Concepción.* Founded by Doña Inés Muñoz de Rivera, the popular and revered wife of Martín de Alcántara and sister-in-law of Francisco Pizarro. Obeyed Franciscan canonical rules. The convent received tribute payments from the Indians on the encomienda of Anahuancas in Jauja. By 1594 approximately 200 women lived there; in 1700 there were more than 1050. The second *convento grande.*

1584   *Monasterio de la Santíssima Trinidad* (Bernardinas). Founded by Doña Lucrecia de Sansoles, wife of Juan de Rivas from La Paz where he held the *encomienda* of Viacha, and her daughter, Mencía de Vargas, the widow of Tomás González de Cuenca and encomendera of Pucarani. Only thirty nuns were permitted to take vows. All were Spanish and from well-known families: mestizas, moras, or cuateronas were excluded. They followed strict Cistercian rules of order.

1589   *Recogimiento or Casa de Divorciadas.* Founded by the Portuguese Francisco de Saldaña for poor orphan girls and women who wished to separate from their husbands. Until 1609 the building formed part of the Monasterio de Santa Clara, which Saldaña also helped found. At that point the recogimiento moved to its new location, where it remained active until 1665.

1592   *Recogimiento de María Magdalena.* Founded by María Esquivel, who had donated her inheritance to found the Hospital de San Diego. Built as an annex to the hospital, the recogimiento served "repentant" or "lost" women and those involved in divorce or annulment litigation. In 1610, due to a lack of financial security, the house closed down.

1603   *Hospital de Santa Cruz de Nuestra Señora de Atocha.* Also known as *La Casa de Niños Expósitos* or the *Casa de los Huérfanos.* An orphanage for abandoned children founded by Luis Pescador. It was maintained by charitable donations until 1659, when Don Mateo Pastor de Velasco and Doña Francisca Vélez Michel y Roldán created a foundation for the school and orphanage and placed it under the patronage of the Tribunal of the Inquisition.

1603   *Monasterio de las Descalzas de San José.* Founded by Doña Inés de Rivera, following the rules of the Concepciónistas. In principle, an observant (or recollection) convent with no more than thirteen nuns, however the population increased significantly over the course of the seventeenth century.

1605   *Monasterio de Santa Clara.* Founded by Francisco de Saldaña and Archbishop Santo Toribio de Mogrovejo. Until 1609 the *Casa de Divorciadas* formed part of the convent. Considered one of the wealthiest and most populated of the *conventos grandes* in Lima.

1615   *Colegio de Santa Teresa de la Caridad.* Also known as the Colegio de la Caridad and perhaps a later rendition of the sixteenth-century Recogimiento de Santa María del Socorro, which formed an annex to the Hospital de la Caridad and garnered support from the hospital's confraternal order. Doña Isabel Porras y Marmolejo, once the abbess of the *Casa de Divorciadas*, and renowned for her piety, governed the school. The girls dressed in the Carmelite habit.

1619   *Recogimiento or Colegio del Carmen.* Founded by the Milanese Catalina María Gómez de Silva and her husband as a recogimiento and school for girls of Spanish nobility. By 1630, thirty girls occupied the house. The school became part of the *Monasterio de Carmelitas Descalças* in 1643.

1624   *Monasterio de Santa Catalina de Sena.* Under Dominican rule. Founded with the money donated initially by Doña María de Celis in 1589, and later by Doña Lucia and Doña Clara Guerra de la Daga as well as Don Juan de Robles, the Rector General del Santo Oficio. A scandal erupted when the members of the Royal Audiencia granted the license for its foundation without royal approval.

1637 *Recogimiento de los Remedios.* A school for young girls founded by Jorge de Andrade for poor and orphaned *doncellas* and supported by the Jesuits and the Confraternity of Nuestra Señora de la O.

1640 *Monasterio de Nuestra Señora del Prado.* Cloistered nuns under strict rules of the Augustinians, located in Callao. Founded by Archbishop Villagómez. Doña Angela de Zarate y Recalde, the sister of the Marqués de Valparaiso, along with four other nuns left the *Monasterio de la Encarnación* to live a more cloistered life.

1643 *Monasterio de Carmelitas Descalças.* To become a convent, the founders, including Catalina María Gómez de Silva, and donors had to wait nearly twenty years to receive the necessary royal license. Some of the first nuns had been educated in the *Colegio del Carmen.* Also referred to as Carmen Alto.

1669 *Beaterio de Santa Rosa de Santa María.* Doña Luisa Antonia Coronel and other pious individuals supported the foundation of this beaterio, which occurred the year after Santa Rosa, the patron saint of Lima and America, was beatified. It became a convent in 1708.

1670 *Recogimiento or Beaterio de las Amparadas de la Concepción.* Founded by Viceroy Conde de Lemos to provide asylum for women separated from their husbands, for "repentant" women, and as a school to educate girls. It also housed lay pious women dedicated to the spiritual exercises advocated by their Jesuit chaplain, Francisco del Castillo.

1671 *Beaterio de las Mercedarias.* Doña Ana María Zavaleta founded the institution in which twenty-one women lived. It was later granted a license to become a convent.

n.d. *Hospicio de San Pedro de Alcántara.* Founded as a convalescent center for ill Spanish and mestiza women who had been hospitalized, and also served as an asylum for poor women.

1672 *Beaterio de las Nazarenas.* Founded by Antonia Lucía Maldonado de Quintanilla in Callao. It became a convent in 1738.

1674 *Beaterio de Nerias.* Founded by Doña Ana de Robles, who had been influenced by her confessor in the congregation of San Felipe Neri. The beaterio converted into the *Monasterio de Trinitarias Descalças* in 1682.

1680 *Beaterio de Santa Rosa de Viterbo.* Founded by Madre Manuela de Jesús, from Panama. Various attempts were made to raise this beaterio to the conventual level (under the order of the Poor Clares) shortly after its foundation, but it remained a beaterio throughout the eighteenth century.

1682 *Monasterio de Trinitarias Descalças.* It originated as a beaterio in 1674 under the direction of Doña Ana de Robles, who paid for the construction of the cells and chapel. Doña Ana and her eleven companions professed in 1683.

1685 *Beaterio de Jesús, María y José.* Founded by the beato Nicolás de Ayllón and his wife, María Jacinta Montoya. Initially it served as a home and school for doncellas, as well as shelter house for poor women. In 1698 it received the license to become a convent under the Capuchin Order, but the process was delayed until 1713 when Capuchin nuns from Spain arrived.

1686   *Monasterio de Santa Ana.* Also referred to as Carmen Bajo or Carmen Nuevo. Four nuns left the *Monasterio de Carmelitas Descalças* once they received the patronage of a prominent member of the Inquisition.

1688   *Beaterio de Nuestra Señora del Patrocinio.* Founded by Father Francisco Villagómez of the Congregation of San Felipe Neri, who donated properties for the beaterio. The beatas followed the rules of the Third Order Franciscans.

1691   *Beaterio de Nuestra Señora de Copacabana.* Doña Francisca Ygnacia Manchipura de Carabaxal, was one of five founders. A descendant of the caciques from the Pueblo of Maranga (Magdalena), Doña Francisca donated a large sum of money to found the institution. The beaterio was dedicated to noble women of Andean descent wishing to lead a religious life. The beaterio also operated as a school.

1704   *Beaterio del Corazón de Jesús.* Founded by Gregorio Cabañas of the Congregation of San Felipe Neri. The beaterio housed sixteen beatas.

1713   *Monasterio de las Capuchinas.* María Jacinta Montoya saw her dream come true when the beaterio she and Nicolás de Ayllón had founded in 1685 became a convent.

Population of Nuns, Servants, Slaves, and Seglares in Lima's Convents and Beaterios in the Seventeenth Century

	Black Veil	White Veil	Novices	Donadas	Servants	Slaves	Seglares	Total
			LA ENCARNACIÓN					
1625	206	39	—	43	—	—	—	288
1631	220	—	—	—	—	250	—	470
1637	214	36	35	43	94	—	34	456
1651	202	30	20	58	116	146	68	640
1660	100:27*	27:8	—	33:16	128	—	158	497
1669	215:17	25:8	—	19:10	36	68	42	440
1690	205:15	24	—	30	250	—	—	524
1700	202:6	21	—	29	280	144	135	817
			LA CONCEPCIÓN					
1625	170	16	—	44	—	—	—	230
1631	196	—	—	—	330	—	—	526
1637	209	15	41	133	297	—	15	710
1651	236	11	12	58	120	108	29	574
1660	263:18	7:11	—	26	—	362	—	687
1669	284:11	16:10	—	19:20	137	185	39	721
1690	230:12	30	—	30	250	—	70	622
1700	247:10	14	—	47	290	271	147:15	1041
			SANTA CLARA					
1625	126	16	—	21	—	—	—	163
1631	170	—	—	—	180	—	—	350
1637	201	26	27	39	147	—	6	446
1651	261	21	10	—	175	98	46	611
1660	263:26	17:11	—	57	174	110	36	694
1669	259:20	21:20	—	30:18	148	128	76	720
1690	184:10	20	—	50	280	—	80	624
1700	172:9	20	—	48	148	130	90:15	632

	Black Veil	White Veil	Novices	Donadas	Servants	Slaves	Seglares	Total
			SAN JOSÉ					
1625	53	10	—	11	—	—	—	74
1637	60	11	12	7	115	—	—	205
1651	52	12	4	25	72	30	4	199
1660	53:7	14	—	24	80	—	—	178
1669	51:6	19:5	—	33:5	83	96	10	308
1690	53:4	20	—	30	—	—	—	107
1700	53:5	14	—	71	95	56	34	328
			LA TRINIDAD					
1625	92	7	—	10	—	—	—	109
1631	100	—	—	—	76	—	—	176
1637	95	11	15	15	141	—	—	277
1651	95	6	11	3	34	71	—	220
1660	97:13	4	—	3	39	28	—	184
1669	89:16	5:3	—	1	37	46	—	197
1690	90:10	20	—	20	250	—	—	390
1700	83:4	5	—	6	78	82	20	278
			STA. CATALINA					
1631	27	—	—	—	42	—	—	69
1637	42	6	18	3	56	—	—	125
1651	60	8	14	6	40	—	—	128
1660	88:11	9	—	1	59	22	—	190
1669	98:11	11	—	—	73	34	2	229
1690	140:6	20	—	20	100	—	30	316
1700	140:6	13	—	15	166	—	54	394
			DEL PRADO					
1651	28	4	3	1	8	6	2	52
1660	33	6	—	—	16	1	—	56
1669	31	—	—	—	16	—	—	47
1690	33	10	—	—	20	—	—	63
1700	31:2	4	—	—	30	—	—	67
			CARMEN DE SAN JOSÉ					
1660	17	3	—	—	—	1	—	21
1669	17:1	3	—	—	—	1	—	22
1690	23	3	—	—	—	4	—	30
1700	18	3	—	—	6	—	—	27
			TRINITARIAS DESCALZAS					
1700	26:2	—	—	—	13	—	—	41
			CARMEN DE SANTA ANA					
1700	19:2	—	—	—	9	—	—	30

	Beatas	Servants	Slaves	Seglares	Total
BEATERIO DE MERCEDARIAS					
1700	20	10:8+	—	7	45
BEATERIO DE JESÚS, MARÍA Y JOSÉ					
1700	22:4	8	4	—	38
BEATERIO DE STA. ROSA DE SANTA MARIA					
1700	10	—	16	5	31
BEATERIO DE JESÚS NAZARENO					
1700	13	4	—	—	17
BEATERIO DE STA. ROSA DE VITERBO					
1700	16	5	—	—	21
BEATERIO DE NRA. SRA. DE COPACABANA					
1700	5	3	—	8	16
BEATERIO DEL PATROCINIO					
1700	10	3	—	—	13

	Recogidas	Servants	Slaves	Seglares	Total
RECOGIMIENTO DE LAS AMPARADAS					
1700	32	—	2	—	34

SOURCES: AGI, Lima 40; Vargas Ugarte, *Historia de la Iglesia*, II: 258; Lavallé, "Recherches," vol. II; *Numeración general*, 357–58.

NOTE: *The second number indicates the novices of the white or black veil. For example, in the Monasterio de la Encarnacion, there were one hundred nuns of the black veil and twenty-seven novices of the black veil. + indicates male servants.

Demographic Data Based on the
Censuses of 1614 and 1700

I. 1614 Census

A detailed breakdown is not available for 1600; however, the 1614 Lima census enumerated by Miguel de Contreras presents the following demographic distribution (augmented by Salinas's "divorciadas," found in Bronner's listing of the data, Bronner, "The Population of Lima," 109):

	Men	Women	Total Lay persons
Spaniards	5,257	4,359	9,616
Blacks	4,529	5,857	10,386
Mulattoes	326	418	744
Indians	1,116	862	1,978
Mestizos	97	95	192
SUBTOTAL	11,325	11,591	22,916
Clergy:			
Monastic	894	820	1,714
"other"	300	—	300
In *Caridad*	—	79	79
In *Divorciadas*	—	13	13
Nuns' servants	—	425	425
SUBTOTAL	1,194	1,337	2,531
TOTAL	12,519	12,928	25,447

II. 1700 Census

Discrepancies in the totals of the *Numeración*, 355–58, render an accurate count difficult. The totals listed on pp. 355–58 differ from those on pp. 2–3 and the overall summation. In order to reach my estimate for the general population, I used the figures on pp. 355–58 in order to be consistent with the figures in Appendix B. If the eleven barrios are summed, excluding the El Cercado totals, the estimate approximates 29,300, with 15,300 females (52.2 percent) and 14,000 males (47.7 percent).

Institutions and inhabitants listed were: twelve hospitals [including two schools for

VIII. Comulgarán cada ocho dias, y serán los Domingos por la mañana; y los Sábados por la tarde á la hora que se les señalare, se exâminarán y confesarán. Y en las nueve fiestas de nuestra Señora, y en las de Christo Nuestro Señor, harán la misma diligencia, confesando y comulgando en sus dias, ó en sus vísperas: y estas comuniones no han de quitar las de los Domingos.

IX. Todos los Viérnes por la noche, despues de haber hecho su examen, tomarán diciplina las que no estubieren achacosas, ó enfermas, y este exercicio sera por todo el año. Pero en la Quaresma, harán diciplina los miercoles, y viernes por la noche, y todas en comunidad: conque se fervorizaran unas á otras.

X. En las penitencias, diciplinas, silicios, y demas mortificaciones, seguiran, el consejo y parecer de sus Padres espirituales, y Confesores, y no harán mortificacion, ni penitencia alguna extraordinaria sin licencia, y de la Madre.

XI. Los Viernes por la tarde entre año, oirán platica cada quince dias: y en el tiempo Santo de la Quaresma, tendrán los Miercoles, y Viernes por al tarde platica, q. la harán los Padres de la Compañía.

XII. Todos los Sábados del año ayunarán en reverencia de Nuestra Señora su Madre, y amparo: y lo mismo harán todas las vísperas de sus festividades, comiendo de pescado, aunque no sean dias de precepto.

XIII. Estarán sujetas á la obediencia de la Madre Abadesa, y Vicaria, y quanto se les mandare la obedecerán con humildad y rendimiento, sin réplicas ni porfias.

XIV. No saldrán á la Reja ni á la puerta sin licencia de la Madre Abadesa, ni tendrán trato, ni comunicacion alguna con personas del siglo.

XV. A sus padres, madres y hermanos verán las Pascuas con licencia de la Madre, y asistiendo la hermana que señalare: y esto ha de ser en el estradico, que está entre las dos puertas, sin dar lugar á que entren dentro de la clausura: y la Madre Abadesa no dará licencia, para ver ni hablar otras personas fuera de las dichas, ni á estas fuera de los tiempos señalados en esta regla.

XVI. No enviarán recaudos á los de fuera, ni escribirán papeles, ni los recibirán sin licencia de la Madre Abadesa, y que pasen por su registro.

XVII. El trage será decente y modesto, que no tenga nada de profano: y el tocado una toca blanca. No se pondrán color, ni otro aliño, que desdiga de la vida que siguen. El vestido exterior será de estameña blanca, con escapulario azul de la misma estameña y una imágen de la Purísima Concepcion, pendiente de un cordon azul y blanco, de modo que caiga encima del pecho la Santísima Imágen. Y el interior será de algun color modesto, pero no de seda.

XVIII. No usarán de puntas aunque sean pequeñas en pañuelos, camisas, ni en ropa alguna de su uso y vestido: solo se permitirán en la ropa de los altares y sacristía.

XIX. Cada año, por espacio de ocho dias, se retirarán á tener unos exercicios espirituales, en la forma que se los dieren los Padres espirituales; y estos dias asistirán con las demás solamente al comer y cenar, y lo restante del dia estarán retiradas en leccion espiritual, y en tener quatro horas de oracion y en prepararse para una confesion general que harán de solo lo tocante á aquel año; y la distribucion del tiempo de los exercicios será segun el órden que se les diere.

XX. Al tiempo de comer y de cenar leerán en el Refectorio en un libro de vidas de Santos, ó exemplos suyos, que como se dá en aquel tiempo sustento al cuerpo, se dé alguna refeccion al alma con lo que oyeren.

XXI. No estando enfermas acudirán todas al Refectorio al tiempo de comer y cenar, aunque no sea mas de para oír lo que allí se leyere.

XXII. Los Miércoles, Viérnes y Sábados entre año, podrán hacer algunas mortificaciones en el Refectorio, como comer en el suelo: ponerse en cruz: besar los pies á sus compañeras: postrarse á la puerta para que la pisen: todos actos de humildad y que avivan y alientan el espíritu.

XXIII. Quando tocaren á comer y cenar, antes de sentarse á comer, harán en pie breve oracion; y despues de haber comido, harán la misma oracion en la forma que ántes, dando gracias á Nuestro Señor por el sustento que las dá.

XXIV. Todas acudan en comunidad á la Sala de labor en los tiempos señalados; y para las demas acciones y exercicios públicos, conforme la distribucion del tiempo.

XXV. Acudirán á los oficios domésticos con voluntad sin repugnancia, procurando hacerlos como quienes los hacen por Nuestro Señor y su Santísima Madre.

XXVI. La Madre Abadesa señalará al principio de cada mes á las que han de cuidar del Refectorio, de la Cocina, de la Enfermería, de la Despensa, de la Escucha y Celadora que cuida de la limpieza de la Casa. Y cada mes se irán remudando estos oficios, para que les sea mas facil y menos gravoso el tenerlos. Y ninguna, estando con salud, se escuse de ellos, procurando cada qual servir los mas trabajosos y humildes, por tener mas que ofrecer á Nuestro Señor, y en que agradarle, exercitando la caridad con sus hermanas.

XXVII. La Puerta esté siempre cerrada, y solo se abra para lo que fuere necesario. Y no se permita que ninguna hable en aquellos lugares con persona alguna.

XXVIII. Quando entrare el Médico á visitar á alguna enferma, ó el Barbero á sangrarla, le acompañarán (si la Madre Abadesa no pudiere) la Vicaria con otra que la Madre nombrare, y los asistirán sin dexarlos de vista hasta que vuelvan á salir.

XXIX. La misma diligencia y cuidado se tendrá quando entraren á confesar á alguna, ó quando entraren los Mayordomos y oficiales que acudieren á ver los reparos de la Casa, acompañándolos dos de las nombradas por la Madre Abadesa; y siempre sean dos las que acompañen, señaladas por dicha Madre.

XXX. Las llaves de la Portería se entregarán á la Madre Abadesa á las Ave Marias por la noche; y no se abrirán las Puertas hasta que sea de dia.

XXXI. Todas las noches, antes de acostarse, requiera la Madre Abadesa ó la Vicaria la puerta principal, y las del Coro y Sacristia.

XXXII. Todos los dias despues de la oracion mental, así por mañana, como por la tarde, rezarán una salve por el Rey Nuestro Señor Don Carlos II, y la Reyna Nuestra Señora Doña Mariana de Austria su Madre, y los Señores sus succesores. Y en todos quantos exercicios hicieren encomendarán á Nuestro Señor y á su Purísima Madre á sus Magestades como á únicos Patronos de esta Casa.

XXXIII. Cada mes rezarán un Rosario y ofrecerán una Comunion con las demas obras de aquel dia por el Excmo. Señor Conde de Lemos, Fundador de esta Casa.

XXXIV. Cada dia rezarán cinco Padre nuestros y cinco Ave Marias por todos los Bienhechores de esta Casa. Y la Madre Abadesa tendrá cuidado de acordar y encomendar estas oraciones, como las demas que pareciere hacer por sus Bienhechores.

XXXV. Los Jueves y Domingos por la tarde, tendrán entre sí algun tiempo de divertimiento, para alivio y descanso, conversando entre sí de cosas buenas y santas, y usando de algun entretenimiento decente y honesto.

XXXVI. Ninguna entrará á la Celda de otra, sino es con licencia de la Abadesa; y si entrare, esté poco tiempo dentro y tenga la puerta abierta.

XXXVII. Si alguna estuviere enferma, se irá á curar á la Enfermería; y las que la visitaren, será con licencia de la Abadesa; y hablarán de cosas santas y honestas que puedan alegrar y consolar á la enferma.

XXXVIII. No entrarán niños ni niñas, á ver á sus madres ó parientas dentro de la clausura; y solo se les podrá permitir que las vean dos ó tres veces al año, en la puerta de la Portería, estando la Portera presente.

XXXIX. Ninguna tenga particular amistad con otra, sino todas se amen en el Señor, y tengan una alma y un corazon; y si alguna faltare en esto andando en cuentos y chismes, la dará la Madre Abadesa una gravísima penitencia; y sino se enmendare avisará al Capellan de la Casa y al Padre para que se ponga eficaz remedio.

XXXX. Todas miren por la pobreza, no desperdiciando las cosas, por decir que la Casa es la que las da, ni envien cosa alguna fuera.

XXXXI. Todo lo que trabajaren ha de ser para la Casa, supuesto que ella las ha de asistir con todo lo necesario para su sustento, vestuario y para la curacion de sus enfermedades.

Lo que han de comer y cenar

Los dias de carne se las dará un asado, locro, ó picadillo, y un plato de olla con su verdura; y á las que quisieren se les podrá dar una escudilla de caldo.

De noche cenarán una ensalada, mazamorra ó otro plato semejante y un plato de locro.

Los dias de pescado es les darán tres platos y dos de potajes ó legumbres y uno de pescado ó huevos &c. y el uno de los potajes podrá ser con dulce.

A la colacion se les podrá dar una ensalada cocida y locro falso, y un plato de miel, ó unas pasas.

Los de Nuestra Señora y los primeros de Pascua, se les puede añadir el ordinario otro plato como un pastel ó tamal y alguna fruta.

Regla de la Madre Abadesa

I. Tenga entendido que el mayor servicio que puede hacer á Nuestro Señor y que sea de mayor agrado de la Virgen Santísima Nuestra Señora, es tener gran cuidado con el gobierno de la Casa, procurando con suma diligencia se eviten pecados y faltas, por leves que parezcan.

II. En todas las acciones dé buen exemplo á las demas, siendo la primera en los actos de comunidad, en la virtud, en la observancia de los preceptos divinos, y en la guarda de sus reglas.

III. Procure que todas sus hijas se conserven en union, paz y caridad, evitando qualquier lance que pueda ser de disgusto entre las hermanas, amándolas á todas igualmente, no particularizandose con alguna, y que todas guarden con exâctitud sus reglas y distribuciones.

IV. No permita que entre dia (fuera de los tiempos señalados) tengan conversaciones entre si, ni falten al silencio, ni dé lugar á que esten ociosas, que el ocio es origen de todos los males.

V. Algunas veces entre dia viste la Casa las oficinas para ver si es menester alguna cosa en ellas para proveerlas: y vea si los oficios se hacen con cuidado.

VI. Las faltas que viere las avise y reprehenda como Madre, no disimulando las que supiere, porque el disimulo es una tácita licencia y condescendencia para otras mayores; y quando fuere necesario dará sus penitencias por las faltas, conforme la calidad de ellas, advirtiéndolas con amor y corrigiéndolas con agrado y deseo de la enmienda.

VII. No consienta que en las puertas se hable con persona alguna y cuide que siempre esten cerradas.

VIII. Quando hubieren de hablar á sus parientes, conforme la Regla advierta, que sea con su licencia y que sin ella no pueden hablar á ninguna persona.

IX. Todos los papeles que escribieren á sus parientes ó Padres espirituales ó otra qualquiera persona y los que hubieren de recibir sea con su licencia, registrándolos antes que se den; excepto los de sus padres espirituales; y no permita se escriban cosas vanas y sin fruto.

X. Todas las noches antes de acostarse, visite la Casa y requiera las puertas que caen á la calle.

XI. Procure que no les falte lo necesario de sustento y vestido, pidiéndolo al Mayordomo. Excuse y quite todo lo superfluo; que no se gaste, ni desperdicie vanamente lo que se les da.

XII. Tenga especial cuidado con el regalo y curacion de las enfermas, asistiéndolas, y haciendo, que otras las asistan como pide la caridad.

XIII. Si por enfermedad ó achaque no pudiere visitar la Casa, ni acudir personalmente á las obligaciones de su oficio, encomiende este cuidado á otra de quien tuviere satisfaccion.

XIV. Las faltas que por su persona ó por graves no pudiere remediar, las avise sin encarecer ni exâgerar al Padre espiritual que cuida de toda la Casa para que se ponga el mas conveniente remedio.

XV. Tenga especial cuidado de que á las que entraren á tener exercicios por algunos dias, se les acuda con puntualidad, no permitiendo se les haga falta en cosa alguna de comida y hospedage, y que una de las hermanas les lleve lo que hubieren menester y componga el aposento y Oratorio.

XVI. Advierta, que las que entraren de fuera á tener exercicios, no han de comunicar, ni tener conversaciones entre dia con las hermanas que viven dentro, por que no van á perder vanamente el tiempo, sino á encomendarse á Nuestro Señor y tener quatro horas de oracion cada dia, y en los demas exercicios que en su distribucion tuvieren señalados.

XVII. No consienta que las que van á tener exercicios anden por la Casa: de su quarto han de baxar derechas al coro, á oir Misa y comulgar, y tomar los puntos y meditacion que el Padre espiritual las diere: y del coro se han de volver á su quarto.

XVIII. A medio dia despues de comer podrá enviar la Madre Abadesa á una ó dos de las hermanas para que tengan un rato de conversacion espiritual, con la que estuviere en exercicios, con que tendrán al dia algun alivio y descanso.

Reglas de la Sacristana

Procure que las alhajas de la Iglesia y Sacristia esten con toda decencia y limpieza, y lo que diere al sacristan para adorno del altar y para las Misas, lo dará por cuenta y tendrá cuidado de que se vuelvan con puntualidad.

Tenga catálogo y libro de todas las alhajas de la Iglesia y sacrista y cuide no se desperdicien. Quando faltare alguna cosa necesaria la pida á la Madre Abadesa ó al Mayordomo.

Tocará con puntualidad la campana á todas las horas que estan señaladas para las distribuciones de exercicios espirituales, y sala de labor, para que todas acudan á ellas.

Tenga prevenidas luces en el Coro para quando fueren de noche á rezar, á tener oracion, á hacer exâmen de la conciencia, y demas funciones, y que el Coro se barra, esté limpio y con aseo.

Reglas de la Portera

I. Tenga siempre cerrada la puerta con llave, y no la abra sino quando hubieren de entrar, ó salir.

II. Quando tocaren á la puerta acuda con puntualidad como quien va á abrir á nuestro Señor, y no abra la puerta hasta haber visto por la rejilla quien llama, y si es necesario abrir.

III. A todas las personas que llegaren á la puerta las despache y despida con agrado y caridad con palabras benignas: de modo que todos vayan edificados aunque se les niegue alguna cosa.

IV. Las cartas y papeles que traxeren para las de Casa, las llevará á la Madre Abadesa, sin decir nada á quien se escribe, ni que lo entienda, por si no fuere conveniente que lo sepa.

V. No dará recaudos de las de casa á los de fuera, ni de los de fuera á las de casa sin licencia de la Madre Abadesa, ni permitirá que en la puerta haya parlas, ni voces descompasadas.

VI. Luego que den las Ave Marias cerrará las puertas, y entregará las llaves á la Madre Abadesa.

VII. Quando hubiere de entrar Médico ó Confesor ó otra qualquiera persona de las de afuera, avisará á la Madre Abadesa para que acudan las que los han de acompañar, y no permita que entre ninguno sin que asistan las acompañadoras.

VIII. Quando hubieren de sacar alguna cosa de Casa ó traerla de fuera para las de Casa, avísese de ello á la Madre Abadesa.

IX. No permita que esten á la puerta mercachifles ni vendedoras: procure que aquel lugar esté con silencio y edificacion.

X. No permita que por el torno de la portería hable ninguna de adentro con persona de fuera, sino es en cosas necesarias para la Casa y estando la portera presente.

Reglas de la Refectolera

I. Tenga catálogo y inventario de todas las alhajas que sirven en el refectorio para dar cuenta de ellas quando fuere necesario y para entregarlas por cuenta á la que la sucediere en el oficio.

II. Procure que el refectorio esté limpo y aseado, y todas las demas cosas que sirven en él: que el agua esté prevenida en los cántaros y jarros: y si faltare alguna cosa, la pida con tiempo.

III. Mudará manteles limpios por lo menos cada ocho dias &c. y tendrá lugar dispuesto donde se laven las manos, y toallas para enjugarlas.

IV. Hará señal con la campana á los tiempos señalados para comer y cenar, y avisará á las que sirven así á la primera como á la segunda mesa.

Reglas de la Despensera y Cocinera

I. En el repartir y distribuir las cosas, guarde el órden que tuviere de la Madre Abadesa, y procure con todas igualdad, teniendo especial cuidado con las enfermas y convalecientes.

II. Guarde con cuidado las cosas que se le entregaren, teniendo atencion á que no se dañen, ni desperdicien, y avise con tiempo para que se provea lo que fuere necesario para el sustento y lo demas.

III. Haya mucha limpieza en la cocina y despensa; y en las cosas tocantes á ella y á las que la ayudaren: edifiquelas con las palabras y con el exemplo, siendo la primera en las acciones mas humildes.

IV. Tenga catálogo de las cosas que tiene y que sirven en su oficina, entregándolas por cuenta á las que la sucedieren.

LAVS DEO

Distribucion del tiempo.
Para por la mañana
De cinco y media á seis, levantarse.
De seis á la media, oracion mental todas juntas.
De seis y media á siete y media, componer sus camas, aposentos, y lo demas que tuvieren que hacer.
De siete y media á ocho, oir misa todas juntas.
De ocho á la media, descansar y rezar sus devociones.
De ocho y media á las doce, acudir todas á la sala de labor, y hacer lo que tuvieren que coser, y las demas á sus oficios.
De doce á una á comer, y tener un rato de conversacion devota entre sí, contando algunos casos de edificacion y exemplos.
De una á dos descansar.

Para por la tarde
De dos á la media, rezar su Rosario todas juntas á coro.
De dos y media á las tres, leer leccion espiritual en algunos libros devotos.
De tres á cinco y media, acudir á la sala de labor como por la mañana.
De cinco y media á seis, descansar.
De seis á la media, rezar todas juntas la Letania de Nuestra Señora y sus devociones.
De seis y media á siete, tener oracion mental todas.
De siete á ocho, ocuparse cada una en lo que tuviere que hacer.
De ocho á nueve, cenar y tener un rato de recreacion y conversacion entre sí, como media hora.
De nueve á la media leer un quarto en Contemptus mundi ó en Meditaciones de Arnaya ó Novísimos del Padre Salazar.
De nueve y quarto á la media, hacer el exâmen de conciencia todas juntas, y acabar con un acto de contricion.
Y la noche que fuere de disciplina tenerla despues del exâmen por espacio de medio quarto de hora ó un Miserere rezado despacio.
A las nueve y media, acostarse puntuales sin andar hablando por las camas, ni por los aposentos.
A las diez, las visitará la Madre Abadesa ó la Vicaria para ver si estan acostadas y las hechará Agua bendita.
A las que esto hicieren se les promete segura la vida eterna.

Recogimiento Patterns for First-Time Deposit: Divorciadas, 1569–1713, Lima

	1569–1650*		1651–1713	
Place Deposit	No.	% Total	No.	% Total
Recogimientos				
Divorciadas	30	35	3	2
La Magdalena	2	3	—	—
Las Amparadas	—	—	36	20
Private Homes	22	39	95	52
Hospitals				
La Caridad	7	13	14	8
Santa Ana	—	—	1	—
Convents	3	5	24	13
Beaterios	—	—	9	5
Jail	3	5	—	—
TOTAL	57	100	182	100

SOURCE: AAL, Divorcios, Leg. 1–63. This table is based upon a 20 percent sample of all divorce records between 1569 and 1713. The 20 percent totals by period are: 1569–1650 (n = 81); 1651–1700 (n = 225); 1701–13 (n = 28). When calculating specific data on place of deposit, some cases had no data. For 1569 to 1650, 24 out of 81 (29 percent) contained no data; for 1651 to 1713, 71 of 253 (28 percent) no data. For numerical totals see Appendix F for a discussion of statistical methods.

*Some figures cover slightly different periods: for Divorciadas (1589–1665); Beaterios (1670–1713); Las Amparadas (1670–1713).

Statistical Methodology

The database consists of 334 divorces (divorcios); 31 annulments (nulidades); 114 marital litigation suits (litigios matrimoniales); 37 concubinage (amancebamiento) cases; 26 slave complaints (causas de negros); 1 bigamy (bigamía); 10 criminal marital suits (matrimonios criminales); 15 betrothal disputes (esponsales de matrimonios). The 334 divorce cases are derived from a 20 percent sample of the total number counted between 1569 and 1650 (81 out of 399); between 1651 and 1700 (225 out of 1128); and for the period from 1701 to 1713, 28 cases (28 out of 143) (see Tables 2 and 4 for a breakdown by decade). Records range in length from one folio to two hundred folios. The cases examined represented a sampling based upon length of cases; the shorter ones more often involved nonelite women, while the longer suits represented elite women disputing the return of large dowries.

Unlike censuses, divorce records are often fragmentary, and racial, class, and occupational data spotty. The initial folios generally provide the plaintiff's initial testimony, which contains the reasons for the legal suit. It is possible to learn about the locations of deposit from the auto or order of deposit issued by the ecclesiastical judge, as well as from written requests for transfers. Once recogida, the woman would generally state where she was staying. *Litigios matrimoniales* were usually filed before the woman decided to seek a permanent separation.

Notes

For full publication information on works cited, see the Bibliography, pages 273–306. When citations involving the same archive and series appear in the same footnote, they are not repeated. The following abbreviations are used in the Notes:

AAL   Archivo Arzobispal de Lima
ABP   Archivo de la Beneficencia Pública del Perú
ADA   Archivo Diocesano de Avila (Spain)
AFL   Archivo Franciscano de Lima
AGI   Archivo General de Indias (Seville)
AGN   Archivo General de la Nación (Peru)
AGS   Archivo General de Simancas (Spain)
AHN   Archivo Histórico Nacional (Madrid, Spain)
AML   Archivo de la Municipalidad de Lima
BLAC   [Nettie Lee] Benson Latin American Collection
BNP   Biblioteca Nacional del Perú
BZ   Biblioteca de Zabálburu (Madrid, Spain)
CDFS   *Colección de documentos para la historía de la formación social de hispano-américa, 1493–1810*
CDI   *Colección de documentos inéditos relativos al descubrimiento y conquista de América*
CI   *Cedulario indiano*
CLAHR   *Colonial Latin American Historical Review*
CLAR   *Colonial Latin American Review*
CLG   *Gobernantes del Perú, Cartas y papeles, siglo XVI*
CN   Causas de Negros series in AAL
D   Divorcios series in AAL
DI   *Documentos inéditos del siglo XVI para la historia de México*
HAHR   *Hispanic American Historical Review*
HIEP   *La Iglesia de España en el Perú: Colección de documentos*
JbLA   *Jahrbuch für Geschichte von Staat, Wirtschaft, und Gesellschaft Lateinamerikas*
JCB   John Carter Brown Library

LL   Lilly Library
NL   Newberry Library
RANP   *Revista del Archivo Nacional del Perú*
Recop.   *Recopilación de las leyes de los reynos de las Indias*

Preface

1. *Diccionario de la lengua*, 520–21; Corominas y Pascual, *Diccionario crítico*, 121.

2. See Eiximenis' *Lo Llibre de les dones*, published as *Carro de las donas*. Cerda's *Libro intítulado* referred only to the 1542 translation of Eiximenis, which had now become the standard edition. See also Luján, *Coloquios matrimoniales*; Pérez de Valdivia, *Aviso*; León, *La perfecta casada*; and Acosta Africano, *Tratado en loor*.

3. Unlike nuns, beatas lacked close ecclesiastical supervision, and the foundation of their communities required less capital investment. They were housed in beaterios that were more modest than convents and officially accommodated only thirty-three women. The foundation of a beaterio required approval of local ecclesiastical authorities but could be accomplished quickly, while convents needed the approval of local secular and ecclesiastical authorities, the archbishop, the king, and the pope.

4. On the construction of gendered social categories see Scott, "Gender," 1065, 1068; Hacking, "Making Up People," 230; and de Lauretis, "The Violence of Rhetoric," 1–2, on categories as representations of violence.

5. Linguistic evidence of the transculturation process within the Andean context can be seen by 1560 in Domingo de Santo Tomás' Spanish/Quechua *Lexicon*, and in González Holguín's *Vocabulario* (1608). Holguín's dictionary demonstrates a profound Andean understanding of recogimiento as a mystical practice, enclosure, a virtue, and modest, moral conduct. See Santo Tomás, *Lexicon*, 197, "recoger. tantani gui o aylloni gui"; González Holguín, *Vocabulario*, II: 654–55. González Holguín lists a number of definitions pertinent to this study: (1) recoger allegando lo apartado. Corini corircuni. (2) Recogerse a su casa. Ripucuni. (3) Recogido o encogido modesto. Quentiquenti soncco o qquenticuk soncco mana tuqui tuqui. (4) Recoger y reprimir los sentidos. Yuyaycunacta nitiycucuni harcaycucuni. (5) Recogida casa lugar religión. Alli cauçay huaci ccacicacuyhuaci. (6) Recogerse a estrecha vida. Ñitiy ñitay o quentiyquentiy cauçayman harcaycucuni qquentiycucuni, ñitiycucuni. (7) Recogida o estrecha vida. Ñitiy ñitiylla cauçay harcay harcay qquentiy qquenti cauçay.

6. Compare Lima with the cases of French Indochina and the Netherlands Indies, where colonial authorities in the nineteenth century developed exclusionary policies toward interracial unions and their offspring. See Stoler, "Sexual Affronts."

7. The term "made-up" women derives from Hacking, "Making Up People," 230.

8. A few published accounts written by women helped qualify their religious and social experiences of recogimiento in convents and beaterios. Providencia's, *Relación del orígen* and Santísima Trinidad, *Historia de la fundación*, provided interesting insights. The beatification papers of Isabel Porras de Marmolejo, Nicolás de Ayllón, and Francisco del Castillo, housed in the AAL, include witness reports that detail the perceptions of beatas. The Inquisition trial of María Jacinta de Montoya in the Archivo Histórico Nacional of Madrid is also important for her views on mysticism, recogimiento, and administrative policies. Several fascinating documents at the Archivo

Franciscano (Peru) provided dramatic insights into individual holy women's interpretations of recogimiento as a spiritual praxis.

    9. Carroll, *Through the Looking Glass*, ch. 6.

Introduction

    1. It is not possible to give an "original" date when popular usage of these meanings began. These definitions derive from the following etymological dictionaries: Covarrubias Orozco, *Tesoro de la lengua castellana;* Moliner, *Diccionario del uso del español,* 955; Alonso, *Enciclopedia del idioma,* 3536; Corominas and Pascual, *Diccionario crítico etimológico,* 120–21; *Diccionario de la lengua española,* 1114. For the concept's dissemination in Europe, see Perceval, *A Dictionary in Spanish and English,* 205r; and Stevens, *New Spanish and English Dictionary.* French dictionaries translated recogimiento as *recueil, retirement,* or *assemblement.* Oudin, *Tesoro de las dos lenguas;* Palet, *Diccionario muy copioso*; and for Spanish America, Molina, *Vocabulario en lengua castellana;* Santo Tomás, *Lexicon,* 197; González Holguín, *Vocabulario.*

    2. The actual recording of the meaning into the dictionary occurred post facto, or after that particular usage had long entered mainstream vocabulary. For example, "recogida" in Alonso's, *Enciclopedia del idioma,* 3536, is defined as "a woman who lives in a determined house," and states that this meaning became popular from the eighteenth to the twentieth centuries, when in fact it is in evidence by the 1560s in Spain. By "popular renderings" I refer to usages found in other early modern sources, particularly ecclesiastical litigation records.

    3. See Johnson and Lipsett-Rivera, "Introduction," *The Faces of Honor,* 1–17.

    4. Koselleck, *Futures Past,* 73–91. He said: "It can be shown for German-speaking areas from 1770 onward that both new meanings for old words and neologisms proliferate, altering with the linguistic arsenal of the entire political and social space of experience, and establishing new horizons of expectation," 77. Although Koselleck concentrated on political concepts, his method works equally well for cultural and social ideals.

    5. "Surveying the space of meaning of each of the central concepts . . . exposes, therefore, a contemporary polemical thrust; intentions with respect to the future; and enduring elements of past social organization, whose specific arrangement discloses a statement's meaning," Koselleck, *Futures Past,* 77.

    6. Williams, *Marxism and Literature,* 160–62.

    7. Foucault, "Truth and Power," *The Foucault Reader,* 59. See idem, "Space, Knowledge and Power," *The Foucault Reader,* 239–56. Knowledge and power interact in historically specific ways that vary significantly in different domains. It is the historian's task to understand the components that form those expressions of knowledge and power.

    8. Foucault assiduously avoided defining terms, but delineated certain characteristics of power in *Power/Knowledge,* 142.

    9. Foucault, "Nietzsche, Genealogy, History," 82; Sawicki, *Disciplining Foucault,* 14, 44; Flynn, "Foucault's Mapping," 33–37.

    10. On notions of honor in the Mediterranean, see Pitt-Rivers, *The Fate of Shechem;* for Spain, see Maravall, *Poder, honor y élite.* For Mexico, see Seed, *To Love,*

Honor, and Obey; and on the colonial Pueblo Indians, Gutiérrez, *When Jesus Came,* 194–240. Gutiérrez defines "calidad" as a general estimation of social worth based upon a person's social status, religion, race, ethnicity, legitimacy, occupation, and ownership of land, *When Jesus Came,* 205.

11. Twinam, *Public Lives, Private Secrets;* Mannarelli, *Pecados públicos.*

12. For studies of female honor in early modern Italy, see Ferrante, "Honor Regained," 46–72; and Cavallo and Cerutti, "Female Honor," 73–109. On the complex distinctions between cultural concepts in early modern Italy, see Cohen, "Honor and Gender," 599–600.

13. Pitt-Rivers, "Honour and Shame." Patricia Seed distinguishes between honor as status and as a virtue and argues, within the context of betrothal disputes, that its engendered application for women related to sexual purity, *To Love, Honor, and Obey,* 61–67; Ramón Gutiérrez contends that "honor (*honor*) was strictly a male attribute whiles shame (*vergüenza*) was intrinsic to females," *When Jesus Came,* 209. Ruggiero, "Wives on Deposit," 258, demonstrates that husbands achieved "their real objective of restoring their honor through the system of deposit," but it would be interesting to know the ways in which women maintained and restored *their* sense of honor. On the point that contemporary Mediterranean notions are too casually transplanted, see Twinam, "The Negotiation," 71.

14. AAL, D, Leg. 49, 1680, "Doña Theresa Gutiérres vs. Don Luis Balcasar."

15. Lyndal Roper argues that in early modern Augsburg, "women could be made subject to men's 'will' and men's 'honour,' but they could also lay claim to honour, desire and even will. For men and women alike, these terms had social and economic meaning as well as sexual import, but their significance differed for each sex, and their meaning could change with the context of the telling," Roper, *Oedipus and the Devil,* 73. Gowing argues that gendered differences in conceptualizing and recounting sexual conduct and defining virtue were significant in early modern London, "Gender and the Language of Insult," 7, 9. See also idem, "Language, Power and the Law," 28, 30, 36. On sexuality and marriage in colonial Latin America, see the articles in Lavrin, *Sexuality and Marriage.*

16. See the excellent article by Gal, "Between Speech and Silence," 175–203. Although he does not analyze the ways cultural codes were expressed in violent verbal exchanges, I agree with Stern's assertion that "traditional codes of gender right, obligation, and honor associated with the honor/shame complex may themselves have been contested and multiple," *The Secret,* 386, n. 25.

17. Butler, *Gender Trouble,* 196–97.

18. De Lauretis, "The Violence of Rhetoric," 32. Richard Boyer has argued that "people learn the process of politics by discovering that power is contested—however cynically—over ideals; politics takes on meaning in the interaction between the people and institutions that actually impinge on their lives," Boyer, "Women, *La Mala Vida,*" 255.

19. Martinez-Alier (now Stolke), "Elopement and Seduction," 112; Silverblatt, "Lessons of Gender," 639–50.

20. Silverblatt, "Lessons of Gender," 643.

21. Verena Martinez-Alier was one of the first Latin American scholars to develop a sensitivity to such differences. See her discussion of perceptions of honor, sexual

identity, and race among Cuban women of color in her path-breaking article, "Elopement and Seduction," 109–10, 112–13, 117.

22. For a discussion of the historical conceptualizations of "race," see Williams, *Keywords*, 248. For the influence of these notions on Latin American thought, see Graham, "Introduction," in *The Idea of Race*, 1–5; and Stepan, *The Hour of Eugenics*. On the employment of nineteenth-century constructs of race to interpret the colonial period, see Mörner, *Race Mixture*, which notes a shift in attitudes toward mestizos before and after 1550, but does not analyze the changes in the social construction of the meaning of "mestizo."

23. For the classic discussion of race mixture in Latin America, see Mörner, *Race Mixture*, and an article that specifically tackles social stratification and economic factors, idem, "Economic Factors and Stratification," 335–69. For a discussion of "estates" and "class," see Chance and Taylor, "Estate and Class," 454–87; McCaa, Schwartz, and Grubessich, "Race and Class," 421–33; and Seed, "Social Dimensions of Race," 569–606. On the problems of the changing meanings and relationship of racial and ethnic categories, see Cahill, "Colour by Numbers," 325–46. See also the debate "Race, Class and Gender: A Conversation," that includes two important pieces, including Kuznesof, "Ethnic and Gender Influences," 153–76; Schwartz, "Colonial Identities," 185–201; and Kuznesof's reply in "More Conversation," 129–33. Two recent studies examine gender, race, and class in relation to the cultural value honor: Gutiérrez, *When Jesus Came*, 194–206; and Seed, *To Love, Honor, and Obey*, 61–74.

24. See the excellent essay by Sawicki, "Foucault, Feminism," 286–313.

25. Sawicki, *Disciplining Foucault*, 9–10.

26. Stern, *The Secret*, 18.

27. Blunt and Rose, "Introduction," 5. See Jean Franco's study of the "master narrative" evident in the Catholic Church's mapping of knowledge, and individual women's responses to those narratives in colonial Mexico, in *Plotting Women*, 3–76.

28. This quotation comes from his *Tratado en loor*, fol. 77, cited in Fitzmaurice-Kelly, "Women in Sixteenth-Century Spain," 559.

29. Boyer, "Women, *La Mala Vida*," 253–54; Walby, "Theorizing Patriarchy," 227.

30. Sawicki, *Disciplining Foucault*, 65; Butler, *Gender Trouble*, 100–101.

31. Downs, "If 'Woman,'" 449.

32. One might argue that most people "accepted" as an unquestioned cultural notion that men were the pre-eminent group, with greater prestige, authority, and social control, while women were the "lesser sex" and subordinate. See Ortner, "Gender Hegemonies," 39, who writes, "I have continued to consider the cultural assertion/acceptance of male superiority to be definitive. If men in a given society have a culturally higher status, then by definition this is a "male dominant" or gender asymmetrical society, regardless of how much de facto power women may exert."

33. Ortner also argues that the "phenomenon of gender status" is relative and differentiated and that gender asymmetry is not universal, Ortner, "Gender Hegemonies"; Butler, *Gender Trouble*, particularly her chapter "Subversive Bodily Acts."

34. Przybylowicz, Hartsock and McCallum, "Introduction: The Construction," 6; Scott, "Deconstructing Equality," 41, 43, 46–47.

35. Blunt and Rose, "Introduction," 5.

36. Foucault, *Discipline and Punish*.

37. Identities are constructed within larger discourses. Michel Foucault would not have used the term "identities," but "subject positions." See idem, *The Archaeology of Knowledge*, 115–16. I agree with Stuart Hall's assertion that identities are "never singular but multiply constructed across different, often intersecting and antagonistic, discourses, practices and positions," that they are relationally constructed and are always in a process of becoming. See idem, "Introduction: Who Needs 'Identity,'" 4. I also concur with the idea that a multiplicity of identities can coexist and inform one another in their construction, See Grossberg, "Identity and Cultural Studies," 88–90. On "institutional" identities, see Morris, "At Henry Parkes Motel," 2, 5–6, 37.

38. Sherill Cohen has shown the interconnection between secular and religious houses in early modern Italy. See idem, *Evolution*, 5. See also Michael Katz, who has written: "An adequate interpretation must encompass not only the asylum, not only prisons, mental hospitals, and poorhouses, but also public schools, academies, the YMCA, and ultimately, the family. Striking parallels exist between the timing, theory and shape of those developments that affect deviants, dependents, children, adolescents, and families. An understanding of any of them depends upon an exploration of their interconnection." Katz, "Origins," 18.

39. AAL, Litigios Matrimoniales, Leg. 4, 1707. Inés's father-in-law was the cacique principal of Guatica and Maranga in the Valley of Magdalena, within the jurisdiction of El Cercado.

40. Lavrin, "Women in Colonial Latin America," 321–55. Her academic dossier ranges from an examination of the effects of eighteenth-century ecclesiastical reforms on New Spain's convents, to the administration of properties held by the Convent of Santa Clara in Querétaro, to the spiritual contributions of individual nuns. For example, see Lavrin, "El Convento de Santa Clara," 76–117; "The Role of Nunneries," 371–93; "La vida femenina," 27–51.

41. On Valladolid, Spain, see Lehfeldt, "Sacred and Secular Spaces." Her study asserts that the spiritual experiences of holy women were often tempered by "secular" or economic concerns. On Brazil, see Soeiro, "The Social and Economic Role," 209–32. See Burns, "Apuntes," 67–95; and *Colonial Habits*.

42. See, for example, Muriel, *Hospitales de la Nueva España*; *Conventos de monjas en la Nueva España*; and *Los recogimientos*. Asunción Lavrin has indicated the need for additional studies on beaterios and recogimientos in her article "Female Religious," 188–90.

43. Cohen, *Evolution*, 3.

44. Foucault, "Truth and Power," 59; "Nietzsche, Genealogy, History," 80–84. Perceptions at the time of the institution's foundation may have varied from one colonial city to another, but patterns for recogimientos in Mexico City seem to corroborate those of Lima. For Quito, Viforcas, "Los recogimientos," discusses changes in the functional application of the recogimiento and its decline. Unfortunately, her work fails to address how recogidas were redefined over the course of the 150 years that her study encompasses.

45. Several scholars disagree with Foucault's argument that imprisonment, a "carceral archipelago," and disciplinary mentality were articulated only after 1800 with the advent of "modernization." His main critic for the early modern period is Spierenburg, *The Prison Experience*, 1–5. Sherill Cohen believes that incarcerating/protective institutions predate the modern period, and that women's institutions of early mod-

ern Europe "preceded and anticipated many later developments in the creation of institutions," *Evolution*, 5. On "labeling" and crime, see Larner, "Crimen Exceptum."

46. Cohen, *Evolution*, 6; Bercé et al., *L'Italie au 17e siècle*, 251–75.

47. Muriel, *Los recogimientos*, 45, stated: "Esto nos lleva a clasificar los recogimientos en dos clases: los de protección y ayuda a la mujer y los de corrección. Los primeros son de tipo voluntario y los segundos como penitenciarios que son, los que reciben a las mujeres sentenciadas por diversos tribunales de la Nueva España." For a recently published article that takes exception to this dichotomy—as I do for Lima—see Penyak, "Safe Harbors."

48. For Mexico, see the example of the Recogimiento de Santa Mónica for "señoras casadas," which also housed doncellas and "mujeres de mala vida y adúlteras." Even in the sixteenth century, the institution served as a voluntary and involuntary asylum; Muriel, *Los recogimientos*, 75. Goffman, *Asylums*, 4–7, argues that imprisonment could simultaneously serve to diminish vagrancy, to discipline immoral behavior, and to segregate socially marginalized individuals from the rest of society, thus transgressing imaginary functional typologies of "differences" among institutions.

49. Giddens, *The Constitution of Society*, 60–61, 110–19.

50. Vargas Ugarte, *Historia de la Iglesia*; Castillo, *Un místico;* Vargas Ugarte, *Historia del culto de María;* idem, *Vida del siervo de Dios.*

51. Bellido, *El clero diocesano*. On the Inquisition, see the articles in Ramos, *Catolicismo y extirpación de idolatrías.* On San Martín de Porras, see Busto Duthurburu, *San Martín de Porras;* Cussen, "Fray Martín de Porres"; and on Santa Rosa de Lima, see Wood, "Chains of Virtue."

52. For essays on Mexico, Colombia, and Venezuela, see Lavrin, *Sexuality and Marriage.* For several recent works on Peru, see Stavig, "Living in Offense"; and Spurling, "Honor, Sexuality."

53. I concur with Richard Boyer's point that it is difficult to distinguish a "system" of alliances among secular and religious authorities. They often harbored conflicting or competing views of orthodox Catholicism. Boyer, "Escribiendo la historia."

54. Ahlgren, *Teresa of Avila,* 167.

55. Burke, "Urban History," 69–82. For an overview of the historiographic literature, see Bronner, "Urban Society," 7–72; and for a good social history of urban inhabitants, see *Cities and Society.*

56. Stoler, "Rethinking Colonial Categories," 323, 331–34.

57. For two examples, see Mannarelli, "Sexualidad y desigualdades"; Stoler, "Sexual Affronts."

58. Minchom, *The People of Quito;* Cope, *The Limits;* King, "Colonial Cities," 7, 13–16.

59. Andrien, *Crisis and Decline*, 633–59; Bronner, "Church, Crown, and Commerce," 75–89; Hamnett, "Church Wealth"; Hampe Martínez, "Sobre encomenderos."

60. For general works on Lima, see Bromley and Barbagelata, *Evolución urbana;* Flores Galindo, *Aristocracia y plebe;* Pérez Cantó, *Lima en el siglo XVIII.* A number of studies have focused upon specific social groups in Lima. On African and creole slaves, see Bowser, *The African Slave;* Tardieu, *Los negros y la Iglesia;* on Spaniards, see Lockhart, *Spanish Peru;* on urban Indians, see Lowry, "Forging an Indian Nation"; Charney, "El indio urbano," and "Negotiating Roots"; and on Andean women, see Silverblatt, *Moon, Sun, and Witches.*

61. Martín, *Daughters;* Mannarelli, *Pecados públicos.* See also García y García, *La mujer peruana.*

62. Bronner, "The Population of Lima," 107–19.

63. Ortíz, *Contrapunteo cubano.* For critiques of his definition of transculturation, see Hoeg, "Cultural Counterpoint," 65; Iznaga, *Transculturación,* 43–49.

64. Ortíz, *Contrapunteo cubano,* 103.

65. Ibid., 136–37. More recently, literary scholars have adapted the term in their interpretation of literary texts. In a book published in 1992, Mary Louise Pratt defined the term "to describe how subordinated or marginal groups select and invent from materials transmitted to them by a dominant or metropolitan culture," Pratt, *Imperial Eyes,* 6. See also Spitta, *Between Two Waters,* 1–28, who gives an excellent critique of Ortíz's definition.

66. Osorio, "El callejón de la soledad," 200, posits transculturation as the "permanent exchange of practices, ideas and behaviors that yielded hybrid urban cultures." Unlike my study, which analyzes one Iberian concept and the *process* of transmission of that concept over space and time—whether on an ideal, imperial, or conjugal level—Osorio looks at a variety of different practices associated with sorcery and medicine at a given historical moment in colonial Lima. Her work does not demonstrate the process of change or the transfiguration of their own practices, merely the end result: cultural hybridity.

67. Williams, *Marxism and Literature,* 121–27.

68. Quoted in Pagden, *European Encounters,* 39–40.

Chapter 1: Negotiating Enclosure

1. Zumárraga to Charles V, 27/VIII/1529, in García Icazbalceta, *Don fray Juan de Zumárraga,* II: 199. For an important biography of Juan de Zumárraga, see Greenleaf, *Zumárraga and the Mexican Inquisition.*

2. For different explanations, see García Icazbalceta, "La instrucción pública en México durante el siglo XVI," in: *Obras,* I: 163–265, and idem, "El colegio de niñas de Mexico," in *Obras,* II: 428–34; Ricard, *The Spiritual Conquest,* 210–12; Gonzalbo Aizpuru, *Las mujeres en la Nueva España,* 291ff; Kobayashi, *La educación;* Gómez Canedo, *La educación de los marginados;* Muriel, *La sociedad novohispana.*

3. Several scholars have focused upon theological and humanist influences that informed the Franciscan missionaries who interacted with their Nahua subjects. See Ricard, *The Spiritual Conquest;* Phelan, *The Millennial Kingdom;* Brading, *The First America;* and Baudot, *La pugna franciscana.*

4. The essence of the term "mysticism" is the notion that individuals can directly experience a heightened sense of reality unmediated by the institutional church or by the external senses.

5. According to Melquíades Andrés Martín, two important sources of inspiration for Osuna were Gómez García's *Carro de dos vidas* (1500), and the Benedictine monk, abbot of Monserrat and cousin to Cardinal Cisneros, Francisco Garsías de Cisneros (1455–1510), who wrote the *Exercitatorio de la vida espiritual* (1500). See Andrés Martín, *Los recogidos,* 15, 22–23. Osuna and other Spanish mystics were influenced by the Brethren of the Common Life, who also recommended abandoning the world to turn one's heart inward toward God. Osuna's contemporary, Erasmus, advocated a life of

contemplation, but more specifically as a rejection of ritual, ceremony, and dogma. Andrés Martín asserts that Erasmus should not be claimed as the source of inspiration for "la interiorización de la espiritualidad española"; Andrés Martín, "Pensamiento teológico," III–2: 352. For an excellent study on Erasmus and his influence in Spain, see Bataillon, *Erasmo y España*.

6. On the influence of the hermetic tradition in Spain, see Saint-Saëns, *La nostalgie du désert*.

7. La Salceda was a major center for the recogidos. The 1502 constitution called these houses "casas recolegidas." The revised 1523 constitution termed them "casas de recogimiento." By 1550, the term "recoleto" became increasingly synonymous with the cloistered observant reformed orders such as the Carmelites. To be recollectus or recogido was also considered a positive accomplishment for an aspiring priest or nun. See Meseguer Fernández, "Programa de gobierno," 18, n. 35; and Carrión, "Casas de Recolección," 264, 267. Nebrija's *Dictionarium ex hispaniensi*, fol. cx, defines "recolligo" (+is, +egi) "por recoger o tornar a coger recollectio +onis+ por aquella obra de coger assi." Cardinal Francisco Jiménez de Cisneros patronized the Franciscans of La Salceda and bequeathed his magnificent library to them; Andrés Martín, *Los recogidos*, 48.

8. When Osuna became a member of the Friars Minor around 1513, the order was divided into Conventuals and Observants, the minority. Cardinal Cisneros's reforms, culminating in the Bull of Union in 1517, made the Observants the main branch of the Franciscans.

9. "El intento de la humildad es evacuar al hombre de sí mismo, y el recogimiento no hace otra cosa sino vaciarnos de nosotros mismos, para que Dios se extiende más en el corazón," Osuna, *Tercer abecedario*, ch. XIX, 551–52.

10. The terms "recoleto" and "recogido" shared the Latin root *recollere*, meaning cloistered or enclosed; Meseguer Fernández, "Programa de gobierno," 18, n. 35.

11. For a general, multivolume work on the Spanish Church, see García Villoslada, *Historia de la Iglesia en España*. On the development of distinct theological traditions in sixteenth-century Spain, see Andrés Martín, *La teología española*.

12. Five editions of Osuna's *Abecedario* were published in twenty-five years. On the dissemination and popularity of his work, see Muñiz Rodríguez, *Experiencia de Dios*. His works also had an influence upon the discalced (barefoot) reform movement that developed in many of the regular orders.

13. Both recogimiento and alumbrismo emphasized meditative practices, however major differences distinguished these two schools. Alumbrismo (illuminism) was a more radical rejection of orthodox Christian dogma, including vocal prayer and other activities associated with ritual and ceremony. Isabel de la Cruz, considered to be the "mother of alumbrismo," developed the notion of "dejamiento" or abandoning oneself to God, in a similar way to that described by Osuna but without the mystical or spiritual depth and stages that Osuna said formed an essential part of the "internal path." Osuna rejected alumbrismo and dejamiento. The Inquisition did not attack the recojidos, but found many of those who practiced dejamiento to be suspect. See García Villoslada, *Historia de la Iglesia en España*, III–2: 330–31.

14. Carrión, "Casas de Recolección," 267. In the province of Castile alone there were eight. The first reformed Franciscan foundations were based at Salceda, situated near Guadalajara, and accommodated up to twenty-four friars. Five smaller hermit-

ages were built in the hills surrounding Salceda, where friars could spend long periods in total seclusion.

15. On the contact between Martín de Valencia, Juan de Guadalupe, Francisco de los Angeles Quiñones, and Juan de Zumárraga, see Gil, *Primeras 'Doctrinas*,' 71–77; Andrés Martín, "La espiritualidad de los 'doce' en Extremadura"; and idem, "Contenido y transcripción," 403ff.

16. His predecessor, Garsías de Cisneros, advocated "contemplación" for "los mundanos" in, idem, *Exercitatorio*, ch. XL.

17. The popularity of behavioral manuals during the Italian Renaissance influenced earlier Spanish writers. Before 1500 important treatises included: Catalan Bishop Françesch de Eiximenis, *Llibre de les dones*, a fourteenth-century work that inspired humanist Juan Luis Vives in the sixteenth century; Martín de Córdoba (1400–76), *Jardín de las nobles doncellas*, written in support of Isabel the Catholic's accession to the throne; as well as Fernando de Talavera, *De vestir y de calzar* (1480), which recommended a dress code for women.

18. For a feminist interpretation of the concept of the "fourth estate," see Shahar, *The Fourth Estate*; on women in the sixteenth and seventeenth centuries, see Vigil, *La vida de las mujeres*, 5–17.

19. Hawkesworth, *Beyond Oppression*, 21–22; Wiesner, *Women and Gender*, 13.

20. Cohen, *Evolution*, 25.

21. Guevara's *Reloj de príncipes* (1529), cxliii, stated that women should not always be shut inside, although they should not walk about too freely. A Franciscan, he regularly visited the court of Charles V. His books were enormously popular and were translated and disseminated throughout Europe.

22. Fitzmaurice-Kelly, "Women in Sixteenth-Century Spain"; Vigil, *La vida*, 17. See Fray Martín de Córdoba, *Jardín de las nobles doncellas* (1542) as an example of a treatise praising female virtues. Christine de Pisan (1364–1430?) is generally credited with beginning a four-century-long tradition of select literate elite women who defended women's position against male defamation and subjugation and spoke out against this mistreatment. See Kelly, "Early Feminist Theory."

23. Fitzmaurice-Kelly, "Women in Sixteenth-Century Spain," 557–61.

24. Juan Luis Vives's *Libro llamado* included a discussion of seclusion as a desired virtue, particularly for doncellas, or unmarried, virginal girls, but he rarely employed the term "recogimiento" to express this concept.

25. Covarrubias Orozco, *Tesoro*, 313–14.

26. See Talavera's *De vestir y de calzar*.

27. Martínez de Toledo (1398–1466), *Archipreste*. See also Talavera, *Reforma de trages*.

28. "No sola ha de ser quieta en las cosas de afuera mas en lo interior del ánima ha que amar mucho la quietud y seguir el recogimiento del corazón todo lo que mas pudiere." Osuna, *Norte*, 183v. "Según la diversidad de los estados y variedad de los condiciones de los hombres puede elegir cada uno para sí lugar secreto para que allí en paz y en silencio huelgue pero es verdad que el principal secreto es, que el ánimo lançe de sí y de su morada todo cuydado humano y mundano, y toda cogitación vana e inpescible, y todas las cosas que le pueden inpedir de venir aquella adonde atiende," Garsías de Cisneros, *Exercitatorio*, ch. XXXIX.

29. "En su casa haga un lugar secreto donde recogida en sus pensamiento[s] llame y adore a Dios." Eiximenis, . . . *Carro de las donas*, III: iii.

30. "Si geres que dure tu castidad sigue y busca su fruto: que es tener la ayna entera y hazer la apartando la de las criaturas que la distrassen solo dios la recoge, tornando la a reintegrar, el qual por esto dize en la escritura que lo llamamos capitan de nuestra virginidad y el capitan quiere recoger su gente, porque toda virtud unida y recogida tiene mas fuerza que desparziada y derramada." Osuna, *Norte*, 30r.

31. Citing examples of noble women from the Bible, he said: "Graciosa como Ra-chael, casta como Judith, muy encerrada como Hester, que quiere dezir escondida porque guarde bien tu casa temerosa como Abigail, humilde como Ruth, piadosa-mente devota como Ana, diligente como Martha." On widows, he said: "Antigua-mente las viudas amaban a las yglesias estavan allí retraydas mas les cumple es vivir puerta cerrada y guardar sus casas y hazerse allí medio emparedadas cortando quanto mas pudieran qualquier comunicación." Osuna, *Norte*, 41r; 183v.

32. Fitzmaurice-Kelly, "Women in Sixteenth-Century Spain," 576.

33. King, *Women of the Renaissance*, 168–72.

34. Grendler, *Schooling*, 92–102; King, "The Religious Retreat."

35. Guevara, *Reloj de príncipes*, ch. xxvii; Also cited in Fitzmaurice-Kelly, "Women in Sixteenth-Century Spain," 561.

36. It was probably written around 1396 but published in Barcelona in 1495. His advocacy of female education may be the result of close commercial and cultural ties between the kingdom of Aragon and Italy. See Eiximenis's *Lo Llibre de les dones*. A Spanish translation, published in 1542 and called *Carro de las donas*, plagiarized passages from Vives's *Instrucción de la mujer cristiana*, and invented new ones. Twenty-one chapters were added to the original six from the Catalan text. See Fitzmaurice-Kelly, "Vives and the 'Carro de las Donas.'"

37. Bergmann, "The Exclusion of the Feminine," 124–36.

38. Vives, *Instrucción*, 21–31; Ortega Costa, "Spanish Women," 90.

39. His dialogues "Puerperio" and "El abad y la erúdita" give clear examples of this. Vigil, *La vida*, 45; Bataillon, *Erasmo*, I: 298–300. Melquíades Andrés Martín notes that the treatise *Exercitatorio de la vida espiritual* by Garsías de Cisneros (1500) antedated both Luther and Erasmus in advocating women as active participants in religion. See Andrés Martín, "Pensamiento teológico," III: 2, 333.

40. One of the earliest documented recogimientos dates from 1292 in Seville: "Un recogimiento de mugeres virtuosas que se aplicaban a doctrinar niñas." See Miura Andrades, "Formas de vida religiosa femenina," 144. On Cisneros's foundations, see Quintanilla y Mendoza, *Archetypo de virtudes*, 189 (copy at BLAC).

41. Her bound letters on illuminism, or alumbrismo, were confiscated when she was arrested by the Inquisition. See Cazalla, *Proceso*, 91, n. 6; 95, n. 55. María de Cazalla said acerbically, "Mas sy por leer una Epístola en romançe se oviese de ynputar a delito o se oviese de dezir que predicavan, pocas mugeres avríe devotas o que supiesen leer que no fuesen notadas desto," *Proceso*, 200. See also idem, 43, 55, 228. See also Alcalá, "María de Cazalla." Educated women often feigned illiteracy to escape prosecution or condemnation, See Kagan, *Lucrecia's Dreams*, 23–24.

42. She recognized that preaching was forbidden, but stressed that no law prohib-ited women from writing and reading about spiritual matters among themselves. She

considered the beata Isabel de la Cruz as important a spiritual authority as Saint Paul. Isabel de la Cruz, considered to be the mother of alumbrismo, was a Franciscan tertiary.

43. When the edict against the alumbrados appeared in 1525, she quoted passages from his writings but did not directly cite Erasmus, See Bataillon, *Erasmo*, I: 210. A later witness stated that María "lo tiene por evangelio y no querría otro se leyese ni predicase ni trasladase, sino él y que algunos *Coloquios* hizo ella volver en romançe, para dar a cierta persona y le oyó dezir que Erasmo se avía de canonizar." *Proceso*, 170. After 1527, his books were translated and disseminated throughout Spain; Bataillon, *Erasmo*, 279ff.

44. Aristotle believed this. Córdoba, *Jardín*, 203, claimed that women are more devout than men and they are formed from nobler material. See also Perry, *Gender and Disorder*, 24.

45. For an overview on holy women throughout early modern Europe, see Po-Chia Hsia, *The World of Catholic Renewal*, ch. 9, "Holy Women, Beatas, Demoniacs." See also Muñoz Fernández, *Beatas y santas neocastellanas*, 19–49.

46. Terciaries were lay women or men who belonged to a Third Order of the regular clergy. They were not subject to the strict rules (particularly enclosure) of the regular clergy.

47. José María Miura Andrade argues that beatas and emparedadas were a well-established tradition long before their spiritual flowering between 1530 and 1570 as Melquiades Andrés Martín has suggested. See idem, "Formas de vida religiosa," 146. By the mid–fourteenth century beaterios were reported in Seville. They continued to be founded in the sixteenth and seventeenth centuries; see Avellá Cháfer, "Beatas y beaterios," 100, 118–121. Beatas received papal authority on 7 October 1452 to join the Carmelite Order; see Steggink, "Beaterios y monasterios carmelitas," 150. The earliest known Dominican beaterio in Avila is cited in documents around 1460. Many became monasteries after 1452 when Nicolas V, in his bull *Cum Nulla* placed beaterios under canonical rule. González y González, *El Monasterio*, I: 42–43.

48. The Council of Trent emphasized female monastic enclosure; the papal bull issued afterward extended this requirement to terciaries or beatas.

49. Quintanilla y Mendoza, *Archetypo*, III, 96.

50. On his patronage of holy women like the famous Dominican beata Sor María de Santo Domingo, the Beata de Piedrahita, see Bilinkoff, "A Spanish Prophetess," 30ff; Bataillon, *Erasmo y España*, I: 49; Saínz Rodríguez, *La siembra mística*, 28, 35–36, 53. On the influence of Catherine of Siena in Spain, see Jiménez de Cisneros, *Obra de las epístolas* (copy at NL); and Huerga, *Santa Catalina de Siena*.

51. On the Beata de Piedrahita, see Bilinkoff, "A Spanish Prophetess," 21–34; Meseguer Fernández, "El período fundacional (1478–1517)," I: 360–61. On the influence of extraordinary women on lay spirituality, see Pérez Villanueva, "La Crisis del Santo Oficio (1621–1700)," I: 1090–91.

52. Bilinkoff, "A Spanish Prophetess," 27; Bataillon, "L'Iñiguiste et la beata," 65.

53. On Isabel's patronage of beatas in general, see Gómez Canedo, *La educación*, 110. On Isabel's donation to a beaterio in Espinar in 1503, see AGS, Casa Real (Obràs y Bosques), Leg. 3, fol. 517; to the Dominican Beaterio of Fajardas in Medina del Campo in 1504, Leg. 3, fols. 385, 414; to the beatas of Santa María de los Nieves in Córdoba, ten thousand maravedis in March 1504, Leg. 3, fol. 338.

54. AGS, Casa Real (Obras y Bosques), Leg. 2, fols. 118, 242, 1502. In 1502, Vitoria was paid quite substantial sums (thirty reales on one occasion and ten thousand maravedis on another, within the same year), "para algunas cosas de su servicio de la Reyna." Seven years later, she was still on the household payroll. See idem, Leg. 7, fol. 618, 1509.

55. For instance, in 1508, the provincial, Tomás de Matienzo prohibited the beata María de Santo Domingo from entering convents and having contact with other holy women, "donde se debe evitar el trato con mujeres, y que éstas pretendan intervenir en asuntos de reforma, pues son cosas que tocan a los prelados, no a las mujeres, cuya cabeza es el varón." Beltrán de Heredia, *Historia de la reforma*, 73.

56. She is reported to have said that "estando en el acto carnal con su marido estava más allegada a Dios que si estoviese en la más alta oraçion del mundo." *Proceso*, 33. See also ibid., 31, 64. Marriage over the monastic life was espoused by Juan Luis Vives and Erasmus. Other theologians were not able to resolve their own doubts about the value of the monastic life over secular piety. On the ambivalence of her position as a holy woman / woman who has given birth, María said, "[If] it were so evil to give birth, then God would have removed this vituperation. Birth does not prove or disprove faith; it is the intention from within that matters"; *Proceso*, 227. The beguines advocated education for men and women, mysticism, and the expression of female spirituality in society, through charitable works, see McDonnell, *The Beguines and Beghards*; Devlin, "Feminine Lay Piety," 184, 191; *Meister Eckhart and the Beguine Mystics*.

57. "Es común decir en el pueblo, si a uno que le veen recogido y virtuoso y se casa: mira, por v[uest]ra vida, hulano es santo y se casa, confía destos santos; hulana es sancta y pare." *Proceso*, 86.

58. McKendrick and MacKay, "Visionaries and Affective Spirituality," 94–95; Giles, "Francisca Hernández."

59. See Márquez, *Los alumbrados*, Appendix I, "Edicto de los alumbrados de Toledo (23 de septiembre de 1525)," 273–83; Andrés Martín, "Pensamiento teológico," vol. III–2, 343–53. The Inquisition thought various theological traditions had directly influenced alumbrismo; namely, the Beguines, the Brethren of the Common Life, and Lutheranism. On the beatas, see Longhurst, "La beata Isabel de la Cruz"; and Ortega Costa, "Spanish Women," 92–93.

60. See Beltrán de Heredia, "La Beata de Piedrahita," which differs from the position taken by Bernardino Llorca in "La beata de Piedrahita." See also Andrés Martín, *La teología española*, II: 153–54; Bataillon, *Erasmo y España*, I: 199–200. On the influence of María de Santo Domingo's *Libro* on María de Cazalla, see *Proceso*, 95, n. 55.

61. Various studies have interpreted the diverse expressions of postconquest native cultures in New Spain. Three of the more influential authors are Farriss, *Maya Society*; Gruzinski, *La colonización de lo imaginario*; and Lockhart, *The Nahuas after the Conquest*.

62. AGS, Patronato Real, Leg. 68, Docs. 47, 48, 14/X/1501 for a substantial donation made by the king and queen to the church-schools (*yglesias-colegiales*). See also Garrida Aranda, *Moriscos e indios*, who sees similarities in Crown policy between Granada and New Spain.

63. "[J]unto con las dichas iglesias una casa en que todos los niños que hubiere en cada una de las dichas poblaciones, se junten cada día dos veces, para que allí el dicho capellán los muestre a leer y a escribir y santiguar y signar y la confesión y el Paternos-

ter y el Avemaría y el Credo y Salve Regina." *Instrucción para el gobernador y los oficiales sobre el gobierno de las Indias,* Alcalá de Henares, 20/III/1503 and Zaragoza, 29/III/1503, CDFS, I: 11. Also cited in Kobayashi, *La educación,* 218.

64. Cardinal Cisneros commented upon the conversion of moriscos called *elches* (those forcibly baptized), between 1499 and 1501, when more than twenty thousand were baptized, Quintanilla y Mendoza, *Archetypo,* 55–56. See also Baudot, *La pugna,* 20–23; Garrido Aranda, *Moriscos e indios,* 35. A conflict over conversion policies and ecclesiastical jurisdiction with Archbishop Talavera forced the Franciscans to leave Granada and go to Extremadura, where, fortunately, they were able to garner more support for their spiritual projects.

65. His evangelical fervor included a desire to teach the "Barbary moors"; Mendieta, *Historia eclesiástica,* Libro III, ch. 8. Both the extraordinary enthusiasm and pride in the nobility of their mission to New Spain and their efforts among the moriscos in Spain were praised in a letter from the Franciscans in New Spain to Charles V more than fifty years later: "[No] dexaremos de dezir una cosa, aunque sea en nuestra propia estimación, que cuando se ganó el Reino de Granada los primeros ministros que aquella iglesia tuvó fueron los religiosos de nuestra orden, e comenzaron a plantar la fe, con gran fundamento de vida y doctrina, y después que la codicia pusó clérigos alzaron los religiosos la mano de ellos, y ya sabrá vuestra alteza lo que han aprovechado en la cristiandad, pues se están tan moros como el primer día." 20/XI/1555, Provincial and other friars to the Consejo de Indias, cited in Garrido Aranda, *Moriscos e indios,* 36. See also Brading, *The First America,* 103–4.

66. In Granada, secular clerics were entrusted with educating children, so that perhaps later in the sixteenth century (with the Tridentine reforms) they became more aware of this gap. See Garrido Aranda, *Moriscos e indios,* Apéndice V, 125–27, "Orden que se tiene en el catecismo y doctrina de los moriscos de este arzobispado" [n.d.], which states that those of the female sex, while more difficult to teach, should be given guidance before confession and gathered together for instruction within their parish.

67. Apparently, Franciscans in Santo Domingo instructed only the sons of caciques, which leads one to believe that the education of girls occurred on a systematic basis only once they arrived at New Spain; Gómez Canedo, "Aspectos característicos," 446.

68. Erasmus spent time at the University of Louvain. While Gante did not know Erasmus personally, he had read his writings. See Chávez, *Fray Pedro de Gante,* 49–71; de la Torre Villar, "Fray Pedro de Gante." See Pedro de Gante's letter to Emperor Charles V describing his educational experiences: Pedro de Gante to Charles V, 31/X/1532, *Cartas de Indias,* 52.

69. The chronicler Gerónimo de Mendieta, writing in the latter half of the sixteenth century, also valued female education and praised Gante's efforts in this regard; Mendieta, *Historia eclesiástica,* Lib. III, ch. 52. King, *Women of the Renaissance,* 169, mentions a mixed school in Flanders run by the Beguines in the fifteenth century. The Beguine movement flourished mainly in northern Europe and then proceeded southward to Provence and across the Pyrenees into Catalonia by the beginning of the fourteenth century. Aragonese and Valencian beguines influenced the foundation of beaterios in other Spanish kingdoms. Rodrigo Albornoz, the accountant (*contador*) responsible for paying the clergy's salaries, suggested to Emperor Charles V that "[p]odría Vuestra Magestad mandar para un monasterio de mugeres en que se instru-

yen las hijas de señores principales y sepan la feé y aprendan á hazer cosas de sus manos y quien las tenga en orden y concierto hasta las casar, como hazen á las beguinas en Flandes." Letter to Charles V, 15/XII/1525, DI, XIII, 70.

70. Apparently, Moctehzuma I instated ordinances and rules to this effect, Durán, *Historia de las Indias*, II, ch. 26, 213.

71. Ibid., I, ch. 2, 22ff.

72. Hellbom, *La participación cultural*, 129–30; Kellogg, "The Woman's Room," 568–69. Toribio de Benavente (also known as Motolinia), *Historia de los indios*, trat. I, ch. 9, no. 107. Torquemada, *Monarquía indiana*, II: 221, says that girls dedicated to *ichpochcalli*, the house of the gods, did not always live communally, whereas those of *calmécac* did. Others dedicated themselves to temple activities out of penitence or for disciplinary reasons; Kobayashi, *La educación*, 104–6. Some were designated at birth to sweep and care for the incense vessels in the temple once they reached adulthood. On this subject, see the extract from Fernando de Alva Ixtlilxóchitl's chronicle in Escalante, ed. *Educación e ideología*, 45–46; Alberti Manzanares, "Mujeres sacerdotisas aztecas."

73. Martín de Valencia to Charles V, Guatitan, 17/XI/1532, *Cartas de Indias*, 56; *Códice franciscano*, 57. See also Pedro de Gante to Charles V, 31/X/1532, *Historia de la Iglesia*, II: 200. The students came from the *pipiltzin* class, but poor Nahua girls *de buena conducta* were also accepted. This policy was completely modified between 1536 and 1538 when the recogimientos began accepting all girls, Muriel, *La sociedad novohispana*, 73.

74. Zumárraga to Charles V, 1529, in García Izcazbalceta, *Zumárraga*, II, 199. The main one was in Texcoco, with others in Otumba, Tepeapulco, Huejotcingo, Tlaxcala, Cholula, Coyoacán, and most probably in Chalco, Xochimilco, Cuauhtitlán, Tehuacán, and Tlalmanalco; Gómez Canedo, *La educación*, 130. See also Ortega, "Las primeras maestras," 376. The main recogimiento in Texcoco was called the Colegio de la Madre de Dios; Muriel, *La sociedad novohispana*, 64–67.

75. According to Mendieta in his *Historia eclesiástica*, Libro IV, ch. 16, only boys learned to read and write, but Sahagún stated that "muchas de ellas supieron leer y escribir"; Gomez Canedo, *La educación*, 126; Kobayashi, *La educación*, 285–86; García Icazbalceta, "La instrucción pública," *Obras*, I: 183. On Nahua converts serving as teachers, see Zumárraga to Charles V, 27/VIII/1529, In *Zumárraga*, 199. In a letter written in 1531 to Friar Matías Vueinssens in France, Martín de Valencia said: "Las mujeres son de mucha honestidad y tienen naturalmente una mujeril vergüenza. Sus confesiones (en especial las de las mujeres) son de increíble pureza y de una nunca oída claridad"; Mendieta, *Historia eclesiástica*, Lib. V, pt. 1, ch. 15. See also Lib. IV, ch. 16. In a letter to Charles V in 1532, Pedro de Gante commented upon the strict enclosure (recogimiento) of the five hundred to six hundred boys they taught each day, Gante to Charles V, 31/X/1532, *Cartas de Indias*, 52. Writing in 1576, Sahagún said that the strict discipline employed by the Franciscans recalled the Nahua religious instruction for the calmécac, Sahagún, *Historia general*, III: 161.

76. Gómez Canedo, *La educación*, 98; Muriel, *La sociedad novohispana*, 56.

77. Mendieta, *Historia eclesiástica*, Lib. IV, ch. 30. The girls were taught "con la doctrina cristiana, los oficios mujeriles de las españolas, y manera de vivir honesta y virtuosamente." Zumárraga believed that once educated, women would teach their husbands and children. Zumárraga to Emperor Charles, 25/XI/1536, García Icazbal-

ceta, *Zumárraga*, IV, 125, 127; Zumárraga to Bishops, 30/XI/1537, *Zumárraga*, III, 107–8, 130–31. At this time, women of all backgrounds were encouraged to occupy themselves in "oficios mujeriles" because word had reached Spain that "las mugeres nobles de Mexico vivía con sobrada ociosidad." González Dávila, *Teatro eclesiástico*, I: 37–38. Empress Isabel had sent an edict in 1530 encouraging all "noble" women, Spanish and Nahua, to spin and weave with linen she provided. See Méndez, *Book of Bodily Exercises*, pt. 2, ch. 9, 43; García Icazbalceta, *Bibliografía mexicana*, 228. On teacher's salaries, see Ortega, "Las primeras maestras," 377.

78. They may have been the *ichpochtlayacanqui*, or leaders of young girls, who had served as teachers in the temples. Kellogg, "The Woman's Room," 566; Mendieta, *Historia eclesiástica*, book IV, ch. 16.

79. Ortega, "Las primeras maestras," 265, 268. *Emparedamiento* is a medieval term referring to institutions that provided asylum for both religious and secular women. Most frequently, they were constructed as an annex to the exterior wall of a parish church. They were not subject to canonical rule, but nonetheless, women living there made strict vows of chastity and lived under extremely spartan conditions. The earliest known reference to an emparedamiento is in Gonzalo de Berceo's "La Vida de Santa Oría," in which he described the self-imposed enclosure of a woman named Oría, who lived in a small cell with two or three openings that allowed her to receive food, the sacraments, and a minimal amount of light; idem, *Obras completas*. Emparedamientos were popular throughout the fourteenth and fifteenth centuries. By 1500 one could be found in virtually every Andalucian parish; Miura Andrades, "Formas de vida religiosa," 144–45. The terms "beaterio" and "emparedamiento" were used synonymously during the sixteenth century.

80. Motolinia, *Historia de los indios*, trat. III, ch. 15. "Sabed que con deseo de servir a Nuestro Señor e industriar en las cosas de nuestra santa fe católica a las indias naturales de esa tierra, e a instancia e ruego nuestro, pasan a ella dos religiosas emparedadas de la ciudad de Salamanca, y la una de ellas lleva dos sobrinas suyas. Y para donde estén ellas y las naturales de esa tierra que recogieren, es nuestra voluntad de les mandar hacer una casa e monasterio en la dicha ciudad de México," Royal decree, Empress Isabel to the Audiencia, 4/II/1530, Torquemada, *Monarquía indiana*, II, libro V, ch. 9, 356. She wanted one thousand donzellas to be instructed in the Catholic faith; *Teatro eclesiástico de México*, I: 37. Zamora, "Contenido franciscano," cites documents from the series México, Leg. 1088, corresponding to the years 1529 and 1530 and describing the selection and preparations of the beatas' voyage to New Spain and Isabel's active participation in this process. Another important source, Ortega, "Las primeras maestras," 264–65, includes transcriptions of royal decrees issued by Empress Isabel to this effect in 1530. See also CDI, XLI: 113–19. Two of the other beatas were Juana Graciano and Elena de Medrano, a Franciscan terciary who professed in the Convent of Santa Isabel de Salamanca; Ana de Mesa and Luisa de San Francisco were from Seville, "Contenido franciscano," 39; Muriel, *La sociedad novohispana*, 59–60. Several traveled with daughters or young nieces.

81. Gómez Canedo, *La educación*, 107–8.

82. Mendieta, *Historia eclesiástica*, Lib. IV, ch. 16, "[A]sí estas beatas ó matronas han servido y ayudado en muchas cosas en el ministerio de la Iglesia para utilidad de las almas . . . de enseñar la doctrina cristiana y otras oraciones y devociones que ellas deprendieron, á las mozas y á otras mujeres que no las sabían, y en adestrar como

madres y guiar las confradías que tienen." He referred, in glowing terms, to one particular "devotísima india" named Ana de la Cruz.

83. Royal decree, Isabel to Zumárraga, "Sobre que no visiten las beatas que enseñan a las indias, los religiosos de San Francisco," 27/XI/1532, *Un cedulario mexicano*, 27. She repeated the order in 1534, Isabel to Audiencia, Madrid, 28/XI/1534, *Un cedulario mexicano*, 38.

84. Isabel to Audiencia, Madrid, 27/XI/1532, *Un cedulario mexicano*, 28, at the bequest of the beata Juana Velázquez.

85. Charles V to Audiencia, Toledo, 21/V/1534, *Un cedulario mexicano*, 35–36. See also Gómez Canedo, *La educación*, 115. Muriel, *La sociedad novohispana*, 69–70, lists six single and two married women: Elvira Díaz de Olmedilla, María Ramírez, Juana Rodríguez, Magdalena de Urbina, Isabel Martínez, Gerónima Valmaseda, Juana Guerra, and Elena de Loyola.

86. Zumárraga to Charles V, México, 25/XI/1536, García Icazbalceta, *Zumárraga*, IV: 127–29. This contrasts markedly with Empress Isabel's continued enthusiasm for the project. One month earlier she had written, "También he holgado de lo que decís que hay grandes congregaciones de niñas y muchachas hijas de caciques y principales en ocho o diez casas de a trescientas y cuatrocientas en cada una que aprenden y dicen muy bien la doctrina cristiana y horas de nuestra Señora, como monjas a sus tiempos, en tono, y que vienen a oírlas sus padres y que doctrinadas y enseñadas las que tienen edad las casáis con los muchachos que así criais, y visto lo que me suplicáis mandé proveer a las beatas y ministras que enseñan estas indias alguna limosna para sus necesidades y enfermedades." 3/IX/1536; Empress to Zumárraga, *Un cedulario mexicano*, 42. Empress Isabel continually insisted that a convent for the beatas be constructed in Mexico City, but her wish was not realized; Isabel to Audiencia, 27/XI/1532, Madrid, *Un cedulario mexicano*, 26–27.

87. Zumárraga to Bishops of Mexico, 30IX/1537, García Icazbalceta, *Zumárraga*, III: 106–7.

88. Zumárraga to Charles V, México, 25/XI/1536, García Icazbalceta, *Zumárraga*, IV: 127–29; Instructions from Juan de Zumárraga to friars Juan de Oseguera and Cristóbal de Almazán, s.f., *Zumárraga*, IV: 243. On 30 November 1537, he wrote a joint petition with the other bishops of New Spain to the emperor requesting approval for a convent of Franciscan nuns, so that the indigenous women "serían enteros cristianos . . . y tomarían doctrina de la honestidad y recogimiento de las dichas monjas, y sus padres las darían de mejor voluntad que las dan en estos monasterios, donde no hay esa guarda, ni encerramiento, ni paredes altas"; García Icazbalceta, *Zumárraga*, III: 107. See also *Un cedulario mexicano*, 44–69.

89. The title of the well-known book by Lewis Hanke. See also his article "The Contribution of Bishop Zumárraga"; Greenleaf, *Zumárraga and the Mexican Inquisition*, 26–41.

90. He patronized the Beatas of Santa Isabel in Durango and several female family members belonged to their order. These beatas offered shelter to his nieces and other women who could not marry properly and even provided Zumárraga with teachers for the schools in New Spain; *Zumárraga and his Family*, xv.

91. See Zumárraga, *Doctrina breve muy provechosa* (JCB), which says: "[T]hey also participate in this specie of idolatry: the business of the witches whom they say there are in our land: and they have been condemned and burned. And in the village of Du-

rango where I was born, there was another heretic called Amboto or beatas who said they lived on charity. A bad heretic friar of our Order by the name of Allonso Puertio took advantage of a lot of people: especially simple women: and of some and of others they said they roamed at night from village to village dancing about."

92. Valencia consulted with the Beata del Barco de Avila for divinatory purposes before setting forth on his spiritual mission. Maravall, "La utopía político-religiosa," 218. His biographer, Francisco Jiménez, was careful to distinguish his form of "arrobamiento" from hers.

93. Ortega Costa, "Spanish Women," 97.

94. Bataillon, *Erasmo y España*, II: 819–27; Greenleaf, *Zumárraga and the Mexican Inquisition*, 38–40.

95. *Un cedulario mexicano*, 78, Charles V to Provincial of San Francisco, Valladolid, 23/VIII/1538, "Decís que os parece cosa provechosa y muy necesaria para la instrucción de las hijas de los naturales que haya en esa ciudad de México un monasterio de monjas profesas, de la manera que están en estos reinos. Acá ha parecido que por agora no debe haber en las Indias monasterio de monjas, y así he mandado que no se haga ninguno." Also cited in *Un desconocido cedulario*, 122. Despite royal disapproval, the first convent in the Americas, La Concepción de la Madre de Dios, was established in Mexico City in 1540–41; Muriel, *Conventos*, 36–37.

96. On the pitfalls in interpreting Nahua "reality" from postconquest chronicles, see Gruzinski, *La colonización de lo imaginario*, 11.

97. See soldier/chronicler Bernal Díaz del Castillo's description of the "house of enclosure" in Tenochtitlán, *Historia verdadera*, ch. XCII, 195. For the description of Fray Agustín de Vetancurt, see Escalante, ed., *Educación*, 49.

98. The chronicle of the "Anonymous Jesuit" also described women participating in processions in the Tahuantinsuyo in a similar fashion. See Manzanares Alberti, "Una institución exclusivamente femenina," 153–90.

99. Motolinía, *Historia de los indios*, trat. I, ch. 9, no. 111: "[A] las espaldas de los principales templos había una sala aparte de mujeres, no cerrada, porque no acostumbraban puertas, pero honestas y muy guardadas; las cuales servían a los templos por votos que habían hecho."

100. "Instrucción dada por Don Fray Juan de Zumárraga a Fray Juan de Oseguera y Fray Cristóbal de Almazán, como procuradores al Concilio Universal," s.d., García Icazbalceta, *Zumárraga*, IV: 242, described caciques taking young girls from their parents: "[Y] ellos las encierran y ponen donde no vean sol ni luna, no las dejando jamás salir ni hablar a nadie ni oír doctrina ni recibir baptismo hasta que viejas las despiden." He instructed the beata, Luisa de San Francisco, to remove the girls from these homes in order to instruct them properly. See also Zumárraga to Charles V, México, 1536, *Documentos inéditos*, 61–62; Zumárraga to Juan de Samano, the king's secretary, 20/XII/1537, in *Cartas de Indias*, 169: "[Y] un monasterio grande en que quepan mucho número de niñas hijas de indios, tomadas á sus padres desde seys o siete años abaxo, para que sean criadas, doctrinadas é yndustriadas en el dicho monasterio cerrado, porque es asy la condición y costumbre de los indios, que tienen comúnmente todos los principales á sus mujeres e hijas en estrecho ençerramiento, y asy las darían de mejor gana que las dan."

101. Sahagún, *Florentine Codex*, book VI, ch. 18, 19; Kartunnen and Lockhart, *The*

Art of Nahuatl Speech, has several examples of old women giving advice to young girls, 111, 172.

102. León-Portilla, *The Aztec Image of Self,* 192–93, trans. from Sahagún, *Florentine Codex,* book VI, ch. 18.

103. Burkhart, *The Slippery Earth,* 150.

104. Ibid.

105. Ibid.

106. For an example, see Olmos, *Tratado de hechicerías;* and Baudot, "Fray Andrés de Olmos."

107. See Mathes, *The America's First Academic Library,* 56–63.

108. Baudot, *La pugna,* 169.

109. Sahagún, *Psalmodia Christiana,* 237–41.

110. This usage comes from Gruzinski, *La colonización de lo imaginario.*

111. Zumárraga even suggested hanging those caciques who refused to obey; Gomez Canedo, *La educación,* 121; Zumárraga to Council of Indies, 24/XI/1536, García Icazbalceta, *Zumárraga,* IV: 119–23.

112. Zumárraga to Juan de Samano, 20/XII/1537, in *Cartas de Indias,* 169–70; Zumárraga to Prince Philip, México, 2/VI/1544, García Icazbalceta, *Zumárraga,* IV: 177–78. Noble parents played a large role in selecting the marriage partners of their sons and daughters. See Sahagún, *Florentine Codex,* Lib. VI, ch. 23; López Austin, *The Human Body,* I: 301; Durán, *Historia de la Indias,* I, ch. 21, 190–91; Kellogg, "Cognatic Kinship and Religion," 667–68. Richard Trexler, "From the Mouths of Babes," 569, describes how, in 1554, a number of noble leaders protested the formation of a new nobility—in other words, boys who had been reared in the monasteries.

113. On the friars attitudes, see Zumárraga to Cap. de Tolosa, 12/VI/1531; González Dávila, *Teatro eclesiástico,* I: 43, Motolinía, *Historia de los indios,* trat. II, ch. 7.

114. León-Portilla, *Los franciscanos,* 39.

115. Gómez Canedo, *La educación,* 123; Kobayashi, *La educación,* 289–90. See also García Icazbalceta, *Zumárraga,* IV: 177–78, 205, 239.

116. Muriel, *La sociedad novohispana,* 75.

117. Zumárraga to Charles V, 17/IV/1540, García Icazbalceta, *Zumárraga,* III: 187–206, Donation of houses to the Hospital del Amor de Dios, 13/V/1541, ibid., 209–17; Instructions given by Juan de Zumárraga to friars Juan de Oseguera and Cristóbal de Almazán, s.f., ibid., IV: 231–45.

118. Greenleaf, *Zumárraga and the Mexican Inquisition,* 13–15, 36–37; Zumárraga to Prince Philip, México, 4/XII/1547, García Icazbalceta, *Zumárraga,* IV: 205.

119. Gómez Canedo, *La educación,* 123, 150–51; Zumárraga to Prince Philip, 1547, García Icazbalceta, *Zumárraga,* IV: 205.

120. For studies on the civil war period, see Fernández de Oviedo, *Historía general y natural de las Indias;* Hemming, *The Conquest of the Incas,* particularly, 210–13, on the siege of Cuzco.

121. Lowry, "Forging an Indian Nation," 59.

122. Varón, *La ilusión del poder,* 260. Don Gonzalo reported in 1559 that the altercations and cultural displacement had cost the lives of four thousand of his people, Rostworowski, "Dos probanzas," 125.

123. Varón, *La ilusión del poder,* 260.

124. On the description of houses of enclosure in Caxas, northern Peru, see Jérez, "Verdadera relación," 38. Later chroniclers Bernabé Cobo, the Anonymous Jesuit, and Antonio de la Calancha, made similar analogies in describing *acllahuasi*. See Alberti Manzanares, "La influencia económica," 557–58; "Una institución exclusivamente femenina"; and "Mujer y religión."

125. Cabello Balboa, *Miscelánea Antártica*, 348–49; Zuidema, *Inca Civilization*, 51–60. The highest rank were always Incas and considered the wives of the sun. Some were chosen as the Incas' secondary wives, and others were selected to be the wives of curacas; still others worked as servants or were chosen because of their ability to sing or play an instrument.

126. Hemming, *The Conquest of the Incas*, 32–33; Silverblatt, *Moon, Sun, and Witches*, 90–108.

127. Silverblatt, *Moon, Sun, and Witches*, 103.

128. When Hernando Pizarro arrived at Pachacamac he saw "casas de mujeres encerradas" in each village, some dedicated to the worship of the sun. Others housed women for the caciques, "que están recogidas de los caciques comarcanos, para cuando pasa el señor de la tierra sacan de allí las mejores para presentárselas; y sacadas aquéllas, meten otras tantas," Hernando Pizarro to Audiencia, *Los cronistas*, 259–60.

129. Alberti Manzanares, "La influencia económica," 583–84.

130. Vargas Ugarte, *Historia de la Iglesia*, I: 166–68, 213–16.

131. Puente Brunke, *Encomienda y encomenderos*.

132. On the construction of residences for Lima's early elite, see Lockhart, *Spanish Peru*, 107–8. See also Cobo, "Fundación de Lima," 305.

133. For New Spain, see Viceroy Antonio de Mendoza's account in Vasco de Puga, *Provisiones*, 293; García Icazbalceta, "El Colegio de San Juan de Letrán," in: *Obras*, II: 427–34; Gómez Canedo, *La educación*; Gonzalbo Aizpuru, *Las mujeres en la Nueva España*; and Martin, *Los vagabundos*.

134. In Mendoza's "Relación" (1548), written to his successor, he suggested that the latter support the Colegio de la Caridad, founded specifically for orphaned mestizas, Vasco de Puga, *Provisiones*, 293; CDI, VI: 488. For a list of the first seven mestiza and (one) Spanish schoolgirls, see Muriel, *La sociedad novohispana*, 138. Although founded for mestizas, a preference for Spanish girls was instated in the revised 1550 constitution. Eventually, only Spanish girls were permitted to enter. See "Constituciones para el colegio de niñas de Nuestra Señora de la Caridad," in Gonzalbo, *El Humanismo*, 125–36.

135. The reformer Juan de Avila's program of "Doctrina Christiana" established an educational system for children and adults later taken up by the Society of Jesus. Avila did little to address female education. See Coleman, "Moral Formation."

136. Kobayashi, *La educación*, 143.

137. In reality, a major effort to found schools for girls did not begin until the eighteenth century, and yet, by 1850 more than 86 percent of Spanish women were still illiterate, Kagan, *Students and Society*, 27–29.

138. Several lukewarm attempts were made, including a royal decree issued in 1612, *Recop.*, Lib. I, tít. III, ley xviiii, "Que se hagan y conserven Casas de Recogimiento en que se crien las Indias," Philip III, 10/VI/1612.

139. Pérez de Valdivia, *Aviso*. See Alison Weber's intelligent analysis of Pérez de Valdivia's treatise in "Between Ecstasy and Exorcism." On beatas in Seville in the seventeenth-century, see Perry, *Gender and Disorder*, 97–104, 109–17.

140. Indigenous beatas probably followed the Nahua tradition; Sahagún, *Florentine Codex*, VI, ch. 39; Mendieta, *Historia eclesiástica*, Lib. IV, ch. 16.

141. Whereas the Council of Trent (1546–63) (Session 25, Chapter 5, items 16–17), and the Nueva Recopilación de Leyes (1568) (lib. 7, tít. 27, ley 5) reinforced the notion that all religious women should remain secluded, not until the *motu propio* of Pope Pius V (1566), restated in the Council of Toledo (1582) (XLVI), were beatas ordered to abide by Third Order canon law, thus requiring them to be cloistered like nuns, and restricting public spiritual activities. The church wished to phase beatas out of existence.

142. Andrés Martín, *Los recogidos*, 19.

143. Nalle, *God in La Mancha*, 98–99.

144. Nietzsche challenged the obsessive historical pursuit of origins in the attempt to locate some essential primordial truth. See Nietzsche, "Preface" to idem, *On the Genealogy of Morals*, 15–23. See also Michel Foucault's interpretation of Nietzsche's argument in "Nietzsche, Genealogy and History," 78, 83–84.

145. Koselleck, *Futures Past*, 76.

Chapter 2: Lost Between Two Worlds

1. He said of them, "[T]odos los que fueron assí desterrados perecieron en el destierro, que ninguno dellos bolbió a su tierra"; Garcilaso de la Vega, *Historia del Perú*, III: 245. See also the elegantly written rendition in Brading, *The First America*, 255, 268–271. The year 1572 was also significant because Viceroy Toledo ordered the capture and execution of the last Inca, Manco Inca.

2. Chimpu Ocllo was the granddaughter of Túpac Yupanqui and the daughter of Huallpa Túpac Yupanqui, the younger brother of Huayna Cápac.

3. Varner, *El Inca*, 105–6.

4. See for example Francisco de Toledo's characterization in his letter to the king in 1574, cited in Levillier, *Don Francisco de Toledo*, I: 243–44.

5. For a recent study that examines the impact of the moral reformation of the poor in sixteenth-century Europe and its impact on colonial perceptions of the Indian, see Megged, "Poverty and Welfare."

6. Altman, *Emigrants and Society*, 150–55. Perry, *Gender and Disorder*, 52, notes that once municipal officials began to perceive that unwed mothers and illegitimate children presented a potential charitable burden, they began to penalize single mothers more heavily for immoral conduct. In the wake of post-Tridentine reforms many were henceforth labeled as "wayward" or "marginal" women.

The rate of recorded illegitimacy in sixteenth-century Spain varied tremendously from region to region, but was no doubt under-represented statistically. After 1550, in Talavera the rate averaged between five and seven percent. Many were foundlings taken in by a midwife to be baptized. See González Muñoz, *La población de Talavera*. In the popular working-class parish of San Martín in Seville, the percentage of illegitimate children from 1550 to 1600 averaged 16 percent. Most were categorized as "hijo de Dios," "hijo de la Iglesia," "hijo de Dios y Santa María," or "hijo de la tierra." See García-Baquero López, *Estudio demográfico*, 107–13. The illegitimacy rate in Cáceres from 1560 to 1599 for hidalgos was 6 percent of all births and 3 percent of all taxpayers (*pecheros*). See Rodríguez Sánchez, *Cáceres*, 111.

7. Calvo, "The Warmth of the Hearth," 306. Altman, *Emigrants and Society*, 151, argues that at the beginning of the sixteenth century society was still fluid enough that illegitimate children could become the principal heirs, but the growing number of entails meant that the legal incorporation of illegitimate children into the family became less common throughout the century.

8. Lewin, "Natural and Spurious Children," 351–52, argues that "so-called bastardy could be converted into legitimacy." See also Altman, *Emigrants and Society*, 150–55.

9. On preconquest marital politics, see Silverblatt, *Moon, Sun, and Witches*; for the early colonial period, see Rostworowski, *Doña Francisca Pizarro*; Varón Gabai, *La ilusión del poder*, 248ff, 251ff. Varón argues that the Huaylas nobility actively sought marriage negotiations, albeit with the Incas or Spaniards, 252.

10. Concubinage (*barraganía*) was common in Spain. See Córdoba de la Llave, "Las relaciones extraconyugales." Konetzke, "Los mestizos en la legislación colonial," 120, cites an order that the governor of Santo Domingo, Nicolás Ovando, gave to promote mixed marriages. See also a letter written in 1539 by the bishop of Cuzco, Fray Vicente Valverde, to the same effect, ibid., 114. Even in the 1530s and 1540s officials were not in total agreement over policies toward intermarriage.

11. Garcilaso, *Historia general del Perú*, II: 113–14. Some did marry: Garcilaso de la Vega's father did not marry his mistress, Chimpu Ocllo (baptized Palla Isabel Yupanqui), but Juan de Betanzos, a principal chronicler, married Angelina Yupanqui. See Rosenblat, *La población indígena*, II: 82–87 for a listing of some of the key Peruvian conquerors, their concubines, and the names of their children. Apparently, of all the conquerors, only the hidalgo Alonso de Mesa married an Andean woman; Lockhart, *The Men of Cajamarca*, 229. When it seemed politically advantageous, Francisco Pizarro forced Inés Huaylas to marry a Spaniard of an inferior position; Varón, *La ilusión del poder*, 254.

12. Varner, *El Inca*, 107; Rubio Mañé, "Noticias de una hermana," 626, 630. I thank Magdalena Chocano for providing this reference.

13. Rosenblat, *La población indígena*, II: 87, whose source is Salvador de Madariaga's *Cuadro histórico de las Indias*. On the other hand, young Spanish women were often willing to marry decrepit, battle-scarred conquerors with the full intention, once their husbands died, of collecting the inheritance and securing a younger, more virile second husband. Contemporaries called this "to exchange an old pot for a new one," Varner, *El Inca*, 109. In fact, Garcilaso's stepmother employed this strategy; see Garcilaso, *Historia general del Perú*, I: 113–14. On the term "su india," see Harth-Terré, "El mestizaje y la miscegenación," 133: "*Su india* es la locución frecuente en el asiento del bautismo del jigo de un español habido en india. Y este significaba que era la concubina familiar. Y era *india* a diferencia de *criada*, o *moza*, cuando se trata de la mujer morena o de la española."

14. Kuznesof, "Ethnic and Gender Influences," 155, 159. Spanish-Nahua unions also occurred; see Carrasco, "Indian-Spanish Marriages."

15. Konetzke, "El mestizaje y su importancia en el desarrollo," 24. Some exceptions can be found. See the testimonies of two Spaniards who married their indigenous *compañeras* in the Yucatán when Charles V ordered that all encomenderos had to marry; Rubio Mañé, "Noticias de una hermana," 631, n. 9.

16. James Lockhart states that 95 percent of the first generation of mestizos were illegitimate; *Spanish Peru*, 167.

17. For this suggestion, see Mannarelli, "Sexualidad y desigualdades," I: 230. Additional research on this topic is needed.

18. Elizabeth Kuznesof argues that "until about 1570, gender as a social characteristic was stronger than race," and "the determination of race for the first five or six generations of Spanish Americans was substantially driven by gender"; idem, "Ethnic and Gender Influences," 156, 168. My research indicates that race is in fact a critical factor by 1550, and should be given equal consideration.

19. Hall, "Introduction," 4; Boyer, "Respect and Identity," 491–92; see also Cope, *The Limits*, who "unpacks" the significance and insignificance of racial categories in sixteenth- and seventeenth-century Mexico City. Also key to this discussion are articles by Cahill, "Colour by Numbers"; Kuznesof, "Ethnic and Gender Influences"; and Schwartz, "Colonial Identities."

20. On the social and economic variations within the Spanish world, see Lockhart, *Spanish Peru*, and *The Men of Cajamarca*. I agree with Stuart Schwartz's definition that class in the colonial period "refers to social hierarchies which are not necessarily based upon access and control of the means of production," "Colonial Identities," 196, n. 3.

21. In its strictest sense, "mestizo" meant "mixed"; see Covarrubias Orozco, *Tesoro*, 802, which defines "mestizo" as "el que es engendrado de diversas especies de animales; del verbo *misceo, -es*, por mezclarse." As a fiscal category, it signified exemption from paying tribute. See Stephens, *Dictionary*, 152–56, for various historical and contemporary interpretations of the term. Most of the meanings listed in this dictionary include definitions based on physical appearance and skin color.

22. CI, IV: 342; also cited in CDFS, I: 147, no. 80, Monzón, 3/X/1533; CDFS, I: 168, no. 93, Madrid, 17/VIII/1535.

23. DI, 152–53; Gómez Canedo, *La educación*, 221. In eighteenth-century Oaxaca, mestizo still remained synonymous with illegitimate; see Stephens, *Dictionary*, 156.

24. On the *comunero* rebellion, see Elliott, *Imperial Spain*, 151–59. Emma Solano Ruíz argued that concepts of "poor" and "poverty" as well as attitudes toward social assistance evolved differently in urban and rural areas in Spain. Epidemics, bad harvests, and a lack of access to cultivable land at the beginning of the sixteenth century forced migration to cities and may have exacerbated these differences; idem, "Aspectos de la pobreza," 353–55.

25. Vives was influenced by Luther, Zwingli, Thomas More, and other social reformers and dedicated his book to the city of Bruges, where he lived for some time. His ideas were, however, in part also based upon his experiences in Valencia, which had for centuries made special provisions to protect orphans and collect taxes for poor relief; see Tobriner, *A Sixteenth-Century Urban Report*, 19.

26. Domingo de Soto, *Deliberación*, ch. III. See also Jütte, *Poverty and Deviancy*.

27. A derivation of "coger" (recollere), one of its primary meanings was "juntar o congregar personas o cosas separadas o dispersas"; Martín, *Enciclopedia*, III: 3536, which cites two mid-sixteenth-century sources. See also Perceval, *A Dictionary*, 205r.

28. "Casa, cobertizo o corral de un pueblo, destinado a albergue de mendigos," Alonso, *Enciclopedia*, 3536.

29. Diego González Holguín's Quechua/Spanish dictionary included a definition of recoger as: "to gather together the poor in a home," 654.

30. Martin, *Los vagabundos*, 57–68.

31. Hernández Iglesias, *La beneficencia en España*, I: 13, 26–27, 165, 176–77, 254–55.

32. Vives wrote, "No aprenden solamente á leer y escribir, sino en primer lugar la piedad cristiana, y á formar juicio recto a las cosas"; Vives, *Tratado*, 118–19. In Valencia, St. Vincent Ferrer had established schools for orphans (often in béguinages) around 1410. In reality, only a handful of hospices or schools for foundling or underprivileged children existed in Spain prior to 1550. Schools and orphanages before 1550 included the Hospital de Santa Cruz in Toledo (founded 1504) to educate and raise orphans; the Colegio de las Once Mil Vírgenes in Salamanca for poor orphan girls (founded 1505); and, the Casa de Expósitos, a hospital in Santiago de Compostela (founded 1524). The foundation of charitable institutions increased dramatically, particularly during and after the reign of Philip II. See Jiménez Salas, *Historia*, 205, and in particular, the "Indice de Fundaciones del siglo XVI al siglo XVIII," 259–336.

33. Cohen, *Evolution*, 154.

34. Juan Luis Vives dedicated chapter 6 in his book *La mujer cristiana* to the ideal attributes of the doncella and her education. He had been influenced by the Catalan moralist Françesc de Eiximenis, who wrote the *Llibre de les Dones*. See also Córdoba, *El jardín de las nobles doncellas,* part II, ch. i; III, ch. iii; Mariló Vigil, *La vida,* 47.

35. Ruiz Martínez, "La moderación," 61.

36. Chastity was considered the highest virtue even among foundling girls. Vives said in *Socorro de los pobres* that girls should be educated toward "la modestia, sobriedad o templanza, cortesía, pudor y vergüenza y, lo principal de todo, guardar la castidad, persuadidas de que éste es el único bien de las mujeres."

37. Vives, *La mujer cristiana*, 64.

38. Bergmann, "The Exclusion of the Feminine," 124–36.

39. On violence and subversion, see Mannarelli, "Sexualidad y desigualdades," 225–48; Busto Duthurburu, "La mestiza del Capitán Hernando de Soto," 113–17. Soto's mestiza daughter, Doña Leonor Tocto Chimbo, remained in her parents' household until her father embarked for Spain, at which time she went to live with the famous Doña María de Escobar, "para que la enseñase en policía y en cosas de nuestra sancta fe," 114.

40. This chapter does not consider the legal, social and cultural relationship between single Indian mothers and their mestizo children in Lima. Further research is needed to explore the development of a matrifocal kinship system that resulted from the conquest. Karen Powers argues that scholars considering gender relations need to reconfigure the "women as victims" paradigm that permeates the historiographical literature on the sixteenth century. See Powers, "Gender and the Crucible of 'Conquest,'" 1–5.

41. "De aquestas mujeres hay las que bastan; aunque el lugar es tan grande, unas viven de su trabajo, y otras se meten en cosas graves; hay en éstas muchos lazos y nudos encubiertos. . . . Son mujeres de secreto, pues saben, cuando fulana se casa a título de doncella, si está cancelado el signo de su título." Deleito y Piñuela, *La mala vida,* 69. Vives mentions in *La mujer cristiana,* that the doncella should live in "apartamento," and "no debe ser violado jamás por 'aquellas dueñas de tocas largas reverendas,'" 38.

42. The tendency to raise illegitimate children in the household—whether of the hidalgo or lower classes—was also a common practice in Spain. See Altman, *Emigrants and Society*, 153. This is certainly the case with Francisco, Juan and Gonzalo Pizarros'

children; Lockhart, *The Men of Cajamarca*, 154, 174, 186. One of Francisco's sons by Angelina Yupanqui remained with his mother; idem, 154. The word "remediar" has a long history in Spanish religious tradition. Etymologically re-medeor signifies to cure an illness, especially those sicknesses within the soul. Nuestra Señora de los Remedios became the most popular cult of the Virgin in sixteenth-century Spain; Porres Alonso, "Advocación y culto," 4–5, 9–10.

43. Isabel Suárez Chimpu Ocllo, her new husband, Juan del Pedroche, as well as Francisca's mother, María Pilcosisa, most likely resided in the household also; Rubio Mañé, "Noticias," 626, 630, 632, 645; Varner, *El Inca*, 106–7.

44. Instances occurred in Spain of men being deceived and marrying young women no longer virgins. To allay any lingering doubt that a suitor might have, parents, concerned about family honor, drew up a notarized document attesting to the purity of the potential bride-to-be. The false doncella endured as a popular topic in Spanish literature from the sixteenth through the eighteenth centuries; see Deleito y Piñuela, *La mala vida*, 20.

45. The right of women to inherit encomiendas was never clearly expressed, but women in Peru did so. Not only Spanish women, but mestizas could, and did inherit from both their husbands and fathers. See *Recop.*, libro VI, ley II, tít., xi, 4–5/III/1552: "[C]uando falleciere alguno y dejase dos, tres o más hijos, o hijas, y el mayor que debiese suceder en los yndios entrase en Religión o tuviese otro impedimento, deberá pasar al segundo y assi consiguiente hasta acabar los varones; sucediendo lo mismo en las hijas por falta de aquéllos, y por la de unas y otras la mujer." For an application in New Spain, see CDFS, I: 251, 28/X/1548, Prince Philip to Audiencia of New Spain, which says that if a conqueror dies and leaves only a wife and daughters, he can distribute the fruits of the encomienda between them. This applied to illegitimate and legitimate daughters.

46. Puente Brunke, *Encomienda y encomenderos*, Cuadro I, "Encomenderos indios y mestizos," 33.

47. Lockhart, *Spanish Peru*, 6.

48. Zárate, *Historia del descubrimiento*, ch. 7, 467; Cieza de León, *Crónica del Perú: Primera parte*, ch. 71.

49. Cobo, "Historia," I: 53–54.

50. ibid., I: 53.

51. Lockhart, *Spanish Peru*, 151–52; Cook, *Demographic Collapse*, 151.

52. CI, Royal decree, 18/II/1549, Valladolid, 400. See also Ayala, *Diccionario*, IV, 729b, "Casados," and royal decrees to this effect dated 19/X/1544; 29/VII/1565; 10/V/1569; 29/VI/1579.

53. The quotation in the text comes from the Conde de Nieva to Philip II, 1561, Lima, CLG, I: 387. Authorities distinguished between "pobres vergonzantes" (the honest poor) and "pobres escandalosos" (the scandalous poor). The marqués de Cañete expressed his concern in a letter written in 1556: "[En] esta ciudad hallo que hay tantos pobres vergonzantes y la mayor con pasión y lástima en el mundo por que ansi en los que vienen de España como en las otras partes ocurren todos aqui y e sabido asi de Religiosos como de otras personas que es grande la necesidad pasan especialmente algunos que vienen con muchos hijos para remediar." AGI, Lima, 28-A, Marqués del Cañete to Philip II, Lima, 15/IX/1556, 6v. Viceroy Toledo (1569–81) expressed the sen-

timent that too many "poor" were living off the rich: "[L]os pobres escandalosos fuesen de mejor condición que los ricos para no hazer dellos justiçia por no tener con que seguirlos"; AGI, Lima 28-B, Lib. IV, Toledo to Philip II, Lima, 1/III/1572, fol. 424v.

54. CDFS, no. 196, Madrid, 19/XI/1551, Royal decree: "[Q]ue los españoles vagamundos asienten y se ocupen en oficios"; Conde de Nieva to Philip II, 16/VI/1561, "Con relación de las personas vagas y de mal vivir que enviaba a España," CLG, I: 386–87; and "De la instrucción del Virrey del Perú, que manda no consienta en aquella tierra españoles vagamundos y olgazanes, sino que sirvan o aprendan oficios, o los echen de la tierra," 1568, in CI, I: 423–24. These are only a few examples of social categories created to differentiate and distinguish colonists according to gender, class, and race at this time. The work of Ann Laura Stoler, "Rethinking Colonial Categories," 323, 331–34; and idem, "Sexual Affronts," 514–20, has been particularly useful in formulating my questions and methodology for this chapter.

55. Ayala, *Diccionario*, 748-B, "Peccados públicos," 1541, "Dando parte el Rey a Don Antonio de Mendoza, Virrey de Nueva España de ser informado que en aquella tierra muchas personas quando caminaban, assi por ella como por mar llevaban consigo mugeres de los naturales dando mal exemplo, de que Dios era deservido: le mando lo proveyese de manera que se excusase y hubiese toda honestidad, avisando de lo que determinase." See also CLG, I: 422–23, Conde de Nieva to the king, 4/V/1562, Lima, "Acerca de la conveniencia de perpetuar las encomiendas o repartimientos de indios," which argued that mestizos inheriting encomiendas on such a large scale would "constitute a danger to the tranquility of the Republic," also cited in Konetzke, "Los mestizos en la legislación colonial," 122–23. See also Konetzke, "El Mestizaje y su importancia," 220, which refers to a comment made by García Fernández de Torrequemada, the alguacil of Cuzco, about Spanish-native marriages.

56. Varner, *El Inca*, 105.

57. CDFS, I: 256, Royal Decree, 27/II/1549, Valladolid, "Que ningún mulato, ni mestizo, ni hombre que no fuere legítimo pueda tener indios, ni oficio real ní público"; Solórzano, *Política indiana*, libro III, cap. xix, 1–6; CDFS, I: 259, Valladolid, 1/VI/1549: "[P]ara que ningún mestizo que no sea vecino o hijo legítimo, pueda cargar indios"; Ots Capdequí, *El estado español*, 125–26. Encomenderos in New Spain had pressed the Crown to allow their illegitimate sons the right to inherit encomiendas, but had not been successful, DI, 110.

58. This subscribes to Linda Lewin's argument that inheritance laws in Brazil fluctuated as a reflection of changing notions about the role demography, patriarchal prerogatives, and the state played; Lewin, "Natural and Spurious Children," 352.

59. *Novíssima Recopilación*, part IV, tit. 5, leyes 5, 6, 7; part IV, tit. 19, ley 5; part VI, tit. 13, leyes 8, 9, 11. LL, Latin American mss. Peru, Actas Notariales, No. 753, Reconocimiento de una hija natural de Diego de Ovando, 1551. Fathers with no legitimate heir often legitimized their mestizo sons. See Varner, *El Inca*, 108, for several examples. See also Lockhart, *The Men of Cajamarca*, which provides examples of Sebastián de Benalcázar, 127; Francisco Pizarro, 154; Gonzalo Pizarro, 186; Diego de Maldonado, 222, all of whom legitimized or legally recognized some of their mestizo children. Some fathers recognized their mestizo children in their wills. See the case of the artisan Martín de Florencia in *The Men of Cajamarca*, 378–79.

60. Lockhart, *The Men of Cajamarca*, Francisco Pizarro, 154; Martín Pizarro, 418–19.

61. Ibid., 245.

62. See, for example, the case of Francisca Pizarro, Busto Duthurburu, "Una huérfana mestiza," 103–6. Born around 1535, she remained with her mother until 1548 when one of her dead father's relatives removed her from her mother's custody, 106.

63. To discourage abandonment, a law stated that the father could be absent from the household for only two years; *Novíssima Recopilación*, Libro 10, tit. 1. See also Lockhart, *Spanish Peru*, 168.

64. Domínguez Ortíz, "Delitos y súplicos," 26.

65. Lockhart, *Spanish Peru*, 165. This institution had medieval antecedents in Valencia and Zaragoza, but was further advanced by Philip II in 1577. The municipal council designated a person of upstanding moral character and financial solvency to act as a guardian to "la niñez desvalida," particularly orphans. His task was to search in hostals, plazas, butcheries, and homes for abandoned or mendicant children and to take them to an asylum specifically founded for them. Girls and boys were housed and educated in separate quarters; when they reached a certain age, they were put to work; Arco "Una notable institución," III: 189–202; Jiménez Salas, *Historia de la asistencia*, 135, 142, n. 47.

66. *Recop.*, libro 7, tit. 4, ley 4, cites royal decrees on educational policy passed in 1553, 1555, 1558, and 1569. See also CDFS, I, Royal decree, Valladolid, 3/X/1555, 333–34; CDI, Series II, vol. 22, tít. xvi, "Sobre los mestizos," 331–34.

67. Santo Tomás, *Lexicon*, 197.

68. Molina was, in fact, referring to the practice of forcibly congregating (recogiendo, or gathering together) Indians by the friars in New Spain in the immediate postconquest years to administer mass baptisms, Molina, *Vocabulario*, 102r.

69. The judges included Melchor Cano, Domingo de Soto, and Bartolomé de Carranza. The Council of the Indies had decided not to publish Sepúlveda's work, *Democrates secundus*, because it supported Indian slavery, and this debate brought the matter to a conclusion.

70. Busto Duthurburu, "La primera generación mestiza," 67–79.

71. Elite mestizos, particularly those in Cuzco, although not quite Spanish, still received differential treatment. The best-educated priests tutored Garcilaso and other aristocratic mestizo boys, and they hoped to impress Spanish culture upon what they saw as a new and extremely talented generation of young charges; Varner, *El Inca*, 103, 116ff. Juan de Cuéllar voluntarily undertook the instruction of these boys in 1552.

72. CDFS, I, doc. 235, Royal decree, 18/II/1555, 328–29. Domingo de Santo Tomás wrote: "[H]ay necesidad de dar horden en los hijos e hijas de los españoles e indias naturaleza desta tierra que son muchos . . . y andan como indios y entre los indios y si no se da horden como se haga una casa donde los varones se crien y se les enseñe doctrina y buenas costumbres, para que siendo de hedad para ello se pongan a oficios y no anden en perjuizio suyo y de la república perdidos y las niñas se recojan y no andan distraídas y perdidas, porque empiezan y a andado, asi los unos como los otros." Also cited in Vargas Ugarte, *Historia de la Iglesia*, I: 310.

73. AGN, Real Audiencia, Causas Civiles, Leg. 5, Cuad. 28, 1560, Autos promovidos por Elvira de Coca, hija y heredera de Sebastián de Coca.

74. Ayala, *Diccionario*, 740B, "mestizas," 2/XII/1578, "noticióse S.M. en las Provincias del Perú avía muchas a quienes sus Padres dejaron sus haciendas en confianza de personas particulares para que las casasen o remediasen, los quales no cumplían con sus obligaciones aprovechandose de las referidas haciendas, lo que era causa de andar

multitud de mestizas perdidas y sin guardar la honestidad y recogimiento que convenía pues no teniendo quien las amparase usaban de demasiada libertad por su mala inclinación; y que las que estaban en Monasterios tenian menos clausura de la que debian, y algunas se salían de las casas permaneciendo fugitivas dellos muchos dias: Mandó a las Audiencias tuviesen en adelante mucho cuidado de proveer el remedio de lo referido ordenando se las restituyese las haciendas que se las debiesen y con ellas se las diese estado donde viviesen recogidamente, y que las que estuviessen en los Monasterios no saliesen dellos."

75. The Ovandos of Cáceres were a well-known hidalgo family with connections throughout America. Many of the males had illegitimate offspring, including Diego de Ovando, son of Alonso de Ovando and María López. See LL, Doc. 753, 1551, "Reconocimiento de una hija natural"; Altman, *Emigrants and Society*, 148, 152; idem, "Spanish Hidalgos."

76. Altman, *Emigrants and Society*, 148, 153.

77. In the 1530s many religious orders were more tolerant. In his request to the king to found convents in New Spain, Archbishop Zumárraga specified that mestizas would form the upper choir and indigenous women the lower choir; Zumárraga to Bishops of Mexico, Oaxaca and Guatemala, 30/XI/537, García Icazbalceta, *Zumárraga*, III: 116.

78. In medieval Spain young girls from noble families were educated in convents. After 1550, Spanish convents began to provide more social assistance for needy Spanish females. The Cortes of Madrid, for example, requested in 1552 that orphans be allowed to enter convents as recogidas: "[M]uchas veces queden doncellas huérfanas sin madre y a veces sin padre; se recogen en monasterios para criarse allí, para ser remediadas, y estar con el recato y honestidad que conviene, y aprenden buenas costumbres." Apparently the bishops and provincials of the orders resisted such a change. The Cortes bypassed them and appealed directly to the king. See Jiménez Salas, *Historia de la asistencia*, 142, n. 46. In the Americas, what had been an informal practice was formalized in a papal bull of Gregory XIII dated 20/VIII/1575, allowing Spanish girls to be educated in convents. The Monasterio de la Concepción (founded 1573) practiced the same exclusionary racist policy as La Encarnación.

79. Calancha, *Crónica moralizada*, III, 971. Vargas Ugarte, *Historia general del Perú*, II: 92.

80. In Mexico, the convent La Concepción de la Madre de Dios (founded 1541) admitted Spanish, creole, and a few noble mestizas in 1542, including the two daughters of Isabel Moctezuma and Juan Cano; Muriel, *La sociedad novohispana*, 208.

81. AGN, Superior Gobierno, Leg. 4, Cuaderno 64, 1656; Angulo, "Libro original que contiene la fundación del monasterio de monxas de señora Sta. Clara desta cibdad del Cuzco." This manuscript was transcribed and published by Domingo Angulo in an article by the same title in *RANP* 11, no. 1 (1939): 55–95; and 11, no. 2 (1939): 157–84. Ots Capdequí, *Instituciones sociales*, 256–57, cites legislation from the *Recopilación*, ley 7, tit. 7, lib. 1, that permitted mestizas to become nuns "con la misma calidad." Santa Catalina de Sena, a convent exclusively for Spanish women in Cuzco, was not founded until 1605. See AGI, Lima 93, Juan de Vibero, Cuzco, 24/I/1572; AGI, Lima 324, Report, "Convento de monjas de nra. sra. de los remedios de Sto. Domingo de cuzco," 1606. On the early foundation years of the Convent of Santa Clara in Cuzco, see Burns, "Gender and the Politics," and idem, *Colonial Habits*, 15–40. Burns argues that the

Convent of Santa Clara in Cuzco began denying some mestizas black veil positions in the 1570s. This coincides with changes in imperial legislation and Toledo's policies toward mestizos, Burns, "Gender and the Politics," 29, 33, 36.

82. Angulo, "El Monasterio," 67, 69. On the convent in the city of La Plata, see *La Audiencia de Charcas*, II: 15–16.

83. Ayala, *Diccionario*, 740B, "Mestizas," Royal decree, 25/XII/1557, "Para amparo e instrucción en la vida política y christiana de las muchas que en tierna edad andaban abandonadas en la Provincia del Perú, por haver fallecido sus Padres en el Real Servicio; Mandó Su Magestad al Virrey hiciesse fabricar una casa en la ciudad de los Reyes donde fuessen recogidas, alimentadas e instruídas; a cuyo fin cargasse alguna pensión por voluntad sobre repartimiento de Yndios, o lo que mas conveniente pareciesse al intento."

84. On Guatemala, see CDFS, I: 333–34, Royal decree, Valladolid, 3/X/1555; for Quito, AGI, Quito 8, Doc. 1, 7v, President of the Audiencia to Philip II, 1564, which describes the recogimiento: "En esta ciudad se trata de hacerse una casa de recogimiento donde se recojan muchas doncellas pobres, mestiças y españolas hijas de conquistadores y personas que an servido a Vuestra Magestad." On Chuquisaca, see the entry for Domingo de Santo Tomás in Mendiburu, *Diccionario*, VII: 220–21.

85. Angulo, "Libro original," 81.

86. The Augustinian Prior José de Vibero described the scandal surrounding the rapes of various mestizas by the provisor, Esteban Villalón, HIEP 2, no. 5 (1944): 473–75, "Diligencias y averiguaciones hechas por el cabildo sede vacante del Cuzco sobre quejas del Arzobispo."

87. Between 1560 and 1564, more than 70 percent of the doncellas resided in the convent on a temporary basis. They did not become nuns, but either left because their fathers retrieved them, a pious individual provided them with a home, they died, or they married. AGN, Superior Gobierno, Leg. 4, Cuad. 64, 1656; van Deusen, "Los primeros recogimientos," 277.

88. Burns, "Gender and the Politics," 20–21.

89. van Deusen, "Los primeros recogimientos," 278–79.

90. CDFS, doc. 206, I: 298, Charles V to Viceroy Mendoza, 25/XII/1551.

91. From its inception, the Hospital de la Caridad in Lima resembled European hospitals that functionally adapted to immediate social needs, Pullan, *Rich and Poor*, 208.

92. Orphanages were commonly associated with hospitals or hospices in early modern Europe. See Jiménez Salas, *Historia de la asistencia social*, 195–218.

93. Vargas Ugarte, *Historia de la Iglesia*, I: 309–10; HIEP 2, no. 7 (1944): 289–90, "Carta del cabildo secular de los reyes a S. M. sobre la Cofradía de la Caridad." On the foundation of the important Hermandad de la Caridad y de la Misericordia, which provided dowries for Spanish and mestiza girls, see Armas Medina, *Cristianización del Perú*, 433. Charity was popular on an individual as well as institutional (such as confraternal) level; see Lockhart, *Spanish Peru*, 168. The example of Francisco Hernández Orejuela is interesting. He left part of his estate to his illegitimate mestiza daughter Ana Hernández, but also provided dowry funds for four of the poorest doncellas being sponsored by La Caridad's brotherhood; AGN, Audiencia Real, Causas Civiles, Leg. 15, Cuad. 74, 1575, 33v–34r.

94. AGI, Justicia 403.

95. CDFS, doc. 206, I: 298, Charles V to Viceroy Mendoza, 25/XII/1551. See also HIEP 2, no. 9 (1944): 607, Bartolomé Hernández, Company of Jesus to Council of Indies, 1572, "en ellos se enseña las letras juntamente con mucho recogimiento."

96. AGN, Protocolos Notoriales, Diego Gutiérrez, no. 64 (1553–56), fs. 176–84, "Donación al recogimiento de mestizas." I would like to thank Ilana Aragón Noriega for providing me with this reference. .

97. Eguigüren, *Diccionario histórico cronológico*, I: 46.

98. AGN, Protocolos, no. 64, "Donación al recogimiento."

99. Ibid. The girls' names were: Leonor, daughter of Hernán Guzmán, from Almodóvar del Campo; Ysabel, daughter of Alaçer, from Guadalcanal; Ana, daughter of Pedro Martín "el ciego"; María de Castañeda, the adopted daughter of the founders, Catalina de Castañeda and Antonio Ramos; Ysabel and Catalina, both daughters of Juan de Vega; Catalina; Catalina, daughter of Gaspar de Torres; and Ana.

100. AGN, Protocolos, no. 64, "Donación al recogimiento."

101. Ibid.

102. Bayle, "La educación," 210–11. The pedagogical methods resembled those employed by the Franciscans in New Spain; see Motolinia, *Memoriales*, 192–96.

103. AFL, Leg. 10, 766r, 788v.

104. Doncellas were associated with nobility in the novel *El Caballero Cifar*, written around 1300. The *Siete partidas*, libro II, tit. xiv, ley 3 discusses their ideal conduct at the queen's court. See also Alonso, *Enciclopedia del idioma*, II, 1599; and Boggs, *A Tentative Dictionary*, 198; which cite the term "doncella" in the *Libro de Buen Amor*, Berceo's *Santa Oria* and other medieval sources. They were also portrayed in variety of other ways: doncellas could seek adventure (like Dulcinea in "Don Quijote") or be employed as ladies-in-waiting, messengers, and intermediaries. In some instances they played the role of fortune tellers. See Herdman, *"Dueñas" and "Doncellas,"* 17–56.

105. AGI, Justicia 403, "El Monasterio de San Francisco de la ciudad de los rreies sobre se conforme aesta tasacion y no se entremeta el obispo," 1560.

106. Ibid.

107. Archbishop Loaysa later tried a similar strategy with the Monasterio de la Concepción (founded 1573). He attempted to modify the clause in the original charter of the institution, which would place the convent under his protection and give him control over its extensive properties in Carabayllo and other areas near Lima. Five years later, Pope Gregory XIII intervened on behalf of the nuns of the convent and conceded the right to administer all properties to Inés de Chaves, the first abbess and founder of La Concepción, and to all other abbesses thereafter. For a more detailed account, see Vargas Ugarte, "El Monasterio de la Concepción."

108. For a fascinating analysis of the rivalry between the two factions of the Audiencia (Santillán vs. Saravia) and the Archbishop, see: "Prólogo," by D. J. de la Riva-Agüero, in Lima, Audiencia, *Audiencia de Lima*, ix–lxxiv.

109. AFL, Leg. 10, 763–68, 771; AGI, Justicia 403; AGI Lima 568; HIEP 2, no. 6 (1944): 222–24, "R. C. Al Guardián de S. Francisco. Sobre el Patronazgo de San Juan de la Penitencia en la ciudad de Los Reyes."

110. As Riva-Agüero stated in his "Prólogo," xli, Loaysa and Santillán were "colegas en el mando." Licenciate Santillán was infamous for favoritism and nepotism in his voting policies and continuously changed his votes in the Audiencia. See idem, "Prólogo," xxiii. See also Trelles, *Lucas Martínez Vegazo*, 96–97, which details the attempt

made by Santillán to change his vote, which originally favored the re-establishment of encomienda rights to Lucas Martínez to support for his nephew, Hernando de Santillán.

111. Licentiate Castro to the king, 29/XI/1564, in CLG, III: 19. In 1556 he was reported to be grazing cattle and horses in the valley of Cañete. See also Cook, *Demographic Collapse*, 158; CLA, I: 247, Audiencia of Lima to the king, 20/III/1560.

112. CLG, III: 19, Lic. Castro to Philip II, Lima, 29/XI/1564; III: 280, Lic. Castro to Philip II, Lima, 20/XII/1567.

113. Toledo said: "[L]as mujeres que tenían diferencias con sus maridos con facilidad se iban y han ido (á estar) y están en las dichas casas, y eran recibidas en ellas sin otro mandato ni autoridad de justicia ni superior"; AGI, Lima 28-A, II: 68; see also CLG, III: 522. Although divorce and annulment suits are rare for this period, they do not report any female litigants being deposited in this recogimiento; AAL, D, Leg. 1. However, I found one instance of a "depositada" in another archival series. In the accusations of solicitation waged against friar Mateo de la Quadra in 1572, witnesses testified that the mestiza Magdalena de Pineda entered San Juan de la Penitencia to serve her "retraida o depositada" mistress, Leonor de Figueroa, and while there became sick with a disease called *modorra*. The friar came to tend Magdalena in the recogimiento, and while she convalesced in bed, he attempted to seduce her, AHN, Inquisición, Leg. 1647, exp. 22, 1572.

114. AFL, Leg. 10, 758, Lima, Pedro Cano to the Audiencia, 26/IV/1572.

115. AFL, leg. 10, 755, declaration of Fray Juan de el Campo, et al., to Licentiate Altamirano, 2/V/1571. Santa Clara was founded in 1605.

116. Having already donated the building to the university in 1576, he explained to the king that when he had visited the recogimiento in 1570 he was disappointed by its state of affairs and he and Archbishop Loaysa resolved to apply the rents and houses to a better end. The decision to take action was delayed by his protracted travels throughout the provinces. In his absence, Navarro regained the rights to the repartimiento, thus sealing the financial fate of the recogimiento, *Relaciones geográficas*, I, "Apéndice," CVI, Toledo to Philip II, 3/X/1576.

117. AFL, Leg. 10, 760, Toledo to Real Audiencia, 20/III/1572. See also Madrid, Biblioteca de Zabálburu, 169–64, Account from the viceroy to Philip II, 1572.

118. AGI, Lima 568, Fundación de la Universidad de San Marcos, 12/XII/1576. The following year the fledgling University of San Marcos received a stipend of thirteen thousand pesos from the tribute payments of the Indians of the repartimiento of Jauja for professorships and "other necessities"; AGI, Lima 337, Doctores de la Universidad de San Marcos to Philip II, 2/III/1577.

119. García y García, *La mujer peruana*, gives a popular rendition of the history of Juana Escalante (without quoting any historical sources) and her dedication to the poor of Lima.

120. "[Y] que el aprovechamiento que pudieran recibir las dichas mestizas de la dicha casa, cuando fuera acertada aquella obra, se podría convertir y con más utilidad en los muchachos y mozos mestizos, que hay copia de ellos en letras y ciencias que pueden aprender en la Universidad, á los cuales no tiene menos obligación S.M. de proveer de remedio que á las dichas mestizas." *Relaciones geográficas*, I (apéndice): CVI, Toledo to Philip II, 3/X/1576.

121. López Martínez, "Un motín de mestizos," 372, 376.

122. Licentiate Castro expressed this in a letter to the king, *Gobernantes del Perú*, III (Prólogo).

123. Castro to the king, 2/IX/1567, CLG, 261. Toledo's concern over this matter resulted in a royal decree prohibiting them from carrying weapons, CDFS, no. 306, Madrid, 19/XII/1568. The royal decree to Castro that mestizos be prohibited from carrying arms can be found in CI, IV: 344, 1566.

124. CI, I: 421–23, 1568, "Cedula que manda al Virrey de Perú pueda embiar de aquella tierra a estos reynos las personas que le pareciere que conviene para la quietud della."

125. The concern that mestizos learn an occupation was generalized; CDFS, I, no. 308, Madrid, 15/I/1569.

126. The precedent had been established with the Council of Trent's promotion of seminaries. The First Provincial Council of Lima (1551–52) addressed the same issue, and the Second Provincial Council of 1583 ordered that priests should be entrusted with parochial education, Vargas Ugarte, *Historia de la Iglesia*, I: 330, 334; HIEP 2, no. 10 (1944): 719, "Carta del Arz. Fr. Jerónimo de Loaysa sobre fundación de la Casa de Huérfanos," 7/IV/1575; Valcárcel, *Breve historia*, 79–80; Martín and Pettus, *Scholars and Schools*; Levillier, *Don Francisco de Toledo*, I: 244–45.

127. After reaching Peru in 1569, Viceroy Toledo expressed concern over the numerous "marginalized" individuals he saw: "[L]as muchas gentes que ay en el Reino, españoles mestizos y mulatos que sin que hacerse aplicar a trabajar se sustentan en el andando vagabundos de unas partes a otras. Muchos de los españoles que tienen esta vida son de los que por sus demontos an sido enbiados a españa los quales deviendo alla ser detenidos y castigados por escandalos se dexan y an dexado bolver." BZ, 169–10, "Memorial de govierno temporal," Francisco Toledo to Philip II, n.d.

128. AGI, Lima 324, Ana de la Asunción, monja de la Concepción, to Philip III, 6/IV/1604.

129. "En el dicho convento ay muchas monjas de las más antiguas y primeras de las hijas y nietas de descubridores, conquistadores e vezinos deste reyno y personas que tenían muchos méritos en esta tierra y la ayudaron a descubrir y conquistar como son Doña Ysabel de Alvarado y Doña Ynes de Alvarado hijas del capitán Gómez de Alvarado conquistador destos reynos que murió en servicio de su magestad." AGI, Lima 324, 16/III/1585.

130. For his definition of "residual," see Williams, *Marxism*, 122–23.

131. A papal bull issued by Gregory XIII in 1576 declaring that mestizos could participate in the Church met with resistance from Viceroy Toledo as well as ecclesiastical officials, but a decree issued by Philip II in 1588 definitively resolved the matter; CDFS, I, no. 452, San Lorenzo, 31/VIII/1588. Calancha, *Crónica moralizada*, III, ch. xxiii, 971; Solórzano, *Política Indiana*, Libro 4, ch. 20, núm. 15; Konetzke, "Sobre el problema racial," 200–202. AAL, Monasterio de Santa Catalina, Leg. 1, 1624–37, lists several mestizas who paid annual room and board, but none were nuns of the white or black veil.

132. Further research is needed using wills and notarial records to examine the legal and social power that single Indian mothers and their mestiza daughters exercised in sixteenth-century society.

133. González Holguín, *Vocabulario*, II: 654–55.

134. A total of 3,248 males and females emigrated to Peru from 1540 to 1559, 3,882

between 1560 and 1579 and 3,451 (954 of them women) from 1579 to 1600. Total female immigration to America increased from 16.4 percent between 1540 and 1559 to 28.5 percent during the remainder of the sixteenth century. Lima had 247 Spanish residents in 1540; 690 by 1559, and 1187 by 1579. See Boyd-Bowman, "Patterns of Spanish Emigration," 54, 83. Juan de Salinas Loyola lists thirty-two encomenderos and 2,500 Spaniards in Lima in the 1570s, "Breve relación de la ciudad de Los Reyes de Lima," *Relaciones geográficas*, 56, 58–60. By 1613, a fairly even proportion of the sexes had been reached for the Spanish Lima population; Bronner, "The Population of Lima," 109.

135. Ann Laura Stoler argues that racial tensions heightened once white women arrived in larger numbers to Sumatra. See Stoler, "Rethinking Colonial Categories," 331–32.

Chapter 3: Transgressing Moral Boundaries

1. Hacking, "Making Up People," 222–36.
2. Blunt and Rose, "Introduction," 5. For an interesting discussion of the dilemmas facing Church authorities in dealing with issues related to sexuality, see Lavrin, "Sexuality in Colonial Mexico."
3. Cohen, *Evolution*, 16.
4. Ibid., 56.
5. Osuna, *Norte*, 30r.
6. Malón de Chaide, *Libro de la conversión*.
7. Pérez de Valdivia, *Aviso*, 418.
8. Perry, "Magdalens and Jezebels," 132.
9. Warner, *Alone of All Her Sex*.
10. Navarro, *Abecedario virginal*, 151, "La Virgen María con su modestia de hablar reprehendido a las mugeres habladoras, de quien habló el Espíritu Santo, diziendo: Muger ay charlatana, y habladora, vagabunda, y inquieta, que no puede estar en casa sossegada, y a pie quedo. Lo qual fue bien al contrario en la Virgen, pues fue modestissima, y muy compuesta."
11. See for instance the painting by Piero della Francesca, *Madonna della Misericordia*, ca. 1445–48. See also Navarro, *Abecedario*, describing her benefits for the world: M—medianera; A—auxiliadora; R—restauradora (del mundo); I—iluminadora; A—abogada.
12. Baernstein, "In Widow's Habit."
13. Institutions for *mondane* (prostitutes), *malmaritate* (abandoned or mistreated wives), *a educazione* (women to be educated), and those *in deposito* (women held in custody) were created in Italy; See Cohen, *Evolution*, 20; Ferrante, "Honor Regained," 47.
14. Cohen, *Evolution*, 13, 61.
15. Bercé et al., *L'Italie au 17 siècle*, 272; Russo, *I monasteri femminili*, 143–51.
16. Morgado, *Historia de Sevilla*, 465–66; Perry, *Gender and Disorder*, 141.
17. *Canons and Decrees*, 220–21.
18. On the increase in the number of convents in Seville, see Perry, *Gender and Disorder*, 75, 78. Perry found that more than half of the twenty-eight convents in Seville were founded before 1660. This pattern is generally reflected throughout the rest of

Spain; see Ruíz Martín, "Demografía eclesiástica," in *Diccionario de Historia Eclesiástica de España*, II: 690; and Sánchez Lora, *Mujeres, conventos*, 97–101, which demonstrates the uneven ecclesiastical distribution by province and the exceptional growth of particular orders like Saint Clare.

19. Mary Elizabeth Perry has argued that three types of institutions—brothels, Magdalen houses, and prisons—served "to lessen the threat of unchaste women" in Counter-Reformation Spain; "Magdalens and Jezebels," 125. I am concerned with the differences *among* different types of recogimientos, of which Magdalen houses form a part.

20. A more informal example in the 1570s is the Jesuits' *casa pía*, or temporary shelter for penitent prostitutes; see León, *Grandeza y miseria en Andalucia*, 43–44, who said of the non-Jesuit recogimientos: "[Q]ue solían tratar muy mal en las recogidas, y con estas y otras ocasiones se volvían a su mal estado." The Jesuits also founded the Emparedamiento de San Ildefonso in Seville; Morgado, *Historia de Sevilla*, 472.

21. Casas de Arrepentidas existed beginning from the mid–fourteenth century with the Franciscan Order Na Soriana to "recoger las rameras arrepentidas"; see Rodríguez-Solís, *Historia de la prostitución*, I: 71. State intervention began after 1565; see AGS, Patronato Real, 23–266, "Bula en que Su Santidad autoriza un Monasterio de Arrepentidas," 1566. See also Perry, "Magdalens and Jezebels," 133. On institutions in northern Europe, see Spierenburg, *The Prison Experience*.

22. Archivo General del Palacio Real, Madrid, Sección Administrativa, no. 6: "Order to give wood from the royal forests to Isavel Morena, rectora de las mugeres recogidas," 22/XI/1582, 204r; "Order to the Captain-General of Granada," 27/XII/1582, 212v. I would like to thank Geoffrey Parker for these references.

23. Pérez de Herrera, *Discursos del amparo*; Lis and Soly, *Poverty and Capitalism*; and idem, "Policing."

24. Peréz Baltasar, *Mujeres marginadas*, 19.

25. Pérez de Herrera, *Discursos del amparo*; *Novíssima recopilación*, Pragmática, Philip II, 7/VIII/1565, Ley XIV, Título XXXIX, Libro VII, 706, stated that vagabond or beggar women should be sent to the galera or correctional house for women. On the difference between the significance of "galera" as a galley and correctional house, see Larrieu, "'Galeras' et 'Galera.'"

26. Luis Cabrera de Córdoba claimed that they removed the women's hair and eyebrows and then subjected them to poor rations, excessive work, and daily beatings, "until they see that they are reformed and will behave better than before"; Cabrera de Córdoba, *Relaciones de las cosas sucedidas*; also cited in Pérez Baltasar, *Mujeres marginadas*, 30.

27. San Jerónimo, *Razón y forma de la galera*, 9r, 12v.

28. Cohen, *Evolution*, 21.

29. Atondo, *El amor venal*, 201–3, argues that in Mexico, recogimientos did not acquire repressive, carceral characteristics until the 1620s.

30. Schilling, "'History of Crime,'" 300.

31. Viforcas, "Los recogimientos"; Muriel, *Los recogimientos*, on the Recogimiento de Jesús de la Penitencia (founded 1572) for prostitutes; the Hospital de la Misericordia, a recogimiento for "mujeres perdidas," and "señoras divorciadas," 56–58; the Recogimiento de Santa Mónica for "señoras casadas," 72–78. Interest in founding

recogimientos for distinct "types" of women emerged in Mexico in the 1570s, thus prefiguring their advancement in South America by the 1580s.

32. AML, *Libros e cédulas*, Libro V, Decree, Viceroy Fernando de Torres y Portugal, count of Villar, 15/VII/1586, 160r.

33. For an important biography of Mogrovejo, see Rodríguez Valencia, *Santo Toribio de Mogrovejo*. During much of the same period, Archbishop-Viceroy Pedro Moya de Contreras (archbishop 1573–91, interim viceroy 1584–85) also initiated lasting changes in the Catholic Church of Mexico, implemented Tridentine reforms, and oversaw the Third Mexican Provincial Council in 1585. For an impressive, erudite biography, see Poole, *Pedro Moya de Contreras*.

34. Montalvo, *Breve teatro*, 27–28.

35. Dammert Bellido, *El clero diocesano*; Vargas Ugarte, *Los concilios limeños*, vol. I.

36. Bowser, *The African Slave*, 339–40. On the extent of Church property, see Porras Barrenechea, "Perspectiva y panorama de Lima," in Porras Barrenechea, *Pequeña antología de Lima*, 29.

37. See Appendix C; Montesinos, *Anales del Perú*, II: 197; Bronner, "The Population of Lima, 109.

38. Pedro Cieza de León, "Lima en 1550," in Porras Barrenechea, *Pequeña antología de Lima*, 100; Lizárraga, "Lima al finalizar el siglo xvi," in ibid., 108.

39. Tizón y Bueno, "El plano de Lima," I: 410.

40. Suárez, *Comercio y fraude*, 15–40.

41. AHN, Ayala, *Diccionario*, VII, 732b, "Delincuentes," 6/II/1571.

42. Mannarelli, *Pecados públicos*, 32. On migration and family formation, see Charney, "Holding Together"; "Negotiating Roots"; Jaramillo, "Migraciones y formación de mercados"; Vergara Ormeño, "Migración y trabajo femenino."

43. AGI, Lima 35, marqués de Montesclaros (1607–15) to Philip III, 1/IV/1612, 38r. Montesclaros associated the excessive number of tapadas with the need to finance an "encerramiento" to enclose pernicious women. In 1624 the City Council restated this prohibition: "[Q]ue mugeres no andan tapadas . . . tienen que mostrar su cara . . . el exceso de las tapadas ha crecido tanto que ha causado y causa graves daños y escandalos en esta República y turban e inquietan la asistencia y devolución de los Templos y de las Procesiones y demas actos Religiosos." AML, *Libros de Cédulas y Provisiones*, Libro III, 2da. parte, 1534–1633, 370r. Women were also not supposed to cover themselves with tunics during Holy Week, AAL, Papeles Importantes, Leg. 6, exp. 24, 1611.

44. AML, *Libros de Cédulas y Provisiones*, Libro III, 2da parte, 371v, 379v–82r.

45. AAL, D, Leg. 1, 1569, Marí Pérez vs. Pedro Sánchez is the first recorded divorce still extant in the Archbishopric Archive. She was deposited in an individual's home. On the various functions of the Hospital de la Caridad, see Cobo, "Historia de la fundación," I: 292–96; "Memorial de la Hermandad y Cofradía de la Caridad, 1569," Vargas Ugarte, *Historia de la Iglesia*, I: 407–12.

46. AAL, Nulidades, Leg. 7, 1616, Doña María de Villavicencio vs. Pedro de Miranda. The home of Gerónima de Garay, an elite inhabitant of Huánuco, served as a recogimiento.

47. In 1582 a woman named Isabel López decided to dedicate her life to "mujeres desvalidas" in the Recogimiento de Santa Mónica and shortly thereafter, "se vió poblada por las mujeres que tramitando divorcio eran depositadas en ella"; Muriel,

Los recogimientos, 74. The precise date of the foundation of the Hospital de la Misericordia in the sixteenth century, a recogimiento for "mujeres perdidas y señoras divorciadas" in Mexico City, is uncertain. Muriel, *Los recogimientos*, 56.

48. "[Se] me ha pedido con mucha instancia por parte de una muger principal, interviniendo en ello persona grave y de mucha authoridad (Francisco Saldaña)," Santo Toribio to Pope Sixto V, 8/XI/1590, Rodríguez Valencia, *Santo Toribio*, II: 479–80. See also "Carta del Arzobispo de los Reyes, Sto. Toribio a S. M. sobre remedios de las necesidades del Monasterio de Santa Clara y la Casa de Recogidas," 29/IV/1602, HIEP 4, no. 20 (1946): 432; van Deusen, *Dentro del cerco*, 10–11. On 26 September 1598 the dean of the church, Dr. D. Pedro Muñiz, named Isabel de Porras Marmolejo as the first governess "de las mujeres de diborcio, arrepentidas y demas depositadas que estan y estuvieran en la casa y recogimiento"; AAL, Monasterio de Santa Clara, Leg. 1. The Recogimiento de Santa Mónica in Mexico City served a similar groups of females, including divorciadas, women whose husbands were traveling, orphaned doncellas, and "mujeres de mala vida y adúlteras," Muriel, *Los recogimientos*, 74–75.

49. Viceroy García Hurtado de Mendoza supported the idea of additional convents for the daughters of the conquerors; AGI, Lima 33, no. 7, lib. iii, 67v, Hurtado de Mendoza to Philip II, 19/XI/1593, Lima. The archbishop of Mexico, Pedro Moya de Contreras, expressed similar concerns and helped found the Convent of Jesús María in 1580 for the daughters and granddaughters of the conquerors who lacked adequate dowries to marry. Poole, *Pedro Moya de Contreras*, 56–57.

50. "Relación y memorial que se envía á su santidad por el Arzobispo de los Reyes . . . en conformidad del motu proprio," 1598, García Irigoyen, *Santo Toribio*, II: 245.

51. "Suceden en estas partes muy de ordinario divorcios, que si se entendiese por las partes haber de estar reclusas en el ínterim que se determinaba la causa de divorcio, y asimismo después de declarado deberse hacer el dicho divorcio, cesarían muchos de los dichos pleitos y harían vida maridable." "Carta de Santo Toribio al Papa Sixto V sobre entrada de mujeres seglares en monasterios de monjas, 8/XI/1590," Rodríguez Valencia, *Santo Toribio*, II: 479–80.

52. I have found two cases of young girls housed in the recogimiento between 1589 and 1605. Jerónima de Palma reported staying there on many occasions with her sister (a permanent resident); and Ana de Prado Terán also lived there as a girl; AAL, Beatificaciones, Isabel de Porras Marmolejo, 1633, 67r–69v, 72r–75r.

53. AGI, Patronato, Ramo 33, Philip II to marqués de Cañete, Valladolid, 10/VIII/1592. See also "El Monasterio de Monjas de Santa Clara," 10/VIII/1592, in Angulo, "Cedulario Arzobispal," 215–17; Rodríguez Valencia, *Santo Toribio*, II: 144.

54. The archbishop lived with "recogimiento and incredible honesty," never "visiting women," resisting temptresses' "depraved intentions," and had little to do with nuns. Yet he was deeply concerned with women's welfare; Rodríguez Valencia, *Santo Toribio*, II: 49, 444; Montalvo, *Breve teatro*, 27–28; idem, *El sol del Nuevo Mundo*, 328–29.

55. AGI, Lima 320, Francisco de Saldaña to the king, 23/III/1594; AGI, Lima 581, XIII, 135v–136r, Report of Council of Indies, San Lorenzo, 9/IX/1598. Of the nine slaves, the six males were Antón Biaffara, Juan Bran, Sebastian Raçanga, Antonillo (muchacho), Luis Mocanbique, and Luis (muchacho). The three women included: Ysabel Biaffara, Esperança Valanta, and Ynes Biaffara.

56. Respeto de que/otros tres de monjas que ay en esta ciudad (y una casa de cari-

dad, de mugeres recogidas) se empeçaron con mucho fundamento/metiendose en el-los mugeres de muy gruesas haziendas/y contodo eso pasan gran necesidad y sino fuese por la merced que les ha hecho V. Md. y mis antecesores y yo se huvieran despoblado." He also disliked Archbishop Mogrovejo and considered his donations to be insubstantial compared with the support from the royal government: "[El] Arzobispo (que lo ha deseado y escripto sobre ello a V. Md. el favor que le ha hecho) ha sido hazer juntar algunas limosnas (de poca consideracion) en su Arçobispado, y de su hazienda /me ha dicho saldaña que no le ha dado un solo Real." AGI, Lima 33, Hurtado de Mendoza to Philip II, Lima, 24/IV/1594, 1r–1v. On their mutual dislike and battle over the boundaries of ecclesiastical and secular patronage, see García Irigoyen, *Santo Toribio*, II: 43–55.

57. The repartition of lands and Indians by royal decree is mentioned in a Council of Indies session in 1592 and again in 1597. See AGI Lima 581, X, 172v., Valladolid, 24/VIII/1592; XIII, San Lorenzo, 9/IX/1598, 135v–36r. Viceroy Hurtado de Mendoza mentions the application of "tierras vacas y repartiéndole yndios para su servicio" to the convent in a letter to the king in 1594, AGI, Lima 33, n. 21, Lima, 24/IV/1594. The amount was 42.5 fanegas of land, AAL, Santa Clara, Leg. 1, Report by Francisco de Saldaña, 22/IV/1606. See also AGI, Lima 94, 1604, Lima, Audiencia to the king, "Respondese a la cedula sobre el estado que tiene el Convento de Santa Clara desta Ciudad," which states: "[Le] hizo el marques de Cañete unas tierras q[ue] valen mil pesos de renta esta ya en estado que ay dentro 25 monjas de avito y 7 donadas y 8 esclavas y tiene disposicion para haver hasta 100 monjas."

58. Montalvo, *El sol del Nuevo Mundo*, 332.

59. AAL, Monasterio de Santa Clara, Leg. 1, "Condiciones de la chacara de Sta. Clara," 10/V/1607; "Autos tocantes a las reacusaciones fechas por parte del Monasterio de Santa Clara," "Reacusación a los Sres. canónigos Dres. Juan Dias de Aguilar y Gaspar Sanches de San Juan," 10/VII/1607, 95v, 112r–13v. Don Mateo Gonçales de Pas was the schoolmaster, whom the nuns suspected of collaborating with the recogidas. On the water rights, the convent's lawyer said: "[La] casa del divorcio fuera a verificar como por ella avían hecho un agujero . . . un albañar de una asequía para entrar como en realidad de verdad entraron en la guerta del dicho conbento y sacaron unas calabaças y sapallos y fruta de la dicha guerta el dicho señor maestre escuela deviendo tomar el negocio con las veras que caso tan grave rrequiera. No solo no lo hizo pero con palabras mui secas sin querer oir en la dicha rrazon al dicho señor canonigo se fue dando de mano y diciendo que eran enbustes de las monjas por hacer mal y daño a aquellas pobrecillas del diborcio que tan aflixidas estavan," "El convento recusa . . . " 17/VI/1608, 182 r–v.

60. AAL, Monasterio de Santa Clara, Leg. 3, exp. 12, 1619. "Autos que sigue el Monasterio de Santa Clara para que le rebajen el precio de 11 559 pesos 4 reales que deben pagar por las casas pertenecientes al recogimiento del Divorcio." The nuns refused to pay this amount to the Casa de Divorciadas for the space they had "bought" from them.

61. AAL, Causas Civiles, Leg. 25, exp. 24, 1620, "Beatriz de Molina sobre unas cuentas de su mando"; Causas Civiles, Leg. 28, exp. 6, 1623, "Declinación de jurisdicción q[ue] hace Bernardo de Paz, mayordomo del Monasterio de Santa Clara"; Papeles Importantes, Leg. 9, exp. 5, 1625, "Gobernadora de la Casa de Divorcios." The governess, Doña Ana Ortíz Yllan had not been paid for more than two months by Santa Clara.

62. AAL, Causas Civiles, Leg. 28, exp. 6, 1623, "Declinación de jurisdicción q[ue] hace Bernardo de Paz, mayordomo del Monasterio de Santa Clara," 2v.

63. Rodríguez Valencia, *Santo Toribio*, II: 480.

64. AGI, Quito 76, Bishop Luis López de Solís to Philip III, 1601, Quito, 776r.

65. The author believes that more than three women petitioned for divorces, given the widespread concern on the part of colonial authorities; however, only three records have survived.

66. AHN, Ayala, *Diccionario*, "Prostitución," VIII, fol. 248, no. 347, Royal Decree, 21/VIII/1526; Muriel, *Los recogimientos*, 47.

67. It was called the Recogimiento de Jesús de la Penitencia (1572), Muriel, *Los recogimientos*, 48. For an excellent study of prostitution in colonial Mexico City, see Atondo, *El amor venal*.

68. The recogidas were distinguished as "pecadoras españolas distinguidas," "jovenes españolas," "pecadoras de calidad," and "jóvenes pecadoras convertidas," Muriel, *Los recogimientos*, 51–52.

69. Atondo, *El amor venal*, 37, cites similar terms for colonial Mexico.

70. Years later the marqués de Cañete donated a substantial amount of property, but Viceroy Velasco's donation enabled the chapel to be completed, Mendiburu, *Diccionario*, III: 76; ABP, 7499, "Libro mayor de cuentas, Hospital de San Diego," 24r.

71. ABP, 8400, "Ordenanzas para la Hermandad de San Diego," 182r; 7499, 39v; 8399, "El libro donde están asentadas todas las cosas tocantes a la casa y hospital de Sr. San Diego," 49r.

72. He offered support for the Recogimiento de Jesús de la Penitencia in Mexico, an institution known for its redemptive, not punitive function; Muriel, *Los recogimientos*, 47–53.

73. Hanke, *Los Virreyes españoles*, II: 61; also cited in van Deusen, *Dentro del cerco*, 11.

74. ABP, 8399, 49r.

75. For examples of casta women being admitted to the recogimiento, see AAL, D, Leg. 2, 1604, Doña Luisa del Castillo vs. Martín Marqués; Leg. 2, 1601, Joana Solís, mulata libre, vs. Joan de Borjas, sabe firmar; Leg. 3, 1607, Elvira de Toro vs. Francisco Hernández. The ordinance read: "[L]as que podían ser recibidas eran sólo las españolas y no de otro género de gente," ABP, no. 8399, 51r.

76. The administrator of the Hospital of San Diego referred to it as a "recogimiento de mujeres rameras . . . a manera de carcel para que en el se pusiesen como presos las que fuesen escandalosas en essa República." ABP, no. 8399, Juan Rodríguez de Cepeda, mayordomo del Hospital de San Diego to the City Council of Lima, 26/VI/1603, 39r.

77. Doña Luisa del Castillo petitioned to be transferred to a private home because, she claimed, the governess of La Magdalena had been extremely rude to her. AAL, D, Leg. 2, 1604, Doña Luisa del Castillo vs. Martín Marqués.

78. AAL, D, Leg. 3, 1607, Elvira Rodríguez de Toro vs. Francisco Hernández; Leg. 3, 1609, Juana Barba Cabeza de Baca vs. Pedro de Béjar.

79. ABP, no. 8399, 37r.

80. Mendiburu, *Diccionario*, III: 76.

81. AAL, Causas Civiles, Leg. 25, exp. 24, 1620, Beatríz de Molina sobre unas cuentas de su mando.

82. AGI, Lima 35, marqués de Montesclaros to Philip III, 19/III/1610.

83. Sawicki, *Disciplining Foucault*, 10–12, 42.

84. Many litigants filing for a divorce said that they had left home on previous occasions. For one example, see AAL, D, Leg. 16, 1636, Doña Catalina de Ocadíz Salbatierra vs. Licenciado Josephe Suárez de Figueroa, abogado de la Real Audiencia. Complaints of "unauthorized separations" were common, but many couples lived apart without filing a formal legal complaint (querella). Silvia Arrom has found the same to be true in nineteenth-century Mexico City; *The Women*, 226.

85. AAL, D, Leg. 3, 1607, Gabriel Martínez vs. Catalina Hernández were married for five years but had lived together for only two; Leg. 7, 1617, María de Fontuosa vs. Rodrigo Benítez had been married for fifteen years but separated for nine; Leg. 9, 1626, Petronila de Escobar vs. Diego Velásquez.

86. AAL, D, Leg. 7, 1616, Francisca de Cabeças vs. Gabriel Vallalado Montañes. The eleven-year-old Francisca, from Xauja, escaped to the home of a "señora beata" before appealing to the ecclesiastical judge in Lima to deposit her in an institution. See also Amancebamientos, Leg. 1, 1616. Catalina de Cáceres was married to an absent husband and lived in a friend's home.

87. Doña Ana de Cabrera y Cordova had gone to the Monasterio de Nuestra Señora de los Remedios in the city of La Plata to escape her husband, the wealthy owner of a mill and mines in the "cerro." Later she traveled to Lima, where she petitioned for a divorce and the restitution of her marriage dowry and for the time she had spent in the convent. See AAL, D, Leg. 4, 1610, Doña Ana de Cabrera y Cordova vs. Joan de Padilla.

88. AAL, Monasterio de Santa Clara, Leg. 4, 9/I/1637.

89. AAL, D, Leg. 1, 1609, Alonso Pérez natural de Condesuyo vs. Catalina yndia. See also D, Leg. 15, 1632, Agustina de Barrios vs. Bernardo de Argote. Agustina de Barrios fled to La Caridad because, she claimed, her husband continually beat their slave and she was terrified of his temper.

90. For an interesting study of the meaning of "notorio y conocido" in eighteenth-century Quito, see Herzog, *La administración*.

91. AAL, D, Leg. 20, 1639, Doña Cathalina de Uceda vs. Agustín Francisco Alemán.

92. AAL, D, Leg. 7, 1617, Rosa de Orellanos vs. Juan de Dios.

93. AAL, Causas criminales de matrimonio, Leg. 1, 1610, Juan Borges.

94. D. Juan Saello, master silk weaver, wanted his wife deposited in the Hospital de la Caridad because he could not stand communicating with her any longer. He had thought she had changed after abandoning him and the two children, but he saw she had not when she complained to the corregidor of El Cercado and had four policemen come after him. AAL, Litigios Matrimoniales, Leg. 3.

95. AAL, D, Leg. 9, 1626, Petronila de Escobar vs. Diego de Velásquez.

96. AAL, D, Leg. 1, Pedro López vs. Martha Hernández.

97. AAL, Litigios Matrimoniales, Leg. 1, Bartolomé López vs. Juana María, mestiza libre.

98. AAL, D, Leg. 1, 1569, Marí Pérez vs. Pedro Sánchez. She was deposited "en parte seguro" while he traveled to Huánuco on business; see also Leg. 13, 1629, Doña María de Oría vs. Beníto Gonzáles. This practice was less common by 1650. Delfina González del Riego also argues that the frequent absence of a husband could lead to a serious in-

crease in conjugal tensions; "Fragmentos de la vida cotidiana," 211. In Mexico City, the Recogimiento de Santa Mónica served women who were alone while their husbands traveled, 74.

99. Eiximenis, *Carro de las donas*, Libro III, iiii, "[La] muger casada si a caso está su marido ausente que es ydo a algunos negocios por ninguna vía deve desordenarse en el comer y bever y vestir ante aquellos días deve tener todo recogimiento y honestidad procurando dar buen exemplo a sus criadas parientes y vezinos."

100. AAL, Litigios Matrimoniales, Leg. 1, 1634, Doña Agustina de Ayala Moxica vs. Andres, 1634.

101. AAL, Hospitales, Leg. 3, 1622, see a similar instance in D, Leg. 2, 1604, Doña Luisa del Castillo vs. Martín Marqués. Luisa was six months pregnant and her husband had been "absent from the kingdom" much of that time. Since he had not returned, she requested that the ecclesiastical judge release her from her "unwarranted deposit." In AAL, D, Leg. 5, 1612, Doña Ana de la Torre, "mujer principal de la ciudad," vs. Juan de Reynoso, almirante, "hombre principal y noble," Doña Ana argued that since Juan had returned from Spain, he refused to live with her, nor had he helped her maintain the household or provide for their children.

102. AAL, Causas Criminales de Matrimonio, Leg. 2, 1634, María de San Pedro vs. Benito Pereyra.

103. AAL, Monasterio de La Concepción, Leg. 9, exp. 62, 1648, Autos seguidos por Gracia Caçanga, madre de Luisa criolla, esclava de Francisca de la Cruz, quien trató de ponerla en una panadería para castigarla y de ahi embarcarla a otra cuidad por haberse escapado del convento.

104. Cited in Tardieu, *Los negros y la Iglesia*, I: 371. For an example of the discourse of an enslaved woman, see AAL, CN, Leg. 7, 1635, Jacinta de Horosco, mulata esclava, married to Pedro Rico, negro esclavo, who was taken to Quito. By law, an enslaved woman could request her husband's transfer closer to Lima and, in doing so, might represent herself in court as morally "recogida," honorable, and deserving to have her husband with her. See Rípodas Ardañaz, *El matrimonio*, 378–82, which discusses several major synods that reiterated slaves' rights to have their husband or wife returned if taken a far distance. See also Bowser, *The African Slave*, 261–66.

105. Patricia Seed argues for "insufficient assistance" on the part of church officials in New Spain toward blacks, castas, servants, and slaves: their cases were not entirely ignored, but pursued less vigorously, particularly in instances where enslaved women sought to locate their partners. See *To Love, Honor, and Obey*, 81–82. For petitions in Lima, see the AAL series, "Causas de Negros."

106. AAL, CN, Leg. 3, 1617. Juan Angola, married for eight years to Vitoria Angola, had been absent in Nasca for the entire time. Now back in Lima, he did not want to return to Nasca and said to the judge, "[Yo] estoi presto de ponerme en la carcel arço-bispal donde esté depositada hasta que tenga efecto lo que pido." His owner claimed he fled the hacienda. See also AAL, CN, Leg. 3, 1618, Joan Ramos, moreno libre and Ys-abel Bañon, esclava; Leg. 5, 1625, Agustín criollo and Juana criolla; 1629, Antonio de Morales, mulato esclavo; Leg. 7, 1638, Juan Biojo and Susana Angola. Susana went to a panadería.

107. CN, Leg. 3, 1618, Joan Ramos.

108. CN, Leg. 3, 1625, Agustín Criollo.

109. AAL, CN, Leg. 7, 1635, Jacinta de Horosco.

110. Based upon her analysis of amancebamiento records (in which three blacks out of a total of thirty-two appear), María Emma Mannarelli concludes that their mistreatment "dice de la indiferencia de la gente en general, y de las autoridades en particular, frente al comportamiento sexual de la población esclava"; *Pecados públicos*, 117–18. These same records, in addition to documents from the series "Causas de Negros," suggest precisely the opposite to me: neither the population in general nor the authorities seem to have remained indifferent. For a discussion of the legal recourses available to slaves, see Tardieu, *Los negros y la Iglesia*, II: 729–49.

111. Seed, *To Love, Honor, and Obey*, 79.

112. AAL, Esponsales de Matrimonios, Leg. 1, 1627. The young bridegroom, Don Marío Benites Marsano, argued to the judge that the couple had adhered to the procedures and had even married in the vestibule (*locutorio*) of the convent of Santa Catalina.

113. AAL, Causas Civiles, Leg. 2, exp. 9, 1597, "Autos de María de Chaves, mulata libre." She wanted to marry Simón de Bermúdez, a mulato slave, but her "owners" deposited her in a recogimiento on three separate occasions, in order to convince her to change her mind. Her owners felt (and she eventually agreed with them) that it was not a marriage of equals. Simón, who wanted to marry her, said that her employers were disobeying the Council of Trent's ordinances; 3r, 12r. For a similar case, see Esponsales de Matrimonios, Leg. 1, 1608.

114. AAL, CN, Leg. 3, 1618. Ursula's mother countered by placing a legal complaint against Pasqual. He was apprehended and jailed.

115. AAL, Nulidades, 1604, Rufina de Barrionueva vs. Diego de la Cruz. He requested that the judge "se saque de poder de su padre y madre y se ponga en depósito donde vive recogidamente [h]asta que cumpla la edad de doze años y tenga capacidad para aprobar o reprobar el dicho matrimonio que está consumado." Both were free blacks.

116. AAL, Monasterio de La Concepción, Leg. 8, exp. 17, 1640. Autos de la solicitud elevada por Diego de Castillo, negro libre criollo del puerto del Callao, y Francisca Bazan, negra libre criolla de Lima, residente en el Monasterio de la Concepcion.

117. For comparisons with Mexico, see Boyer, *Lives*, 68ff.

118. AAL, Esponsales de Matrimonio, Leg. 1, 1606; 1613, Doña Gerónima de Allioza; 1617, María Antonia de Espinosa, mestiza; Leg. 3, 1646, Doña María de Torres, 32r; Amancebamientos, Leg. 3, 1632, Leonor de Zamudio.

119. AAL, Esponsales de Matriminios, Leg. 2, 1613 (out of order). On the important cultural difference in attitudes toward casual sexual relations and physical intimacy after a promise of marriage had been made, see Boyer, *Lives*, 94–95.

120. On Mexico, see Seed, *To Love, Honor, and Obey*, 45, 171.

121. AAL, Nulidades, Leg. 3, 1606, Ynés Hernández vs. Francisco de la Llana. Ynés professed on 11 August 1608.

122. AAL, Esponsales de Matrimonios, Leg. 1, 1608. Doña Hierónima Bravo de Sotomayor had been forced to profess in the Monasterio de Santa Clara in Huamanga around 1592. She pressed charges against her father, but was not able to nullify her vows until 1606. In 1608, after her father had died, she married the man of her choice. For Mexico, see Seed, *To Love, Honor, and Obey*, 32–46.

123. AAL, Causas Criminales de Matrimonio, Leg. 3, 1656, Promotor Fiscal vs. Don Joseph de Torres y Bohorques and Doña Josepha de Castro.

124. AAL, Esponsales de Matrimonios, Leg. 1, 1630.
125. AAL, Monasterio de las Bernardas, Leg. 1, 1627.
126. On bigamy in Spain, see Poska, "When Bigamy." For an example of concubinage in Avila, see Archivo Diocesano de Avila, Leg. 55/7/1, 1596. The entire village filed suit against Andrés Palmares and María Povedaña, a couple living in concubinage who faced excommunication. For Lima, see AAL, Amancebamientos, Leg. 1, Valentín de León and Doña Ysabel Vanega both sentenced to exile (*destierro*). In 1673, Juana Lucia, an "yndia ladina" from Chilca (in the jurisdiction of Cañete) had married three times and was jailed while the judge tried to unravel the complex stories, AAL, Sección Matrimonios de Bigamias, Leg. 1, 1673. On bigamy, see also Cook and Cook, *Good Faith*; and Boyer, *Lives*.
127. AAL, D, Leg. 4, 1612, Cristóval Gómez vs. Francisca. Francisca, a morena criolla slave of a priest, was accused of concubinage by her husband, a bricklayer. Married for twenty years, he commented: "[H]ace catorce años está publicamente amancebada y trata con muchas personas y es una negra borracha." Francisca also accused Cristóval of concubinage, but the case remained unresolved. In these cases, women rarely testified, but not for the reasons of "silence," which María Emma Mannarelli has argued. Both parties were considered to be guilty until proven innocent, and were often not given the proper chance to represent themselves. The bias consisted in the nature of the crime and should not be assumed to be a gender bias.
128. In some instances, the couple had been involved for years. One husband, forced to return to his marriage, was terribly distressed to leave his mistress, whom he had known since he was twelve years old; AAL, D, Leg. 20, 1640, Francisca de la Cruz, yndia, vs. Juan de Paredes, yndio. Some couples were punished with exile; AAL, Amancebamientos, Leg. 1, 1606, Valentín de León and Doña Ysabel Vanega.
129. AAL, Amancebamientos, Leg. 1, 1610, Pedro Godoy; 1612, Francisco de Soto; 1613, Francisco de Castañeda; 1616, Pedro Estéban; Leg. 3, 1629, Asencio Gómez; 1630, Bartolomé Rodríguez; Leg. 4, Francisco Escudero Romero.
130. AAL, D, Leg. 26, 1646, Juan de Quiroga, mulato libre, maestro carpintero, vs. Petron Flores, mulata.
131. See also Mannarelli, *Pecados públicos*, 117. Of thirty-two cases examined in the series Amancebamientos, Leg. 1–4, between 1600 and 1650, most did not specify racial status: nineteen, no data; three mulatas; three mulata or negra slaves; four yndias; one negra; and two Spaniards. Male and female occupations included carpenters, iron workers, bakers, sword makers, tavern-keepers, pot makers, and chicken farmers—which indicated that most were artisans. In eight cases, the relationship had occurred with a married woman, and no name or other revealing evidence was presented. The number of amancebamiento trials decreased significantly in the latter half of the seventeenth century; see Leg. 5, 1655–1825. Perhaps more of a systematic attack was brought to bear against the sexual comportment of members of the popular classes between 1600 and 1650, or even particular trades such as tavern-keepers, which corresponds to the increasing regulations against them. Mannarelli's argument that "la identidad de género supuso también matices étnicos y de clase que actuaron en los procesos contra amancebados" also seems feasible; *Pecados públicos*, 118.
132. AAL, Amancebamientos, Leg. 2, 1615, Gerónimo de Ayala, *herrador,* and Luisa Pérez, mulata. He went to the Archbishopric prison and she to the Casa de Divorciadas.

133. For deposits in the Casa de Divorciadas, see AAL, Amancebamientos, Leg. 1, 1612, Francisco de Soto and a nameless married woman; Leg. 2, 1615, Luisa Pérez, mulata and Gerónimo de Ayala, mulato, herrador; 1616, Alonso de Mesa, *pulpero,* and a nameless married woman; Leg. 3, 1628, Gusepe Ruíz, carpintero, and María de Escobar; 1634, Antonia de Escobar; 1635, Francisco de Espinosa, Spaniard, and Ysabel de los Angeles.

134. AAL, Amancebamientos, Leg. 1, 1616, Alonso de Mesa, pulpero, and Catalina de Cáceres; 1615, Bartolomé Fajardo and Dorotea; D, Leg. 13, 1629, Doña Francisca de Mendoça vs. Martín Delgado.

135. In several cases, if the woman had initiated divorce proceedings on the basis of adultery, the husband would counteraccuse the wife of adultery. Agustín López de Amaya argued that Lorenza, his wife, had been caught in bed with her lover and so he had the right to retain her dowry. Once branded as an adultress, whether true or not, Lorenza, like other women, found it difficult to gain support for her case; AAL, D, Leg. 13, 1629, Lorenza de la Cruz vs. Agustín López de Amaya. Richard Boyer argues that female adultery was not well tolerated in Mexico either; *Lives*, 145.

136. Vinall and Noble, "Shrewd and Wanton Women," 141.

137. AAL, Monasterio de La Trinidad, Leg. 1, 30/VIII/1615.

138. Françesc Eiximenis spoke about the male right to kill an adulterous wife, based upon the legal code of the Siete Partidas. He also stated that a woman had the right to abandon her husband if he had committed the same indiscretion, but only if it did not disrupt the household. Viera, "Françesc Eiximenis," 1–20; *Carro de las donas*, Libro II, xvii.

139. AAL, Monasterio de La Trinidad, Leg. 1, 30/VIII/1615; Leg. 2, 5/V/1630.

140. Blunt and Rose, "Introduction," 5. Josefina Muriel found that women in New Spain initiated divorce proceedings more often than men; *Los recogimientos*, 64.

Chapter 4: Breaking the Conjugal Contract

1. AAL, D, Leg. 1, 1594, Hierónima de San Miguel vs. Juan Tejeda Bonifacio, 12v, 13v. Juan petitioned for more than one year to have her deposited in an institution but was unsuccessful.

2. In Spain, recogimiento or depósito in a home was apparently common even in towns such as Avila, ADA, Leg. 56/3/36, 1603, "María Vargas vs. Pedro Sánchez." Leg. 56/6/1, 1606, "María de Arriba vs. Juan Pérez." The language used in Spanish litigation records resembles that in Peru: for instance, "houses of deposit" for divorciadas were also described as "honesta y recogida."

3. "Introduction," Johnson and Lipsett-Rivera, *The Faces of Honor*, 16; Twinam, "The Negotiation," 79. Her analysis of honor is based upon eighteenth-century elites involved in legitimation cases.

4. In her recent book on eighteenth-century elites and illegitimacy, *Public Lives, Private Secrets*, 28, Ann Twinam argues that elites differentiated between private and public in sociological terms, and that family, kinship, and friendship "set the decisive parameters." Those who pertained to the family or were close associates formed part of the private, family sphere; the rest were part of the public world. The testimonies I have read for the sixteenth and seventeenth centuries in Lima suggest that women, of all social ranks, differentiated between public/private in terms of the self, the family,

and others; as well as in a spatial sense: to denote the home as private, and outside the home as public. Yet, those "spheres" could just as easily blend.

5. Mannarelli, *Pecados públicos*, 99; Stern, *The Secret*, 8–9.

6. Goldberg, *Racist Culture*, 186.

7. Butler, *Gender Trouble*, 25. Butler reworks the idea that subjects occupy fixed positions (in this case engendered) but that their continued subjection depends upon action, which may consist of acts of complicity and resistance. See also Stern, *The Secret*, 301–2.

8. Only three sixteenth-century divorce proceedings are still extant in the Archivo Arzobispal: Marí Pérez (1569); María de Torres (1590); and Marta Hernández (1590). The Provincial Council of Lima in 1567 stated: "[Q]ue de los pleitos de divorcio solo el obispo por su persona conozca y sino fuere por causa cierta y manifiesta no se de sentencia de diborcio"; Trujillo Mena, *La legislación eclesiástica*, 299.

9. The Third Lima Council (1583) dedicated several chapters to the sacrament of marriage, emphasizing its indissolubility. "Más no habiendo causas muy graves y manifiestamente probadas, en ninguna manera se aparten los matrimonios ya contraídos, pues el mismo Díos los juntó." *Concilios limenses (1551–1772)*, I: 423. All litigations were placed under the jurisdiction of the bishop with the vicar general or provisor issuing the sentence.

10. "[Q]ue casi todos confiesen q[ue] haunq[ue] tenga algunas obras de entendimiento pero no entiende el fin e las tales obras o a lo menos consta claro q[ue] no entiende la raçon del tal fin haziendo aprehension composicion y division cerca del tal juizio en tal manera q[ue] sepa hazer reflexion sobre sus actos, y alcançar el fin dellos y la razon de tal fin, lo qual como emos probado es la señal por la qual se distingue los honbres de entendimiento de los niños y bovos y brutos. Concluyo q[ue] se prueba bien la falta de juizio y acuídad desta señora con impedimento para no poder entender q[ue] cosa es matrimonio." AGS, Diversos de Castilla, Leg. 39, doc. 34, "Opinion of Licenciado Horozco, Lawyer for Juan Vazqúez de Molina," 4/VII/1548. See also Lewis, "The 'Weakness.'"

11. Lenman and Parker, "The State," 37.

12. AGI, Quito 76, 779r; 781v, 784r; 786v. Corregidores, oídores, and prominent military officials testified in support of the bishop's request to the king for two thousand pesos in tribute to pay for expenses of the fledgling Recogimiento de Santa Marta.

13. AAL, D, Leg. 1, 1601, Francisco Ximénes vs. María de Esquivel; 1601, María de Morales vs. Gregório Arias.

14. AAL, D, Leg. 1, 1601, María de Morales vs. Gregório Arias.

15. Boyer, *Lives*, 128–40.

16. Guevara, *A los recién casados*, 22: "Que los maridos no sean demasiado celosos . . . que de cuando en cuando no es malo cerrarle la puerta, apartarla de la ventana, negarle alguna salida, quitarle alguna sospechosa compañía; mas esto ha de hacer el marido con gran cautela."

17. AAL, D, Leg. 4, 1609, Doña Ynes de Zamudio vs. Cristobal de Barrera, 23v. The original quotation reads: "[Sí] alguna vez le pusé las manos sería moderadamente con ánimo de corregirla alguna imperfección y a medrarla, la qual es permitido a un marido según su derecho."

18. See AAL, D, Leg. 15, 1634, Mariana Cortes vs. Juan de Bocanegra. Mariana had been married for seven years but found it necessary to live with her two sisters and re-

ceive alms from a Dominican friar because her husband would not support her. See also Leg. 26, 1646, María Magdalena, criolla, vs. Francisco de Valladares; 1646, Doña Gabriela de Aguilar vs. Don Pedro de Anpuero Barba, for cases of physical abandonment.

19. See also Stern's discussion of the terrain of contestation in conjugal disputes in eighteenth-century Mexico; *The Secret*, 59–85.

20. The reasons given remained constant in the latter part of the seventeenth century; Lavallé, "Divorcio y nulidad," 427–35; for the eighteenth-century, see Flores Galindo and Chocano, "Las cargas del sacramento," 403–10. For Mexico City, see Muriel, *Los recogimientos*, 64.

21. *Contrahentium libera debet esse voluntas,* or unwilling consent by one of the parties, was the major reason an annulment was granted, but other reasons were commonly argued as well. Martín, *Daughters*, 110–11, explains that the Second Provincial Council of Lima (1567) upheld this law to protect parties against the intense interference and political and economic pressure to marry uninterested parties, especially women with a vast inheritance.

22. A study on divorce and annulment in sixteenth- and seventeenth-century Mexico is needed. For a comparison with eighteenth-century Mexico, see Arrom, *The Women*, 206–58.

23. The testimony of María de Torres (the first notorious "divorciada") in 1599 is very telling in this regard; AAL, D, Leg. 1. See also Martín, *Daughters*, 141–42.

24. AAL, D, Leg. 21, 1641, Juan López, yndia natural de Cañete, vs. Felipe López, del pueblo de Motupe.

25. AAL, Leg. 1, D, 1569, Marí Pérez vs. Pedro Sánchez, 19r, 29r.

26. Because of the tremendous distances and communication lag, a papal bull in 1606 declared that bishops could resolve such matters and should appeal directly to the pope only when necessary. See Rípodas Ardañas, *El matrimonio*, 389–90. AAL, D, Leg. 1, 1569, Marí Pérez vs. Pedro Sánchez. This cultural practice extended to Protestant cultures; see Schilling, "Reform and Supervision," 44–50.

27. Schilling, "Reform and Supervision," 42. By the seventeenth century, the Church had difficulty enforcing the inviolability of marriage in Spain. See Poska, "When Love Goes Wrong."

28. This is similar to asylums in Italy that maintained a claustral regimen. See Ferrante, "Honor Regained," 47.

29. AAL, Beatificaciones, Isabel de Porras y Marmolejo, 1634, 200r.

30. Ibid., 21r–22r.

31. Ibid., 159v–160v.

32. AFL, Registro 17, no. 41, Sor Isabel de Porras Marmalejo, 1634, 506r. Her anonymous biographer wrote, "[S]ería impresa desigual a las fuerças humanas querer ponderar el espíritu y ferbor con que se entregó todo al exercicio de la oración vivía y se sustentava, gozando con Dios muy buenos ratos en su coraçón y de manera se engolfava en el inmenso mar de los divinos atributos, que anegada en ellos, totalmente perdía por entonces el usso de los sentidos en largos extassis que de continuo tenía; donde recebía grandes misericordias del Señor, en perderle de vista el Alma con muchos influencias de gloria, viendo enviçion imaginaria la umanidad de Christo nuestro Señor, unas [veces] glorificado y otros crucificado, y muy de ordinario se sentía estar en unión con Dios sin sesar, unas con más eficacia, y otras con menos, de aquí

le nacía que qualquier cosa que oyesse, o oviesse que tocava a su amado, no era su mano contenerse, sino que le abrasava el coraçon, y a veces dava terribles gritos, y era arrepatada de la fuerça del espíritu y llevada de una partes en otras"; 508v–509r. When her tenure of office ended in the Casa de Divorciadas, she took another administrative post as abbess of the colegio-recogimiento in the Hospital de la Caridad, where she supervised young female students as well as women "of all walks of life or *todos generos* who are enclosed or penitent, recogidas, for different reasons and living virtuously," Córdoba y Salinas, *Crónica franciscana*, 938.

33. AAL, D, Leg. 3, Elvira de Toro vs. Francisco Hernández, 1607–8. She said: "Quiero vivir con ello en el servicio de Dios para ello no he sido atemorizada ni amenazada. . . . Dejo de insistir en el divorcio por aver yntervenido personas religiosas," 56r.

34. AAL, D, Leg. 1, 1600, Ana de Torres vs. Pedro Alonso.

35. Rípodas Ardañaz, *El matrimonio*, 309.

36. See for example, AAL, D, Leg. 9, 1620, Doña Francisca Renxifo vs. Juan Cavallero de la Fuente, hombre noble y hidalgo; Leg. 15, 1634, Doña Juana Ortíz vs. Diego Ybañez de Abila; Leg. 16, 1636, Doña Catalina de Ocadíz Salbatierra vs. Licenciado Josephe Suárez de Figueroa, abogado desta Real Audiencia; Leg. 20, 1640, Doña María Rodríguez Giraldo, whose dowry amounted to twenty thousand pesos, vs. Pedro Gerónimo de Melo. Others held positions that afforded higher status; Leg. 9, 1620, Doña Francisca de Rojas vs. Redro de Ybar, escribano de su Magestad. For examples of husbands in military service, see AAL, D, Leg. 7, 1617, María de los Angeles vs. Juan García, soldado; Leg. 9, 1620, María de Zamudio vs. Juan Nuñez, Coronel; Doña Damiana de Murga vs. Capitán Don Toribio de Vereterra, Condestable Mayor de artillería y alcalde de las casas Reales del puerto del Callao.

37. AAL, D, Leg. 3, 1607, Elvira de Toro, pulpera, vs. Francisco Hernández, sillero; Leg. 3, 1608, Ysabel Rodríguez vs. Diego Zamorano, sombrerero; Leg. 9, María de Oría vs. Benito Gonzales, viajero; Leg. 33, 1639 (out of order in legajo), María de Aspítia, humilde, vs. Francisco Portierra de Morga, pintor.

38. AAL, D, Leg. 9, 1621, María de los Reyes, yndia, vs. Lorenso de Robles, yndio who worked in an obraje.

39. Bernard Lavallé found the same to be true in the annulment records he examined for the years from 1650 to 1700; "Divorcio y nulidad," 434. Litigation costs were higher, the process took much longer, and it was extremely difficult to prove that the litigant had either married against her will or the marriage had never been consummated. For several instances of women arguing that they married against their will and while they were legal minors, see AAL, Nulidades, Leg. 8, 1624, Mariana del Castillo (eleven years old), vs. Hernando de Llanos; 1627, Alonsa de Mesa y Guzmán vs. Martín Rodríguez de Esquibel (under twelve); Leg. 14, 1640, Antonia de Yllezcas vs. Francisco de Matienzos.

40. For cases in Lima and specifically Indians from El Cercado, see AAL, D, Leg. 9, 1622, Juana Chumbi vs. Lorenzo de Heredia; and Leg. 9, 1622, Francisca Vincos vs. Cristoval Vanera. The cases of Indians from provincial areas were generally heard. See D, Leg. 9, 1621, María de los Reyes vs. Lorenso de Robles; and 1623, Francisca Melchora vs. Don Sebastián Quispininabilca.

41. Butler, *Gender Trouble*, 116; Gal, "Between Speech and Silence," 175–203.

42. The term "triangular dialogue" is borrowed from Lyndal Roper, who argues that courtroom narratives were not shaped freely by their authors, but were linked

between husband, wife and the council; idem, "Will and Honor," 55. On the importance of witnesses and what was "well known and public" in legal suits, see Herzog, *La administración*, 96–100, 201–22.

43. Lloyd, "A Feminist Mapping," 257; Sawicki, *Disciplining Foucault*, 14; Butler, *Bodies that Matter*, 2–3.

44. Boyer, "Women, *La Mala Vida*," 253–54.

45. AAL, D, Leg. 16, 1631 (out of order in legajo), María Flores, española, vs. Bernardo Simón, quarteron de mulato; Leg. 17, 1638, Ana de Ayala, free morena, vs. Juan Velásquez, free mulatto; Leg. 15, 1634, Francisca de la Mota vs. Marcos Dominges, portugués; 1636, Doña Juana Ortíz vs. Diego Ybañez de Abila; Juan López, yndia natural de Cañete, vs. Felipe López de Motupe, Leg. 21, 1641. This language continued to be used throughout the century; see D, Leg. 50, 1682, Dionosio de Soria vs. Doña Juana Quintero; D, Leg. 53, 1687, Juana López de la Cueba vs. Juan de Abalos.

46. In principle, elite women described themselves or were described as "una mujer honrrada y de buena vida" or "una muger principal," but sometimes descriptions included racial categorizations such as "es una yndia honrrada y de buena vida." For examples of this discourse, see AAL, D, Leg. 16, 1636, Doña Catalina de Ocadíz Salbatierra vs. Licenciado Josephe Suárez de Figueroa, abogado de la Real Audiencia; Leg. 26, 1646, Ana Criolla, morena libre, vs. Juan Cortés, negro criollo esclavo.

47. D, Leg. 26, 1646, Juan de Quiroga, mulato libre, vs. Petrona Flores, mulata.

48. D, Leg. 16, 1635, María Flores, española, vs. Bernardo Simón, quarteron de mulato.

49. On honor as defined by elites, see Twinam, "The Negotiation," 73; plebeian honor, Johnson, "Dangerous Words," 138–40; on slaves' or working people's notion of honor, Graham, "Honor among Slaves," 219–20.

50. Butler, *Gender Trouble*, 103.

51. For similar instances in early modern Europe, see Abrams, "Whores, Whore-Chasers," 272; Gowing, "Gender and the Language," 1–2, 19. For examples in divorce suits, see AAL, D, Leg. 21, 1650, Doña Lucía de Cardenas vs. Antonio de Caballos: he called her a "mujer ramera."

52. AAL, D, Leg. 1, 1590, Marta Hernández vs. Pedro López. For examples of attacking women's character and sexuality through accusations of witchcraft, see Alberro, "Beatriz de Padilla," 247–56; Behar, "Sexual Witchcraft"; Mannarelli, "Inquisición y mujeres."

53. AAL, D, Leg. 26, 1646, Ana Criolla vs. Juan Cortés.

54. AAL, D, Leg. 17, 1638, Ana de Ayala, morena libre, vs. Juan Velásquez.

55. For comparisons with rural Spain, see ADA, Leg. 56/3/36, 1603, "María Vargas vs. Pedro Sánchez." Leg. 56/6/1, 1606, "María de Arriba vs. Juan Pérez."

56. AAL, D, Leg. 50, 1681, Doña Juana de Aldaña vs. Ygnacio de Castro.

57. Lucia Ferrante, "Honor Regained," 64, argues that this was the case for women in early modern Bologna, but I believe that many women in colonial Lima did not believe this to be true.

58. In Mexico City, Josefina Muriel found a clear differentiation between institutional and private deposit by the type of situation: "a través de los casos estudiados podemos presumir, que en general, iban a este recogimiento [el Recogimiento de la Misericordia], las mujeres cuyos maridos pedían el divorcio o las acusaban de alguna falta grave, que hiciera imposible la vida matrimonial. En cambio, iban a casas de honra las

inocentes víctimas de los maridos y las que pedían el divorcio, que eran en tal caso la parte acusadora"; *Los recogimientos*, 71.

59. In this instance, the politics of location refers to the placement of women in both a social (in terms of identity) and physical space; Blunt and Rose, "Introduction," 7. I am not arguing for an "essential" male or female position relative to the meanings of honor or recogimiento. Rather, I am trying to show the ways in which men and women "position" themselves, in opposition to one another (after all, they are fighting one another in a courtroom).

60. Of the eighty-one divorce cases analyzed for the period from 1569 to 1650, twenty-four yielded no data. Of the rest, twenty-two (39 percent) went to private homes. In the second half of the seventeenth century, deposit in private homes constituted more than fifty percent of all deposits (see Appendix E).

61. Of the total number of women deposited in private homes between 1569 and 1713, some remained in their own home, others went to a relative's house, usually an aunt or a sister. Deposit in their mother's home was the most popular request. Four women requested deposit in a widow's home and three in the home of a beata.

62. Some elite Spanish women, who judged themselves to be "honrada y principal," preferred La Caridad over the Casa de Divorciadas, AAL, D, Leg. 16, 1636, Doña Catalina de Ocadíz Salvatierra vs. Licenciado Josephe Suárez de Figueroa.

63. María de Torres was interred for seven months in La Caridad, and wondered why it was necessary to be under such tight supervision; AAL, D, Leg. 1, 1599, María de Torres vs. Domingo Hernández, 55r. See also AAL, D, Leg. 9, 1621, María Francisca de Angulo vs. Capitán Francisco Crespo. She had been deposited in La Caridad for more than one year "para curarse." Her husband paid sixteen pesos each month for her board and keep. In all cases reviewed thus far, women were transferred from La Caridad to Divorciadas, but rarely vice versa. See AAL, D, Leg. 1, Maria de Torres vs. Domingo Hernandez, 53r; Nulidades, Leg. 1, 1601, María de Sandoval vs. Bartolomé Ruis"; Amancebamientos, 1625, Promotor Fiscal vs. y Florentina Catalán; D, Leg. 9, 1621, María Francisca de Angulo vs. Capitán Francisco Crespo; and 1622, Gerónima de San Francisco vs. Diego Hernández; D, Leg. 15, 1636 (out of order but in the legajo), Ana de Pas vs. Juan Merino; D, Leg. 20, 1639–40, Juana de Quesada vs. Francisco Muños de Alba, AAL, D, Leg. 13, 1630, Doña Juana de Paredes vs. Juan Martinez de Escurrechea; AAL, D, Leg. 20, 1639, Juana de Quesada vs. Francisco Muñoz de Alba. Fewer women resided in the Recogimiento of La Magdalena because of its short duration.

64. AAL, Monasterio de las Descalças de la Trinidad, 1615, Doña Mariana de Mendoça had been married, completed one year as a novice, and then decided to return to her husband; D, Leg. 2, 1605, Doña Catalina de Castro vs. Cristobál Rodríguez Mondragón (Santa Clara); Leg. 9, 1620, Doña Francisca de Rojas vs. Pedro de Aybar. After Francisca received a divorce sentence she went to live in the Monasterio de la Trinidad in 1622 and later to La Encarnación. See also Santa Clara, Leg. 4, 1638, Doña Paula de Ulloa; D, Leg. 4, 1609, Doña Ana de Cabrera y Córdova vs. Joan Porcel de Padilla.

65. AAL, D, Leg. 3, 1608, Ysabel Franca vs. Sebastián de Talabera. See also D, Leg. 26, 1646, Ana Criolla, morena libre, vs. Juan Cortes, negro criollo esclavo. For the period from 1650 to 1700, see Lavallé, "Divorcio y nulidad," 433.

66. Causas de Negros, Leg. 7, 1635, Jacinta de Horosco.

67. AAL, D, Leg. 3, 1608, Ysabel Franca vs. Sebastián de Talabera; Leg. 20, 1640,

Doña Catalina de Uceda vs. Agustín Francisco Alemán; Amancebamientos, Leg. 3, 1635, Ysabel de los Angeles.

68. AAL, D, Leg. 10, 1624, María de Salinas vs. Juan de la Vega.

69. AAL, D, Leg. 16, 1635, María Flores, española, vs. Bernardo Simón, quarteron de mulato; Causas Criminales de Matrimonio, Leg. 1, 1629, María de Benavides.

70. AAL, D, Leg. 21, 1650, Doña Lucía de Cardenas vs. Antonio de Caballos. Antonio requested her transfer from a private residence to the Casa de Divorciadas.

71. AAL, D, Leg. 1, 1599, María de Torres vs. Domingo Hernández Carmena, 31v. She had been deposited in several homes before going to the Casa de Divorciadas.

72. AAL, D, Leg. 1, 1599, María de Torres vs. Domingo Hernández Carmena, 53r. 54r.

73. AAL, D, Leg. 26, 1646, María Magdalena, criolla, vs. Francisco de Valladares, pulpero.

74. AAL, D, Leg. 20, 1640, Doña Francisca de Quiros vs. Don Francisco de Urbina y Flores.

75. AAL, D, Leg. 1, 1598, Anna Ruíz vs. Marcos Fernández Carvallo.

76. AAL, D, Leg. 33, 1660, Juana María de Lorca vs. Juan Pablo de Espinossa.

77. AAL, D, Leg. 20, 1640, Doña Blasa de Guzmán vs. Antonio de la Mota.

78. The recogida Doña Damiana de Murga, housed in the Casa de Divorciadas, asked the judge for permission to be in her mother's company, but her husband responded angrily to his wife's plea, claiming that "she had been influenced against me by her mother, because she bears me ill will" ("me tiene mala voluntad"). AAL, D, Leg. 9, 1621, Doña Damiana de Murga vs. Capitán Don Toribio de Veretera.

79. In a few instances the father of the bride initiated the proceedings against his son-in-law. See AAL, D, Leg. 3, 1608, Ysabel Rodríguez vs. Diego Zamorano, both poor artisans.

80. AAL, D, Leg. 9, 1620, "Doña Francisca Renxifo vs. Juan Cavallero de la Fuente, hombre noble y hidalgo," who said, "[No] a de ser en cassa de la d[ic]ha su madre ni en otra por ebitar los yncombenientes q[ue] quedan dichos sino ade ser metida en el Recogimiento de las Diborciadas para que fue ynstituydo." See also D, Leg. 15, 1633, Gregoria Piñan vs. Gabriel de Montenegro; Leg. 26, 1647, Doña Leonor de Ampuero vs. Joseph Segarra.

81. If her life were at stake, and evidence showed that previous assaults had been made, the husband could be jailed. See AAL, D, Leg. 3, 1608, Ysabel Franca vs. Sebastián de Talabera; Leg. 3, 1607, Elvira de Toro vs. Francisco Hernández; Leg. 4, 1610, Mariana de Serralva vs. Juan Goméz; Leg. 22, 1642, Ana María, mulata libre, vs. Gabriel Zamorano. Men were more likely to be imprisoned for indebtedness or robbery.

82. AAL, D, Leg. 1, 1598, Anna Ruíz vs. Marcos Fernández Carballo, 20r; Leg. 20, 1640, Doña Blasa de Guzmán vs. Antonio de la Mota; Leg. 20, 1640, Doña Maior de Espino vs. Francisco Guisado Bote (three transferrals).

83. AAL, D, Leg. 3, 1608, Ana Colón vs. Antonio de Arratia.

84. AAL, D, Leg. 9, 1623, Doña María de la Paz (onrrada y principal) vs. Juan Hurtado; Leg. 9, Ysabel Galindo vs. Alejandro de Almedia.

85. AAL, D, Leg. 20, 1639, Juana de Quesada vs. Francisco Muñoz de Alba.

86. AAL, D, Leg. 3, 1608, Ysabel Franca vs. Sebastián de Talavera, who was also imprisoned because of indebtedness. See also 1607, Elvira de Toro vs. Francisco Hernández.

87. AAL, D, Leg. 2, 1604, Ysabel Ruíz vs. Pedro Sánchez; Leg. 20, 1640, Doña María Rodríguez Giraldo vs. Pedro Gerónimo de Melo.

88. She wanted "un par de camisas, un poco de pano para un faldelina y una saya de gergeta y unas gervillas and botines" and clothing to protect her from the cold "y esta es un paramo." AAL, D, Leg. 1, 1599, María de Torres vs. Domingo Hernández Carmena, 49v, 56r–56v.

89. AAL, D, Leg. 9, 1620, Francisca Renxifo vs. Juan Cavallero de la Fuente, hombre noble y hidalgo, 31r.

90. AAL, D, Leg. 13, 1629, Doña Francisca de Mendoza vs. Martín Delgado.

91. AAL, Monasterio de Santa Clara, Leg. 1, 1604, Doña Magdalena de Roxas y Sandoval vs. Pedro de Bolanos, 178r–78v.

92. AAL, D, Leg. 26, 1646, María Magdalena, criolla, vs. Francisco de Valladares.

93. AAL, D, Leg. 13, 1629, Lorenza de la Cruz vs. Agustín López de Amaya. See also Leg. 9, 1620, Doña Francisca de Rojas vs. Pedro de Ybar. The abbess of the Monasterio de la Encarnación served as a witness on her behalf, 66r–v.

94. AAL, D, Leg. 13, 1629, Lorenza de la Cruz vs. Agustín López de Amaya.

95. AAL, Amancebamientos, Leg. 2, 1625, Promotor Fiscal vs. Florentina Catalán.

96. On a case of forgery, see AAL, D, Leg. 13, 1629, Doña Francisca de Mendoza vs. Martín Delgado.

97. AAL, D, Leg. 9, 1620, Doña Francisca de Rojas vs. Pedro de Ybar, 66r–66v.

98. AAL, D, Leg. 9, 1623, Ysabel Galindo vs. Alejandro de Almedia.

99. For an example, see AAL, Amancebamientos, 1625, Promotor Fiscal vs. Florentina Catalán.

100. ABP, 8399, 49r; AAL, Causas Criminales, Leg. 11, exp. 23, 1639.

101. Women entering La Magdalena were admitted only if they could prove that they had means to provide for themselves; ABP, 8399, 49v.

102. AAL, Litigios Matrimoniales, Leg. 1, 1634, Doña Agustina de Ayala Moxica vs. Antonio Andrés.

103. AAL, Monasterio de Santa Clara, Leg. 1, exp. 12, 1604, "Autos seguidos por Juana Sandoval," 2r.

104. When Saldaña donated the sum, María wrote the promissory note which the governess and other witnesses signed; AAL, D, Leg. 1, 1599, María de Torres vs. Domingo Hernández, 82r, 83r. For an example of a confraternal donation, see AAL, D, Leg. 13, 1629, Lorenza de la Cruz vs. Agustín López de Amaya.

105. In 1598 the cost each month was eight pesos of silver, AAL, D, 1598, Ana Ruíz vs. Marcos Carvallos, 22r. Convents, which discouraged divorciadas from living there until after 1650, required written ecclesiastical acceptance and a vote of approval by the nuns to allow a woman to enter as a lay member (divorciada or not). Once accepted, she paid 100 to 150 pesos annually.

106. AAL, D, 1620, María de Zamudio vs. Juan Nuñez. Juan told the judge that he was poor and unable to pay her "alimentación" and thus requested that María be deposited "en una casa particular." Some suffered for months without financial assistance in the institution; Doña Juana de Sandoval was "interred" for four months without assistance, Santa Clara, Leg. 1, 1607.

107. AAL, D, Leg. 1, 1598, Ana Ruíz vs. Marcos Carvallos; Leg. 3, Ana Colón vs. Antonio de Arratia.

108. AAL, D, Leg. 2, 1604–06, Joana Solis vs. Joan de Borgas, where Joana feared

that her husband would try to sell her slave. See also Leg. 3, 1607–8, Doña Gabriela de Ordoñez vs. Miguel de Cereces.

109. AAL, D, Leg. 20, 1639, Doña Cathalina de Uceda vs. Agustín Francisco Alemán.

110. AAL, D, Leg. 9, 1622, Gerónima de San Francisco vs. Diego Hernández. At the end of the year Gerónima was deposited in the house of a lawyer in the Real Audiencia.

111. Ibid. Diego's owner claimed that Gerónima did not want to be there, not because she was unable to work but because she did not want to be confined, "sino en libertad ocasionada." "En la Caridad tiene, casa, de comer, cirujano, botica y todo lo necessario y juntamente el Recogimiento q[ue] debe tener la susad[ic]ha sinque le de ocasion a q[ue] ande en la libertad y vida licensiosa q[ue] ella tiene . . . puede resultar inconveniencias y pesadumbres entre ellos."

112. See, for example, the case of Doña Juana de Cardenas, AAL, Nulidades, Leg. 1, 1605; Monasterio de Nuestra Señora del Prado, Leg. 1, 1645, Doña María de Olmos y Ortega, who had lived as a seglar in the convent for many years while awaiting the divorce sentence to arrive from Potosí. Once her sentence had been pronounced, she petitioned to become a nun of the black veil. See also Monasterio de las Descalças de San Joseph, Leg. 1, 1615, Doña Mariana de Mendoça; D, Leg. 5, 1613, Doña María de Salazar vs. Pedro de Ubitarte.

113. AAL, D, Leg. 26, 1646, María Magdalena, criolla, vs. Francisco de Valladares.

114. The Provincial Council of Lima in 1567 stated "[Y] quando asi la diere [un divorcio], la muger ques apartada de su marido póngase en una casa honesta donde biba en cerramiento," Trujillo Mena, La legislación eclesiástica, 299. This was still the case in nineteenth century Mexico; see Arrom, The Women, 216.

115. AAL, D, Leg. 9, 1623, Ysabel Galindo vs. Alejandro de Almedia.

116. Giddens, Central Problems, 123–28.

Chapter 5: Elite Formation and the Politics of Recogimiento

1. Cobo, "Historia," I: 72–73.

2. Lohmann Villena, Los americanos, I: lxxiv, "Distribución por regiones indianas."

3. Fred Bronner argues that by 1630, the beneméritos or conquistadores, officials, and traders formed a three-pronged group that constituted the elite. See Bronner, "Church, Crown, and Commerce," 82.

4. Lockhart, Spanish Peru, 11–34. See Hampe Martínez, "Sobre encomenderos," 126–32; Bronner, "Peruvian Encomenderos," 637, 643, 649.

5. Bronner, "Peruvian Encomenderos," 650; Brading, The First America, 315–18, who bases his discussion of the tremendous wealth in Lima at this time on Córdova y Salinas, Memorial. See also Suárez, "Merchants, Bankers." A variety of studies on colonial elites in Latin America are available. For Chile, see Flusche, Two Families; on Venezuela, Ferry, The Colonial Elite; on Mexico, Hoberman, Mexico's Merchant Elite; Brading, Merchants and Miners; and Israel, Race, Class and Politics, 79–109. For a general look at the relationship between social stratification and economic factors, see Mörner, "Economic Factors."

6. Glave, "Santa Rosa"; Lavallé, Las promesas ambiguas, 105–27, 129–41.

7. Lavallé, Las promesas, 157–224; Bronner, "Church, Crown, and Commerce," 82; Hamnett, "Church Wealth." Burns coined the term "spiritual economy" to show the

inextricable link between the circulation of "economic" and "spiritual" goods in Cuzco's convents and secular society; idem, *Colonial Habits*, 3, 5–6.

8. Ganster, "Churchmen," 145. Lima's elites, as well as "provincial patriarchs," sent their boys to such schools, which gave them additional status; Ramírez, *Provincial Patriarchs*, 176. The Jesuit schools of San Pablo and San Martín catered to the Spanish elite. The Colegio del Príncipe de Esquilache (founded 1620?) solicited sons of caciques most likely to inherit their fathers' titles. The first twelve students remained in school from age ten until they married or became a cacique. The goal was the "españolización" of the indigenous nobility, so that once reintegrated into their community, they could serve as a model of "acculturation." What such a process of "acculturation" involved, and whether Spanish educational norms were really effective cultural strategies, merits further investigation. See Macera, "Noticias sobre la enseñanza," 341. In Mexico, no school for caciques flourished in the seventeenth century; Gonzalbo Aizpuru, *Historia de la educación*, 167.

9. For example, The Colegio de la Caridad, founded in 1549 for abandoned mestizas, later served as a school for creole girls who could prove their legitimacy and purity of blood (*limpieza de sangre*); Gonzalbo, "Tradición y ruptura," 50.

10. Lavallé, *Las promesas ambiguas*, 157–224; idem, "Recherches," vol. 2; Brading, *The First America*, 320–22.

11. See Borges, *Religiosos en Hispanoamérica*, 133.

12. Bronner, "Church, Crown, and Commerce," 86.

13. Lavallé, *Las promesas ambiguas*, 112ff, 133, 135–38; Iwasaki Cauti, "Vidas de santos."

14. The first volume was published in Barcelona in 1639, and Bernardo de Torres wrote part of volume II, published in 1653 after Calancha's death. The original publication was entitled, *Crónica moralizada del Orden de San Agustín en el Perú* (Barcelona: P. Lacavalleria, 1639–53).

15. The policies were codified in the 1613 Synod. See *Sínodos de Lima*. The Jesuit José de Arriaga published his manual in 1621. Both Viceroy Esquilache (who returned to Spain in 1621), and Archbishop Lobo Guerrero (d. 1622) were keenly interested in such a project. See also Mills, "Bad Christians"; and idem, *Idolatry and Its Enemies*. Mills argues that during Pedro Villagómez's (1641–71) tenure as Archbishop, idolatry campaigns continued until about 1667.

16. For examples of family connections between religious and political authorities in the Inquisition, see Ramos, "El Tribunal del Santo Oficio"; idem, "La fortuna del inquisidor."

17. Suárez, "Monopolio, comercio directo," 497.

18. Andrien, *Crisis and Decline*, 4, 18, 28–29. His chapter "The Viceregal Economy in Transition" provides an excellent, well-written synopsis of the discussions surrounding the seventeenth-century crisis in America, and more specifically, the general economic climate in the viceroyalty of Peru. See also Trelles, "Historia económica colonial"; Glave, "El Virreinato peruano"; Tord and Lazo's chapter on "fiscalidad colonial," in *Hacienda, comercio, fiscalidad*, 191–214.

19. Africans and Afro-Peruvians represented 50 percent of the city's population, which reached 27,400 in 1636. See Bowser, *The African Slave*, appendix A, "The Colored Population of Lima," 341. See also Bronner, "The Population," 115; Charney, "El indio urbano."

20. Andrien, *Crisis and Decline*, 21–22, argues that profitability began to decline after 1650 for estate owners, because long-term price controls on wheat eventually had a detrimental effect on the Peruvian economy, thus allowing Chile to make inroads into this market. The natural disasters of 1687 "transformed Chile from a struggling frontier province into the principal wheat producer of Spanish Peru"; *Crisis and Decline*, 27. See also Roel Pineda, *Historia social*. These changes also affected the religious orders. Convents such as La Concepción, Santa Clara, and La Encarnación owned land in the Lurigancho valley. The Jesuits ran sugar estates in Bocanegra, Villa, San Juan del Surco, and Santa Beatriz, all valleys close to Lima; Cushner, *Lords of the Land*, 156–80.

21. Hamnett, "Church Wealth," 113–32; Bronner, "Church, Crown, and Commerce," 82–83; Lavallé, "Recherches," I: 241–51; Hoberman, *Mexico's Merchant Elite*, 237, 281–82.

22. Bronner, "Peruvian Encomenderos," 644–46.

23. Marie Helmer, "Le Callao"; Roel Pineda, *Historia social*, 178–84, 201–8.

24. Rodríguez Vicente, *El tribunal del consulado*, 109–11; also cited in Fred Bronner, "Church, Crown, and Commerce," 80. On the sale of public offices, see Andrien, "The Sale of Fiscal Offices"; Roel Pineda, *Historia social*, 322–23.

25. This compares with a 33 percent increase in the Spanish/mestizo population between 1636 and 1700; Bowser, *The African Slave*, appendix A, "The Colored Population of Lima," 340–41; Bronner, "The Population," 115; Mannarelli, *Pecados públicos*, 68–71, shows that the gender imbalance continued throughout the seventeenth century.

26. Juan de la Cerda, *Libro intitulado*, 246r. See also Luján, *Coloquios matrimoniales*. On the idea of honor as a virtue related to family status in Mexico, see Seed, *To Love, Honor, and Obey*, ch. 4.

27. Guevara, *A los recién casados*, 13–14.

28. Ibid., 7, 12v. See also Dávalos y Figueroa, *Defensa de damas*, reprinted in Cisneros, "Estudio y edición," 93.

29. León, *La perfecta casada*, ch. XXVII. An Augustinian Hebraist, Luis de León, based his advice for women on Scripture rather than on the misogynist patristic Fathers. He saw women as the ultimate authority in maintaining a sense of recogimiento in the home. See also Bergmann, "The Exclusion of the Feminine," 133–35.

30. Granada, *Libro de la oración*. See also the excerpt in Andrés Martín, *Los recogidos*, 405.

31. A study on dowries in Lima is needed.

32. Pilar Gonzalbo's article on dowries included a graph that represented the approximate percentages of women with dowries amounting to: five hundred to two thousand pesos (40 percent); two thousand to five thousand (33 percent); five thousand to ten thousand (14 percent); idem, "Las cargas del matrimonio," 212.

33. His successor, Philip IV, issued a series of laws in 1623 to deal with excessive dowry prices and the number of women unable to sustain such high demands: "[O]rdenamos y mandamos que de aquí [en] adelante los vienes que ubiere mostrencos en cada lugar sirvan y se apliquen para casamientos de mugeres pobres y huérfanas." AGI, Lima 44, Madrid 10/II/1623, 20r.

34. Muriel, *La sociedad novohispana*, 151,155, discusses pious works intended to finance dowries for marriage or entry into a convent for the girls in the Colegio de la Caridad.

35. Vargas Ugarte, "Memorial de la Hermandad y Cofradía de la Caridad, 1569," *Historia de la Iglesia*, I: 310, 407–12. Cobo, "Historia de la fundación," I, ch. xxvii. In 1569, Marí Pérez, a twelve-year-old illegitimate orphan received two hundred pesos from the Hermandad de la Caridad to marry, AAL, D, Leg. 1, 1569.

36. ABP, 8248, "Libro antiguo de las limosnas q[ue] se recogían para dotes de las doncellas y su salida, Cofradía del Rosario"; Vargas Ugarte, *Historia de la Iglesia*, I: 311.

37. Martín, *Daughters*, 121–22.

38. ABP, 8296, "Cofradía de la Puríssima Concepción, Constituciones," 78v, 186r.

39. Martín, *Daughters*, 124–25.

40. The Cofradía de la Caridad and La Puríssima Concepción were two of the most competitive confraternities; ABP, 8296, 78r. The ordinances of the Franciscan confraternity of the Puríssima Concepción (1600) stated that they would give priority to orphans and the "truly poor," but also considered doncellas whose fathers were too old to support them any longer. Only Spanish or quarterona girls who could pass for Spanish were eligible. A provision appended later stated that nieces or relatives of the sodality members could also participate in the lottery.

41. Bayle, "La educación," 206–25; Furlong, *La cultura*, 104–16. On *amigas*, see Martín, *Daughters*, 88–89.

42. La Encarnación (founded 1573) and La Concepción had been admitting daughters of the elite since the 1580s. On convent education in Italy, see Grendler, *Schooling*. See also Russo, *I monasteri femminili*, 38–39, 65–68. Pope Paul V (1605–21) granted convents in France the license to admit female pupils; Rapley, *The Dévotes*, 45–46. Josefina Muriel argues that a number of convents founded in the sixteenth century received *educandas*. The founders of the Real Convento de Jesús María (founded 1580) argued that the convent/school for poor doncellas was a necessary service "to the Republic"; *La sociedad novohispana*, 209. See also 208–11.

43. AAL, Monasterio de la Encarnación, Leg. 4; Vargas Ugarte, *Historia de la Iglesia*, II: 508.

44. In 1630, the 119 nuns of La Encarnación who had just voted to accept seventeen twelve-year-old doncellas argued that they had maintained such a practice since the monastery was founded: "[T]eniendo por bien lo q[ue] se a usado desde los principios q[ue] se fundó este monasterio de q[ue] aya doncellas seglares"; AAL, Monasterio de la Encarnación, Leg. 3, 1630; Martín, *Daughters*, 75.

45. AAL, Monasterio de la Encarnación, Leg. 3, "En este monasterio ay quarto de por si para las seglares donde estan con una religiosa antigua por maestra q[ue] cuyda de todas de día y de noche y las seglares q[ue] ay son dies y siete." Also cited in Martín, *Daughters*, 76.

46. Vargas Ugarte, *Historia de la Iglesia*, II: 509. The eight were La Encarnación, La Concepción, La Trinidad, Santa Clara, Santa Catalina (founded 1624), El Prado (founded 1643), San Joseph (after 1650), and El Carmen (founded 1643 as a convent, originated as the recogimiento/colegio del Carmen).

47. La Encarnación charged one hundred pesos and Santa Clara two hundred pesos a year for room and board, AAL, Monasterio de Santa Clara, Leg. 4, Leg. 5, and Leg. 6. For a general discussion of education in convents, see Asuncion Lavrín, "Female Religious," 185.

48. Literacy might determine whether a novitiate would become a nun of the

black or white veil, Martín, *Daughters*, 180. For Mexico, see Ramos, *Imágen de santidad*, 132–33.

49. Here I interpret the term "estado" to mean her condition as a doncella. Many writers talked about the different "estados" for women: as doncellas, married women, widows, or nuns.

50. AAL, Monasterio de la Encarnación, Leg. 3, 1630. His case is also mentioned in Martín, *Daughters*, 75. See also AAL, Causas Civiles, 1612, "Obligación de Pedro Alfonso del Castillo y Mateo Pastor al Monasterio de la Encarnación," to pay the room and board for María de Castillo to live as a seglar.

51. See BNP, B1747, 1634, "Petición presentada por María de la Torre para que se le conceda licencia para que pueda ingresar en el seglarado del Monasterio de la Concepción." In 1630, the archbishop of Seville granted the Monastery de la Concepción the right to admit seglares; see AAL, Monasterio de la Concepción, Leg. 4, exp. 18, 1630: "Bula que dice que el convento puede criar a las doncellas seglares 'en buenas y sanctas costumbres.'" This contradicts the mandate issued by the archbishop of Lima in the same year.

52. Apparently, Cuzco's convents did not utilize the term "educandas," and seglares were often daughters of the elite, Burns, *Colonial Habits*, 113–14.

53. For an example of the crowded conditions within cells, see Amaya, *La mujer en la conquista*, 334–36.

54. Martín, *Daughters*, 80–82; Suardo, *Diario de Lima*, 54.

55. Between 1600 and 1720, ninety-one female teaching congregations were founded in France. *Conservatorios* that educated "imperiled" girls in Italy were also popular; see Cohen, *Evolution*, 153–55.

56. AGI, Lima 44, Cartas del Virrey, n. 4, lib. iv, 10/II/1623, 15r.

57. Her calculations are for the entire seventeenth century; Mannarelli, *Pecados públicos*, Cuadro V.1, 168 (El Sagrario: total 294 expósitos), 168; and V.2, 170 (San Marcelo: total thirty-eight).

58. BNP, B122, 1637, "Confirmación . . . de una recogimiento para doncellas pobres." Viceroy Conde de Chinchón supported this establishment. See also Muzquiz de Miguel, *El Conde de Chinchón*, 64.

59. Luis Pescador founded the Hospital or Casa de Niñas Expósitas under the aegis of Nuestra Señora de Atocha. On poor children being left on church doorsteps, see AGI, Indiferente General 481, Cámara del Perú, "[H]ospital de Nra. sra. de atocha de la ciudad de los rreyes," 28/III/1605, 396r–396v. On the history of the institution's foundation, see AGI, Lima 322, anonymous account, 23/II/1603, "Luis Pescador professo en el havito del hermano Joan de Dios . . . se fue a Lima donde con las limosnas que recoxio compro un sitio y con licencia del ordinario fundo una iglessia y hospital de la advocacion de N[uest]ra S[eño]ra de Atocha. Los hermanos andan de dia y de noche por las calles/corrales/muladares/rios/y acequias/buscando si la gente desalmada ha hechado alli criaturas/y las han hallado diversas veces/unos en los muladares y acequias/y/otras comiendo de perros/y para el remedio de tan gran daño/y recoger tanvien las criaturas que se hechan alas puertas delas iglessias (con espiritu del cielo) fundo el dicho hospital." See also Vargas Ugarte, *Historia general*, III: 31–32.

60. Cobo, "Historia de la fundación," I: 302–3; Martín, *Daughters*, 92–93.

61. Mannarelli, *Pecados públicos*, 279–83; Bronner, "Church, Crown, and Commerce," 86–87; Vargas Ugarte, *Historia de la Iglesia*, II, 502–3.

62. Martín, *Daughters*, 80, 184, 190.

63. On children in the Casa de Niños Expósitos, see Mannarelli, *Pecados públicos*, 282. For a comparison with the social beneficence system for abandoned white children in Brazil, see Nazzari, "An Urgent Need to Conceal," 110–17.

64. ABP, Cabildos, 1627–1790, Doc. 9207, "Constituciones y Actas del Colegio de la Caridad," 1618, 3r. The hermandad advocated "la división y apartamiento en cassa y vivienda de por sí para la crianza y recogimiento de las dichas niñas y no conbenir que esten juntas en la dicha cassa de la charidad por la frecuentación grande de las mugeres pobres que con tan[ta] deshorden diario entran a curarse de diferentes enfermedades asi cassadas como solteras y de todas edades." Selected educandas had been entrusted to the care of an "abbess" since at least 1601, but their education was less formal and they did not have a separate facility from the Hospital. See Cobo, "Historia de la fundación," I: 292–96; Vargas Ugarte, *Historia de la Iglesia*, I: 310, n. 25. On the merchants' hermandad, see Rodríguez Vicente, *El tribunal del consulado*, 102–6. Its counterpart in Mexico also received substantial financial support from the wealthy merchant sector; see Gonzalbo Aizpuru, *Las mujeres en la Nueva España*, 154–55, 163.

65. In 1615, Don Diego de Sierra donated thirty thousand pesos for the school, and Philip III donated additional capital; Cobo, "Historia de la fundación," I: 293–94. On scholarships, see ABP, 9207, 1618.

66. Cobo, "Historia de la fundación de Lima," I: 270; Mendiburu, *Diccionario*, VII: 342–43; AGI, Lima 301, "Relación de las ciudades, villas y lugares, parroquias y doctrinas que ay en este Arzobispado de Lima," 1619, 8r–8v.

67. AAL, Beatificaciones, Isabel de Porras Marmolejo; Mendiburu, *Diccionario*, VI: 522.

68. AAL, Beatificaciones, Isabel de Porras Marmolejo, 200. María Eugenia, a nun of the black veil in Santa Catalina, attended "Doña Isabel's" school, 169v; two sisters, Doña Elvira and Ana María del Castillo, took the black veil in Santa Clara, 181v, 182v–83r; María Magdalena, became a nun of the black veil in the Monasterio de las Descalças, 187r.

69. AAL, Beatificaciones, Isabel de Porras Marmolejo; Mendiburu, *Diccionario*, VI: 522; Córdoba y Salinas, *Crónica franciscana*, 938–42; Montesinos, *Anales del Perú*, II: 228–31; Cobo, "Historia de la fundación," I: 293–95.

70. Bernabé Cobo refers to Domingo as Pérez de Silva as does the modern author Luis Martín. Foundation documents (AGI, Lima 44) refer to him as Gómez de Silva, so I have followed this example.

71. AGI, Lima 44; Cobo, "Historia de la fundación," I: 270. Borromeo's educational program in northern Italy served as a model for other areas; Grendler, *Schooling*, 360, 375.

72. AGI, Lima 44, II, 12v; Martín, *Daughters*, 87.

73. AGI, Lima 44, 11r–11v, 14r, 15r.

74. Ibid. Curiously, she did not refer to the sixteenth-century Peruvian recogimientos of San Juan de la Penitencia in Lima, nor to San Juan Letrán in Cuzco, and stated that no other recogimiento/colegio existed in Peru in 1619.

75. Ibid., 11r. Books included "libros de coro y de canto misales y breviarios y libros de devoción en romance," 30v.

76. After completing their education, two of her students, the daughters of Francisco del Aquena, became nuns in La Concepción; ibid., 12r-v, 32r.

77. Although each founder had different goals, Jorge de Andrade and Catalina María used similar arguments to solicit funds for their schools; BNP, B122.

78. AGI, Indiferente General 1478, Petition from viceroy count of Chinchón in the names of Miguel Nuñez de Santiago and Jorge de Andrade, 29/XI/1636, includes the approval of the license and the ordinances of the Recogimiento de Nuestra Señora de los Remedios.

79. AGI, Indiferente General 1479, Philip IV to the viceroy, Audiencia, and archbishop, 14/XII/1639.

80. Cerda, *Libro intitulado*, 17r.

81. For an example of the status of girls educated in the recogimientos, see Monasterio de la Concepción, Leg. 3, exp. 24, 1627/32. "Expediente de ingreso de doña Marta de Oviedo, quien se encuentra en el recogimiento de doncellas de la Caridad." Her father requested that she be allowed to enter with a dowry of 1,000 pesos (normally 3,195 pesos for a nun of the black veil), given her qualifications.

82. Cobo, "Historia de la fundación," I: 137.

83. Cobo, "Historia de la fundación," I: 233–34. His estimate of 2,010 women in convents is slightly higher than the 1,591 count recorded in official visits in 1631 (see Appendix B).

84. I estimated the female religious population of Carmen de San José (founded 1643) at twenty.

85. This point is made by Elizabeth Lehfeldt for Valladolid, Spain; "Sacred and Secular Spaces," 1–3. For research on the connection between elite formation and convents in Latin America, see Burns, "Conventos, criollos," 315–17; and idem, *Colonial Habits*, 147–48. For Buenos Aires, see Fraschina, "La dote canónica."

86. Burns, *Colonial Habits*, 80–82. Coversely, the findings of Susan Soeiro for mid-eighteenth century Salvador da Bahia (the capital of Brazil) show that novitiates, many the daughters of merchants, businessmen, bureaucrats and the landed elite, entered the Desterro Convent during a period of economic depression and insecurity, Soeiro, "The Social and Economic Role," 220–21.

87. Hamnett, "Church Wealth"; Bronner, "Church, Crown, and Commerce," 81–85ff; Cushner, *Lords of the Land*.

88. Some scholars have argued that their proliferation resulted from changing inheritance patterns related to primogeniture and insufficient dowry funds for more than one daughter; Perry, *Gender and Disorder*, 78.

89. Sánchez Herrero, "Monjes y frailes," 408, 410, 412; Ruíz Martín, "Demografía eclesiástica," in *Diccionario de historia eclesiástica*, II: 682–733. The clarisas, for example, founded eighty-three new convents in the sixteenth century, forty-eight between 1601 and 1639, and sixteen from 1640 to 1700. In 1591 there were, on the average, between 3.11 and 4.12 nuns for every thousand laywomen in Castile. The number of male religious was much higher; Sánchez Lora, *Mujeres, conventos*, 99–106. On the importance of the orders of Saint Clare and the Conceptionists in New Spain, see Muriel, *Conventos de monjas*, 14, 138, 247.

90. Baernstein, "In Widow's Habit," 787–807; idem, "The Counter-Reformation Convent"; Lehfeldt, "Sacred and Secular," 25–26.

91. Lehfeldt, "Discipline, Vocation, and Patronage," 1012.

92. Sánchez Herrero, "Monjes y frailes," 408, 409; Borges, *Religiosos*, 127–28, 200–207, 217–18, 268–70.

93. San José (1603) was the first recollection house or discalced convent to be founded, followed by del Prado (1640), and Carmelitas Descalças (1643). After a long hiatus came the Trinitarias Descalças (1682), Santa Ana (1686), and Las Mercedarias Capuchinas (1713).

94. Asunción Lavrin, "Female Religious," 165–95; Martín, *Daughters*, ch. 7; Burns, *Colonial Habits*, 119–26.

95. Martín, *Daughters*, 181, says that dowries were between two thousand and twenty-five hundred pesos in most convents in Peru. See also Vargas Ugarte, *Historia de la Iglesia*, II: 113; van Deusen, "Los primeros recogimientos," 265, n. 18.

96. Martín, *Daughters*, 179–80; Burns, *Colonial Habits*, 122.

97. Kathryn Burns found that, by the seventeenth century, almost all female relatives of elite native Andeans were nuns of the white veil; *Colonial Habits*, 124.

98. See Appendix B. See also AAL, Monasterio de Nuestra Señora del Prado, Leg. 1; Monasterio de Santa Catalina de Sena, Leg. 1. A prosopographical study of nuns of the black and white veil might reveal linkages between old and new elites in Lima from 1600 to 1650.

99. AAL, Monasterio de Santa Clara, Leg. 4, exp. 25, 1632. "Autos de ingreso de María Nuñez y Francisca de Guevara para monjas de velo blanco." The petition from Abbess Doña Beatris de Escobar says that although the two were poor and orphaned, "se les acepta porque el monasterio está necesitado de monjas de velo blanco que le sirvan." See also AAL, Monasterio de Santa Clara, Leg. 4, exp. 32, 1632. "Autos de ingreso de Francisca de la Cruz, huérfana, natural del Puerto del Callao, para religiosa de velo blanco."

100. Martín, *Daughters*, 185.

101. Calancha, *Crónica moralizada*, III: chs. 23–28. Well into the 1620s conventual records referred to the fact that the families of the foundresses were beneméritos.

102. Soeiro, "The Social and Economic Role," 218–19, argues that "the convent operated as a social mechanism permitting the elite to restrict marriages, ultimately with the aim of maintaining itself as a self-perpetuating and exclusive body." For another perspective, see Fraschina, "La dote canónica," 70, 101.

103. Calancha, *Crónica moralizada*, III: 1010–24, ch. 28.

104. The Monasterio de San José had a strict population limit and more rigorous spiritual standards than the conventos grandes. The foundresses—Doña Inés de Sosa, daughter of Francisco Velásquez de Talavera and Antonia de Sosa, and Leonor de Ribera and her sister Beatríz de Orozco, daughters of Rodrigo de Orosco, marquis of Martara—left La Concepción to found the observant convent. Their father had been one of the first *pobladores* of Lima, AGI, Lima 321; Mendiburu, *Diccionario*, VII: 368. For Mexico, see Hoberman, *Mexico's Merchant Elite*, 236.

105. They were the daughters of General D. Francisco de Irarrazaval y Andía and Doña Leonor de Zárate y Recalde, who was the daughter of the *comendador* Diego Ortíz de Zárate of the Order of Santiago. Several of the nuns' brothers were encomenderos or held key governmental posts; Mendiburu, *Diccionario*, VIII: 370–71; Calancha and Torres, *Crónicas agustinianas*, 871–73.

106. This is certainly the case with Doña Magdalena Peralta and Doña Juana Bueno, who also entered the Monasterio del Prado, Mendiburu, *Diccionario*, VIII: 372. In eighteenth-century Buenos Aires, the distinction was made between "nobles," "nobles

pobres," or "indigentes" in establishing convents for the daughters of the rising merchant class; Fraschina, "La dote canónica," 68. For Mexico, see Loreto López, "Familia y conventos"; idem, "La fundación del Convento de la Concepción."

107. AGI, Lima 44, Madrid, 1623, 20r–20v: "Encargamos a los prelados yglesias catedrales y collegiales y monasterios capaces de vienes en común así de frailes como de monxas procuren todos juntos y cada uno de por si rremediar y acomodar mugeres pobres y huérfanas en los lugares donde estubieren. Pues entre las obligaciones y limosnas aque están vinculados los vienes y rrentas eclesiásticas en el estado que oy tiene este rreyno es esta una de las más precisas y meritorias."

108. For instance, in spite of one hundred thousand pesos in available capital for the convent of Discalced Carmelites, the license had been denied in 1619, AGI, Lima 37, no. 34, lib. IV, 21/III/1617, 258r–61v, "Poder que da Diego Mayuelo al padre Francisco de Figueroa jesuita, para que en su nombre pida licencia para la fundación del monasterio"; Lima 37, no. 34, lib. IV, 6/III/1617, 262r–69v: "Hacienda que ofrece Diego Mayuelo y su muger, vecinos de Lima para la fundacion del Monasterio de Carmelitas Descalças q[ue] pretenden hacer en ella"; and Lima 38, lib. IV, 358r–63v, which details donations of seventy thousand pesos in capital, land, and slaves plus thirty thousand more for the support of the fourteen nuns in the convent which Doña Leonor de Godoy and her husband, Diego de Mayuelo, were willing to donate; Lima 38, lib. IV, count of Esquilache to Philip III, 12/IV/1619, which states that the viceroy had denied Mayuelo the license to found the Convent of Discalced Carmelites.

109. The city council approved the foundation of the Monasterio de Santa Catalina (under secular authority) in 1624 without royal license, thus causing a major uproar. After this incident, royal decrees from Philip IV in 1626 reiterated his position that no new religious houses be founded; AGI, Lima 41, marquis of Guadálcazar to Philip IV, 8/III/1627; 15/III/1628; AGI, Lima 48, count of Chinchón to Philip IV, 21/IV/1637.

110. AGI, Lima 37, n. 34. lib. IV, 256r–58r: "El Príncipe de Esquilache a S.M. se solicita aclaración a la cédula que prohibe fundar monasterios si sólo se refiere a frailes o también a monjas," 6/IV/1617: "[En] la cédula de prohivición que tenemos los virreyes para no dar licencias para fundaciones de Monasterios no hallo que se estienda a monjas antes parece que admitiendo lo que ha concedido por que la cédula dize que no se de licencias para fundar monasterios y los motivos en q[ue] se funda la prohivición son solamente tocantes a frailes y en ninguno se supone que le ay en fundaciones de monjas."

111. On the attempt to control the power and numbers of the clergy in Spain under Philip IV, see Elliott, *The Count-Duke*, 182–84. The great age of religious foundations in Spain occurred during the second half of the sixteenth century. By 1600, opposition against new foundations increased, and after 1640 the Spanish Crown restricted new foundations because of the economic crisis and the belief that a saturation point had been reached. See Domínguez Ortíz, *The Golden Age of Spain*, 123–24.

112. Vargas Ugarte, *Historia general*, III: 270.

113. After a series of misunderstandings, an agreement was reached in 1643 that patronage should rest with the foundresses. See AGI, Lima 302, "El Arzobispo de Lima da cuenta del estado que tiene la fundación del convento que se pretende tener en Lima de Monjas descalças de Santa Teresa," 7/VI/1642.

114. A handful of nuns from this convent later founded other Carmelite convents in Quito (1652), Chuquisaca (1665), Guatemala (1667), Huamanga (1683), and Santa Teresa in Lima (1686). See Vargas Ugarte, *Historia de la Iglesia*, III: 26, n. 17.

115. She wrote to Archbishop Pedro de Villagómez: "[No] me hallo con fuerça para poder guardar su regla y santo instituto con la perfección que requiere por ser mis años tantos y mis achaques muchos . . . suplico que se me da licencia para salir de la dicha clausura y religion, y porq[ue] mi intento es y ha sido siempre de vivir vida recogida, me señale cerca del d[ic]ho convento una habitación y sustento para que pueda acabar los días de mi vida." AAL, Monasterio de las Carmelitas Descalças, Leg. 1, 20/II/1644.

116. AAL, Monasterio de las Carmelitas Descalças, Leg. 1, 1643.

117. Lehfeldt, "Discipline, Vocation, and Patronage," 1016. She also argues that the effort to impose claustration was not new to sixteenth- and seventeenth-century Spain; the Tridentine reforms resemble those of Ferdinand and Isabel, 1019.

118. For a general overview of the period, see Vargas Ugarte, *Historia de la Iglesia*, II: 458, 472, 474ff.

119. Duviols, *Cultura andina*, xxxiii, 132, 133, 253, 254; Sánchez, *Amancebados*, 55, 125. Both María Ynés and María Susa Ayala, from Chancay, were sentenced to two years of labor in the Hospital de Santa Ana.

120. Vargas Ugarte, *Historia general*, III: 244. While viceroy, the count of Chinchón witnessed one auto-da-fé in 1625 and another in 1639, Castañeda and Hernández, *La Inquisición*, I: 332–36.

121. The three theologians influenced one another and felt a sense of moral and spiritual superiority as Spaniards. See Kottman, *Law and Apocalypse*, 107–9. On the contact between Fray Luis de Granada and Teresa of Avila, see Alvárez, "Fray Luis de León," in Criado de Val, *Santa Teresa*, 493–502. On the influence of other contemporary writers on her, see Andrés Martín, "Proceso de interioridad," 7–23. On Granada's popularity and the number of editions that appeared in Spain, see Rhodes, "Spain's Misfired Canon." Rhodes compares the *Libro* directly with Osuna's *Abecedario*, 57, n. 31. See also Whinnom, "The Problem of the 'Best Seller.'"

122. Kottman, *Law and Apocalypse*, 110–13.

123. Nalle, *God in La Mancha*, 145–47; Iwasaki, "Mujeres al borde," 590, 596–99; Hampe Martínez, "The Diffusion of Books."

124. Iwasaki, "Mujeres al borde," 597–99; Muriel, *Cultura femenina novohispana*, 314–42; Jaffary, "Virtue and Transgression"; Holler, "The Spiritual and Physical Ecstasies."

125. An object of adoration and source of "mystical" knowledge, Santa Rosa attracted followers from modest Spanish, creole and casta families. Elite Spanish women also sought her spiritual advice. See Iwasaki, "Mujeres al borde," 587–90; Martín, *Daughters*, 288. See also the excellent article by Mujica Pinilla, "El ancla de Santa Rosa."

126. Iwasaki, "Mujeres al borde," on Santa Rosa, 584; on beatas: "la cuaterona Isabel de Jesús hizo un original compendio de las teorías de fray Luis de Granada," 597; Inés de Ubitarte also confessed familiarity con his writings, 598; and Inés Velasco, 599.

127. "Si es verdadero el recogimiento, siéntese muy claro, porque acaece alguna operación . . . en que parese que se levanta el alma con el juego, que ya ve lo es las cosas del mundo," *Camino de perfección*, ch. XLVI. Teresa's writings were an important vehicle by which Francisco de Osuna's ideas were disseminated. Andrés Martín, *Los rec-*

ogidos, 621, 624–42. Her dog-eared copy of Osuna's *Tercer abecedario* contained numerous markings and comments in the margins.

128. "Este modo de rezar—aunque sea vocalmente—con mucha más brevedad se recoge el entendimiento, y es oración que trae consigo muchos bienes: llámase recogimiento, porque recoge el alma todas las potencias y se entra dentro de sí con su Dios, y viene con más brevedad a enseñarla su divino Magestad y a darla oración de quietud que de ninguna otra manera"; *Camino de perfección*, ch. XLVI.

129. Ahlgren, *Teresa of Avila*, 10–15, 32–33, 38–39, 41–42.

130. Weber, *Teresa of Avila*, 11–12, 15.

131. Teresa de Avila, *Vida*, 247b; *Camino de perfección*, ch. XVIII.

132. Ahlgren, *Teresa of Avila*, 24–31.

133. Perry, *Gender and Disorder*, 117. I have found a number of cases of individual beatas throughout seventeenth-century Spain, but collective organizations were rare.

134. Alberro, *Inquisición y sociedad*, 491–525; Holler, "'More Sins,'" 211–13.

135. Iwasaki, "Mujeres al borde," 84–85, 88ff; Castañeda and Hernández, *La Inquisición*, I: 335; on Melgarejo's trial in the 1620s, see Iwasaki, "Luisa Melgarejo de Soto"; Glave, "Santa Rosa."

136. Castañeda y Hernández, *La Inquisición*, II: 329.

137. The term "alumbrado" is vague and confusing but should not be conflated with "beatas." Not all beatas were alumbradas. The cases of Luisa Melgarejo and Inés de Ubitarte (a nun in La Encarnación) were suspended; *La Inquisición*, I: 333–36. See also Medina, *Historia del Tribunal*, II: 27–34. Castañeda and Hernández, *La Inquisición*, I: 335. See also Iwasaki, "Luisa Melgarejo de Soto."

138. The full quotation reads: "[C]on boz del Señor, escusar de otros exercicios de trabaxo doméstico y vivir en ocio, cosa sospechosa"; cited in Iwasaki, "Mujeres al borde," 108.

139. Castañeda y Delgado, *La Inquisición*, I: 334. In 1629, Inquisition authorities published an edict describing in detail "superstitious" behaviors; ibid., I: 370–71.

140. Sánchez Lora, *Mujeres, conventos*, 241: "Agotada la mística, el esfuerzo por vivificarla empieza y termina, dramáticamente, en la escala secreta sanjuanista. No estando la casa sosegada, todo será hacer fuerza al proceso a base de violencia y sangre, para sosegar, para aniquilar la otra tendencia horizontal que repugna al aprisionamiento." I am not arguing that female mystics did not continue to practice forms of "interior" spirituality. Biographies and autobiographies of visionaries in Spain, Peru, and Mexico abound with their experiences of ecstatic raptures, visions and physical ailments.

141. *The Book of Foundations*, recounted, in Teresa's words, the foundation of sixteen Discalced Carmelite convents in Spain. Most of her works appeared in Spain in the 1580s and were available in Lima by the beginning of the seventeenth century. Archbishop Hernando de Ugarte held some of her works in his library. See Hampe Martínez, "La biblioteca del arzobispo."

142. Cerda, *Política*, 237r.

143. Soto, *Obligaciones*, 58r: "Impórtales muchísimo a los Religiosos el recogimiento y huyr de tratos seglares, y salidas, pues a penas, y casí nunca volverán al Convento sin desmedro, qual dezía Seneca: Nunca vuelvo a casa las costumbres que saque, que no de balde dize San Bernardo: que al buen frayle el pueblo le es cárcel, y parayso la celda casa de si mismo, y antes lo avía dicho San Hierónymo: y entre las insignias, y

trofeos de vida monástica pone el mismo San Bernardo el recogimiento, y rincón, y la voluntaria pobreza ésto es lo que ennobleze la vida monástica, aún en los muy virtuosos puede hazer impresión tan mal Planeta, y constelación de vulgo: y assí linda cosa es para Religiosos el recogimiento, y poco trato con seglares, porque no buelvan tales a casa quales salieron: y porque la mucha conservación es causa de que sean menospreciados."

144. Cerda, *Política*, 236r–46r.

145. Ibid., *Política*, 238r.

146. Santibañez Salcedo, *El Monasterio*, 22. Chapter III of their constitutions commanded silence during periods of communal labor and specified hours of "mental prayer"; Amaya, *La mujer en la conquista*, 504–5.

147. AAL, Monasterio del Prado, Leg. 1; Calancha wrote: "[Le] fue dando unos ardientes deseos en continuadas ansias de verse en más estrecha Recolección de la que había en la Encarnación, donde si se hallaba santidad y religión y tantas monjas siervas queridas de Dios y de tanta opinión de santidad, la entristecía el haber dentro tantos centenarios de monjas y criadas, con que no podía tener la soledad y quietud que le pedía su retiro y oración." *Crónicas agustinianas*, 875. Did Lima's pattern of monastic patronage resemble patterns in Valladolid, Spain, where wealthy benefactors tended to finance religious houses that emphasized strict enclosure and discipline? Lehfeldt, "Discipline, Vocation, and Patronage," 1025.

148. Santibáñez Salcedo, *El Monasterio*, 22.

149. Calancha, *Crónicas agustinianas*, 795–870.

150. However, the administration of the cult provoked serious confrontations between various authorities over the years; see BNP, B538, 1615: "Expediente sobre la petición presentada por don Nicolás Ruíz Bracamonte para que se proceda al inventario," which provides details on the need to provide more security and a priest to care for the cult. See also Mendiburu, *Diccionario* (1934), IX: 194–95.

151. Calancha, *Crónicas agustinianas*, 875.

152. Ibid., 876.

153. She also received forty thousand pesos from the priest Jorge de Andrade, who had also founded the colegio/recogimiento of Nuestra Señora de los Remedios, Mendiburu, *Diccionario*, VIII: 372.

154. Calancha, *Crónica agustinianas*, 911, 915. For a discussion of Jerónima de la Madre de Dios, see Amaya, *La mujer en la conquista*, 508–10.

155. Calancha, *Crónicas agustinianas*, 883.

156. Ibid., 897.

157. Ibid., 884, 898–99.

158. Ibid., 884. AAL, Monasterio del Prado, Leg. 1. See, for example, the request of Doña María de Olmos y Ortega who wrote: "[Q]ue estoy por seglar en el Convento de Nuestra Señora del Prado y quiero ser religiosa del velo negro se pronuncio sentencia de divorcio q[ue] seguí en la villa de potosí contra martín alonso de olmos mi marido." 28/IX/1645. She took her formal vows a year later.

159. See, for example, the petition of Doña Micaela Jiraldo, doncella from Ica, who had been a "seglar" for eighteen years in La Concepción and wanted to enter El Prado as a nun of the black veil, but, because all the slots were full, requested to be admitted as a nun of the white veil, paying 1,597 pesos in dowry, AAL, Monasterio del Prado, Leg. 1, 6/X/1654.

160. Vargas Ugarte, *Historia de la Iglesia*, II: 471.

161. Calancha, *Crónica moralizada*, III: 986.

162. Ibid., 997.

163. Calancha, *Crónicas agustinianas*, 893–94.

164. Valega, *El virreinato del Perú*, 429–30. See the fictitious rendering in Lavalle, *La hija del Contador*. See also Vargas Ugarte, *Historia de la Iglesia*, II: 460–71.

165. Juan de Soto, *Obligaciones*, 25v–26r.

166. AAL, Monasterio del Prado, Leg. 2. Between 1664 and 1670, two nuns attempted to nullify their vows: a significant number given the fact that only thirty-three nuns inhabited the convent. This evidence supports the fact that a life of recogimiento was not for everyone. See the case of Costança de la Madre de Dios, in 1664, who argued that eight years before, her father forced her to become a nun. She complained that the constitutions of the Monasterio del Prado were too strict, but could not even be persuaded to transfer to the more lax convent of La Encarnación, where she had relatives.

167. Osuna, *Norte*, says, "Excúsanse diciendo que las ofrecen a Dios en un monasterio cuando las meten monjas, y plega a Dios que no las ofrezcan al diablo, porque Dios no recibe sino sacrificio voluntario."

168. Calancha, *Crónicas agustinianas*, 898.

169. Stallybrass and White, *The Politics and Poetics*, 16, 20–21, 191–95.

170. Translated and quoted in Brading, *The First America*, 317.

171. Martín, *Daughters*, 179.

Chapter 6: Contesting the Boundaries of the Sacred and the Worldly

1. Buendía, *Vida admirable*, 215.

2. The Casa de las Amparadas de la Puríssima Concepción was also referred to as the "Casa de las Amparadas" the "Casa de Recogidas" the "Beaterio de las Amparadas" and the "Recogimiento de las Amparadas."

3. García y Sanz, *Vida del Venerable*, 111. Castillo and the count of Lemos maintained an especially close relationship: Castillo was both the viceroy's personal confessor and godfather to two of his children. For a good biography, see Nieto Vélez, *Francisco del Castillo*, 225–42. The viceroy's predecessors—the count of Alba de Liste (1655–61); the count of Santisteban (1661–66)—and later, the count of Castellar (1674–78) were not interested in supporting such a foundation; García y Sanz, *Vida del Venerable*, 112; and Mendiburu, *Diccionario*, II: 320. The *Audiencia* presided between 1666 and 1667, until the count of Lemos arrived.

4. Buendía, *Vida admirable*, 211.

5. AGI, Lima 414, the archbishop to Fiscal, 28/I/1735; Mendiburu, *Diccionario*, II: 320. A plot of land worth 11,000 pesos, an additional 10,200 donation from Lemos himself, and other assistance enabled the foundation of the house to be laid in 1668.

6. Mugaburu, *Diario*, 124.

7. García y Sanz, *Vida del Venerable*, 114.

8. Buendía, *Vida admirable*, 216.

9. Ibid., 219.

10. Ibid. Three of the nine women's names are known: the forty-three-year-old Inés María de Jesús, who became the first abbess; thirty-eight-year-old Isabel María de la Concepción; and twenty-eight-year-old Gertrudis de los Reyes. Nieto Vélez, *Francisco del Castillo*, 133. All three testified in the beatification *proceso* of Francisco del Castillo.

11. Buendía, *Vida admirable*, 220–21; Mugaburu, *Diario*, 126; *Procesión antecedente*, s.f.

12. López, *Sermón panegyrico*, 29v.

13. The notion of concentric circles became more popular as a result of Dante's *Inferno*, but the origin is Ptolomaic.

14. López, *Sermón panegyrico*, 27v–28r.

15. Out of a total of 18,955 women (15,300 lay women plus 3,655 living in convents), 20 percent lived in convents; Cook, *Numeración general*, 357–58.

16. Mexico City, with an estimated population of one hundred thousand circa 1700 (20 percent Spanish and creole and 80 percent Indians and castas), had twenty-nine monasteries and twenty-two convents, which suggests a much lower ratio between religious and secular inhabitants than in Lima; Gemelli Careri, *Viaje*, 22–23.

17. AGI, Lima 414, count of Lemos to Queen Regent Mariana, Lima, 25/I/1669.

18. For examples where women describe themselves, or are described by others, as "recogida" or living in "recogimiento," see AAL, Esponsales de Matrimonios, Leg. 4, 1661, Thomasina de Sotomayor, madre de Doña Josepha de la Fuente vs. Estéban de Miranda; Leg. 5, 1663, Doña Ana Merlo; Leg. 7, 1695, María del Carmen Noriega, negra libre. See also AAL, Nulidades, Leg. 21, 1669, Juana Maldonado, negra esclava, vs. Ygnacio de la Cruz, mulato esclavo. The administrator (*mayordomo*) of Juana's owner described her as "recogida and virtuosa."

19. Maravall, *La cultura del barroco*, 24; Sánchez Lora, *Mujeres, conventos*, 37ff, 456ff.

20. In 1588, Diego de Alcalá, a fifteenth-century Spanish Franciscan, was canonized: the first new saint in sixty-five years. See Burke, "How to Be," 46.

21. Vargas Ugarte, *Historia de la Iglesia*, III: 227–55.

22. Melquiades Andrés Martín has argued for a "rationalization and decline" of mysticism in seventeenth-century Spain; *Historia de la mística*, 445–48.

23. Santo Toribio de Mogrovejo (1538–1606), beatified in 1679 and canonized in 1726; San Martín de Porras (1579–1639), the process for his beatification began around 1650, he was beatified in 1837 and canonized in 1962; San Juan Macías (1585–1645); San Francisco Solano (1549–1602), beatified in 1679 and canonized in 1726; Nicolás de Ayllón (?–1677). A number of other limeñas were considered for beatification including Isabel de Porras Marmolejo in 1665.

24. Lavrin, "La vida femenina," 31. On the beatification process of Santa Rosa, see Hampe Martínez, *Santidad*, and, in particular, his transcription of the "Relación de las fiestas y gastos por la beatificación de Santa Rosa en la ciudad de Lima (28 de mayo de 1669)," 135–41.

25. Graziano, "Una verdad fictícia," 309–10, refers to the 1665 hagiography written by L. Hansen, who drew comparisons between the two.

26. On the decline of Spain after 1648, see Stradling, *Europe and the Decline*, 143–99.

27. Porras Barrenechea, *Fuentes*, 242–46.

28. Córdoba y Salinas, *Crónica franciscana*, 33.

29. Lavrin, "La vida femenina," 33.

30. Molinos had an impact all over Europe, and particularly in parts of Germany; see Andrés Martín, *Los recogidos*, 729. On his link to Osuna's precepts of recogimiento, Molinos said in his *Guía espiritual*: "Estos, recogidos en lo interior de sus almas, con verdadera entrega en las divinas manos, con olvido y total desnudez aun de si mismos, van siempre con levantado espíritu en la presencia del Señor, por fé pura, sin imágen, forma ni figura, pero con gran seguridad, fundada en la interior tranquilidad y sosiego, en cuyo infuso recogimiento tira el espíritu con tanta fuerza, que hace recoger allá dentro el alma, el corazón, el cuerpo y todas las corporales fuerzas"; Molinos, *Guía espiritual*, Libro III, chs. 1, 4; also cited in Andrés Martín, *Los recogidos*, 707.

31. For a discussion of seventeenth-century Spanish mystics, see Sánchez Lora, *Mujeres, conventos*, 403–59; and Manero Sorolla, "Visionarias reales," 305–8. For Italy, see Cabibbo, *La santa dei Tomasi*, 104, 124ff.

32. Nora Jaffary examined ninety-five cases of "false" mystics (forty-nine men and forty-six women) tried by the Inquisition after 1598; Jaffary, "Virtue and Transgression," 10. The numbers in Lima are significantly smaller, which leads one to ask whether the Lima Inquisition did not target "ilusas" and "alumbrados," or their numbers were insignificant. In Lima, beatas in the Beaterio de las Nerias (later the Monasterio de Trinitarias Descalzas in 1682), included María de la Encarnación, known for her "intense contemplation"; Francisca de San José, who released souls from purgatory; and Juana de Jesús María, known for her dedication to the Passion of Christ. See Santísima Trinidad, *Historia de la fundación*, 95ff, 112.

33. Manero Sorolla, "Visionarias reales," 312.

34. AGI, Lima 336, "Expediente que trata de la fundación del convento," 1697. The Beaterio de Jesús, María y José became a convent after nearly forty years and numerous petitions from various parties. María Jacinta wished to observe the Carmelite or Saint Clare rules, but later determined (and others convinced her) that because these orders had convents in Lima, she should choose the Capuchin Order within the observant Franciscans. For a list of petitions, see Vargas Ugarte, *Biblioteca peruana*, V: 158–59.

35. Mendiburu provided a very critical assessment of him: "[D]ejó en Lima muchos recuerdos de su vida mística y de su religiosidad llevada al último grado de la exageración. Y en verdad hacía cosas estravagantes y hasta ridículos que desdecían de la sensatez y manejo circunspecto de un mandatario de su gerarquía"; *Diccionario*, III: 227–28. For contemporary characterizations of the count of Lemos' "piety," see Buendía, *Vida admirable*, 237–42.

36. Basadre, *El Conde*, 293ff.

37. In Spain, Philip IV (1621–65) published a royal decree admonishing municipal authorities to recoger "mugeres perdidas" and place them in correctional houses. Royal decree, Philip IV, 11/VII/1661, *Novíssima recopilación*, Lib. XII, tít. XXVI, ley VIII. This decree applied not only to Madrid but also to other capitals experiencing the same phenomenon. He uses the term "casas de galera" rather than "recogimientos."

38. Mendiburu, *Diccionario*, 2d ed., XI: 415, reports thirteen strong tremors (*temblores*) in Lima between 1668 and 1716. A serious earthquake in 1655, a disastrous one in 1687, and yet another in 1690 brought major epidemics in their wake. In 1673 an epidemic known as the *cordellate* swept Lima, claiming a number of victims, including the Jesuit priest Castillo. See Vargas Ugarte, *Vida del siervo*, 27; see also Angulo, "El terremoto del año 1687"; and idem, "El terremoto del año de 1690."

39. Liñán y Cisneros, *Carta pastoral*, 18 July 1695; 15 October 1695; 9 April 1697; 20 March 1699; Muguburu, *Chronicle*, 313.

40. Díaz de San Miguel, *La gran fee* (JCB).

41. Xaimes de Ribera, *Hazer de si mismo*, 8r; Mispilivar, *Sagrado arbitrio;* Elso, *Sermones varios* (all JCB).

42. Liñán y Cisneros, *Carta pastoral*, 20/III/1699.

43. For an example, ser Echave y Assu, *La estrella de Lima*, 235–36.

44. AGI, Lima 336, "Expediente."

45. Not only was social imparity considered a problem in Lima, but authorities in Mexico City expressed their concern over the number of destitute females. They responded by founding one recogimiento in 1658 for extremely poor women in a precarious state, Muriel, *Los recogimientos*, 78–110.

46. Spaniards represented 53 percent of the population, but that percentage included mestizos. Certainly the latter had risen from 0.08 percent in 1614 to a more significant percentage by 1700, even though the precise number cannot be determined.

47. Lavallé, "Divorcio y nulidad," 427–28, 463–64.

48. Ibid., 436–42.

49. For a sample of cases from 1650 to 1713, see AAL, D, Leg. 29, 1651, Leonora Pasquala yndia "honrada y de buena vida de Guailas"; Leg. 33, 1659, Francisca del Lunar, yndia del Callao vs. Agustín Lunar; Leg. 34, 1661, María de los Santos, yndia, vs. Lásaro Hernándes de la Cruz; Leg. 37, 1664, María Sabina, yndia de Guánuco, vs. Sebastián Sinchi; Leg. 40, 1667, Agustina Barbuja, yndia de Caxamarca, vs. Sebastián Gómez Carvallo, alferes en el presidio del Callao; Leg. 45, 1672, María Antonia, yndia natural del pueblo del Surco, vs. Andrés Ramos, maestro sastre, residentes de Lima; 1672, Juana Madalena, yndia, vs. Francisco Valero; Leg. 47, 1675, Ygnacia María Gomes de la Cruz vs. José de la Paz; Leg. 48, 1676, Catalina de los Reyes vs. Joseph Liscano, yndio; Leg. 52, 1685, Juana María vs. Bartholomé de Esquivel; Leg. 55, 1690, Doña Gregoria Grifo, yndia, vs. Felipe Chamilla, yndio; Leg. 60, 1698, María de la Cruz, yndia, vs. Antonio Baltasar, mestizo; Leg. 60, 1699, María de la Cruz, yndia, vs. Pascual Guaman, mestizo; Leg. 63, 1708, Ysabel de la Peña vs. Joseph Fernández de Almeida.

50. AAL, D, Leg. 38, 1665, Melchora del los Reyes, morena libre, vs. Joseph de Sandoval.

51. AAL, Nulidades, Leg. 21, 1660, Juan Bazarrete, mulato libre, vs. Antonia María, negra esclava; 1661, Juana Maldonado, negra esclava, vs. Ygnacio de la Cruz, mulato esclavo; Ascencia María, yndia del Callao, vs. Cristóbal Lunar, yndio.

52. AAL, CN, Leg. 19, 1678.

53. Ibid., D, Leg. 52, 1685, María Ferrero vs. Francisco Rodrígues Matajudios.

54. Many women relied upon other family members for economic support. See AAL, Litigios Matrimoniales, Leg. 4, 1713, Doña Ana de Cereceda vs. Matias de León. AAL, D, Leg. 30, 1653, Ysabel de la Cruz, morena libre, vs. Graviel Jimenes. Ysabel said that without her son's support she would not be able to survive. Doña Teresa Gutiérrez's attorney described her as "bibiendo siempre en un perpetuo enserramiento, recogimiento y virtud a expensas de lo que su madre le embiaba," D, Leg. 49, 1680, Doña Teresa Gutiérrez vs. Don Luis Balcasar. See also D, Leg. 53, 1686, Bernarda de la Cruz, mulata libre, vs. Pablo de Alarcón, negro esclavo; Leg. 53, 1688, María de la Cruz vs. Pasqual de Alarcón.

55. AAL, D, Leg. 49, 1678, Michaela Flores vs. Ignacio de Valenzuela. Also cited in Lavallé, "Divorcio y nulidad," 442.

56. Ibid., Leg. 56, 1691, Valeriana Pimentel vs. Roque Ventura, maestro cerrujero, said that she was forced to work to feed and clothe herself during her eighteen years of marriage, but that she kept her part of the marital obligation.

57. Ibid., Leg. 38, 1654, Doña Francisca Crespo vs. Benito de Dueñas. Her case is also cited in Lavallé, "Divorcio y nulidad," 442.

58. AGI, Lima 336, "Expediente." On the growing number of abandoned, free and freed parda women who went to the Hospital de San Bartolomé to die, see van Deusen, "The 'Alienated' Body," 28.

59. On conversion efforts of "worldly" women, see AAL, Beatificaciones, Francisco del Castillo, 740r, 741r, testimony of Inés María de Jesús, for her description of Father Castillo's conversion work, which often concentrated upon poor and lost (perdida) women. Antonia Lucía Maldonado de Quintanilla (she adopted the surname del Espíritu Santo), founder of the Beaterio de las Nazarenas, gave advice to young women. See Providencia, *Relación*, ch. XIV, 56–58.

60. Lavallé, "Divorcio y nulidad," 430. In her analysis based upon the 1700 *Numeración general*, María Pilar Pérez Cantó calculated that nearly 60 percent of the total population was composed of women; *Lima en el siglo XVIII*, 53–54.

61. Peralta y Barnuevo, *Imágen política*, 14r.

62. The work was dedicated to the Viceroy Don Melchor de Navarra y Rocaful, Duque de la Palata (1681–89); see Montalvo, *El sol*, 37.

63. AGI, Lima 520, Archbishop Almoguera to Charles II, 10/VII/1675; also cited in Hamnett, "Estates and Loans," 116–17.

64. On loans in Mexico, see Lavrín, "El Convento de Santa Clara"; for Cuzco, see Burns, "Apuntes."

65. Andrien, "The Sale of Juros," 1–19; idem, *Crisis and Decline*, 27–28.

66. AGI, Lima 333, abbess of the Monjas Bernardas to the king, 1656.

67. AGI, Lima 333, Lima, abbesses to the king, 6/XII/1664.

68. Viceroy La Palata called convents "provincia tan dilatada y dificultosa de comprender y gobernar, que ya se ha desesperado de su dirección." Archbishop Liñán y Cisneros (1678–1705) found it impossible to regulate conventual income; Mendiburu, *Diccionario*, VI: 4.

69. Lavallé, "La population conventuelle," 167–96. The number of women and young girls wishing to "pisar el suelo" or "step on the floor" as "seglares" or "educandas" increased substantially after 1640 in convents such as Santa Catalina and Nuestra Señora del Prado; see AAL, Monasterio de Nuestra Señora del Prado, Leg. 1, 2; AAL, Monasterio de Santa Catalina de Sena, Leg. 1, 2. See also Cook, *Numeración general*, 357–58. From 1690 to 1700 Archbishop Liñán y Cisneros tried to pressure convents to reduce the number of nonreligious women by restricting the entrance of nuns, but his strategy backfired. The number of nonreligious women only continued to increase; Mendiburu, *Diccionario*, VI: 4. The demographic "secularization" of convents in Lima is echoed in Spanish Naples; Russo, *I monasteri femminili*, 107–9. The term "seglar" was sometimes synonymous with "recogida."

70. van Deusen, *Dentro del cerco*, 29.

71. This is true for Santa Clara, Santa Catalina, and La Concepción, which quad-

rupled, and for the recollection convent of San José. I suspect that the numbers for the year 1669 for La Encarnación are underrepresented.

72. AAL, CN, Leg. 18, 1676. Doña María de Lara y Figueroa lived as a "seglar recogida" in the Monasterio de la Trinidad; D, Leg. 49, 1680, Doña Theresa Matoso vs. Capitán Francisco Ramírez. See also AAL, Monasterio de la Concepción, Leg. 26, exp. 50, 1692, Solicitud de María de la Rosa, india depositada en la Concepción.

73. AAL, D, Leg. 47, 1675, Doña Cathalina de Castro vs. Juan de Montesinos Salazar. Their daughter had resided as a seglar in the Monasterio de la Concepción.

74. Ibid., Leg. 33, 1660, Doña Angela de Casteñeda vs. Juan de Figueroa; Leg. 49, 1680, Doña Theresa Matoso vs. Capitán Francisco Ramírez; Leg. 49, 1680, Doña Luisa de Santileses vs. Capitán Bartolomé Calderón; Leg. 63, 1708, Ysabel de la Peña vs. Joseph Fernández de Almeida. Litigios Matrimoniales, Leg. 4, Doña María de Aguado y Cárdenas, convent unspecified; Doña María de Médrez, 1710, Monasterio de la Trinidad. See also AAL, Santa Clara, Leg. 13, exp. 1, 1669, Autos de ingreso de doña Maria Romero, casada, para seglar en el monasterio; Leg. 13, exp. 19, 1669, Autos de ingreso de Juana de Caceres. In both cases, the women claimed their husbands had threatened to kill them.

75. AAL, Monasterio de Santa Clara, Leg. 9, exp. 143, 1656, Autos de ingreso de Doña Micaela Bravo, divorciada, para religiosa de velo negro en el monasterio de Santa Clara. AAL, D, Leg. 33, 1660, Doña Angela de Castañeda vs. Juan de Figueroa; Leg. 37, 1664, Doña Andrea de la Cueba y Espinossa vs. Cristobal de Escarnilla. Doña Andrea took her vows in the Monasterio de Santa Catalina; D, Leg. 38, 1665, Doña Agustina de Dueñas vs. Bernardo de Ortega; Agustina became a nun of the white veil in Santa Clara. See also AAL, Santa Clara, Leg. 13, exp. 83, 1671, Autos de ingreso de Dona Josefa de Guadalupe, casada para religiosa del velo blanco; Santa Clara, Leg. 14, exp. 23, 1672, Casada Petronila Lopez de Paredes entrando como seglar. Her husband consented; Monasterio de la Encarnación, Leg. 13, exp. 41, 1675, Autos de ingreso de Doña Sebastiana de Paredes y Angulo como monja de velo blanco en el Monasterio.

76. AAL, Santa Clara, Leg. 22, exp. 21, 1688, Autos sobre la solicitud de Maria de la Cruz samba libre, en la causa de divorico que sigue contra Pascual Alarcon, negro esclavo de Doña María Iñigo. María de la Cruz argued that her husband attacked her with a knife while deposited in a private home and requested safekeeping in Santa Clara.

77. See AAL, Litigios Matrimoniales, Leg. 3, of a woman labeled as "una mujer muy baja con quien tiene hijos," accused of concubinage who was deposited in the Monasterio de la Encarnación. See also Litigios Matrimoniales, Leg. 4, María Bruna, 1701, negra libre in the Monasterio de la Encarnación; María Magdalena, mestiza, 1702, in the Monasterio de la Encarnación; María Santos, 1715, in the Monasterio de la Concepción. María Carrión, married to a master barber with a moderate income, requested to be deposited in a convent where she could work during her divorce proceedings; D, Leg. 63, 1712.

78. AAL, La Encarnación, Leg. 11, exp. 106, 1666, Autos de ingreso de Doña María Josefa de Jesús, huérfana recogida en el Colegio de las Niñas de la Caridad, monja de velo blanco. See also the example of Alfonsa de Atocha, deposited in 1703 in the Hospital de Nuestra Señora de Atocha, then taken to the Monasterio de la Encarnación to be raised "con todo recogimiento y virtud," returned at age eight to the hospi-

tal/orphanage. Eventually she became a nun of the white veil in La Encarnacíon; Mannarelli, *Hechiceras*, 83–84.

79. AAL, D, Leg. 48, 1678, El Sargento Mathias Polanco vs. Theresa Salgado.
80. AAL, CN, Leg. 15, 11/X/1669.
81. Ibid., Leg. 23, 13/I/1690.
82. van Deusen, *Dentro del cerco*, Cuadro I, "Proporción de religiosas, seglares y sirvientes, Lima 1700," indicates that the ratio of religious woman to seglar and serviente (which includes the category donada) for the three largest convents was La Concepción: 433: 608; La Encarnación: 370: 453; Santa Clara: 306: 326.
83. The 1614 census lists 1,375 mulatas, indias, and mestizas (I excluded the black population because the census does not distinguish between enslaved and free women) and 425 servants in convents. The 1700 *Numeración* count for the lay population is 3,311 indias, mulatas, castas, and free blacks; in institutions, a total of 1,342 non-Spanish, free criadas, and donadas. The number of slaves in convents and beaterios (735) represents 17 percent of the total female slave population in 1700 (3, 663). See Appendices B and C for an elaboration of statistics.
84. AAL, CN, Leg. 21, 1684; Leg. 23, 1690.
85. Ibid., Leg. 13, 24/I/1661.
86. AAL, Monasterio de Santa Clara, Leg. 11, exp. 71, 1663, Autos que sigue Feliciana de Salinas, negra, contra Doña María de Salinas, monja del monasterio de Santa Clara, para que se le reconozca como persona libre.
87. AAL, CN, Leg. 17, 1673.
88. AAL, Esponsales de Matrimonios, Leg. 7, 1694, María del Carmen Noriega, negra libre.
89. They were either pardas, morenas, or quarteronas. Jean-Pierre Tardieu, *Los negros*, I: 394, calculated the following racial proportion of donadas entering La Encarnación and Santa Clara between 1642 and 1699:

	LA ENCARNACIÓN	SANTA CLARA
negras	1	5
mulatas	25	18
cuarteronas	4	13

90. Nuns or family members might offer anywhere between two hundred and five hundred pesos. In Cuzco, a five-hundred-peso fee for donadas seems to have been the norm; Burns, *Colonial Habits*, 120.
91. AAL, Monasterio de La Concepción, Leg. 23, exp. 27, 1683. Expediente de ingreso de Melchora del Santíssimo Sacramento, morena libre.
92. The example of Teresa is cited in Tardieu, *Los negros*, I: 397.
93. Ibid., 398.
94. AAL, Monasterio de La Encarnación, 1688, Autos de ingreso de Juana Josepha como donada. Also cited in Tardieu, *Los negros*, I: 396–97.
95. AAL, Monasterio de Santa Clara, Leg. 11, exp. 53, 1698, Autos de ingreso de la parda María de Vargas, criada del monasterio, para religiosa donada.
96. AAL, Monasterio de Santa Clara, Leg. 21, exp. 66, 1699, Autos de ingreso de Maria de Mora para religiosa donada.

97. Tardieu, *Los negros*, I: 395–96.

98. AAL, Monasterio de Santa Clara, Leg. 21, exp. 56, 1698, Autos de profesión de la parda Maria de Urrutia (de Huánuco) para monja donada; Leg. 21, exp. 67, 1699, Autos de profesión de Juana Villarroel para monja donada.

99. AAL, Monasterio de la Concepción, Leg. 23, exp. 18, 1683, Solicitud que presentan Lucia Bravo de Laguna y Catalina de la Madre de Dios para ser donadas, quarteronas libres; Leg. 23, exp. 20, 1683, Solicitud que presenta Maria Ustaque de Zárate, mulata, para donada; Leg. 22, exp. 26, 1680, Solicitud de Polonia de Estrada, india. See also Monasterio de La Concepción, Leg. 21, exp. 24, 1678, Solicitud que presenta Maria de la Cueva, india para el hábito de donada.

100. AGI, Lima 79, Carta no. 57, "Monjas de la Concepción quieren fundar una recolección, piden licencia," 15/I/1681; AGI, Lima 79, Carta no. 58, Viceroy Melchor Liñan y Cisneros to Charles II, 1681; AGI, Lima 334, "La petición de las monjas carmelitas descalzas que quieren fundar otro convento con un límite de veintiuno en el año 1672."

101. López, *Sermón panegyrico*, 8v.

102. Santísima Trinidad, *Historia de la fundación*, 95–119. These biographical accounts were compiled in 1744 by some of the first beatas/nuns to enter the beaterio/convent.

103. Three observant convents, whose constitutions limited the number of nuns to thirty-three, felt pressured to alter their ordinances and allow more nuns to enter in spite of their express desire to live "en mayor estrecha y recogimiento." For example, in 1652, the nuns of the Monasterio de San Joseph requested that their limit be raised from thirty-three to sixty-two. See AGI, Lima 56, no. 23, 14r, Vceroy count of Salvatierra to the king, 15 August 1652.

104. By the 1620s, Inquisition authorities had curtailed individual and collective activities of beatas in Toledo, Extremadura, and Jaén, and labeled them an historical anomaly.

105. The time it took for a beaterio to become a convent varied tremendously; some never achieved conventual status. In Lima, the Monasterio de la Encarnación (founded 1561) and the Monasterio de la Concepción (founded 1573) began as beaterios (see Appendix B).

106. For examples of individual beatas, see "Fray Francisco García, Comendador de la Merced de los Reyes dá licencia a Mariana Núñez de Jesús, beata de la órden, para que pueda hacer su Codicilio," Barriga, *Los Mercedarios*, III: 369; AAL, Monasterio del Prado, Leg. 1, 1643, María de Jesús, beata del órden de San Agustín, who petitioned the ecclesiastical judge to have her fourteen-year-old daughter removed from the Monasterio de La Trinidad, where she had been working as a servant (criada) for a nun.

107. The prioress of the Beaterio de Santa Rosa provided six hundred pesos in her will to Doña Magdalena Balmaseda, an unmarried virgin over thirty years of age who, because she was poor, could not afford to become a beata, but who had always been "muy recogida" and had frequented Mass since childhood. AAL, Celibato, Leg. 1, exp. 25, May 1699. Unable to marry, and with "pains in her aged state," she took a formal vow of celibacy before the ecclesiastical judge once she had received the inheritance.

108. A number of small, informal beaterios existed in the vicinity of Cuzco, but the Beaterio de las Nazarenas served as the most important lay pious house in the late seventeenth century. In 1713, the beatas claimed to have been caring for orphaned children for forty years; AGI, 531, Cartas y Expedientes del Cabildo Eclésiastico del Cuzco,

Cabildo of Cuzco to the king, 11/IX/1713. For a listing of smaller, less opulent beaterios in Cuzco, see Urteaga, *Cuzco 1689*, 230–33; and Cahill, "Popular Religion," 81, n. 36, which includes references to beaterios in Quispicanchis, Yucay, and Corporaque.

109. For a detailed explanation of the "beaterio phenomenon" in Lima, see van Deusen, "Defining the Sacred."

110. Bronner, "Church, Crown, and Commerce," 82–83. The foundation of a beaterio required approval of local ecclesiastical authorities, which could be accomplished quickly. Convents needed the approval of local secular and ecclesiastical authorities, the archbishop, king, and pope.

111. Suárez, "El poder de los velos," 165–74.

112. A majority of convents in Lima were either promoted or supported financially by women; Lavrin, "Female Religious," 170. Capital for the Beaterio de Nerias (1674) came from Doña Ana de Robles; Doña Luisa de Antonia Coronel supported the Beaterio de Santa Rosa de Santa María (1669); and Doña Ana María Zavaleta founded the Beaterio de las Mercedarias (1671) at her own expense; Doña Francisca Ygnacia Manchipura de Carbaxal was one of five founders of the Beaterio de Nuestra Señora de Copacabana (1691).

113. The founder of the Beaterio de las Nerias, Ana de Robles, contributed her earnings from the panadería she owned and operated. See Santísima Trinidad, *Historia de la fundación*, 33.

114. Arenal and Schlau, *Untold Sisters*, 297–98. Transcribed and translated portions of Josefa de la Providencia's work appear in *Untold Sisters*. See also Providencia, *Relación*, ch. I, 3–4.

115. Providencia, *Relación*, ch. II.

116. Ibid., 23ff, details how the beatas should imitate the passion and suffering of Christ.

117. AFL, no. 30, s.f. "Razón de la fundación de Beatherio de Nuestra Señora de Copacabana de la illustre Ciudad de los Reyes, Lima." In the seventeenth century her cult blossomed; Friar Alonso Ramos Gavilán's history of the cult of Nuestra Señora de Copacabana (1621) and the Augustinian Francisco Valverde's poem (1641) are two examples of seventeenth-century literary works.

118. Mendiburu, *Diccionario*, V: 311. The Conde de Lemos donated fifty-five hundred pesos; see also Lohmann Villena, *El Conde*, 293.

119. Vargas Ugarte, *Biblioteca peruana*, IV: 157. The *Numeración general* of 1700 lists eighteen beatas, including four Indian beatas and four "demandantes" (the equivalent to a novice), 358. The Beaterio de Copacabana predates other foundations for noble Indian women. In Mexico City, the Monasterio de Corpus Christi for noble Indian women was founded in 1724. The Beaterio de Nuestra Señora del Rosario also catered exclusively to Indian women in Guatemala; see Lavrin, "Female Religious," 188. AGI, Lima 336, "Expediente." Montoya actively promoted indigenous education and admission of indigenous women into convents. AHN, Inquisición, Leg. 1649, no. 51, "Proceso . . . María Jacinta de la Santíssima Trinidad," 16v–17r. The Beaterio de Jesús, María y José became a convent after nearly forty years and numerous petitions from various parties. María Jacinta wished to observe the Carmelite or Saint Clare rules, but later determined (and others convinced her) that because these orders had convents in Lima, she should choose the Capuchin Order within the observant Franciscans. For a list of several petitions, see Vargas Ugarte, *Biblioteca peruana*, V: 158–59.

120. The Beaterio de Copacabana (1691) was founded for some of the daughters of the coastal indigenous elite and contained a school that catered to indígenas, but some girls of Spanish descent were admitted. The Beaterio or Recogimiento de las Amparadas de la Concepción was conceived as a beaterio, recogimiento, prison, school, and depository for women in the process of getting a divorce. The Beaterio de Jesús, María y José catered to young disadvantaged girls of mixed parentage.

121. This replicates a pattern in early modern Italy; Papi, "Mendicant Friars," 89.

122. The forty-three-year-old sevillana Inés María de Jesús became the first abbess; Nieto Vélez, *Francisco del Castillo*, 133; AAL, Beatificaciones, Francisco del Castillo, 219r.

123. This includes the Beaterios of Patrocinio, Las Rosas, Las Mercedarias, and Las Nerias.

124. Beaterios may have provided a safe haven for some widows who might have felt that their new status would not bring economic or social benefits; see Papi, "Mendicant Friars," 86–87.

125. See Expediente que trata de la fundación, 1697, AGI, Lima 336; Providencia, *Relación*, 24–25, 121. For a more detailed discussion of how the founders in Lima envisioned their beaterios, see van Deusen, "Manifestaciones," 62–70.

126. The Lima tribunal began to suspect beatas associated with alumbrismo in the late sixteenth century, but few were actually tried until 1620; Castañeda and Hernández, *La Inquisición de Lima*, I: 322; on beatas tried after 1620 as "alumbradas" or visionaries, see I: 332–36.

127. AAL, Beatificaciones, Nicolás de Ayllón, 1701, 13r; AHN, Inquisition, Leg. 1649, no. 51, 3v. Some discrepancy over the date of her "conversion," as she called it, exists. She says she was twenty-four years old in 1672, but in fact this age corresponds to 1669; ibid., 39v; 42v. Their vows of celibacy were not formally sanctioned by the Church, which may be why Inquisition authorities questioned her so closely on the matter.

128. AHN, Inquisición, Leg. 1649, no. 51, 6r–6v; 15v–16r. The couple purchased the property from the well-known Alloza family; Vargas Ugarte, *Vida del siervo*, 44.

129. AAL, Beatificaciones, Nicolás de Ayllón, 1701.

130. Vargas Ugarte, *Vida del siervo*, 51.

131. AHN, Inquisición, Leg. 1649, no. 51, 8r–8v.

132. Echave y Assu, *La estrella*, 235. With only six hours of sleep each day, the recogidas practiced nearly eighteen hours of spiritual exercises and other disciplines, including daily communion.

133. AGI, Lima 336, "Expediente."

134. AHN, Inquisición, Leg. 1649, no. 51, 34v.

135. She claimed to follow Teresa of Avila's recommendations on this matter; AHN, Inquisición, Leg. 1649, no. 51, 15v–16r.

136. Echave y Assu, *La estrella*, 235.

137. AHN, Inquisición, Leg. 1649, no. 51, 44r–45r. "Se an expelido de la congregazion las Doncellas siguientes Da. Beatris de Azedo, Da. Ignacia de Mendoza, Da. Jacoba de Zespedes, Da. Michaela de Atensio, Da. Nicolasa de Cardenas, Da. Maria Zadala y Da. Joepha Corea; Y ten an sido expelidas Beatris de Dios Padre, Juana Josepha, Joespha Maria, Juana de San Lorenzo, Francisca de la Candelaria, Thomasa de Santa Rosa, dos Rosas, una Jacoba y dos mas."

138. Despite such rigid standards, servants and seglares resided there. The 1700 *Numeración general* reports twelve servants and slaves to serve sixteen religious women and girls.

139. Perry, *Gender and Disorder*, 102, n. 25. Ana de Robles was the foundress and first abbess of the Beaterio de las Nerias. On her strict regimen, see Santísima Trinidad, *Historia de la fundación*, 40, 137. Antonia Lucia del Espíritu Santo governed the Beaterio de las Nazarenas.

140. García y Sanz, *Vida del Venerable*, 111.

141. They were known as "capuchinas laicas" because they emulated the monastic state; Muriel, *Los recogimientos*, 94–98, 105.

142. For a brief history of the institution, see "Examen histórico-crítico"; Martín, *Daughters*, 163–69.

143. AGI, Lima 414, count of Lemos to Queen Regent Mariana, 25/I/1669.

144. AGI, Lima 414, Copy of an original, count of Lemos to the queen regent, 13/III/1668.

145. AGI, Lima 414, count of Lemos to the king, 23/III/1670.

146. The Recogimiento de Santa María Magdalena (1692) incarcerated and punished prostitutes and delinquents sentenced by the Sala de Crímen of the Royal Audiencia; Muriel, *Los recogimientos*, 110.

147. AGI, Lima 414, Archbishop Melchor Liñán de Cisneros to Charles II, 17/X/1680;, see also a copy in Lima 79, carta no. 52.

148. AAL, "Reglas de la Casa de las Amparadas de la Concepción," 1. The last page indicates that this version was a copy "de un exemplar impresso, y antiguíssimo, q[ue] existe en esta comisión de mi cargo"; Lima, 14/I/1795. See Appendix F. Ignatius of Loyola was suspicious of Jesuit priests teaching nuns or lay women in convents. In fact, he dictated his *Spiritual Exercises* to women from the pulpit. Some European convents followed the guidelines he established; see Iparraguirre, *Historia de la práctica*, I: 304.

149. Father Antonio Ruíz de Montoya, called the "Apostle of Paraguay," studied with the famous mystic Gregorio López, one of the Jesuit interpreters of recogimiento; Andrés Martín, *Los recogidos*, 275, 727; Castillo, *Un místico*, 150. In his autobiography, Castillo recounted that his teacher, Montoya, began studying the *Spiritual Exercises* of Ignatius of Loyola in the Colegio de San Pablo in 1605 and even then was known for his "intense spirit of recogimiento"; *Un místico*, 106. Montoya wrote the *Silex del divino amor y rapto del ánima* for his disciple Castillo, who frequently used it. On Castillo's thoughts on Saint John of the Cross and Saint Teresa of Avila, see *Un místico*, 42–43.

150. Loyola founded and wrote the articles of the constitution of the Casa (Recogimiento) de Santa Marta in 1543; Loyola, *Obras completas*, 558–68. Castillo's support for the beaterio may have also stemmed from the fact that two of his nieces were beatas. One became prioress of a beaterio in 1678 and the other, Sor María de Jesús, lived in the Beaterio de las Rosas; AAL, Beatificaciones, Francisco del Castillo, 1677, testimony, Joseph de Buendía, 467r; Castillo, *Un místico*, 5, n. 3.

151. AAL, Beatificaciones, Francisco del Castillo, testimony of Joseph de Buendía, 479v.

152. AAL, Beatificaciones, Francisco del Castillo, testimony of Agustina del Christo, morena criolla, Lima, 1680, 29/III/1680, 847v–5or. María del Espíritu Santo, 3/III/1679, 664v–69r, became a Franciscan tertiary after she heard him preach: "[E]stuvo en su moredad muy metida en las delicias y que tenía una oración que no podia

dejar y que desde oyó al dicho siervo de Dios trata de servir a Dios y con su gracia ha procurado continuar hasta ahora."

153. AAL, Beatificaciones, Francisco del Castillo, testimony of Sor Inés María de Jesús, 11/VIII/1679, 737r.

154. Lima 414, Report, 4/I/1681, was signed by many prominent officials. It tallied forty recogidas and seventy schoolgirls.

155. Mendiburu, *Diccionario*, II: 465; VI: 543. The 1700 census probably underestimated the population.

156. García y Sanz, *Vida*, 112. Strict enclosure was rigorously enforced in the Recogimiento de San Miguel de Belem in Mexico City; Muriel, *Los recogimientos*, 94–95, 105.

157. AAL, "Reglas." The recogidas were to be strictly segregated from the permanent "hermanas"; "Regla de la Madre Abadesa," no. 16–18.

158. AGI, Lima 414, Archbishop Melchor Liñán de Cisneros to Charles II, Lima, 17/X/1680.

159. AAL, "Reglas," XXII.

160. Ibid., "Reglas." The Recogimiento de San Miguel de Belem (1683) had a similar regimen; Muriel, *Los recogimientos*, 95.

161. The Beaterio de Copacabana also maintained an educational center, but specified that it should serve daughters of the elite indigenous nobility.

162. For an example of a woman fleeing from her home, see AAL, Litigios Matrimoniales, Leg. 4, 1702, Bentura Veltrán maestre sastre vs. María Magdalena Ortega, mestiza. On cases of women describing marital life as a form of slavery, see Lavallé, "Divorcio y nulidad," 442–43. For an example of an abandoned wife, see AAL, Beatificaciones, Nicolás de Ayllón, 17r. Doña Juana de Zandoval found asylum in the Casa de Amparadas when her husband went to Chile. Only recently married, she had no means of support, and sought refuge there. I have found only a few instances of deposit in the Beaterios of Patrocinio, Mercedarias, Las Rosas, and Copacabana between 1670 and 1713.

163. Of 140 divorce cases (*divorcios*) (194 total minus 54 no data) between 1671 and 1713, Las Amparadas represented 20 percent of first-time deposits. However, if one includes multiple deposits and transfers the numbers increase: 36 women (first-time); 26 (second-time); and 6 (third deposit) out of a total of 140 women. After 1708, when the crisis with the Monasterio de las Rosas occurred, other beaterios began accepting divorciadas with more frequency.

164. This calculation is based upon a total of fifty-two (sixty-four total minus twelve no data) marital litigation suits (*litigios matrimoniales*) from 1670 to 1713. Of these fifty-two, twenty-four were deposited for the first time in the Casa de las Amparadas during those years.

165. The majority of the sixty-eight divorciadas (thirty-six women for the first deposit; twenty-six for the second deposit; and six for the third deposit) deposited in the Casa de Amparadas between 1670 and 1713 did not come from the elite sector of society. Nearly 60 percent (forty) provided no racial data, but many of those sixty-eight recogidas used the title doña. The title doña should *not* be equated with race but merely considered a measure of higher economic status (not necessarily of the elite, or "Spanish"). Nearly 40 percent of the women who designated race were categorized as either "yndias" or "castas": including "sambas," "quarteronas," "pardas," and "negras criollas."

166. AAL, D, Leg. 33, 1660, Doña Angela de Casteñeda vs. Juan de Figueroa; Leg. 49, 1680, Doña Theresa Matoso vs. Capitán Francisco Ramírez; Leg. 49, 1680, Doña Luisa de Santileses vs. Capitán Bartolomé Calderón; Leg. 63, 1708, Ysabel de la Peña vs. Joseph Fernández de Almeida; Litigios Matrimoniales, Leg. 4, Doña María de Aguado y Cárdenas, convent unspecified; Doña María de Médrez, 1710, Monasterio de la Trinidad. On a request for a transfer from the Casa de Amparadas to a convent, see AAL, D, Leg. 44, 1669, Doña Beatris Buitrón vs. Gregorio de Olibares.

167. Of the various instances of women transferred to the Casa de Amparadas between 1670 and 1713, one had been interned in the Hospital de la Caridad and another deposited in the Monasterio de la Concepción; the remainder had temporarily resided in private homes, either of a female friend, an "honorable woman," a relative, or their mother. In such instances, husbands ordered their wives to be redeposited because they felt threatened.

168. AAL, D, Leg. 56, 1691, Doña María Petronila de Liebana, yndia, vs. Salvador Vargas. Salvador Vargas was disturbed by the fact that his wife had been in Las Amparadas for more than four months, "living like an unmarried woman."

169. AAL, Litigios Matrimoniales, Leg. 4, Nicolás de Banzes vs. Paula de Liñán. He accused her of only wanting to "parlar con las Mozuelas que son de mal vivir las quales entran a todas oras de puertas adentro."

170. He said, "[M]ientras dicha su madre comunica a dicha mi mujer se han de aumentar los disturbios que tenemos y porque he tenido noticia que por los techos de dichas sus cassas se hablan y comunican . . . dicha mi muger esta con todo gusto en dicho recogimiento y yo no la pueda solicitar para que hagamos vida según Dios nos manda." AAL, Litigios Matrimoniales, Leg. 4, 1701, Pedro de Cárdenas vs. María Bruna, negros libres.

171. AAL, D, Leg. 53, 1686, Doña Francisca Zambrano vs. Pablo de Retes.

172. Ibid.

173. Ibid. "Pues que no aya clausura en el Beaterio que si la ay aunque no expressa por del Pontificie, la tienen subordinada por virtud y voluntad al Prelado no hacer cosa que no sea sin voluntad y licencia suya."

174. Ibid., Leg. 56, 1691, Doña María Ortíz vs. Juan de Peñaranda; Leg. 62, 1707, Doña María Romero vs. Francisco de la Sarte.

175. Ibid., Leg. 50, 1681, Doña Juana de Aldaña vs. Ygnacio de Castro.

176. Ibid., Leg. 45, 1672, Juana Magdalena, yndia, vs. Francisco Valero.

177. AAL, Litigios Matrimoniales, Leg. 4, 1702, María Magdalena vs. Francisco de Escobar.

178. Several divorciadas mention "siervas de Dios." See AAL, D, Leg. 60, 1698, Luisa Sivico, samba libre, vs. Clemente de Atiense, pardo libre. She requested a transfer.

179. Ibid., Leg. 53, 1687, Agustina de Vargas vs. Domingo Basarate. Agustina requested a transfer from the Casa de las Amparadas to a private home because the "recogidas estan gravemente disgustados y en ánimo de hacer una grande demoración con dicho mi marido." See also D, Leg. 54, 1689, Doña Joana de la Rosa Nabarrete vs. Don Bartholomé Mosquera. Several of the beatas recounted Father Castillo's efforts to console recogidas wishing to leave; AAL, Beatificaciones, Francisco de Castillo, testimonies of Isabel María de la Concepción, 741v, 742r; and Gertrúdis de los Reyes, 747v.

180. AAL, Beatificaciones, Francisco del Castillo, testimony of Gertrudis de los Reyes, 747r.

181. Ibid., 743r. For an example of a disagreement between two servants, Francisca Davila and Andrea Portillo, and the intervention of Castillo, see 752v.

182. The count of Lemos suggested to King Charles II that an additional four thousand pesos from the city tax on meat (*sisa de carne*), which until that time had been applied to the fortification of Callao, could subsidize the salary of the governess and at least twelve recogidas; AGI, Lima 68, Dispatches, count of Lemos, no. 5, carta 14, 11/III/1668; Lima 414, count of Lemos to the king, 13/III/1668; 24/VIII/1671. The Jesuit chaplain Nicolás de la Cruz (d. 1706) replaced Castillo and administered the house for more than twenty-five years; Mendiburu, *Diccionario*, II: 464–65.

183. AGI, Lima 414, count of Castellar to Charles II, 21/III/1675; count of Castellar to Charles II, 31/I/1677; Jesuit provincial to the king, 30/III/1677; Summary of six letters sent from various prelates and ecclesiastics about the need to provide four thousand pesos in two-year installments from the one-third share of the vacant bishopric, which entered the royal treasury, 15/XII/1677; Lima 78, no. 17, Report from Archbishop Melchor de Liñán y Cisneros to Charles II, 26/VIII/1678. Archbishop Juan de Almoguera (d. 1676) also favored more permanent support of the Casa.

184. AGI, Lima 414, "Ynforme de la Abadesa, Monjas y Combento de las Recogidas," 6/XI/1679.

185. "Examen histórico-crítico," 246ff.

186. Angulo, "El terremoto de 1687," 41.

187. Angulo, *Santa Rosa*, 17.

188. AGI, Lima 535, "Recomienda las solicitudes hechas para la fundación de un monasterio sobre el Beaterio de Santa Rosa"; count of la Monclova to Charles II, 7/XI/1690, also printed in Moreyra y Paz-Soldán, *Colección de cartas*, I: 77–78, no. 27B. See also AGI, Lima 304, count of la Monclova to Charles II, 13/VIII/1695, cited in Moreyra y Paz-Soldán, *Colección de cartas*, II: 59–60.

189. See the collection of requests from prominent individuals and a list of their donations that amounted to more than four hundred thousand pesos in AGI, Lima 537. See also BNP, C4169, 1709, "Tanto de la exclamación que hice sobre la mudada de las monjas de mi madre Santa Rosa, a la Casa de las Recoxidas," 2r–2v. They received two thousand pesos annually from the income from an hacienda de pan llevar in the Bocanegra valley, and donations from entrepreneurs Joseph Solano de Herrera and Domingo de Cueto. See also "Relación de la fundación del real monasterio de Santa Rosa de Santa María de la ciudad de los Reyes, hecha en 2 de febrero de 1708," in Angulo, *Santa Rosa*, 61–67.

190. BNP, C3823, 1710, "Información dada por parte del Sgto. Mayor D. Francisco de Oyague . . . sobre calificar haberse hecho el tránsito de dichas religiosas, del sitio en que estaban al de los recogidas amparadas," 1r, 5r–5v.

191. Ibid.,

192. Ibid., C4169, 1709, 4v.

193. His testimony on behalf of her beatification illustrates his devotion to her cult. See Millones, *Una partecita del cielo,* which provides a transcription of his testimony. Apparently, the beatas of Santa Rosa had requested the site while the count of Lemos was viceroy, but he had opted to build the Casa de Amparadas there; see Mendiburu, *Diccionario*, V: 311.

194. Alonso Messía replaced Nicolás de la Cruz as chaplain when he died in 1708.

195. Mendiburu, *Diccionario*, V: 310. Messía served as confessor to the count of la

Monclova and his daughter, Josefa de Portocarrero. Josefa was the foundress of the Monasterio de las Rosas. See Madre Toribia de Santa Rosa, "Breve relación de la vida de Sor Josefa de Santa Rosa" (Manuscript, 1912), housed in the Monasterio de las Rosas de Santa Rosa. I would like to thank the nuns for giving me permission to see this document.

196. BNP, C3823, 1710. Oyague said: "[L]as conduxo a la casa de donde fueron sacadas las recoxidas amparadas, y respeto de que la función se dio sin consentimiento mío," 1v.

197. AGI, 414, 12/I/1720, "Da quenta a Vuestra Magestad del cumplimiento dado su Real Orden para el Reestablecimiento del Colegio y Recogimiento de las Amparadas." The schoolmaster Garcés was also involved.

198. Ladrón de Guevara also supported the efforts of Josefa de Portocarrero to found the convent.

199. AGI, Lima 414, 9/XI/1714; Vargas Ugarte, *Historia de la Iglesia*, IV: 19–20.

200. AGI, Lima 414, "Avisa del recibo," 14/I/1730; Lima 414, 7/XII/1730, "La Madre y Preposita de Recoxidas de la Ciudad de Lima informa a Vuestra Magestad del Estado que hoy tiene aquel Recogimiento." The abbess, Estefanía de San Joseph, referred to another royal decree in 1721 to return all property to the recogidas, but that did not occur. See also AGI, Lima 414, 14/I/1733, Viceroy Villa García to Philip V, which discusses the matter. They were supposed to receive income from the tax on snow but that did not take effect.

201. AGI, Lima 414, 7/XII/1730, "La Madre Preposita de Recoxidas"; Lima 414, "Avisa del recivo del Real Cédula del 31/III/1732."

202. AGI, Lima 414, 15/XII/1733, the marquis of Castelfuerte to the king; 21/VII/1736, Viceroy marquis of Villa García to the king.

203. AGI, Lima 521, Report from Archbishop Soloaga to the king, 26/VII/1736.

204. Williams, *Marxism*, 122–23.

Conclusions

1. Frezier, "Lima en 1713," 217. See also Bernales Ballesteros, *La ciudad*, 130; Ugarte Elespuru, *Lima y lo limeño*, 190.

2. See Peralta y Barnuevo, *Imágen política*, 12r–12v.

3. Flores Galindo, *Aristocracia*, who argued that a period of "decadence," indicating a serious divide between rich and poor, began around 1750. I would argue that this was already in evidence by 1700.

4. Torrecilla, *Enciclopedia canónica*, II: 166, "rameras o meretrices": "[L]as Rameras pueden licitamente pedir, y recibir el precio justo por el uso de su cuerpo, aunque pecan en *entregar* el tal uso, y que en tal caso, no tienen obligación de restituir." In Spain, *ramerías* were houses for "public" women; *Diccionario de la lengua española*, 1102. See Muriel, *Los recogimientos*, 115, 186; and on reas weaving cotton in the Recogimiento de Santa María Magdalena of Mexico City, 120. In the Recogimiento de Santa María Egipciaca in Puebla, the recogidas were forced to "hilar diariamente cuatro onzas de algodón," and they complained about this fact to authorities in 1772, 155.

5. Muriel, *Los recogimientos*, 116. The "modern" penitential notion of recogimiento was also replicated on a smaller scale in provincial areas of New Spain; Muriel, *Los recogimientos*, 146.

6. Pérez Baltasar, *Mujeres marginadas*, 29, 93ff.

7. Muriel, *Los recogimientos*, 81, 94. The patron of the Recogimiento de Belem (founded 1683) for "mujeres pobres de cualquier calidad" was the Real Sala de Crimen, but when the founder died, the archbishop intervened in 1726 and patronage remained with the archbishop. The reasoning was that "sí la Sala de Crimen heredaba su obra la convertiría en cárcel." In Mexico City, the Recogimiento de Santa María Magdalena for prostitutes and delinquents (founded 1692) eventually converted into a penal institution under the protection of the Sala del Crimen.

8. AGI, Lima 414, marquis of Villa García to the king, 21/VII/1736; Lima 639, count of Villa García to the king, 26/V/1739. See AAL, Litigios Matrimoniales, IV, V. See also Flores Gallindo and Chocano, "Las cargas." Beaterios continued to handle marital *depósitos* during the nineteenth century; see Hünefeldt, "Los beaterios."

9. Hünefeldt, *Paying the Price*, 161–64.

10. Pérez Baltasar, *Mujeres marginadas*, 69–70; Muriel, *Los recogimientos*, 115–16; AGI, Lima 414, Viceroy Villa García to the king, 21/VII/1736, "[Se] funde una casa galera para recogimiento de mujeres públicas."

11. The emphasis is mine. Muriel, *Los recogimiento*s, 116, quotes a statement made by Viceroy Iturrigaray.

12. On mystical treatises that influenced Santa Rosa and other holy women and men in Lima, see Flores Araoz, *Santa Rosa de Lima*, 58–79; on works on Luis de Granada published in Lima, 71; on works relating to Santa Rosa, Angulo, *Santa Rosa de Santa María*; Hampe, *Santidad*, 69–70.

13. Ahlgren, *Teresa of Avila*, 171.

14. Ewick and Silbey, "Subversive Stories," 198, argue that "narrativity" has been celebrated for embodying qualities of particularity and ambiguity. Narratives provide a "promising vehicle for introducing legal decision-makers to a more complex, ambiguous legal subject."

15. Stern, *The Secret*, 19.

16. Lewis, "Blackness," 86–87.

17. I agree with Elizabeth Kuznesof that the "interplay between gender, race and class has not yet been clearly understood"; idem, "Ethnic and Gender Influences," 159. On the importance of class, see Schwartz, "Colonial Identities," 185–201.

18. For two important works that explore this fluidity, see Cope, *The Limits*; Boyer, *Lives of the Bigamists*.

19. Deans-Smith, "Culture, Power," 258; various essays in Johnson and Lipsett-Rivera, *The Faces of Honor;* and Boyer, "Respect and Identity."

20. See the illuminating article by Canning, "Feminist History."

21. On racial blurring and "drift" in the seventeenth and eighteenth centuries, see Kuznesof, "Ethnic and Gender Influences," 167–68; Cope, *The Limits*.

22. For example, consider differences in interpretations of "honor" in Patricia Seed's *To Love, Honor, and Obey*, based upon betrothal disputes; Ramón Gutiérrez's *When Jesus Came*, and Richard Boyer's "La Mala Vida." See also the essays by Boyer and Lipsett-Rivera in Johnson and Lipsett-Rivera, *The Faces of Honor.*

23. Seed, *To Love, Honor, and Obey*, 123ff.

24. This hypothesis requires further research.

25. Inquisition authorities still meted out severe punishment in some bigamy

cases. For instance, Juliana, a forty-year-old black slave, had married while in Chile. Once caught and accused of bigamy she served as a cook while in the secret Inquisitorial prison, and was sentenced to one hundred lashes and two years of service in the Hospital de la Caridad for her crime, AHN, Lib. 1032, "Relaciones de Causa," 191r–92r.

26. AAL, D, Leg. 63, 1712, María Carrión vs. Diego Ortíz.

27. AAL, Litigios Matrimoniales, Leg. 4, 1706, Juan de Monzón vs. Doña Ysabel de Torres.

28. For one example, see AAL, Leg. 37, 1664, Agustina de Dueñas vs. Bernardo de Orte; Agustina went to La Caridad while her husband traveled. One husband placed his mistress "in recogimiento" in two distinct convents and the Hospital de la Caridad each time he left town; AAL, D, Leg. 63, 1712, Doña Angela de Requena.

29. AAL, Litigios Matrimoniales, Leg. 3, 1681, Tomasa María de Gadea vs. Graviel Ruíz. In cases where no financial support or housing was available, a woman could find temporary lodging in the Casa de los Pobres (founded 1689), a refuge center. It was described by a contemporary as "fundada para señoras pobres, a quienes la fortuna las desposee de todos medios para sustentarse, aquí hallan alivio, y recurso de su necesidad"; Echave y Assu, *La estrella*, 239.

30. AAL, CN, Leg. 18, 25/VI/1676.

31. Doña María Larios, Juana de la Rosa, and Ana de Mendoza requested deposit in the homes of widows; AAL, D, Leg. 47, 1675, Doña María Larios vs. Luis Sánchez; Leg. 53, 1688, Petronila Muñoz negra esclava, vs. Alexo Bentura de la Cueva, negro libre. Petronila wished to go to the home of her owner (*amo*); Leg. 57, 1694, Juana de la Rosa, negra libre, vs. Nicholás de Alocer; Leg. 61, 1702, Ana de Mendoza vs. Melchor Bisente de Mendolasa. María Bernarda sought consolation from a Franciscan beata named Sisilia de los Angeles; Leg. 63, 1713, María Bernarda, yndia, vs. Andrés Lescano, mestizo.

32. Some women still experienced threats from their husbands and no longer felt safe in private homes. See CN, Leg. 22, exp. 21, 1688, Autos sobre la solicitud de Maria de la Cruz samba libre, en la causa de divorico que sigue contra Pascual Alarcon, negro esclavo de Doña Maria Iñigo. Maria said her husband tried to kill her with a knife while deposited in a private home.

33. AAL, Dispensas Matrimoniales, Leg. 1, exp. 104, 1677.

34. AAL, Santa Clara, Leg. 16, exp. 46, 1679.

35. For a discussion of personal appeals, usually directed to the king, in seventeenth-century Castile, see MacKay, *The Limits*, 142–43.

36. AGI, Quito 182, doc. 68, "El Ob[is]po de Quito ynforma los yncombientes que se siguen de que la Cassa de recogidas en aquella ciudad no se govierne unicam[en]te por la dirección del Ordinario." 8/VI/1725.

37. The Real Recogimiento de Santa Rosa de Viterbo, Ciudad Real, Chiapas (1712), with patronage vested in the king, was established to "recoger en ella a las mujeres que con su licenciosa y escandalosa vida . . . dañaban las costumbres de la república"; Muriel, *Los recogimientos*, 179; a recogimiento in Michoacán, established for "mujeres licenciosas y poco recatadas," began operation between 1729 and 1737; Guadalajara, Casa de Recogidas, began receiving "mujeres perdidas" around the mid–eighteenth century, *Los recogimientos*, 184–85; Guanajuato, *Los recogimientos*, 186–87.

38. AGI, Lima 529, Avisa el rezivo de la Real Cedula de 31/XII/1736 en que se le mando remitese el testamento . . . 8/VIII/1737.

39. Martínez Compañón's, *Trujillo del Perú*, includes a floor plan of the eighteenth-century recogimiento in Trujillo.

40. AGI, Chile 107, Cabildo Secular to the king, 28/IX/1708, in response to a letter
written the previous year encouraging the council to found a recogimiento for "scandalous" women; Herraéz S. de Escariche, *Beneficencia de España*, contains a plan of the
eighteenth-century recogimiento established in Santiago de Chile.

41. Andrien, *Crisis and Decline*, 34.

42. Maza, *La ciudad de México*, 18–20. Minchom, *The People of Quito*, 145–50, presents data demonstrating a higher number of women in eighteenth-century Quito, but
because census figures are either unavailable or inaccurate, it is difficult to determine
the gender ratio for the earlier period. Clark and Slack argue in *English Towns*, 64, 88,
that English towns often had more women than men, and many were temporary migrants in search of work or a husband.

43. Vetancurt, *Teatro mexicano*.

44. See Pescador, *De bautizados*, who explores the concentration of single women
in certain areas of Mexico City.

45. Sallmann, *Visions indiennes*, 9.

46. Ida Altman explored this in the last chapter of *Emigrants and Society*.

47. See Cabibbo, *La santa dei Tomasi*, 120, which refers to the nuns who read C.
Tomasi, *Immagini de' cinque santi clementini Gaetano, Francesco, Filippo, Luigi, Rosa*
(Rome, 1671), 384. See also BNM, Mss. 8293, Varios Manuscritos acera de los merce-
darios, "Noticia de la Venerable Heremita María de Santa Rosa, solitaria en la sierra de
Elvira," 354rff.

48. For example, see Salazar, *Política española*, proposition 3: "[T]he principal
reason why Spain has been able to acquire the kingdoms it rules, and the fundamental
reason of state that it uses to conserve them, is religion."

Glossary

aclla: Young woman chosen to serve the Inca state.

acllahuasi: House of women chosen to serve the Inca state.

alcabala: Sales tax.

alcalde: An authority who represents local community government and generally sits on the city council.

alumbrados: Lit., illuminists. Those who rejected any mediation of Church officials, meditation on the Passion, fasting, or penance, and focused instead on abandonment of the will (*dejamiento*) toward God in a direct, interior manner.

ama de leche: Wet nurse.

amancebamiento: Concubinage, or living in a separate household with a married partner, or without being married. Synonymous with illicit sexual relations.

arras: A gift paid by the prospective husband to his wife for taking her virginity.

arrepentida: Penitent woman.

audiencia: A Spanish viceregal court and governing body, made up of judges (*oidores*) and a president.

auto-da-fé: A public procession in which the condemned marched through the streets as part of the punishment meted out by the Inquisition.

ayllu: Andean kinship group composed of those claiming descent from a common ancestor.

bachiller: A man holding a bachelor's degree. The academic distinction of most parish priests.

barrio: Neighborhood in a city.

beata: A lay pious woman who took informal religious vows.

beaterio: Community or house of women living under informal religious vows.

begriffsgeschichte: Analysis of the meanings of political concepts.

benemérito: Descendent of an original settler.

bienes gananciales: Property held in common.

cabildo: Elected secular or ecclesiastical council.

cacicazgo: Hereditary office held by a cacique.

cacique: Native lord or governor. Used interchangeably with *curaca*.

calidad: Individual's social standing or rank based on religion, race, ethnicity, gender, legitimacy, personal virtue, occupation, wealth, and relationship to others (e.g., as father or mother).

casas de misericordia: Asylums where the poor, according to their age, condition, and gender could be trained to work under the direction of state officials.

casa pías o públicas: Pious houses, also referred to as *recogimientos,* founded and operated by members of the Jesuit order.

casas de recogimiento: Houses of religious retreat, asylum, or involuntary imprisonment.

casta: Person of non-European ancestry; especially person of mixed Indian, African, and European ancestry.

cédula: Written authorization; usually short for *real cédula,* or a royal decree.

censos: Loans.

cihuatlamacazque: Priestesses in the major Aztec temples.

cofradía: Religious sodality or confraternity established to promote a particular devotion. A member was a *cofrade.*

colegios: Schools for daughters of the elite. In some instances, used interchangeably with *recogimientos.*

conventos grandes: Colloquial term for the largest, most populous colonial convents (e.g., La Concepción, La Encarnación, and Santa Clara), as distinct from the relatively small, observant ones (e.g., El Prado or Santa Ana).

conventos recoletos: Convents with a small population, strict vows of obedience and poverty, and only minimal contact with people in secular society. Also called observant convents.

corregidor: Royal district governor; a Spanish magistrate, charged with administering a district (*corregimiento*).

criada: Servant in a convent.

criollo/a: American-born person of Spanish or African descent.

crónicas conventuales: Conventual chronicles.

cuarterona: A woman of one-quarter non-Spanish blood.

curaca: Native Andean lord or governor. Used interchangeably with *cacique.* Also spelled *kuraka.*

dejamiento: Abandonment of the will; a mystical praxis advocated by the *alumbrados.*

depositada: A woman sent to an institution for disciplinary reasons, because her husband was traveling, or because she had petitioned for an annulment or a divorce. Synonymous with *recogida* and *divorciada.*

depósito: Custody, safekeeping; a legal practice of enclosing women, before marriage, or while marital litigation remained in progress.

distraída: Wayward woman.

divorciada: Women involved in divorce litigation living in deposit (*déposito*) throughout the duration of the case.

donada: A convent servant who brought a small dowry and professed simple vows. Nearly always a woman of color.

doncella: An unmarried virgin.

doncella mestiza: An unmarried virgin of mixed Spanish and native descent.

educandas: Girls educated in convent schools.

emparedamiento: A medieval concept applying to a place of enclosure: usually a room or cell separated by a wall and located adjacent to a parish church. A space of enclosure for a woman.

encerramiento: Enclosure.

encomendero: The possessor of an encomienda, a grant from the Spanish Crown of the right to receive labor and tribute from a particular group of native peoples.

estado: Estate, as in medieval hierarchical ordering of society; also, rank, status, class.

estancias de pan llevar: Wheat-producing estates, particularly in the fertile valleys surrounding Lima.

expósito: An abandoned child, often left in hospitals or in the vestibule of a church.

lo femenino: The increasing variation in forms of spiritual and secular expressions of the female self.

forastero: Indian who did not live in his or her pueblo of origin.

galera: A self-financing correctional house.

género: Class, type. For example, *todos los géneros* refers to people of all walks of life.

gente de razón: People of reason, rational people; non-Indians, especially Spaniards.

gobernador: Governor; here specifically an Indian governor in a cabecera.

hermana: Used synonymously with a *beata,* one who did not live in a formal communal setting; sometimes used interchangeably with *donadas* in convents.

hermandad: Religious brotherhood/sisterhood; less important than a *cofradía.*

hidalgo: Person of the lower nobility.

hija natural, hijo natural: A daughter or son born to parents who were not married at the time of the child's birth. Also synonymous with *hija/o ilegítima/o.*

huérfana/o: An orphan.

india: Native female Andean. Term created by Spaniards to encompass people of pure Andean ancestry.

interioridad: Profound spiritual contemplation.

juez eclesiástico: An ecclesiastical magistrate.

lega/o: Lay sisters or brothers.

limeña/o: Person from Lima.

limpieza de sangre: Purity of blood based on Christian descent.

litigios matrimoniales: Formal complaints of violence or breach of the conjugal contract.

marginada/o: A marginalized individual.

mestizaje: A term for cultural, ethnic, or "racial" mixture.

mestizo: Usually a person of mixed Spanish and Indian ancestry.

mitayo: An Indian forced to perform labor services.

morena: A casta woman of predominantly African descent.

mujeres de mal vivir: Prostitutes.

mujeres públicas: Prostitutes.

mulato: A person of mixed African and European ancestry; a free population but, like Indians, subject to the tribute tax.

lo mundano: Worldly, pertaining to the world, or *el siglo.*

obraje: Textile factory.

oidor: Audiencia judge.

panadería: Bakery.

parda: Woman of African and Spanish descent; Spaniards generally considered them darker-skinned than *mulatas.*

parroquia: Parish.

patria potestas: Legal right of the father over his daughters.

pecados públicos: Public sins.

penitenciada: A woman sent into a convent or beaterio for correction; the term is virtually synonymous with *depositada.*

perdidas: Lost women.

pisar el suelo: Literally, to step on the ground. The practice of lay women or girls paying room and board to live in a convent.

procurador: Defender of the legal rights and privileges of individuals, councils, and religious orders.

procurador de indios: Attorney representing native Andeans.

promotor eclesiástico: Ecclesiastical lawyer.

promotor fiscal: Chief adviser on canon law and on lawsuits before the bishop's court.

provisor eclesiástico: Ecclesiastical judge responsible for marital litigation cases.

pulperías: Popular taverns.

querella: A legal complaint.

quieta: Internal silence, silence.

recoger: To separate oneself or abstract the spirit from all that is earthly or that which might impede meditation or contemplation. To separate oneself from excessive communication and contact with people. To retire to a specific location. To gather together again, or for a second time. To bring together or congregate things or people who are dispersed. To provide asylum. To place oneself in retreat. To withdraw from the world.

recogerse: To still the senses or the "self." To gather within the self in an act of recollection or mental prayer.

recogida: n. A woman who retires to a particular house, on a voluntary or involuntary basis.

recogida: adj. Virtuous. Self-contained. Enclosed. Moral.

recogimiento: A house of spiritual retreat. A house of women called recogidas. A covered area extending from a wall, a house, or barn in a village destined to shelter beggars or mendicants. A house for women with a specific purpose, on either a voluntary or involuntary basis. A school. Quiescent conduct. An act of contemplation.

recollectio: Physical reclusion.

reconocimiento: Legal recognition of a child.

reducción: Congregation or village, where natives were forcibly relocated.

remediada: A woman cleansed of any aberrant tendencies.

repartimiento: Large administrative unit of natives who paid tribute and provided labor to an encomendero or the Crown.

seglarado: The area in convents designated to house lay women and girls.

seglares: Lay women and girls in convents, akin to the term *recogida.*

sevicia: Extreme physical violence or mistreatment.

siglo: Nuns used the term, derived from the Latin *seculum,* to refer to the secular world beyond their cloisters.

siglo de oro: The Golden Century

tablilla: A public listing of those individuals who had committed an immoral or criminal action and faced excommunication.

tapadas: Women who wore a shawl covering everything except one eye.

vaga[b]mundo: A vagabond.

vecino: Resident member of a town; here reserved for non-Indians.

velo blanco: Literally, "white veil," the term for a half-dowry nun. Women in this category were second to the nuns of the black veil in their convent's hierarchy and ranked above donadas, servants, and slaves.

velo negro: Literally, "black veil," the term for a full-dowry nun (also known as a *monja de coro,* or "choir nun").

vergüenza: Modesty or shame.

via media: The middle path: a term associated with *beatas* who often took religious vows but were not cloistered.

visita: Tour of inspection by a bishop or his delegate (pastor visit). Tour of inspection commissioned by the Crown.

zamba, zambo: A woman or man considered to be of mixed European and African descent. Also spelled *samba/o.*

Bibliography

Archival Manuscripts

PERU

Archivo Arzobispal de Lima (AAL)
Amancebamientos, Leg. 1, 1589–1612; 2, 1612–19; 3, 1621–37; 4, 1641–54; 5, 1655–1825.
Beaterios y Monasterios, Varios. Leg. 1.
Beaterios
    Las Amparadas and Las Camilas, Leg. 1.
    Copacabana, Leg. 1, 1692–1829
    Patrocinio, Leg. 1, 1692–1859
    Mercedarias, Leg. 1, 1713–95
Beatificaciones
    "Isabel Porras de Marmolejo"
    "Francisco del Castillo"
    "Nicolás de Ayllón"
Causas Civiles, Leg. II, exp. 9, 1597; XXV, exp. 24, 1620; Leg. XXVIII, exp. 6, 1623.
Causas Criminales de Matrimonios, Leg. 1, 1607–29; 2, 1632–48; 3, 1652–59; 4, 1661–69; 5, 1670–99; 6, 1703–43.
Causas de Negros, Leg. 1, 2, 3, 1616–18; Leg. 5, 1623–29; Leg. 7, 1635–39; Leg. 9, 1643–46; 13, 1660–64; 14, 1665–68; 15, 1669; 17, 1673–75; 18, 1676–78; 19, 1677–79; 20, 1680–86; 21, 1684–86; 23, 1691–93.
Celibato, Leg. 1.
Cofradías. Leg. X.
Dispensas Matrimoniales, Leg. 1, 1603–99.
Divorcios, Leg. 1, 1569–1601; 2, 1602–6; 3, 1607–8; 4, 1609–11; 5, 1612; 6, 1613; 7, 1614–17; 8, 1618–19; 9, 1620–23; 10, 1624; 11, 1625; 12, 1626–28; 13, 1629–30; 13A, 1630; 14, 1631; 15, 1632–34; 16, 1635–36; 17, 1637; 18, 1637; 19, 1638; 20, 1639–40; 21, 1641; 22, 1642; 23, 1642; 24, 1643–44; 25, 1645; 26, 1646–47; 27, 1648; 28, 1649; 29, 1650–52; 30, 1653–54; 31, 1655–56; 32, 1657–58; 33, 1659–60; 34, 1661; 35, 1662; 36, 1663; 37, 1664; 38, 1665; 39, 1666; 40, 1667; 44, 1670; 45, 1671–72; 46, 1673–74; 47, 1675; 48, 1676–77; 49, 1679–80;

50, 1681–82; 52, 1685; 53, 1686–88; 55, 1689–90; 56, 1691–92; 57, 1694; 59, 1696–97; 61, 1701–2; 62, 1703–7; 63, 1708–13; 64, 1714–20.

Esponsales de Matrimonios, Leg. 1, 1606–30; Leg. 2, 1630–35; Leg. 3, 1635–46; Leg. 4, 1647–61; Leg. 5, 1663–66; Leg. 6, 1672–91; Leg. 7, 1691–98; Leg. 8, 1701–27; Leg. 8A, 1700–24.

Hospitales, Leg. 1, 2, 3.

Litigios Matrimoniales, Leg. 1, 2, 2A, 3, 4.

Matrimonios de Bigamias, Leg. 1.

Monasterios

 Carmen (Santa Ana), Leg. 1, 1635–79.

 La Concepción, Leg. 1, 1603–14; 2, 1615–22; 3, 1623–27.

 Las Descalcas (San José), Leg. 1, 1605–32.

 La Encarnación, 3, 1630–32; 4, 1633–37.

 Jesús, María, y José, Leg. 1, 1713–1848.

 Mercedarias, Leg. 1, 1713–99.

 La Trinidad, Leg. 1, 1600–1626.

 Descalças de la Trinidad, Leg. 1, 2.

 Nuestra Señora del Prado, Leg. 1, 1622–48; 2, 1651–73; 3, 1674–89.

 Santa Catalina de Sena, Leg. 1, 1624–39.

 Santa Clara, Leg. 1, 1596–1615; 2, 1602–14; 3, 1615–22; 4, 1623–33; 5, 1634–38; 6, 1639–42; 7, 1642; Leg. 8, 1643–46; 12, 1665–69; 13, 1670–72.

 Santa Rosa, Leg. 1, 1642–1748; 2, 1700.

 Santa Teresa (Carmelitas Descalças), Leg. 1, 1647–1749.

Nulidades, Legs. 1, 2, 3, 7.

Papeles Importantes, Leg. IX.

Archivo de la Beneficencia Pública del Perú (ABP)

Dotes

 Cofradía de la Puríssima Concepción, 8296

 Cofradía del Rosario, 8248

 Cofradía de Nuestra Señora de la O, 8236

Hospitales

 Hospital de San Diego, 8399, 8400.

Archivo de la Municipalidad de Lima (AML)

Libros e cédulas y provisiones de esa Ciudad de los Reyes q[ue] Comienza el año 1613. Libro III, 2da. parte (1534–1633), V.

Archivo Franciscano de Lima (AFL)

 Registro 10

 Registro 17, no. 41, Sor Isabel de Porras Marmolejo

 Registro 30

Archivo General de la Nación (AGN)

Protocolos Notoriales, Diego Gutíerrez, no. 64 (1553–56).

Real Audiencia, Causas Civiles, Leg. 5, Cuad. 28, 1560.

Superior Gobierno, 4, Cuaderno 64, 1656, "Libro original que contiene la fundación del monasterio de monxas de señora Sta. Clara desta cibdad del Cuzco . . ."

Biblioteca Nacional del Perú (BNP)
B122, 1634, 1637, 1747.
C4169, 1709.
C3823, 1710.

SPAIN

Archivo Diocesano de Ávila, Spain (ADAS)
55/7/1, 56/3/36, 56/6/1.

Archivo General de Indias (AGI).
Justicia 403.
Lima, 28-A; 28-B; 33; 35; 37; 38; 40; 41; 44; 48; 56; 78; 79; 93; 94; 301; 320; 321; 322; 324; 328; 333; 334; 336; 337; 414; 415; 520; 521; 535; 537; 568; 581.
Quito 8, Doc. 1
Patronato, Ramo 33.

Archivo General de Simancas (AGS)
Patronato Real, 23, fol. 78, 68, Docs. 47, 48.
Casa Real (Obras y Bosques), 2, fols. 118, 242; 3, fols. 338, 385, 414, 517; 7, fol. 618.
Diversos de Castilla, Leg. 39, doc. 34.

Archivo General del Palacio Real, Madrid
Sección Administrativa, no. 6.

Archivo Histórico Nacional (AHN)
Manuscript. Ayala, Manuel de. "Diccionario de gobierno y legislación de Indias norte de los acertamientos y actos positivos de la experiencia."
Inquisición. Leg. 1647, exp. 22; Leg. 1649, exp. 51.

Biblioteca de Zabálburu (Madrid)
Caja 169, fol. 10.

Biblioteca Nacional de Madrid (BNM)
Mss. 8293, Varios manuscritos acerca de los mercedarios.

UNITED STATES

John Carter Brown Library, Providence, Rhode Island.
Lilly Library, University of Indiana, Bloomington.
    Latin American Manuscripts. Peru, Actas Notariales, No. 753.
Nettie Lee Benson Latin American Collection, Austin, Texas.
Newberry Library, Chicago, Illinois.

Primary Printed Sources and Contemporary Writings

Acosta Africano, Cristóbal. *Tratado en loor de las mugeres y de la castidad, onestidad, constancia, silencio y justicia.* Venice: Presso Giacomo Cornetti, 1592.
Angulo, Domingo, ed. "Cedulario Arzobispal de la Arquidiócesis de Lima," *RANP,* III (1925), 27–102, 273–329.
———. "Libro original que contiene la fundación del monasterio de monxas de se-

ñora Santa Clara desta ciudad del Cuzco," *RANP,* XI: 1 (1939), 55–95; XI: 2 (1939), 157–84.

Bachelier, Le Sieur. "Lima en 1709," in Porras Barrenechea, *Pequeña antología de Lima,* 203–12.

Benavente, Toribio de (also known as Motolinía.) *Historia de los indios de La Nueva España y de los naturales de ella.* Edmundo O'Gorman, ed. (Serie de Historiadores y Cronistas de Indias, no. 2.) México: UNAM, 1971.

——. *Memoriales de Fray Toribio de Motolinia.* México: Casa de Luis García Pimentel, 1903.

Berceo, Gonzalo de. *Obras completas.* Logroño: Instituto de Estudios Riojanos, 1977.

Buendía, José. *Vida admirable y prodigiosas virtudes del Venerable Padre Francisco del Castillo.* Madrid: Antonio Román, 1693.

Cabello Balboa, Miguel. *Miscelánea Antártica: una historia del Perú antiguo.* Lima: Universidad Nacional Mayor de San Marcos, Instituto de Etnología, 1951.

Cabrera de Córdoba, Luis. *Relaciones de las cosas sucedidas en la Corte de España desde 1599 hasta 1614.* Madrid: J. Martín Alegría, 1857.

Calancha, Antonio de la. *Crónica moralizada de Antonio de la Calancha.* Ignacio Prado Pastor, ed. Barcelona, 1639. Lima, 1653. Facsimile edition. 6 vols. Lima: Universidad Nacional Mayor de San Marcos, 1974–81.

Calancha, Antonio de la, and Bernardo de Torres. *Crónicas agustinianas del Perú.* Manuel Merino, ed. Lima, 1653. Madrid: C.S.I.C., 1972.

Castillo, Francisco del. *Un místico del siglo XVII (autobiografía del Castillo de la Compañía de Jesús).* Rúben Vargas Ugarte, ed. Lima: Imprenta Gil, 1960.

Cazalla, María de. *Proceso de la Inquisición contra María Cazalla.* Milagros Ortega-Costa, ed. Madrid: Fundación Universitaria Española, 1978.

Cedulario indiano. Compiled by Diego de Encinas. 1596. Reprint. 4 vols. Madrid: Ediciones Cultura Hispánica, 1945.

Cerda, Juan de la. *Libro intítulado vida política de todos los estados de mugeres.* Alcalá de Henares: Casa de Juan Gracián, 1599.

Cieza del León, Pedro. *Crónica del Perú: Primera parte.* Seville, 1553. Lima: Pontificia Universidad Católica del Perú, 1986.

——. "Lima en 1550," in *Pequeña antología de Lima,* 98–101.

Cisneros, Garsías de. *Exercitatorio de la vida espiritual.* 1500. Reprint. Julian González de Soto, ed. Barcelona: Librería Religiosa, 1857.

Cobo, Bernabé. "Historia de la fundación de la ciudad de Lima," in *Monografías históricas sobre la ciudad de Lima.* Lima: Imprenta Gil, 1935, I: 1–317.

Códice franciscano, siglo XVI. México: Editorial Salvador Chávez Hayhoe, 1941.

Concilios limenses (1551–1772). Rubén Vargas Ugarte, ed. 3 vols. Lima, 1951–54.

"Constituciones para el colegio de niñas de Nuestra Señora de la Caridad," in Pilar Gonzalbo, *El Humanismo y la educación en la Nueva España.* México: Consejo Nacional de Fomento Educativo, 1985, 125–36.

Cook, Noble David, ed. *Numeración general de todas las personas de ambos sexos, edades y calidades q[ue] se ha echo en esta ciudad de Lima año de 1700.* Lima: COFIDE, 1985.

Córdoba, Martín de. *Jardín de nobles doncellas.* 1480. Reprint. Harriet Goldberg, ed. Chapel Hill: University of North Carolina Department of Romance Languages, 1974.

Córdoba y Salinas, Diego de. *Crónica franciscana de las provincias del Perú.* 1651. Reprint. Lino G. Canedo, ed. Washington, D.C.: Academy of American Franciscans History, 1957.

Un desconocido cedulario del siglo XVI. México: Casa de Pedro Ocharte, 1563.

Díaz de San Miguel y Solier, Nicolás Antonio. *La gran fee del centurion español: sermón moral, que en la capilla del Santo Oficio de la Inquisición.* Lima, 1695.

Díaz del Castillo, Bernál. *Historia verdadera de la conquista de la Nueva España.* Carmelo Saenz de Santa María, ed. Madrid: Instituto "Gonzalo Fernández de Oviedo," 1982.

Echave y Assu, Francisco de. *La estrella de Lima convertida en sol sobre sus tres coronas.* Antwerp: Juan Baptista Verdussen, 1688.

Eiximenis, Françesc de. *Lo Llibre de les dones.* Critical edition by Frank Naccarato under the direction of Joan Corominas. Barcelona, 1495. Barcelona: Department de Filologia Catalana, Universitat de Barcelona, 1981.

———. *Carro de las donas.* Juan de Villaquirán, trans. Valladolid, 1542.

Elso, Gerónimo de. *Sermones varios.* Madrid: Joseph Rodríguez de Escobar, 1731.

Fernández de Oviedo y Valdés, Gonzalo. *Historia general y natural de las Indias.* Juan Pérez de Tudela Bueso, ed. Madrid: Ediciones Atlas, 1959.

Frezier, Amédée François. "Lima en 1713," in *Pequeña antología de Lima,* 212–27.

———. *A Voyage to the South-Sea and Along the Coasts of Chile and Peru in the Years 1712, 1713 and 1714.* London: Jonah Bowyer, 1717.

García, Gómez. *Carro de dos vidas.* Seville: Ioannes Pegnicer de Nurenberga and Magno Herbst de Fils, 1500.

García y Sanz, Pedro. *Vida del Venerable u Apostólico Francisco del Castillo de la Compañía de Jesús.* Rome: Tipografía de Juan Cesaretti, 1863.

Garcilaso de la Vega. *Historia general del Perú (Segunda parte de los Comentarios reales de los Incas).* Angel Rosenblat, ed. Córdoba, 1616. 3 vols. Buenos Aires: Emecé Editores, 1944.

Gemelli Careri, Giovanni Francesco. *Viaje a la Nueva España.* 1708. Reprint. México: Universidad Nacional Autónoma de México, 1976.

Granada, Fray Luis de. *Libro de la oración y meditación.* Salamanca: En Casa de Domingo de Portonarijs, 1577.

Guevara, Antonio. *Libro llamado Reloj de príncipes.* Valladolid, 1529.

Guevara, Antonio de. *A los recién casados.* Madrid, 1868.

Hernando de Talavera. *Reforma de trages.* Baeça: Juan de la Cuesta, 1638.

———. *De vestir y de calzar.* 1480.

Jérez, Francisco de. "Verdadera relación," (1534) in *Los cronistas de la conquista.* Horacio H. Urteaga, ed. Paris: Desclée de Brouwer, 1938.

Jiménez de Cisneros, Francisco. *Obra de las epístolas y oraciones de la bien aventurada virgen sancta Catalina de Sena de la órden de los predicadores.* Toledo, 1512.

Karttunen, Frances, and James Lockhart, eds. *The Art of Nahuatl Speech: The Bancroft Dialogues.* Los Angeles: UCLA Latin American Center Publications, 1987.

León, Luis de. *La perfecta casada.* Salamanca: Casa de Juan Fernández, 1583.

———. *La perfecta casada.* Salamanca: En Casa de G. Foquel, 1587.

———. *La perfecta casada.* 1586. Reprint. Eduardo Juliá Martínez, ed. Madrid: Librería General de Victoriano Suárez, 1946.

León, Pedro de. *Grandeza y miseria en Andalucia, testimonio de una encrucijada histórica (1578–1616).* Pedro Herrera Puga, ed. Granada, 1981.

Liñan y Cisernos, Melchor. *Carta pastoral.* [Lima, 1703].

———. *Carta pastoral que escrive.* [Lima, 1697].

Lizárraga, Reginaldo de. "Lima al finalizar el siglo XVI," in *Pequeña antología de Lima,* 107–16.

López, Francisco. *Sermón panegyrico de la fundación del convento de Santa Ana de Carmelitas Descalças de la Ciudad de Lima.* Lima: Joseph de Contreras, 1687.

Loyola, Ignacio de. *Obras completas de San Ignacio de Loyola.* 1543. Madrid: Biblioteca de Autores Cristianos, 1947.

Luján, Pedro de. *Coloquios matrimoniales.* Toledo: Casa de Miguel Ferrer, 1563.

Malón de Chaide, Pedro. *Libro de la conversión de la Magdalena.* Alcalá de Henares: Juan Gracián [for] Diego Guillén, 1593.

Martínez Compañón y Bujanda, Baltasar Jaime. *Trujillo del Perú.* facsimile ed. 9 vols. Madrid: Ediciones de Cultura Hispánica, 1985.

Martínez de Toledo, Alfonso (also known as Corvacho.) *Archipreste de Talavera que habla de los vicios de las malas mugeres: y complexiones de los hombres.* Seville, 1547.

Meléndez, Juan. *Tesoros verdaderos de las Indias.* Rome: Imprenta Nicolás Angel Tinassio, 1681.

Memorias de los Virreyes que han governado el Perú, durante el tiempo del colonaje español. Manuel Atanasio Fuentes, ed. Lima: Libreria Central de Felipe Bailly, 1859.

Mendieta, Gerónimo de. *Historia eclesiástica indiana.* México: Antigua Libreria, 1870.

Mispilivar, Bernardo de. *Sagrado arbitrio, commutación de comedias de corpus.* Lima: Luis de Lyra, 1679.

Molinos, Miguel de. *Guía espiritual.* José Ignacio Tellechea Idigoras, ed. Barcelona, 1675. Madrid: Universidad Pontificia de Salamanca, 1976.

Montalvo, Francisco Antonio de. *Breve teatro de las acciones mas notables de la vida del bienaventurado Toribio Arçobispo de Lima.* Rome: Nicolás Angel Tinassio, 1683.

———. *El sol del Nuevo Mundo.* Rome: Imprenta de Angel Bernavo, 1683.

Montesinos, Fernando. *Anales del Perú.* 2 vols. Madrid: Imprenta del Horno, 1906.

Morgado, Alonso. *Historia de Sevilla.* Seville: Andrea Pescioni and Juan de León, 1587.

Mugaburu, Josephe and Francisco. *Diario de Lima (1640–1694).* Lima: Imprenta Vázquez, 1935.

Navarro, Antonio. *Abecedario virginal de excelencias del santíssimo nombre de María.* Madrid: Pedro Madrigal, 1604.

Olmos, Andrés de. *Tratado de hechicerías y sortilegios de Fray Andrés de Olmos.* México: Mission Archéologique et Ethnologique Française au Mexique, 1979.

Osuna, Francisco de. *Norte de los estados.* Seville: Bartolomé Pérez, 1531.

———. *Tercer abecedario espiritual.* 1528. Reprint. Melquiades Andrés Martín, ed. Madrid: Biblioteca de Autores Españoles, 1972.

Peralta Barnùevo y Rocha Benavides, Pedro de. *Imágen política del goviero del Excelentíssimo Señor D. Diego Ladrón de Guevara.* Lima: Gerónimo de Contreras, 1714.

Pérez de Valdivia, Diego. *Aviso de gente recogida.* 1585. Madrid: Imp. del Reyno, 1678.

Pérez de Herrera, Cristóbal. *Discursos del amparo de los legítimos pobres, y reducción de los fingidos.* Madrid: L. Sánchez, 1598.

Procesión antecedente al día, que se colocó el Santíssimo Sacramento del Altar, en la Capilla, de la Casa Real de Mugeres Amparadas de la Puríssima. Lima, 1670.

Providencia, Josefa de la. *Relación del orígen y fundación del monasterio del Señor San*

Joaquín de Religiosas Nazarenas Carmelitas Descalzas de esta Ciudad de Lima. Lima: Imp. Real de los Niños Expósitos, 1793.

Puga, Vasco de. *Provisiones, cédulas e instrucciones para el govierno de la Nueva España.* Madrid: Cultura Hispánica, 1945.

Quintanilla y Mendoza, Pedro de. *Archetypo de virtudes, espejo de prelados; El venerable padre y siervo de Dios Fray Francisco Xímenez de Cisneros.* Palermo: Nicolás Bua, 1653.

Quiroga, Pedro de. *Coloquios de la verdad.* Daisy Ripodas Ardanaz, ed. Valladolid: Instituto de Cooperación Iberoamericana, 1992.

Sahagún, Bernardino de. *Florentine Codex. Historia general de las cosas de la Nueva España.* Juan Carlos Temprano, ed. 1547. 2 vols. Madrid: Historia 16, 1990.

———. *Psalmodia Christiana (Christian Psalmody).* Arthur J. O. Anderson, trans. 1583. Salt Lake City: University of Utah Press, 1993.

Salazar, Juan de. *Política española.* [Lograno, 1619]. Madrid: M. Herrero García, 1945.

Salinas y Córdova, Buenaventura de. *Memorial de las historias del Nuevo Mundo.* Lima: Gerónymo de Contreras, 1630.

San Jerónimo, Madre Magdalena. *Razón y forma de la galera, y casa real, que el Rey, Nuestro Señor manda hazer en estos Reynos para castigo de las mugeres vagantes, y ladronas, alcahuetas, hechiceras, y otras semejantes.* Salamanca: Artus Taberniel, 1608.

Santísima Trinidad, María Josefa de la. *Historia de la fundación del Monasterio de Trinitarias Descalzas de Lima.* 1744. Isabel de la Presentación, ed. Lima: Editorial San Antonio, 1957.

Sínodos de Lima de 1613 y 1636/Bartolomé Lobo Guerrero, Fernando Arías de Ugarte. Madrid: Centro de Estudios Históricos del CSIC, 1987.

Solórzano Pereira, Juan de. *Libro primero de la recopilación de las cédulas, provisiones y ordenanzas reales.* 1622. Reprint. Buenos Aires: Universidad de Buenos Aires, 1945.

———. *Política indiana.* 1648. Reprint. 2 vols. Madrid: Talleres Voluntad, 1930.

Soto, Domingo de. *Deliberación en la causa de los pobres.* Salamanca, 1545.

Soto, Juan de. *Obligaciones de todos los estados y oficios, con los remedios y consejos mas eficaces.* Alcalá de Henares: Andrés Sánchez de Ezpeleta, 1619.

Suardo, Juan Antonio. *Diario de Lima de Juan Antonio Suardo (1629–1639).* Rubén Vargas Ugarte, ed. Lima: Imprenta C. Vásquez, 1935.

Teresa of Avila, Saint. *Obras de Santa Teresa.* Efrén de la Madre de Dios and Ofilio del Niño Jesús, eds. 3 vols. Madrid, 1951–59.

Torquemada, Juan de. *Monarquía indiana.* Seville, 1615. 4th edition. México, 1969.

Trujillo Mena, Valentín, ed. *La legislación eclesiástica en el Virreynato del Perú durante el siglo XVI.* Lima: Ed. Lumen, 1981.

Vetancurt, Augustín de. *Teatro mexicano: descripción breve de los sucessos exemplares históricos, políticos, militares y religiosos del Nuevo Mundo Occidental de las Indias.* México: Doña María de Benavides, viuda de Juan de Ribera, 1698.

Vives, Juan Luis. *On Assistance to the Poor.* Alice Tobriner, trans. Chicago: University of Chicago, School of Service Administration, 1971.

———. *Libro llamado instrucción de la mujer cristiana.* 1524. Juan Justiniano, trans. Madrid: Signo, 1936.

———. *Tratado del socorro de los pobres.* 1526. Juan de Gonzalo Nieto é Ivarra, trans. Valencia: Editorial Prometeo, 1781.

Xaimes de Ribera, Joan. *Hazer de si mismo espejo.* Lima: Imp. de Manuel de los Olivos, 1689.

Zárate, Agustín de. *Historia del descubrimiento y conquista del Perú.* Antwerp, 1555. Madrid: Biblioteca de Autores Cristianos, 1923.

Zumárraga, Juan de. *Doctrina breve muy provechosa.* México, 1544.

———. *Zumárraga and His Family: Letters of Vizcaya, 1536–1548.* Transcribed and with an introduction by Richard E. Greenleaf. Translated by Neal Kaveny. Washington, D.C.: Academy of American Franciscan History, 1979.

Dictionaries and Other Reference Materials

Alonso, Martín. *Enciclopedia del idioma.* Madrid: Aguilar, 1947.

Boggs, Ralph Steele. *A Tentative Dictionary of Medieval Spanish.* 2 vols. Chapel Hill, 1946.

Busto Duthurburu, José Antonio del. *Diccionario histórico biográfico de los conquistadores del Perú.* 2 vols. Lima: Libreria Studium Ediciones, 1986–.

Canons and Decrees of the Council of Trent. H. J. Schroeder, trans. St. Louis and London: Herder Books, 1941.

Corominas, Joan, and José A. Pascual. *Diccionario crítico etimológico castellano e hispánico.* Madrid: Editorial Gredos, 1980.

Covarrubias Orozco, Sebastián de. *Tesoro de la lengua castellana, o española según la impresión de 1611.* Benito Remigio Noydens, ed. Madrid: Luis Sánchez, 1674.

Diccionario de historia eclesiástica de España. Quintín Aldea Vaquero, Tomás Marín Martínez and José Vives Gatell, eds. 4 vols. Madrid: Instituto Enrique Flórez, Consejo Superior de Investigaciones Científicas, 1972–75.

Diccionario de la lengua castellana en que se explica el verdadero sentido de las voces, su naturaleza y calidad. Real Academia Española, ed. 1726. Reprint. Madrid: Real Academia Española, 1964.

Diccionario de la lengua española. Real Academia Española. 19th ed. Madrid: Real Academia Española, 1970.

Diccionario histórico de la lengua española. Madrid: Academia Española, 1933.

Diccionario Porrúa de historia, biografía y geografía de México. 3 vols. 5th edition. México: Editorial Porrúa, 1986.

Domingo de Santo Tomás. *Lexicon, o vocabulario de la lengua general del Perú.* 1560. Raúl Porras Barrenechea, ed. Lima: Instituto de Historia, 1951.

García Icazbalceta, Joaquín. *Bibliografía mexicana del siglo XVI. Catálogo razonado de libros impresos en México de 1539 a 1600.* México: Fondo de Cultura Económica, 1954.

González Holguín, Diego. *Vocabulario de la lengua general de todo el Perú llamada lengua Qquichua o del Inca.* 1608. Raúl Porras Barrenechea, ed. 2 vols. Lima: Imp. Santa María, 1952.

Mendiburu, Manuel de. *Diccionario histórico-biográfico del Perú.* 8 vols. Lima: Imprenta "Bolognesi" and J. Francisco Solís, 1874–90.

Mir y Noguera, Juan. *Diccionario de frases de los autores clásicos españoles.* Buenos Aires: Joaquín Gil, 1942.

Molina, Alonso de. *Vocabulario en lengua castellana y mexicana.* México: Antonio de Spinosa, 1571.

Moliner, María. *Diccionario del uso del español.* Madrid: Editorial Gredos, 1981.

Nebrija, Antonio de. *Dictionarium ex hispaniesnsi.* Burgos, 1512.

Oelschlager, Victor R. B. *A Medieval Spanish Word List; A Preliminary Dated Vocabulary of First Appearances up to Berceo.* Madison: University of Wisconsin Press, 1940.

Oudin, César. *Tesoro de las dos lenguas española y francesa.* 1616. Brussels, 1660.

Palet, Joan. *Diccionario muy copioso de la lengua española y francesa.* Paris: Guillemot, 1604.

Perceval, Richard. *A Dictionary in Spanish and English.* John Mensheu, ed. London: E. Bollifant, 1599.

Santo Tomás, Domingo de. *Lexicon, o vocabulario de la lengua general del Perú.* 1560. Facsimile ed. Raúl Porras Barrenechea, ed. Lima: Instituto de Historia, 1951.

Stephens, Thomas M. *Dictionary of Latin American Racial and Ethnic Terminology.* Gainesville: University of Florida Press, 1989.

Stevens, John. *New Spanish and English Dictionary.* London: G. Sawbridge, 1706.

Torrecilla, Martín de. *Encyclopedia canónica, civil, moral, regular y orthodoxa.* 2 vols. Madrid: Blas de Villanueva, 1721.

Collected Works

Cartas de Indias. Madrid: Ministerio de Fomento, Imp. de Manuel G. Hernández, 1877.

Charcas. Audiencia. *La Audiencia de Charcas: correspondencia de presidentes y oidores.* Madrid: Imprenta de Juan Pueyo, 1922.

Colección de bulas, breves y otros documentos relativos a la Iglesia de América y Filipinas. Francisco Javier Hernáez, ed. 2 vols. Brussels: Imprenta de Alfredo Vromant, 1879.

Colección de documentos inéditos relativos al descubrimiento y conquista de América y Oceanía. 42 vols. Madrid: Ministerio de Ultramar, 1864–84.

Colección de documentos para la historia de la formación social de hispanoamérica, 1493–1810. Richard Konetzke, ed. 2 vols. Madrid: Consejo Superior de Investigaciones Científicas, 1953–62.

Documentos inéditos del siglo XVI para la historia de México. Mariano Cuevas, ed. México: Museo Nacional de Antropología, Historia y Etnología, 1914.

Gobernantes del Perú, Cartas y papeles, siglo XVI; documentos del Archivo General de Indias. Robert Levillier, ed. 14 vols. Madrid: Sucesores de Rivadeneyra, 1921–26.

La Iglesia de España en el Perú: colección de documentos para la historia de la Iglesia en el Perú. Emilio Lissón Chávez, ed. 9 vols. in 5. Seville, 1943–47.

Lima. Audiencia. *Audiencia de Lima: correspondencia de presidentes y oidores, documentos del Archivo de Indias.* Robert Levillier, ed. Madrid: Imprenta de Juan Pueyo, 1922.

Manuscritos peruanos en las bibliotecas de América. Rubén Vargas Ugarte, ed. Buenos Aires: A. Baiocco, 1945.

Moreyra y Paz-Soldán, Manuel. *Colección de cartas de virreyes: Conde de Monclova.* Manuel Moreyra y Paz-Soldán and Guillermo Cespedes del Castillo, eds. 3 vols. Lima: Instituto Histórico del Perú, 1954–55.

Novísima recopilación de las leyes de España. 6 vols. Madrid: Boletín Oficial del Estado, 1975.

Recopilación de las leyes de los reynos de las Indias. 4 vols. Madrid, 1681. Reprint. Madrid: Ediciones Cultura Hispánica, 1973.

Relaciones geográficas de Indias. Marco Jiménez de la Espada, ed. 4 vols. Madrid: Tip. de M. G. Hernández, 1881–97.

Books

Actas del III Coloquio de Historia Medieval Andaluza: la sociedad medieval andaluza: grupos no privilegiados. Jaén: Diputación Provincial de Jaén, 1984.

Aguirre Beltrán, Gonzalo. *La población negra de México, 1519–1810; estudio etnohistórico.* México: Ediciones Fuente Cultural, [1946].

Ahlgren, Gillian T. W. *Teresa of Avila and the Politics of Sanctity.* Ithaca: Cornell University Press, 1996.

Altman, Ida. *Emigrants and Society; Extremadura and Spanish America in the Sixteenth Century.* Berkeley: University of California Press, 1989.

Amaya, Fernández Fernández, et al., eds. *La mujer en la conquista y la evangelización en el Perú (Lima 1550–1650).* Lima: Universidad Católica del Perú, 1997.

Andrés Martín, Melquiades. *Historia de la mística de la Edad de Oro en España y América.* Madrid: Biblioteca de Autores Cristianos, 1994.

———. *Los recogidos: nueva visión de la mística española (1500–1700).* Madrid: Fundación Universitaria Española, 1975.

———. *La teología española en el siglo XVI.* 2 vols. Madrid: Editorial Católica, 1976–77.

Andrien, Kenneth. *Crisis and Decline: The Viceroyalty of Peru in the Seventeenth Century.* Albuquerque: University of New Mexico Press, 1985.

Angulo, Domingo. *Santa Rosa de Santa María. Estudio bibliográfico.* Lima: Sanmartí y Compañía, 1917.

Arenal, Electa, and Stacey Schlau, eds. *Untold Sisters: Hispanic Nuns in Their Own Works.* Amanda Powell, trans. Albuquerque: University of New Mexico Press, 1989.

Ariès, Philippe. *Centuries of Childhood: A Social History of Family Life.* Robert Baldick, trans. New York: Alfred A. Knopf, 1962.

Armas Medina, Fernando de. *Cristianización del Perú (1532–1660).* Seville: C.E.H.A., 1953.

Arrom, Silvia. *The Women of Mexico City, 1790–1857.* Stanford: Stanford University Press, 1985.

Atondo Rodríguez, Ana María. *El amor venal y la condición femenina en el México colonial.* México: Instituto Nacional de Antropología e Historia, 1992.

Barriga, Victor M. *Los mercedarios ilustres en el Perú.* 3 vols. Arequipa: Editorial La Colmena, 1944.

Basadre, Jorge. *El Conde de Lemos y su tiempo.* Lima: Editorial Huascarán, 1948.

Bataillon, Marcel. *Erasmo y España: estudios sobre la historia espiritual del siglo XVI.* México: Fondo de Cultura Económica, 1950.

Baudot, Georges. *La pugna franciscana por México.* México, 1992.

Beltrán de Heredia, Vicente. *Historia de la reforma de la provincia de España (1450–1550).* Rome: Instituto Storico Dominicano, 1939.

Bercé, Y. M., G. Delille, J. M. Sallmann, and J. C. Waquet, eds. *L'Italie au 17e siècle.* Paris, 1989.

Bernales Ballesteros, Jorge. *Lima: la ciudad y sus monumentos.* Seville: Consejo Superior de Investigaciones Científicas, Escuela de Estudios Hispano-Americanos, 1972.

Bilinkoff, Jodi. *The Avila of Teresa: Religious Reforms in a Sixteenth Century City.* Ithaca: Cornell University Press, 1989.

Blunt, Alison, and Gillian Rose, eds. *Writing Women and Space: Colonial and Postcolonial Geographies*. New York and London: Guilford Press, 1994.

Bonilla, Heraclio, ed. *Las crisis económicas en la historia del Perú*. Lima: Centro Latinoamericano de Historia Económica y Social, 1986.

Borges, Pedro. *Religiosos en Hispanoamérica*. Madrid: Editorial MAPFRE, 1992.

Bourdieu, Pierre. *Outline of a Theory of Practice*. Richard Nice, trans. Cambridge: Cambridge University Press, 1977.

Bowser, Frederick. *The African Slave in Colonial Peru, 1524–1650*. Stanford: Stanford University Press, 1974.

Boyd-Bowman, Peter. *Patterns of Spanish Emigration to the New World (1493–1580)*. Buffalo: Special Studies Council on International Studies, State University of New York at Buffalo, April 1973.

Boyer, Richard. *Lives of the Bigamists: Marriage, Family and Community in Colonial Mexico*. Albuquerque: University of New Mexico Press, 1995.

Brading, David. *The First America: The Spanish Monarchy, Creole Patriots and the Liberal State, 1492–1867*. Cambridge: Cambridge University Press, 1991.

———. *Miners and Merchants in Bourbon Mexico, 1763–1810*. Cambridge: Cambridge University Press, 1971.

Bromley, Juan, and José Barbagelata. *Evolución urbana de la ciudad de Lima*. Lima: Consejo Provincial de Lima, 1935.

Burkhart, Louise M. *The Slippery Earth: Nahua-Christian Moral Dialogue in Sixteenth-Century Mexico*. Tucson: University of Arizona Press, 1989.

Burns, Kathryn. *Colonial Habits: Convents and the Spiritual Economy of Cuzco, Peru*. Durham: Duke University Press, 1999.

Busto Duthurburu, Antonio del. *San Martín de Porras (Martín de Porras Velásquez)*. Lima: Pontificia Universidad Católica del Perú, 1992.

Butler, Judith. *Bodies that Matter: On the Discursive Limits of Sex*. New York and London: Routledge, 1993.

———. *Gender Trouble: Feminism and the Subversion of Identity*. New York and London: Routledge, 1990.

Cabibbo, Sara. *La santa dei Tomasi: storia di suor María Crocifissa (1645–1699)*. Torino: Giulio Einaudi, 1989.

Carmona García, Juan I. *El sistema de la hospitalidad pública en la Sevilla del antiguo regímen*. Seville: Diputación Provincial de Sevilla, 1979.

Castañeda Delgado, Paulino, and Pilar Hernández Aparicio. *La Inquisición de Lima (1570–1635)*. Vol. 1. Madrid: Editorial Deimos, 1989.

Chávez, Ezequiel. *Fray Pedro de Gante; el ambiente geográfico, histórico y social de su vida y de su obra hasta el año de 1523*. México: Editorial Jus, 1943.

Clark, Peter, and Paul Slack. *English Towns in Transition, 1500–1700*. London: Oxford University Press, 1976.

Cohen, Sherrill. *The Evolution of Women's Asylums since 1500: From Refuges for Ex-Prostitutes to Shelters for Battered Women*. New York and Oxford: Oxford University Press, 1992.

Cook, Alexandra Parma and Noble David. *Good Faith and Truthful Ignorance: A Case of Transatlantic Bigamy*. Durham: Duke Univerity Press, 1991.

Cook, Noble David. *Demographic Collapse, Indian Peru 1520–1620*. Cambridge: Cambridge University Press, 1981.

Cope, R. Douglas. *The Limits of Racial Domination: Plebeian Society in Colonial Mexico City: 1660–1720*. Madison: University of Wisconsin Press, 1994.

Criado de Val, Manuel, ed. *Santa Teresa y la literatura mística hispánica. Actas del I Congreso Internacional sobre Santa Teresa y la mística hispánica*. Madrid: EDI–6, 1984.

Cuevas, Mariano. *Historia de la Iglesia en México*. 5 vols. México: Imprenta del Asilo Patricio Sanz, 1921–28.

Cushner, Nicholas. *Lords of the Land: Sugar, Wine and Jesuit Estates of Colonial Peru, 1600–1767*. Albany: State University of New York Press, 1980.

Dammert Bellido, José. *El clero diocesano en el Perú del siglo XVI*. Lima: Centro de Estudios y Publicaciones, 1996.

Deleito y Piñuela, José. *La mala vida en la Espana de Felipe IV*. Madrid: Espasa-Calpe, 1948.

Díaz-Plaja, Guillermo. *El espíritu del barroco*. Barcelona: Editoral Crítica, 1983.

Dominguez Ortíz, A. *The Golden Age of Spain, 1516–1659*. London: Weidenfeld, 1971.

Durán, Diego. *Historia de las Indias de la Nueva España e Islas de la Tierra Firme*. Angel María Garibay K., ed. México: Ed. Porrúa, 1967.

Duviols, Pierre. *Cultura andina y represión: procesos y visitas de idolatrías y hechicerías. Cajatambo siglo XVII*. Cusco: Bartolomé de las Casas, 1986.

Eguigüren, Luis Antonio. *Diccionario histórico cronológico de la Real y Pontificia Universidad de San Marcos y sus colegios: crónica e investigación*. 2 vols. Lima: Imp. de Torres Aguirre, 1940–.

Elliott, J. H. *The Count-Duke of Olivares: The Statesman in an Age of Decline*. New Haven and London: Yale University Press, 1986.

———. *Imperial Spain, 1469–1716*. New York: Penguin Books, 1976.

Encinas, Diego de. *Cedulario indiano recopilado por Diego de Encinas*. 1596. Madrid: Ed. Cultura Hispánica, 1945–46.

Escalante, Pablo, ed. *Educación e ideología en el México antiguo: fragmentos para la reconstrucción de una historia*. México: Consejo Nacional de Fomento Educativo, 1985.

Farriss, Nancy. *Maya Society under Colonial Rule: The Collective Enterprise of Survival*. Princeton: Princeton University Press, 1984.

Ferry, Robert J. *The Colonial Elite of Early Caracas: Formation and Crisis 1567–1767*. Berkeley: University of California Press, 1989.

Flores Galindo, Alberto. *Aristocracia y plebe, Lima, 1760–1830*. Lima: Mosca Azul Editores, 1984.

Flusche, Della M. *Two Families in Colonial Chile*. Lewison: Edwin Mellon Press, 1989.

Flynn, Maureen. *Sacred Charity: Confraternities and Social Welfare in Spain, 1400–1700*. Ithaca: Cornell University Press, 1989.

Foucault, Michel. *The Archaeology of Knowledge and the Discourse on Language*. New York: Pantheon Books, 1972.

———. *Discipline and Punish: The Birth of the Prison*. Alan Sheridan, trans. New York: Vintage Books, 1979.

———. *The Foucault Reader*. Paul Rabinow, ed. New York: Pantheon Books, 1984.

Franciscanos extremeños en el Nuevo Mundo. Guadalupe: Monasterio de Santa María de Guadalupe, 1987.

Franco, Jean. *Plotting Women: Gender and Representation in Mexico*. New York: Columbia University Press, 1989.

Fúrlong, Guillermo. *La cultura femenina en la época colonial.* Buenos Aires: Editorial Kapelusz, 1951.

García Ayluardo, Clara, and Manuel Ramos, eds. *Manifestaciones religiosas en el mundo colonial americano.* Vol. 1, *Espiritualidad barroca colonial: santos y demonios en América.* México: Universidad Iberoamericana: INAH: CONDUMEX, 1993.

García Icazbalceta, Joaquín. *Don fray Juan de Zumárraga: primer obispo y arzobispo de México.* 4 vols. México: Editorial Porrúa, 1947.

———. *Obras de D. J. García Icazbalceta.* 10 vols. México: Imprenta de Victoriano Agüeros, 1896–99.

García Irigoyen, Carlos. *Santo Toribio: obra escrita con motivo del tercer centenario de la muerte del santo arzobispo de Lima.* 4 vols. Lima: Imprenta y Librería de San Pedro, 1906–7.

García Villoslada, Ricardo, ed. *Historia de la Iglesia en España.* 5 vols. Madrid: Edica, 1979–.

García y García, Elvira. *La mujer peruana a través de los siglos; serie historiada de estudios y observaciones.* 2 vols. Lima: Imprenta Americana, 1924–25.

García-Baquero López, Gregorio. *Estudio demográfico de la parroquia de San Martín de Sevilla, 1551–1749.* Seville: Diputación Provincial de Sevilla, 1982.

Garrido Aranda, Antonio. *Moriscos e indios: precedentes hispánicos de la evangelización en México.* México: Universidad Nacional Autónoma de México, 1980.

———. *Organización de la Iglesia en el Reino de Granada y su proyección en Indias, siglo XVI.* Seville: Escuela de Estudios Hispano-Americanos de Sevilla, 1979.

Gatrell, V. A. C., Bruce Lenman, and Geoffrey Parker, eds. *Crime and the Law: The Social History of Crime in Western Europe since 1500.* London: Europa Publications, 1980.

Giddens, Anthony. *Central Problems in Social Theory.* London: Macmillan Press, 1979.

———. *The Constitution of Society: Outline of the Theory of Structuration.* Berkeley: University of California Press, 1984.

Gies, Frances and Joseph. *Marriage and the Family in the Middle Ages.* New York: Harper and Row Publishers, 1987.

Gil, Fernándo. *Primeras 'Doctrinas' del Nuevo Mundo; Estudio histórico-teológico de las obras de fray Juan de Zumárraga (+1548).* Buenos Aires: Universidad Católica Argentina, Publicaciones de la Facultad de Teología, 1993.

Giles, Mary, ed. *Women in the Inquisition: Spain and the New World.* Baltimore: Johns Hopkins University Press, 1999.

Ginzburg, Carlo. *Clues, Myths, and the Historical Method.* John and Anne Tedeschi, trans. Baltimore: Johns Hopkins University Press, 1989.

Glave, Luis Miguel. *De Rosa y espinas: economía, sociedad y mentalidades andinas, siglo XVII.* Lima: Instituto de Estudios Peruanos, 1998.

Goffman, Erving. *Asylums: Essays on the Social Situation of Mental Patients and Other Inmates.* Chicago: Aldine Publishing Co., 1961.

Goldberg, David. *Racist Culture: Philosophy and the Politics of Meaning.* Cambridge: Blackwell Press, 1993.

Gómez Canedo, Lino. *La educación de los marginados durante la época colonial; escuelas y colegios para indios y mestizos en la Nueva España.* México: Ed. Porrúa, 1982.

Gonzalbo Aizpuru, Pilar. *La educación de la mujer en la Nueva España.* México: Secretaría de Educación Pública, 1985.

————. *Historia de la educación en la época colonial: el mundo indígena*. México: El Colegio de México, 1990.

————. *Las mujeres en la Nueva España: educación y vida cotidiana*. México: El Colegio de México, 1987.

Gonzalbo Aizpuru, Pilar, ed. *Familias novohispanas, siglos XVI al XIX*. México: El Colegio de México, 1991.

González Dávila, Gil. *Teatro eclesiástico de la primitiva Iglesia de la Nueva España en las Indias Occidentales*. 2 vols. Madrid: José Porrúa Turanzas, 1959.

González Muñoz, María del Carmen. *La población de Talavera de la Reina (siglos XVI–XX), estudio socio-demográfico*. Toledo: Diputación Provincial, 1974.

González y González, Nicolás. *El Monasterio de la Encarnación de Avila, Siglos XV y XVI*. 2 vols. Avila: Caja Central de Ahorros y Prestamos de Avila, 1976.

Greenleaf, Richard. *Zumárraga and the Mexican Inquisition, 1536–1543*. Washington, D.C.: Academy of American Franciscan History, 1961.

Grendler, Paul F. *Schooling in Renaissance Italy: Literacy and Learning, 1300–1600*. Baltimore: Johns Hopkins University Press, 1989.

Gruzinski, Serge. *La colonización de lo imaginario: sociedades indígenas y occidentalización en el México español, siglos XVI–XVIII*. Jorge Ferreiro, trans. México: Fondo de Cultura Económica, 1991.

Gutiérrez, Ramón. *When Jesus Came the Corn Mothers Went Away: Marriage, Sexuality, and Power in New Mexico, 1500–1846*. Stanford: Stanford University Press, 1991.

Hall, Stuart, and Paul du Gay, eds. *Questions of Cultural Identity*. London: Sage Publications, 1996.

Hampe Martínez, Teodoro. *Santidad e identidad criolla: estudio del proceso de canonización de Santa Rosa*. Cuzco: Centro de Estudios Regionales Andinos Bartolomé de Las Casas, 1998.

Hanke, Lewis, ed. *Los virreyes españoles en América durante el gobierno de la Casa de Austria*. Madrid: Atlas, 1976–.

Harth-Terre, Emilio. *Hospitales mayores en Lima en el primer siglo de su fundación*. Buenos Aires, 1964.

Hawkesworth, M. E. *Beyond Oppression: Feminist Theory and Political Strategy*. New York: Continuum Press, 1990.

Hekman, Susan J., ed. *Feminist Interpretations of Michel Foucault*. University Park: Pennsylvania State University Press, 1996.

Hellbom, Anna-Britta. *La participación cultural de las mujeres: indias y mestizas en el México precortesiano y postrevolucionario*. Stockholm: Ethnographical Museum, 1967.

Hernández Iglesias, Fermín. *La beneficencia en España*. 2 vols. Madrid: Establecimientos Tipográficos de Manuel Minuesa, 1876.

Herráez S. de Escariche, Julia. *Beneficencia de España en Indias*. Seville: Escuela de Estudios Hispanoamericanos, 1949.

Herzog, Tamar. *La administración como un fenómeno social: la justicia penal de la ciudad de Quito (1650–1750)*. Madrid: Centro de Estudios Constitucionales, 1995.

Hoberman, Luisa. *Mexico's Merchant Elite, 1590–1660: Silver, State and Society*. Durham and London: Duke University Press, 1991.

Hoberman, Louisa Schell, and Susan Migden Socolow, eds. *Cities and Society in Colonial Latin America*. Albuquerque: University of New Mexico Press, 1986.

Hsia, R. Po-chia. *The World of Catholic Renewal, 1540–1770.* Cambridge: Cambridge University Press, 1998.

Huerga, Alvaro. *Historía de los alumbrados: los alumbrados de Hispanoamérica (1570–1605).* 3 vols. Madrid: Fundación Universitaria Española, 1986.

————. *Historia de la Reforma de la Provincia de España (1450–1550).* Rome: Instituto Storico Dominicano, 1939.

————. *Santa Catalina de Siena en la historia de la espiritualidad hispana.* Rome, 1969.

Hünefeldt, Christine. *Paying the Price of Freedom: Family and Labor among Lima's Slaves, 1800–1854.* Berkeley: University of California Press, 1994.

Iparraguirre, Ignacio. *Historia de la práctica de los ejercicios espirituales de San Ignacio de Loyola.* 2 vols. Bilbao: Artes Gráficos Grijelmo, 1955.

Israel, Jonathan. *Race, Class and Politics in Colonial Mexico, 1610–1670.* Oxford: Oxford University Press, 1975.

Iznaga, Diana. *Transculturation in Fernando Ortíz.* Havana: Editorial de Ciencias Sociales, 1989.

Jiménez Salas, María. *Historia de la asistencia social en la España moderna.* Madrid, 1958.

Johnson, Lyman L., and Sonya Lipsett-Rivera, eds. *The Faces of Honor: Sex, Shame, and Violence in Colonial Latin America.* Albuquerque: University of New Mexico Press, 1998.

Jütte, Robert. *Poverty and Deviancy in Early Modern Europe.* Cambridge: Cambridge University Press, 1994.

Kagan, Richard L. *Lucrecia's Dreams: Politics and Prophecy in Sixteenth-Century Spain.* Berkeley: University of California Press, 1990.

————. *Students and Society in Early Modern Spain.* Baltimore: Johns Hopkins University Press, 1974.

King, Margaret. *Women of the Renaissance.* Chicago: University of Chicago Press, 1991.

Kobayashi, José María. *La educación como conquista (empresa franciscana en México).* México: El Colegio de México, 1974.

Koselleck, Reinhart. *Futures Past: On the Semantics of Historical Time.* Keith Tribe, trans. Cambridge: MIT Press, 1985.

Kottman, Karl A. *Law and Apocalypse: The Moral Thought of Luis of León (1527?–1591).* The Hague, Netherlands: Martinus Nijhoff, 1972.

Lavallé, Bernard. *Las promesas ambiguas: criollismo colonial en los Andes.* Lima: Pontificia Universidad Católica del Perú, 1993.

Lavalle, José Antonio de. *La hija del contador.* Lima: La Novela Peruana, 1923.

Lavrin, Asunción, ed. *Sexuality and Marriage in Colonial Latin America.* London and Lincoln: University of Nebraska Press, 1989.

Lemlij, Moisés, and Luis Millones, eds. *Historia, memoria y ficción.* Lima: Seminario Interdisciplinario de Estudios Andinos, 1996.

León-Portilla, Miguel. *The Aztec Image of Self and Society: An Introduction to Nahua Culture.* J. Jorge Klor de Alva, ed. Salt Lake City: University of Utah Press, 1992.

————. *Los franciscanos vistos por el hombre náhuatl: testimonios indígenas del siglo XVI.* México: Universidad Nacional Autónoma de México, 1985.

Levillier, Robert. *Don Francisco de Toledo: supremo organizador del Perú, su vida, su obra (1512–1582).* Madrid: Espasa-Calpe, 1935.

Lis, Catharina, and Hugo Soly. *Poverty and Capitalism in Pre-industrial Europe.* Sussex: Harvester Press, 1979.

Lockhart, James. *The Men of Cajamarca: A Social and Biographical Study of the First Conquerors of Peru*. Austin: University of Texas Press, 1972.

―――. *The Nahuas after the Conquest: A Social and Cultural History of the Indians of Central Mexico, Sixteenth through Eighteenth Centuries*. Stanford University Press, 1992.

―――. *Spanish Peru, 1532–1560: A Colonial Society*. Madison: University of Wisconsin Press, 1968.

Lohman Villena, Guillermo. *Los americanos en las órdenes nobiliarias (1529–1900)*. 2 vols. Madrid: Instituto Gonzalo Fernández de Oviedo, 1947.

―――. *El Conde de Lemos: virrey del Perú*. Madrid: Estades, 1946.

López Austin, Alfredo. *The Human Body and Ideology: Concepts of the Ancient Nahuas*. Thelma Ortíz de Montellano and Bernard Ortíz de Montellano, trans. Salt Lake City: University of Utah Press, 1988.

Lorente, Sebastián. *Historia del Perú bajo la dinastia Austriaca, 1598–1700*. 3 vols. Paris: Imprenta A. E. Rochette, 1870.

Madariaga, Salvador de. *Cuadro histórico de las Indias*. Buenos Aires: Eidtorial Sudamericana, 1945.

Mannarelli, María Emma. *Hechiceras, beatas y expósitas: mujeres y poder inquisitorial en Lima*. Lima: Ediciones del Congreso del Perú, 1998.

―――. *Pecados públicos: la ilegitimidad en Lima, siglo XVII*. Lima: Flora Tristan, 1993.

Maravall, José Antonio. *La cultura del barroco: analísis de una estructura histórica*. Barcelona: Editorial Ariel, 1975.

―――. *Poder, honor y élites en el siglo XVII*. Madrid: Siglo Veintiuno de España, 1979.

Marianella, Conchita Herdman. *"Dueñas" and "Doncellas": A Study of the "Doña Rodríguez" Episode in "Don Quixote."* Chapel Hill: University of North Carolina, Dept. of Romance Languages, 1979.

Márquez, Antonio. *Los alumbrados; orígenes y filosofía, 1525–1559*. Madrid: CSIC, 1970.

Marshall, Sherrin, ed. *Women in Reformation and Counter-Reformation Europe: Public and Private Worlds*. Bloomington: Indiana Press, 1989.

Martín, Luis. *Daughters of the Conquistadores: Women of the Viceroyalty of Peru*. Albuquerque: University of New Mexico Press, 1983.

Martín, Luis, and Jo Ann Geurin Pettus. *Scholars and Schools in Colonial Peru*. San Antonio: Southern Methodist University, School of Continuing Education, 1973.

Martin, Norman F. *Los vagabundos en la Nueva España, siglo XVI*. México: Editorial Jus, 1957.

Mathes, W. Michael. *The America's First Academic Library: Santa Cruz de Tlatelolco*. Sacramento: California State Library Association, 1985.

Maza, Francisco de la. *La ciudad de México en el siglo XVII*. México: Fondo de Cultura Económica, 1968.

McDonnell, Ernest W. *The Beguines and Beghards in Medieval Culture, with Special Emphasis on the Belgian Scene*. New York: Octagon Books, 1969.

McGinn, Bernard, ed. *Meister Eckhart and the Beguine Mystics: Hadewijch of Brabant, Mechthild of Magdeburg and Marguerite Porete*. New York: Continuum Press, 1994.

Medina, José Toribio. *Historia del Tribunal de la Inquisición de Lima*. 2 vols. Santiago: Fondo Histórico y Bibliográfico J. T. Medina, 1956.

Medina, Manuel Ramos, ed. *El monacato femenino en el imperio español: monasterios, beaterios, recogimientos y colegios*. México: Centro de Estudios de Historia de México, 1995.

Méndez, Cristóbal. *Book of Bodily Exercises*. Francisco Guerra, trans. New Haven: Elizabeth Licht, 1960.

Millones, Luis. *Una partecita del cielo: la vida de Santa Rosa de Lima narrada por don Gonzalo de la Maza a quien ella llamaba padre*. Lima: Editorial Horizonte, 1993.

Mills, Kenneth. *Idolatry and Its Enemies: Colonial Andean Religion and Extirpation, 1640–1750*. Princeton: Princeton University Press, 1997.

Minchom, Martin. *The People of Quito, 1690–1810: Change and Unrest in the Underclass*. Boulder: Westview Press, 1994.

Mörner, Magnus. *Race Mixture in the History of Latin America*. Boston: Little, Brown and Co., 1967.

———, ed. *El mestizaje en la historia de Iberoamérica*. México: Instituto Panamericano de Geografía e Historia, 1961.

Muir, Edward, and Guido Ruggiero, eds. *Sex and Gender in Historical Perspective*. Baltimore and London: Johns Hopkins University Press, 1990.

Muñiz Rodríguez, Vicente. *Experiencia de Dios y lenguaje en el Tercer Abecedario Espiritual de Francisco de Osuna*. Salamanca: Universidad de Salamanca, 1986.

Muñoz Fernández, Angela. *Beatas y santas neocastellanas: ambivalencias de la religión y políticas correctoras del poder (ss. xiv–xvi)*. Madrid: Comunidad de Madrid, 1994.

Muriel de la Torre, Josefina. *Conventos de monjas en la Nueva España*. México: Editorial Santiago, 1946. 2d ed., México: Editorial Jus, 1995.

———. *Cultura femenina novohispana*. México: Universidad Nacional Autónoma de México, 1982.

———. *Hospitales de la Nueva España*. 2 vols. México: Editorial Jus, 1956–60.

———. *Los recogimientos de mujeres: respuesta a una problemática social novohispana*. México: Universidad Nacional Autónoma de México, 1974.

———. *La sociedad novohispana y sus colegios de niñas*. México: Universidad Nacional Autónoma de México, 1995.

Muzquiz de Miguel, José Luis. *El Conde de Chinchón: Virrey del Perú*. Madrid, 1945.

Nalle, Sara. *God in La Mancha: Religious Reform and the People of Cuenca, 1500–1650*. Baltimore and London: Johns Hopkins University Press, 1992.

Nieto Vélez, Armando. *Francisco del Castillo: El apóstol de Lima*. Lima: Pontificia Universidad Católica del Perú, 1992.

Nietzsche, Friedrich Wilhem. *On the Genealogy of Morals; Ecce Homo*. Walter Kaufmann, ed. New York: Vintage Books, 1967.

Orozco, Emilio. *Manierismo y barroco*. Madrid: Ed. Cátedra, 1975.

Ortíz, Fernando. *Contrapunteo cubano del tabaco y el azúcar*. Havana: Editorial Jesús Montero, 1940.

Ots Capdequí, José. *El estado español en las Indias*. 3d ed. Buenos Aires: 1957.

———. *Historia del derecho español en América y del derecho indiano*. Madrid, 1969.

———. *Instituciones sociales de la América española en el período colonial*. Buenos Aires: Imprenta López, 1934.

Pagden, Anthony. *European Encounters with the New World: From Renaissance to Romanticism*. New Haven: Yale University Press, 1993.

Parker, Geoffrey, and Lesley M. Smith, eds. *General Crisis of the Seventeenth Century*. 2d ed. London and New York: Routledge, 1997.

Pérez Baltasar, María Dolores. *Mujeres marginadas: las casas de recogidas en Madrid.* Madrid: Gráficas Lormo, 1984.

Pérez Cantó, María Pilar. *Lima en el siglo XVIII: estudio socioeconómico.* Madrid: Ediciones de la Universidad Autónoma de Madrid, 1985.

Pérez Villanueva, Joaquín, and Bartolomé Escandell Bonet, eds. *Historia de la Inquisición en España y América.* 2 vols. Madrid: Biblioteca de Autores Cristianos, Centro de Estudios Inquistoriales, 1984–.

Perry, Mary Elizabeth. *Gender and Disorder in Early Modern Seville.* Princeton: Princeton University Press, 1990.

Pescador, Juan. *De bautizados a fieles difuntos: familia y mentalidades en una parroquia urbana, Santa Catarina de México, 1528–1820.* México: Colegio de México, 1992.

Phelan, John Leddy. *The Millennial Kingdom of the Franciscans in the New World.* Berkeley: University of California Press, 1970.

Pitt-Rivers, Julian. *The Fate of Shechem or the Politics of Sex: Essays in the Anthropology of the Mediterranean.* Cambridge: Cambridge University Press, 1977.

Poole, Stafford. *Pedro Moya de Contreras: Catholic Reform and Royal Power in New Spain, 1571–1591.* Berkeley: University of California Press, 1987.

Porras Barrenechea, Raúl. *Fuentes históricas peruanas: apuntes de un curso universitario.* Lima: Instituto Raúl Porras Barrenechea, 1963.

———, comp. *Pequeña antología de Lima: el río, el puente y la alameda.* Lima: Instituto Raúl Porras Barrenechea, 1965.

Puente Brunke, José de la. *Encomienda y encomenderos en el Perú: estudio social y político de una institución colonial.* Seville: Diputación Provincial de Sevilla, 1992.

Pullan, Brian S. *Rich and Poor in Renaissance Venice: The Social Institutions of a Catholic State to 1620.* Oxford: Blackwell Press, 1971.

Ramírez, Susan E. *Provincial Patriarchs: Land Tenure and the Economics of Power in Colonial Peru.* Albuquerque: University of New Mexico Press, 1986.

Ramos, Gabriela, comp. *La venida del reino: religión, evangelización y cultura en América, siglos XVI–XX.* Cuzco: Centro de Estudios Regionales Andinos Bartolomé de las Casas, 1994.

Ramos, Gabriela, and Henrique Urbano, comps. *Catolicismo y extirpación de idolatrías: siglos XVI–XVIII.* Cusco: Centro de Estudios Rurales de Bartolomé de las Casas, 1993.

Ramos, Manuel. *Imagen de santidad en un mundo profano.* México: Universidad Iberoamericano, Departamento de Historia, 1990.

Ramos Escandón, Carmen, et al., eds. *Presencia y transparencia: la mujer en la historia de México.* México: El Colegio de México, 1987.

Rapley, Elizabeth. *The Dévotes: Women and Church in Seventeenth-Century France.* Montreal and Buffalo: McGill-Queen's University Press, 1990.

Ricard, Robert. *The Spiritual Conquest of Mexico.* Leslie Byrd Simpson, trans. Berkeley: University of California Press, 1966.

Rípodas Ardañas, Daisy. *El matrimonio en Indias: realidad social y regulación jurídica.* Buenos Aires: Fundación para la Educación, la Ciencia y la Cultura, 1977.

Rodríguez Sánchez, Angel. *Cáceres: población y comportamientos demográficos en el siglo XVI.* Cáceres: Editorial Extremadura, 1977.

Rodríguez Valencia, Vicente. *Santo Toribio de Mogrovejo; organizador y apóstol de Sur-América.* 2 vols. Madrid: Consejo Superior de Investigaciones Científicas, 1957.

Rodríguez Vicente, María Encarnación. *El tribunal del consulado de Lima en la primera mitad del siglo XVII.* Madrid: Ediciones Cultura Hispánica, 1960.

Rodríguez-Solís, E. *Historia de la prostitución en España y América.* 2 vols. Madrid: Biblioteca Nueva, 1892–93.

Roel Pineda, Virgilio. *Historia social y económica de la colonia.* Lima: Editorial Gráfica Labor, 1970.

Roper, Lyndal. *Oedipus and the Devil: Witchcraft, Sexuality and Religion in Early Modern Europe.* London and New York: Routledge, 1994.

Rosenblat, Angel. *La población indígena y el mestizaje en América.* Buenos Aires: Editorial Nova, 1964.

Rostworowski de Diez Canseco, María. *Doña Francisca Pizarro: una ilustre mestiza, 1534–1598.* Lima: Instituto de Estudios Peruanos, 1989.

Russo, Carla. *I monasteri femminili di clausura a Napoli nel secolo XVII.* Naples: Universita de Napoli, Instituto di Storia Medioevale e Moderna, 1970.

Saint-Saëns, Alain. *La nostalgie du désert: l'idéal érémetique en Castille au Siècle d'Or.* San Francisco: Edwin Mellen University Press, 1992.

————, ed. *Religion, Body and Gender in Early Modern Spain.* San Francisco: Mellen Research University Press, 1991.

Saínz Rodríguez, Pedro. *La siembra mística del Cardinal Cisneros y las reformas en la Iglesia.* Madrid: Universidad Pontificia de Salamanca, Fundación Universidad Española, 1977.

Sallmann, J. M., ed. *Visions indiennes, visions baroques: les métissages de l'inconscient.* Paris, 1992.

Sánchez, Ana. *Amancebados, hechiceros y rebeldes (Chancay, siglo XVII).* Cusco: Centro Bartolomé de las Casas, 1991.

Sánchez Lora, José L. *Mujeres, conventos y formas de la religiosidad barroca.* Madrid: Fundación Universitaria Española, 1988.

Santibañez Salcedo, Alberto. *El monasterio de Nuestra Señora del Prado.* Lima: Escuela Tipográfica Salesiana, 1943.

Sawicki, Jana. *Disciplining Foucault: Feminism, Power and the Body.* New York and London: Routledge, 1991.

Seed, Patricia. *To Love, Honor, and Obey in Colonial Mexico; Conflicts over Marriage Choice, 1574–1821.* Stanford: Stanford University Press, 1988.

Shahar, Shulamith. *The Fourth Estate: A History of Women in the Middle Ages.* London and New York: Methuen Press, 1983.

Silverblatt, Irene. *Moon, Sun, and Witches: Gender Ideologies and Class in Inca and Colonial Peru.* Princeton: Princeton University Press, 1987.

Spierenburg, Pieter. *The Prison Experience: Disciplinary Institutions and Their Inmates in Early Modern Europe.* New Brunswick and London: Rutgers University Press, 1991.

Spitta, Silvia. *Between Two Waters: Narratives of Transculturation in Latin America.* Houston: Rice University Press, 1995.

Stallybrass, Peter, and Allon White. *The Politics and Poetics of Transgression.* Ithaca: Cornell University Press, 1993.

Stepan, Nancy Leys. *"The Hour of Eugenics": Race, Gender and Nation in Latin America.* Ithaca: Cornell University Press, 1991.

Stern, Steve. *The Secret History of Gender: Women, Men and Power in Late Colonial Mexico.* Chapel Hill: University of North Carolina Press, 1995.

Stradling, R. A. *Europe and the Decline of Spain: A Study of the Spanish System, 1580–1720.* London: George Allen and Unwin, 1981.

Suárez, Margarita. *Comercio y fraude en el Perú colonial: las estrategias mercantiles de un banquero.* Lima: Instituto de Estudios Peruanos, 1995.

Tardieu, Jean Pierre. *Los negros y la Iglesia en el Perú siglos XVI–XVII.* 2 vols. Quito: Centro Cultural Afroecuatoriano, 1997.

Tobriner, Sister Alice. *A Sixteenth-Century Urban Report.* Chicago: University of Chicago, School of Social Service Administration, 1971.

Tord, Javier, and Carlos Lazo. *Hacienda, comercio, fiscalidad, y luchas sociales (Perú colonial).* Lima: Biblioteca Peruana de Historia Económica y Sociedad, 1981.

Trelles A., Efraín. *Lucas Martínez Vegazo: funcionamiento de una encomienda peruana inicial.* Lima: Pontificia Universidad Católica, 1983.

Troyansky, David. *Old Age in the Old Regime: Image and Experience in Eighteenth-Century France.* Ithaca: Cornell University Press, 1989.

Twinam, Ann. *Public Lives, Private Secrets: Gender, Honor, Sexuality, and Illegitimacy in Colonial Spanish America.* Stanford: Stanford University Press, 1999.

Ugarte Elespuru, Juan Manuel. *Lima y lo limeño.* Lima: Editorial Universitaria, 1966.

Urteaga, Horacio, ed. *Cuzco 1689: economía y sociedad en el sur andino.* Cuzco: Centro de Estudios Rurales Andinos "Bartolomé de Las Casas," 1982.

Valcárcel, Carlos Daniel. *Breve historia de la educación peruana.* Lima: Colección Ciencias Histórico-Sociales, 1975.

———. *Historia de la educación colonial.* 2 vols. Lima, 1968.

Valega, José M. *El virreinato del Perú: historia crítica de la época colonial, en todos sus aspectos.* Lima: Editorial Cultura Ecléctica, 1939.

van Deusen, Nancy E. *Dentro del cerco de los muros: el recogimiento en la época colonial.* Lima: Centro de Documentación sobre la Mujer, 1988.

Vargas Ugarte, Rubén. *Historia de la Iglesia en el Perú.* 5 vols. Lima: Imprenta Santa María, 1953–.

———. *Historia del culto de María en Hispanoámerica y de sus imágenes y santuarios más celebrados.* Lima: Imp. "La Providencia," 1931.

———. *Historia general del Perú.* 6 vols. Lima: Milla Batres, 1966.

———. *Títulos nobiliarios en el Perú.* Lima: Imprenta Gil, 1948.

———. *Vida del siervo de Dios Nicolás Ayllón, o por otro nombre Nicolás de Dios natural de Chiclayo.* Buenos Aires: Imprenta López, 1960.

Varner, John Grier. *El Inca: The Life and Times of Garcilaso de la Vega.* Austin and London: University of Texas Press, 1968.

Varón, Rafael. *La ilusión del poder: apogeo y decadencia de los Pizarro en la conquista del Perú.* Lima: Instituto de Estudios Peruanos, 1996.

Vigil, Mariló. *La vida de las mujeres en los siglos XVI y XVII.* Madrid: Siglo Veintiuno, 1987.

Warner, Marina. *Alone of All Her Sex: The Myth and Cult of the Virgin Mary.* New York: Vintage Books, 1983.

Weber, Alison. *Teresa of Avila and the Rhetoric of Femininity.* Princeton: Princeton University Press, 1990.

Weisser, Michael R. *The Peasants of the Montes: The Roots of Rural Rebellion in Spain.* Chicago: University of Chicago Press, 1976.

Wiesner, Merry E. *Women and Gender in Early Modern Europe.* Cambridge: Cambridge University Press, 1993.

Wilcox, Donald J. *In Search of God and Self: Renaissance and Reformation Thought.* Boston: Houghton Mifflin Co., 1975.

Williams, Raymond. *Keywords: A Vocabulary of Culture and Society.* New York: Oxford University Press, 1983.

————. *Marxism and Literature.* Oxford: Oxford University Press, 1977.

Wiltenburg, J. *Disorderly Women and Female Power in the Street Literature of Early Modern England and Germany.* Charlottesville: University of Virginia Press, 1992.

Zuidema, R. Tom. *Inca Civilization in Cuzco.* Austin: University of Texas Press, 1986.

Secondary Sources: Articles

Abrams, Lynn. "Whores, Whore-Chasers and Swine: The Regulation of Sexuality and the Restoration of Order in the Nineteenth-Century German Court," *Journal of Family History,* XXI: 3 (July 1996), 267–80.

Alberro, Solange. "Beatriz de Padilla: Mistress and Mother," in David G. Sweet and Gary B. Nash, *Struggle and Survival in Colonial America.* Berkeley: University of California Press, 1981, 165–88.

Alberti Manzanares, Pilar. "La influencia económica y política de las acllacuna en el Incanato," *Revista de Indias,* XLV: 176 (July 1985), 557–85.

————. "Una institución exclusivamente femenina en la época incaíca: las acllacuna," *Revista Española de Antropología Americana,* XVI (1986), 153–90.

————. "Mujer y religión: Vestales y Acllacuna, dos instituciones religiosas de mujeres," *Revista Española de Antropología Americana,* XVII (1987), 155–96.

————. "Mujeres sacerdotistas Aztecas: Las cihuatlamacazque mencionadas en dos manuscritos inéditos." *Estudios de Cultura Náhuatl,* 24 (1994), 171–85.

Alcalá, Angel. "María de Cazalla: The Grevious Price of Victory," in Giles, *Women in the Inquisition,* 98–118.

Altman, Ida. "Spanish Hidalgos and America: The Ovandos of Cáceres," *Americas,* XLIII: 3 (1987), 323–44.

Alvárez, Tomás. "Fray Luis de León y Santa Teresa: el profesor salmantino ante la monja escritora," in *Santa Teresa,* 493–502.

Amelang, James S. "Los usos de la autobiografía: Monjas y beatas en la Cataluña moderna," in James S. Amelang and Mary Nash, *Historia y género: las mujeres en la Europa moderna y contemporánea.* Valencia: Institució Valenciana d'Estudis i Investigació, 1990, 191–212.

Andrés Martín, Melquiades. "Contenido y transcripción de la 'Obediencia' e 'Instrucción,'" in *Franciscanos extremeños,* 403–34.

————. "La espiritualidad de los 'doce' en Extremadura y en Nueva España," in *Franciscanos extremeños,* 365–93.

————. "Pensamiento teológico y vivencia religiosa en la reforma española, 1400–1600," in *Historia de la Iglesia en España,* III–2: 269–361.

————. "Proceso de interioridad en la mística española (1500–1535): la reflexión de las potencias al centro del alma, como método dialéctico para la contemplación quieta," in *Santa Teresa,* 7–23.

Andrien, Kenneth. "The Sale of Fiscal Offices and the Decline of Royal Authority in the Viceroyalty of Peru, 1633–1700," *HAHR*, XLII: 1 (February 1982), 49–71.

———. "The Sale of Juros and the Politics of Reform in the Viceroyalty of Peru," *Journal of Latin American Studies*, XLIII (May 1981), 1–19.

Angulo, Domingo. "El terremoto de 1687 . . . información que se hizó por el Cabildo, Justicia y Reximento desta ciudad de Los Reyes," *RANP*, XII: 1 (1939), 3–45; XII: 2 (1939), 131–64.

———. "El terremoto del año de 1690," *RANP*, XIII: 1 (1940), 3–8.

Arco, Ricardo del. "Una notable institución social: el Padre de los Huérfanos," in *Estudios de historia social de España*. Madrid: Consejo Superior de Investigaciones Científicas, 1955, III: 189–222.

Avellá Cháfer, Francisco. "Beatas y beaterios en la ciudad y arzobispado de Sevilla," *Archivo Hispalense*, CXCVIII (January–April 1982), 99–132.

Baernstein, P. Renee. "In Widow's Habit: Women between Convent and Family in Sixteenth-Century Milan," *Sixteenth-Century Journal*, XXV: 4 (winter 1994), 787–807.

Bakewell, Peter J. "Registered Silver Production in the Potosí District, 1550–1735," *JbLA* 12 (1975), 67–103.

Barbier, Jacques. "Elites and Cadres in Bourbon Chile," *HAHR*, LII: 3 (August 1972), 416–35.

Bataillon, Marcel. "L'Iñiguiste et la beata: premier voyage de Calisto à México," *Revista de Historia de América*, XXXI (June 1951), 59–75.

Baudot, Georges. "Fray Andrés de Olmos y su tratado de los pecados mortales en lengua náhuatl," *Estudios de Cultura Nahuatl*, XII (1976), 33–59.

Bayle, Constantino. "La educación de la mujer en América," *Razón y Fé*, CXXIV (1941), 206–25.

Behar, Ruth. "Sexual Witchcraft, Colonialism and Women's Powers: Views from the Mexican Inquisition," in Lavrin, *Sexuality and Marriage in Colonial Latin America*, 178–206.

Beltrán de Heredia, Vicente. "La Beata de Piedrahita no fue alumbrado," *Ciencia Tomista*, LXIII (1942), 249–311.

Bergmann, Emile. "The Exclusion of the Feminine in the Cultural Discourse of the Golden Age: Juan Luis Vives and Fray Luis de León," in Saint-Saëns, *Religion, Body and Gender*, 124–36.

Bilinkoff, Jodi. "A Spanish Prophetess and Her Patrons: The Case of María de Santo Domingo," *Sixteenth Century Journal*, XXIII: 1 (spring 1992), 21–34.

Blank, Stephanie. "Patrons, Clients, and Kin in Seventeenth-Century Caracas: A Methodological Essay in Spanish American Social History," *HAHR*, LIV: 2 (May 1974), 260–83.

Borges, Pedro. "La emigración de eclesiásticos a América en el siglo XVI. Criterios para su estudio," in Francisco de Solano and Fermín del Pino, *América y la España del siglo XVI*. Madrid: CSIC, 1983, II: 47–62.

Boyd-Bowman, Peter. "Patterns of Spanish Emigration to the Indies until 1600," *HAHR*, LXVI: 4 (November 1976), 580–604.

Boyer, Richard. "Escribiendo la historia de la religión y mentalidades en la Nueva España," in *Familia y sexualidad en Nueva España*. México: Fondo de Cultura Económica, 1982, 119–37.

————. "Respect and Identity: Horizontal and Vertical Reference Points in Speech Acts" *Americas,* LIV: 4 (April 1998), 491–509.

————. "Women, *La Mala Vida,* and the Politics of Marriage," in Lavrin, *Sexuality and Marriage in Colonial Latin America,* 252–86.

Bronner, Fred. "Church, Crown, and Commerce in Seventeenth-Century Lima: A Synoptic Interpretation," *JbLA,* XXIX (1992), 75–89.

————. "Peruvian Encomenderos in 1630: Elite Circulation and Consolidation," *HAHR,* LVII: 4 (November 1977), 633–59.

————. "The Population of Lima, 1593–1637: In Quest of a Statistical Benchmark," *Ibero-Amerikanisches Archiv,* V, 2 (1979): 107–19.

————. "Urban Society in Colonial Spanish America: Research Trends," *Latin American Research Review,* XXI: 1 (1986), 7–72.

Burke, Peter. "How to Be a Counter-Reformation Saint," in Kaspar von Greyerz, *Religion and Society in Early Modern Europe, 1500–1800.* London: George Allen & Unwin, 1984, 45–55.

————. "Urban History and Urban Anthropology of Early Modern Europe," in Derek Fraser and Anthony Sutcliffe, *The Pursuit of Urban History.* London: Edward Arnold, 1983, 69–82.

Burns, Kathryn. "Apuntes sobre la economía conventual: el Monasterio de Santa Clara del Cusco," *Allpanchis,* XXIII: 38 (1991), 67–95.

————. "Conventos, criollos y la economía espiritual del Cuzco, siglo XVII," *El monacato femenino,* 315–17.

————. "Gender and the Politics of Mestizaje: The Convent of Santa Clara in Cuzco, Peru," *HAHR,* 78: 1 (1998), 5–44.

Busto Duthurburu, José Antonio del. "Una huérfana mestiza: la hija de Juan Pizarro," *Revista Histórica,* XXVIII (1965), 103–6.

————. "La mestiza del Capitán Hernando de Soto, su familia y los lienzos del Virrey Toledo," *Revista Histórica,* XXVIII (1965), 113–17.

————. "La primera generación mestiza del Perú y una causa de su mal renombre," *Revista Histórica,* XXVIII (1965), 67–79.

Cahill, David. "Colour by Numbers: Racial and Ethnic Categories in the Viceroyalty of Peru, 1532–1824," *Journal of Latin American Studies,* XXVI: 2 (May 1994), 325–46.

————. "Popular Religion and Appropriation: The Example of Corpus Christi in Eighteenth-Century Cuzco," *Latin American Research Review,* XXXI: 2 (1996), 67–110.

Calvo, Thomas. "Concubinato y mestizaje en el medio urbano: el caso de Guadalajara en el siglo XVI," *Revista de Indias,* XLIV: 173 (1984), 204–12.

Canning, Kathleen. "Feminist History after the Linguistic Turn: Historicizing Discourse and Experience," *Signs,* IX: 2 (winter 1994), 368–404.

Carrasco, Pedro. "Indian-Spanish Marriages in the First Century of the Colony," in *Indian Women of Early Mexico,* 87–103.

Carrión, Luis. "Casas de Recolección en la Provincia de la Inmaculada Concepción y estatutos porque se regían," *Archivo Ibero-Americano,* 1st series, XXV (enero–febrero 1918), 264–72.

Castoriadis, Cornelius. "The Institution and the Imaginary: A First Approach," in *The Imaginary Institution of Society.* Cambridge: MIT Press, 1987, 115–64.

Cavallo, Sandra, and Simona Cerutti. "Female Honor and the Social Control of Reproduction in Piedmont between 1600 and 1800," in Muir, *Sex and Gender in Historical Perspective*, 73–109.

Chance, John K., and William B. Taylor. "Estate and Class: A Reply," *Comparative Studies in Society and History*, XXI: 3 (1979), 434–42.

———. "Estate and Class in a Colonial City: Oaxaca in 1792," *Comparative Studies in Society and History*, XIX (1977), 454–87.

Charney, Paul. "Holding Together the Indian Family during Colonial Times in the Lima Valley, Peru." *University of Wisconsin-Milwaukee, Center for Latin America, Discussion Paper Series*, no. 86 (October 1991), 1–36.

———. "El indio urbano: un analísis económico y social de la población india de Lima en 1613," *Histórica*, XII: 1 (July 1988), 5–33.

———. "Negotiating Roots: Indian Migrants in the Lima Valley during the Colonial Period," *CLAHR* (winter 1996), 1–20.

Cisneros, Jaime. "Estudio y edición de la *Defensa de damas*," *Fénix*, IX (1955), 80–196.

Cohen, Elizabeth S. "Honor and Gender in the Streets of Early Modern Rome," *Journal of Interdisciplinary History*, XXII: 4 (spring, 1992), 597–625.

Cohen, Sherill. "Asylums for Women in Counter-Reformation Italy," in *Women in Reformation and Counter-Reformation Europe*, 166–88.

Coleman, David. "Moral Formation and Social Control in the Catholic Reformation: The Case of San Juan de Avila," *Sixteenth Century Journal*, XXVI: 1 (spring 1995), 17–30.

Córdoba de la Llave, Ricardo. "Las relaciones extraconyugales en la sociedad castellana bajomedieval," *Anuario de Estudios Medievales*, XVI (1986), 571–619.

Deans-Smith, Susan. "Culture, Power, and Society in Colonial Mexico," *Latin American Research Review*, XXXIII: 1 (1998), 257–77.

Devlin, Dennis. "Feminine Lay Piety in the High Middle Ages: The Beguines," in John A. Nichols and Lillian Thomas Shank, *Medieval Religious Women*, vol. I, *Distant Echoes*. Kalamazoo: Cistercian Publications, 1985, 183–96.

Domínguez Ortíz, Antonio. "Delitos y súplicos en la Sevilla imperial: la crónica negra de un misionero jesuita," in Antonio Domínguez Ortíz, *Crisis y decadencia de la España de los Austrias*. Barcelona: Ed. Ariel, 1971, 10–71.

Downs, Laura Lee. "If 'Woman' Is Just an Empty Category, then Why Am I Afraid to Walk Alone at Night? Identity Politics Meets the Postmodern Subject," *Comparative Studies in Society and History*, XXXV: 2 (April 1993), 414–37.

Ewick, Patricia, and Susan S. Silbey. "Subversive Stories and Hegemonic Tales: Toward a Sociology of Narrative," *Law and Society Review*, XXVIX: 2 (1995), 197–226.

"Examen histórico-crítico de la fundación, progreso y actual estado de la Real Casa ó Recogimiento de las Amparadas de la Concepción," *Mercurio Peruano*, CXXXI (1792), 231–66.

Ferrante, Lucia. "Honor Regained: Women in the Casa del Soccorso di San Paolo in Sixteenth-Century Bologna," in Muir, *Sex and Gender in Historical Perspective*, 46–72.

Fitzmaurice-Kelly, Julia. "Vives and the 'Carro de las Donas,'" *Revue Hispanique*, LXXXI: 1 (1933), 530–44.

———. "Women in Sixteenth-Century Spain," *Revue Hispanique*, 1st series, LXX (1927), 557–632.

Flores Araoz, José, et al., eds. *Santa Rosa de Lima y su tiempo*. Lima: Banco de Crédito del Perú, 1995.

Flores Galindo, Alberto, and Magdalena Chocano. "Las cargas del sacramento," *Revista Andina*, II: 2 (1984), 403–34.

Flynn, Thomas. "Foucault's Mapping of History," in Gary Gutting, *The Cambridge Companion to Foucault*. Cambridge: Cambridge University Press, 1994, 28–46.

Foucault, Michel. "Nietzsche, Genealogy and History," in Paul Rabinow, *The Foucault Reader*. New York: Pantheon Books, 1984, 76–100.

Fraschina, Alicia. "La dote canónica en el Buenos Aires tardo-colonial: monasterios Santa Catalina de Sena y Nuestra Señora del Pilar, 1745–1810," *CLAHR*, 9:1 (winter 2000), 67–102.

Gal, Susan. "Between Speech and Silence: The Problematics of Research and Language and Gender," in Micaela di Leonardo, *Gender at the Crossroads of Knowledge: Feminist Anthropology in the Post Modern Era*. Berkeley: University of California Press, 1991, 175–203.

Ganster, Paul. "Churchmen," in Hoberman, *Cities and Society*, 137–63.

García Icazbalceta, Joaquín. "El colegio de niñas de México," in idem, *Obras*, II: 428–34.

———. "La instrucción pública en México durante el siglo XVI," in idem, *Obras*, I: 163–265.

García Oro, J. "Conventualismo y observancia: la reforma de las órdenes religiosas en los siglos XV y XVI," in *Historia de la Iglesia en España*, III: 211–349.

Giles, Mary E. "Francisca Hernández and the Sexuality of Religious Dissent," in Giles, *Women in the Inquisition*, 75–97.

Girard, François. "Mujeres y familia en Nueva España," in Ramos Escandón, *Presencia y transparencia*, 61–77.

Glave, Luis Miguel. "Mujer indígena, trabajo doméstico y cambio social en el virreinato peruano del siglo XVII: la ciudad de La Paz y el sur andino en 1684," *Bulletin de l'Institut Français D'Etudes Andines*, XVI: 3–4 (1987), 39–69.

———. "Santa Rosa de Lima y sus espinas: la emergencia de mentalidades urbanas de crisis y la sociedad andina (1600–1630)," in García Ayluardo, *Manifestaciones religiosas*, 53–70.

———. "El Virreinato peruano y la llamada "crisis general" del siglo XVII," in Bonilla, *Las crises económicas de la historia del Perú*, 95–137.

Gómez Canedo, Luis. "Aspectos característicos de la acción franciscana en América," in *Franciscanos extremeños*, 441–63.

Gonzalbo Aizpuru, Pilar. "Las cargas del matrimonio: dotes y vida familiar en la Nueva España," in *Familia y vida privada en la historia de Iberoamérica*. México: El Colegio de México, Universidad Nacional Autónoma de México, 1996, 207–26.

———. "Tradición y ruptura en la educación femenina del siglo XVI," in Ramos Escandón, *Presencia y transparencia*, 33–59.

González del Riego, Delfina. "Fragmentos de la vida cotidiana a través de los procesos de divorcio," *Histórica*, XIX: 2 (Dic. 1995), 197–217.

Gowing, Laura. "Gender and the Language of Insult in Early Modern London," *History Workshop Journal*, XXV (spring 1993), 1–21.

———. "Language, Power and the Law: Women's Slander Litigation in Early Modern London," in Jennifer Kermode and Garthine Walker, *Women, Crime and the Courts in Early Modern England*. Chapel Hill, 1994, 26–47.

Graham, Richard. "Introduction," in Richard Graham, *The Idea of Race in Latin America, 1870–1940*. Austin: University of Texas Press, 1990, 1–5.

Graham, Sandra Lauderdale. "Honor among Slaves," in Johnson, *The Faces of Honor*, 201–28.

Graziano, Frank. "Una verdad fictícia: Santa Rosa de Lima y la hagiografía," in *Historia, memoria y ficción*, 302–11.

Grossberg, Lawrence. "Identity and Cultural Studies: Is That All There Is?" Hall and du Gay, *Questions of Cultural Identity*, 87–107.

Hacking, Ian. "Making Up People," in Thomas C. Heller, Morton Sosna, and David E. Wellbery, *Reconstructing Individualism: Autonomy, Individuality and the Self in Western Thought*. Stanford: Stanford University Press, 1986, 222–36.

Hall, Stuart. "Introduction: Who Needs 'Identity'?" in Hall and du Gay, *Questions of Cultural Identity*, 1–17.

Hamnett, Brian. "Church Wealth in Peru: Estates and Loans in the Archdiocese of Lima in the Seventeenth Century," *JbLA*, X (1973), 113–32.

Hampe Martínez, Teodoro. "La biblioteca del arzobispo Hernando Arias de Ugarte: bagaje intelectual de un prelado criollo," *Thesaurus*, XLII (1987), 337–61.

———. "The Diffusion of Books and Ideas in Colonial Peru," *HAHR*, LXXIII: 2 (May 1993), 211–33.

———. "Sobre encomenderos y repartimientos en la diócesis de Lima a principios del siglo XVII," *JbLA*, XXIII (1986), 121–43.

Hanke, Lewis. "The Contribution of Bishop Zumárraga to Mexican Culture," *Americas*, V (1948), 275–82.

Harth-Terré, Emilio. "El mestizaje y la miscegenación en los primeros años de la fundación de Lima," *Revista Histórica*, XXVIII (1965), 132–44.

Helmer, Marie. "Le Callao (1615–1618)," *JbLA*, II (1965), 145–95.

Hoeg, Jerry. "Cultural Counterpoint: Antonio Benítez Rojo's Postmodern Transculturation," *Journal of Latin American Cultural Studies*, VI: 1 (1997), 65–75.

Holler, Jacqueline. "'More Sins than the Queen of England': Marina de San Miguel before the Mexican Inquisition," in Giles, *Women in the Inquisition*, 209–28.

———. "The Spiritual and Physical Ecstasies of a Sixteenth-Century *Beata*: Marina de San Miguel Confesses before the Mexican Inquisition (Mexico, 1598)," in Richard Boyer and Geoffrey Spurling, *Colonial Lives: Documents on Latin American History, 1550–1850*. New York: Oxford University Press, 2000, 77–100.

Hünefeldt, Christine. "Los beaterios y los conflictos matrimoniales en el siglo XIX limeños," in *La familia en el mundo Iberoamericano*. México: UNAM, Instituto de Investigaciones Sociales, 1994, 227–62.

Iwasaki Cauti, Fernando. "Luisa Melgarejo de Soto y la alegría de ser tu testigo, Señor," *Histórica*, XIX: 2 (Dic. 1995), 219–50.

———. "Mujeres al borde de la perfección: Rosa de Santa María y las alumbradas de Lima," *HAHR*, LXXIII: 4 (1993), 581–613.

———. "Vidas de santos y santas vidas: hagiografías reales e imaginarias en Lima colonial," *Anuario de Estudios Americanos*, LI: 1 (1994), 47–64.

Jaffary, Nora. "Virtue and Transgression: The Certification of Authentic Mysticism in the Mexican Inquisition," *Catholic Southwest: A Journal of History and Culture*, X (1999), 9–28.

Jaramillo, Miguel. "Migraciones y formación de mercados laborales: la fuerza de trabajo indígena de Lima a comienzos del siglo XVII," *Economía*, XV: 29 (June–December 1992), 265–320.

Johnson, Lyman L. "Dangerous Words, Provocative Gestures, and Violent Acts," in Johnson, *The Faces of Honor*, 127–51.

Johnson, Lyman L., and Sonya Lipsett-Rivera. "Introduction," in Johnson and Lipsett-Rivera, *The Faces of Honor*, 1–17.

Katz, Michael B. "Origins of the Institutional State," *Marxist Perspectives*, I (winter 1978), 6–22.

Kellogg, Susan. "Cognatic Kinship and Religion: Women in Aztec Society," in *Smoke and Mist: Mesoamerican Studies in Memory of Thelma Sullivan*. J. K. Josserand and Karen Dakin, eds. Oxford: BAR Press, 1988, 666–81.

———. "The Woman's Room: Some Aspects of Gender Relations in Tenochtitlán in the Late Pre-Hispanic Period," *Ethnohistory*, XLII: 4 (fall 1995), 563–76.

Kelly, Joan. "Early Feminist Theory and the *Querelle des Femmes*, 1400–1789," in *Women, History and Theory: The Essays of Joan Kelly*. Chicago: University of Chicago Press, 1984, 1–18.

King, Anthony D. "Colonial Cities: Global Pivots of Change," in Robert J. Ross and Gerard J. Telkamp, *Colonial Cities: Essays on Urbanism in a Colonial Context*. Dordrecht: Martinus Nijhoff Publishers, 1985, 7–32.

King, Margaret Leah. "The Religious Retreat of Isotta Nogarola, 1418–1466," *Signs*, III: 4 (summer 1978), 807–22.

Konetzke, Richard. "El mestizaje y su importancia en el desarrollo de la población hispano-americano durante la época colonial," *Revista de Indias*, VII: 23 (January–March 1946), 7–44; VII: 24 (April-June 1946), 215–37.

———. "Los mestizos en la legislación colonial," *Revista de Estudios Políticos*, CXII (July–August 1960), 113–30.

Korth, Eugene H., S.J., and Della M. Flusche. "Dowry and Inheritance in Colonial Spanish America: Peninsular Law and Chilean Practice," *Americas*, XLIII (April 1987), 395–410.

Kuznesof, Elizabeth Anne. "Ethnic and Gender Influences on 'Spanish' Creole Society in Colonial Spanish America," *CLAR*, IV: 1 (1995), 153–76.

———. "More Conversation on Race, Class, and Gender." *CLAR*, V: 1 (1996), 129–33.

Larner, Christina. "Crimen Exceptum? The Crime of Witchcraft in Europe," in Gatrell et al., *Crime and the Law*, 49–75.

Larrieu, G. "'Galeras' et 'Galera,'" *Bulletin Hispanique*, CXIV (1962), 698–703.

Larson, Brooke. "La producción doméstica y trabajo femenino indígena en la formación de una economía mercantil colonial," *Historia Boliviana*, III: 2 (1983), 173–85.

Lauretis, Teresa de. "The Violence of Rhetoric: Considerations on Representation and Gender," in Teresa de Lauretis, *Technologies of Gender: Essays on Theory, Film and Fiction*. Bloomington: Indiana University Press, 1987, 31–50.

Lavallé, Bernard. "Divorcio y nulidad de matrimonio en Lima (1650–1700), (La desavenencia conyugal como indicador social)," *Revista Andina*, IV: 2 (December 1986), 427–64.

————. "La population conventuelle de Lima (XVI–XVII siècle): approches et problèmes," in *Lima dans la réalité peruvienne*. Grenoble: AFERPA, 1975, 167–96.

Lavrin, Asunción. "El Convento de Santa Clara de Querétaro: la administración de sus propiedades en el siglo XVII," *Historia Mexicana*, XXV: 1 (1975), 76–117.

————. "Female Religious," in Hoberman, *Cities and Society*, 165–95.

————. "The Role of Nunneries in the Economy of New Spain in the Eighteenth Century," *HAHR*, XLVI: 4 (1966), 371–93.

————. "Sexuality in Colonial Mexico: A Church Dilemma," in Lavrin, *Sexuality and Marriage*, 47–92.

————. "La vida femenina como experiencia religiosa: biografía y hagiografía en Hispanoamérica colonial," *CLAR*, II: 1–2 (1993), 27–51.

————. "Women in Spanish American Colonial Society," in Leslie Bethell, *The Cambridge History of Latin America*, vol. II, *Colonial Latin America*. Cambridge: Cambridge University Press, 1984, 321–55.

Lehfeldt, Elizabeth A. "Discipline, Vocation, and Patronage: Spanish Religious Women in a Tridentine Microclimate," *Sixteenth Century Journal*, XXX: 4 (winter 1999), 1009–30.

Lejarza, P. "La expansión de las clarisas en América y Extremo Oriente," *Archivo Ibero-Americano*, XIV (April–June 1954), 160–83.

Lenman, Bruce, and G. Parker. "The State, the Community and the Criminal Law in Early Modern Europe," in Gatrell et al., *Crime and the Law*, 11–48.

Lewin, Linda. "Natural and Spurious Children in Brazilian Inheritance Law from Colony to Empire: A Methodological Essay," *Americas*, XLVIII: 3 (January 1992), 351–96.

Lewis, Laura. "'Blackness,' 'Femaleness' and Self-Representation: Constructing Persons in a Colonial Mexican Court," *PoLAR*, XVIII: 2 (1995), 81–89.

————. "The 'Weakness' of Women and the Feminization of the Indian in Colonial Mexico," *CLAR*, V: 1 (1996), 73–94.

Lis, Catharina, and Hugo Soly. "Policing the Early Modern Proletariat, 1450–1850," in David Levine, *Proletarianization and Family History*. Orlando, 1984, 163–228.

Llorca, Bernardino. "La beata de Piedrahita," *Ciencia Tomista* (1942), 46–62, 176–78; (1944), 275–85.

Lloyd, Moya. "A Feminist Mapping of Foucaultian Politics," in Susan J. Hekman, *Feminist Interpretations of Michel Foucault*. University Park: Pennsylvania State University Press, 1996, 241–64.

Lohmann Villena, Guillermo. "Informaciones lógicas de Peruanos seguidas ante el Santo Oficio," *Revista del Instituto Peruano de Investigaciones Lógicas*, VIII (1955), 7–110; IX (1956), 115–226.

Longhurst, John. "La beata Isabel de la Cruz ante la Inquisición," *Cuadernos de la Historia de España*, XXV–XXVI (1957), 279–303.

López Martínez, Héctor. "Un motín de mestizos en el Perú (1567)," *Revista de Indias*, XXIV: 97–98 (July–December 1964), 367–81.

Loreto López, Rosalva. "Familia y conventos en Puebla de los Angeles durante las reformas borbónicas: los cambios del siglo XVIII," *Anuario del IEHS*, V (1990), 31–50.

————. "La fundación del Convento de la Concepción: identidad y familias en la sociedad poblana (1593–1643)," in Gonzalbo Aizpuru, *Familias novohispanas*, 163–80.

McCaa, Robert, Stuart Schwartz, and Arturo Grubessich. "Race and Class in Colonial

Latin America: A Critique," *Comparative Studies in Society and History*, XXI: 3 (1979), 421–33.

MacKay, Ruth. *The Limits of Royal Authority: Resistance and Obedience in Seventeenth-Century Castile*. Cambridge: Cambridge University Press, 1999.

Macera, Pablo. "Noticias sobre la enseñanza elemental en el Perú durante el siglo xviii," *Revista Histórica*, XXIX (1966), 327–76.

———. "Sexo y coloniaje," in *Trabajos de historia*. Lima: Instituto de Cultura, 1977, III: 297–352.

Manero Sorolla, María Pilar. "Visionarias reales en la España Áurea," in Augustin Redondo, *Images de la femme en Espagne aux XVIe et XVIIe siècles: des traditions aux renouvellements et à l'émergence d'images nouvelles*. Paris: Presses de la Sorbonne Nouvelle, 1994, 305–18.

Mannarelli, María Emma. "Fragmentos para una historia posible: escrita/crítica/cuerpo en una beata del siglo XVII," in *Historia, memoria y ficción*, 266–80.

———. "La Inquisición y el Colegio de la niñas expósitas de Santa Cruz de Atocha. Siglos XVII y XVIII," in idem, *Hechiceras, beatas y espósitas: mujeres y poder inquisitorial en Lima*. Lima: Congreso del Perú, 1998, 75-84–103.

———. "Inquisición y mujeres: las hechiceras en el Perú durante el siglo XVII," *Revista Andina*, III: 1 (July 1985), 141–54.

———. "Sexualidad y desigualdades genéricas en el Perú del siglo XVI," *Allpanchis*, XXII: 35/36 (1990), I: 225–48.

Martinez-Alier, Verena. "Elopement and Seduction in Nineteenth-Century Cuba," *Past and Present*, LV (1979), 90–129.

Mazet, Claude. "Population et société a Lima aux XVIe et XVIIe siècles: la Paroisse San Sebastián (1562–1689)," *Cahiers de Amerique Latines*, XIII–XIV (1976), 53–100.

McKendrick, Geraldine, and Angus MacKay. "Visionaries and Affective Spirituality during the First Half of the Sixteenth Century," in Mary Elizabeth Perry and Anne J. Cruz, *Cultural Encounters: The Impact of the Inquisition in Spain and the New World*. Berkeley: University of California Press, 1991, 93–104.

Megged, Amos. "Poverty and Welfare in Mesoamerica during the Sixteenth and Seventeenth Centuries: European Archetypes and Colonial Translations," *CLAHR*, VI (winter 1997), 1–29.

Meseguer Fernández, Juan. "El período fundacional (1478–1517)," in Joaquín Pérez Villanueva and Bartolomé Escandell Bonet, *Historia de la Inquisición en España*, I: 281–433.

———. "Programa de gobierno del Padre Francisco de Quiñones, Ministro General, O.F.M., 1523–1528," *Archivo Ibero-Americano*, XXI (enero–marzo 1961), 1–51.

Mills, Kenneth. "Bad Christians in Colonial Peru," *CLAR*, V: 2 (1996), 183–218.

Miura Andrades, José María. "Formas de vida religiosa femenina en la Andalucia medieval: emparedadas y beatas," in Angela Muñoz and María del Mar Graña, *Religiosidad femenina: expectativas y realidades (ss. VIII–XVIII)*. Madrid: Asociación Cultural Al-Mudayna, 1991, 139–64.

Mörner, Magnus. "Economic Factors and Stratification in Colonial Spanish America with Special Regard to Elites," *HAHR*, LXI (May 1983), 335–69.

Morris, Meaghan. "At Henry Parkes Motel," *Cultural Studies*, II: 1 (January 1988), 1–47.

Mujica Pinilla, Ramón. "El ancla de Rosa de Lima: mística y política en torno a la patrona de América," in Flores Araoz, *Santa Rosa de Lima*, 53–211.

Nazzari, Muriel. "An Urgent Need to Conceal: The System of Honor and Shame in Colonial Brazil," in Johnson, *The Faces of Honor*, 103–26.

Ortega, Angel. "Las primeras maestras y sus Colegios-escuelas de niñas en Méjico (1530–35)," *Archivo Ibero-Americano* (March–April 1929), 259–76; (May–June 1929), 365–87.

Ortega Costa, Milagros. "Spanish Women in the Reformation," in Marshall, *Women in Reformation and Counter-Reformation Europe*, 89–119.

Ortiz Díaz, José. "Evolución del concepto del hospital," in *Homenaje al Profesor Giménez Fernández*. Seville: Facultad de Derecho, 1967, I: 229–54.

Ortner, Sherry. "Gender Hegemonies," *Cultural Critique*, XIV (winter 1989–90), 35–80.

Osorio, Alejandra B. "El callejón de la soledad: Vectors of Cultural Hybridity in Seventeenth-Century Lima," in Nicholas Griffiths and Fernando Cervantes, *Spiritual Encounters: Interactions between Christianity and Native Religions in Colonial America*. Lincoln: University of Nebraska Press, 1999, 198–229.

Papi, Anna Benvenuti. "Mendicant Friars and Female Pinzochere in Tuscany: From Social Marginality to Models of Sanctity," in Daniel Bornstein and Roberto Rusconi, *Women and Religion in Medieval and Renaissance Italy*. Chicago: University of Chicago Press, 1996, 84–103.

Penyak, Lee M. "Safe Harbors and Compulsory Custody: *Casas de Depósito* in Mexico, 1750–1865," *HAHR*, LXXIX: 1 (February 1999), 83–99.

Pérez Villanueva, Joaquín. "La Crisis del Santo Oficio (1621–1700)," in *Historia de la Inquisición*, I: 996–1203.

Perry, Mary Elizabeth. "Beatas and the Inquisition in Early Modern Seville," in S. Haliczer, *Inquisition and Society in Early Modern Europe*. London: Croom Helm, 1987, 147–68.

———. "Magdalens and Jezebels in Counter-Reformation Spain," in Anne J. Cruz and Mary Elizabeth Perry, *Culture and Control in Counter-Reformation Spain*. Minneapolis: University of Minnesota Press, 1992, 124–44.

Pitt-Rivers, Julian. "Honour and Social Status," in J. G. Peristany, *Honour and Shame: The Values of Mediterranean Society*. Chicago: University of Chicago Press, 1974, 19–77.

Porras Barrenechea, Raúl. "Perspectiva y panorama de Lima," in Porras Barrenechea, *Pequeña antología de Lima*, 17–44.

Porres Alonso, Bonifacio. "Advocación y culto de la Virgen del Remedio en España," *Hispania Sacra*, XXIII (1970), 3–77.

Poska, Allyson. "When Bigamy Is the Charge: Gallegan Women and the Holy Office," in *Women and the Inquisition*, 189–205.

———. "When Love Goes Wrong: Getting Out of Marriage in Seventeenth-Century Spain," *Journal of Social History*, XXVIX: 4 (summer 1996), 871–82.

Przybylowicz, Donna, Nancy Hartsock, and Pamela McCallum. "Introduction: The Construction of Gender and Modes of Social Division," *Cultural Critique*, XIV (winter 1989–90), 5–14.

Ramos, Gabriela. "La fortuna del inquisidor. Inquisición y poder en el Perú. Un estudio social," *Cuadernos para la historia de la evangelización en América Latina*, IV (1990), 89–122.

———. "El Tribunal del Santo Oficio en el Peru, 1605–1666," *Cuadernos para la historia de la evangelización en América Latina*, III (1989), 93–127.

Rhodes, Elizabeth. "Spain's Misfired Canon: The Case of Luis de Granada's *Libro de la oración y meditación*," *Journal of Hispanic Philology*, XV (1990), 43–66.

Roper, Lyndal. "Will and Honor: Sex, Words and Power in Augsburg Criminal Trials," *Radical History Review*, 43 (1989), 45–71.

Rostworowski de Diez Canseco, María. "Dos probanzas de Don Gonzalo, curaca de Lima (1555–1559)," *Revista Histórica*, XXXIII (1981–82), 105–73.

Rubio Mañé, J. Ignacio. "Noticias de una hermana del Inca Garcilaso de la Vega y de su descendencia en Yucatán." *Boletín del Archivo General de la Nación*, XV (1944), 625–47.

Ruggiero, Kristen. "Wives on Deposit: Internment and the Preservation of Husbands' Honor in Late Nineteenth-Century Buenos Aires," *Journal of Family History*, XVII: 3 (1992), 253–70.

Ruiz Martínez, Cristina. "La moderación como prototipo de santidad: una imagen de la niñez," in Sergio Ortega, *De la santidad a la perversión; o de porqué no se cumplía la ley de Dios en la sociedad novohispana*. México: Editorial Grijalbo, 1986, 49–66.

Sánchez, Ana. "Angela Carranza, alias Angela de Dios: Santidad y poder en la sociedad virreinal peruana (s. XVII)," in Gabriela Ramos and Henrique Urbano, *Catolicismo y extirpación de idolatrias, siglos XVI–XVIII*. Cusco: Centro de Estudios Regionales Andinos "Bartolomé de la Casas," 1993, 263–92.

Sánchez Herrero, José. "Monjes y frailes. Religiosos y religiosas," in *Actas del III Coloquio de Historia Medieval Andaluza*, 405–56.

Sawicki, Jana. "Foucault, Feminism and Questions of Identity," in Gary Gutting, *The Cambridge Companion to Foucault*. Cambridge: Cambridge University Press, 1994, 286–313.

Schilling, Heinz. "'History of Crime' or 'History of Sin'?—Some Reflections on the Social History of Early Modern Church Discipline," in E. I. Kouri and Tom Scott, *Politics and Society in Reformation Europe: Essays for Sir Geoffrey Elton on His Sixty-Fifth Birthday*. London: Macmillan Press, 1987, 289–310.

———. "Reform and Supervision of Family Life in Germany and the Netherlands," in Raymond A. Mentzer, *Sin and the Calvinists: Morals Control and the Consistory in the Reformed Tradition*. Kirksville, Mo.: Sixteenth Century Journal Publishers, 1994, 15–61.

Schwartz, Stuart B. "Colonial Identities and the *Sociedad de Castas*," *CLAR*, IV: 1 (1995), 185–201.

———. "New World Mobility: Social Aspirations and Mobility in the Conquest and Colonization of Spanish America," in Miriam Usher Chrisman and Otto Grundler, *Social Groups and Religious Ideas in the Sixteenth Century*. Kalamazoo: Medieval Institute, Western Michigan University, 1978, 23–37.

Scott, Joan. "Deconstructing Equality-versus-Difference: Or, the Uses of Poststructuralist Theory for Feminism," *Feminist Studies*, XIV: 1 (spring 1988), 33–50.

———. "Gender: A Useful Category of Historical Analysis," *American Historical Review*, XCI: 5 (1986), 1053–75.

Seed, Patricia. "Social Dimensions of Race: Mexico City, 1753," *HAHR*, LXII: 4 (1982), 569–606.

Silva, María Beatriz Nizza da. "Divorce in Colonial Brazil: The Case of São Paulo," in Lavrin, *Sexuality and Marriage in Colonial Latin America*, 313–40.

Silverblatt, Irene. "Lessons of Gender and Ethnohistory in Mesoamerica," *Ethnohistory*, XLII: 4 (fall 1995), 639–50.

Soeiro, Susan A. "The Social and Economic Role of the Convent: Women and Nuns in Colonial Bahia, 1677–1800," *HAHR*, LIV: 2 (May 1974), 209–32.

Solomon, Frank. "Indian Women of Early Colonial Quito as Seen through Their Testaments," *Americas*, XLIV: 3 (January 1988), 326–29.

Solono Ruiz, Emma. "Aspectos de la pobreza y la asistencia a los pobres en Jaén a fines de la Edad Media," in *Actas del III Coloquio de Historia Medieval Andaluza*, 353–66.

Spurling, Geoffrey. "Honor, Sexuality and the Colonial Church: The Sins of Dr. González, Cathedral Canon," in Johnson and Lipsett-Rivera, *The Faces of Honor*, 45–67.

Stavig, Ward. "Living in Offense of Our Lord: Indigenous Sexual Values and Marital Life in the Colonial Crucible," *HAHR*, LXXIV: 4 (1995), 597–622.

Steggink, Otmar. "Beaterios y monasterios carmelitas españoles en los siglos XVI y XVII," *Carmelus*, II (1963), 149–65.

Stoler, Ann Laura. "Carnal Knowledge and Imperial Power: Gender, Race and Morality in Colonial Asia," in Micaela di Leonardo, *Gender at the Crossroads of Feminist Anthropology in the Postmodern Era*. Berkeley: University of California Press, 1991, 51–101.

———. "Rethinking Colonial Categories: European Communities and the Boundaries of Rule," in Nicholas B. Dirks, *Colonialism and Culture*. Ann Arbor: University of Michigan Press, 1992, 319–52.

———. "Sexual Affronts and Racial Frontiers: European Identities and the Cultural Politics of Exclusion in Colonial Southeast Asia," *Comparative Studies in Society and History*, XXXIV: 3 (July 1992), 514–51.

Suárez, Margarita. "Monopolio, comercio directo y fraude: la élite mercantil de Lima en la primera mitad del siglo XVII," *Revista Andina*, XI: 2 (December 1993), 487–502.

———. "El poder de los velos: monasterios y finanzas en Lima, siglo XVII," in Patricia Portocarrero Suárez, *Estrategias de desarrollo: intentando cambiar la vida*. Lima: Flora Tristán, 1993, 165–74.

Tizón y Bueno, Ricardo. "El plano de Lima," in *Monografías históricas sobre la ciudad de Lima*. Lima: Imprenta Gil, 1935, I: 401–36.

Torre Villar, Ernesto de la. "Fray Pedro de Gante, maestro y civilizador de América," *Estudios de Historia Novohispana*, V (1974), 9–77.

Trelles, Efraín. "Historia económica colonial: balance y perspectivas," in Bonilla, *Las crises económicas en la historia del Perú*, 13–31.

Trexler, Richard. "From the Mouths of Babes: Christianization by Children in Sixteenth-Century New Spain," in Richard Trexler, *Church and Community 1200–1600: Studies in the History of Florence and New Spain*. Rome: Edizioni di Storia e Letteratura, 1987, 549–73.

Twinam, Ann. "The Negotiation of Honor: Elites, Sexuality, and Illegitimacy in Eighteenth-Century Spanish America," in Johnson, *The Faces of Honor*, 68–102.

van Deusen, Nancy. "The 'Alienated' Body: Slaves and Free *Castas* in the Hospital de San Bartolomé of Lima, 1680 to 1700," *Americas*, LVI: 1 (July 1999), 1-30.

———. "Defining the Sacred and the Worldly: *Beatas* and *Recogidas* in Late-Seventeenth-Century Lima." *Colonial Latin American Review* (fall 1997), 441-77.

———. "Manifestaciones de la religiosidad femenina del siglo XVII: las beatas de Lima," *Histórica*, XXXII: 2 (July 1999), 47–78.

————. "Los primeros recogimientos para doncellas mestizas en Lima y Cusco, 1550–1580," *Allpanchis*, XXXV–XXXVI (1990), 249–91.

Varavall, J. A. "La utopía político-religiosa de los franciscanos en Nueva España," *Estudios Americanos*, II (1949), 199–227.

Vargas Ugarte, Rubén. "El Monasterio de la Concepción de la Ciudad de los Reyes," *Revista de Indias*, VI (1945), 419–44.

Velasco, B. "Fundación del convento de terciarias franciscanas de Santa Isabel de Cuellar," *Archivo Ibero-Americano*, ser. 2, XXXI (1971), 477–81.

Vergara Ormeño, Teresa. "Migración y trabajo femenino a principios del siglo XVII: el caso de las indias en Lima," *Histórica*, XXI: 1 (July 1997), 135–57.

Viera, D. "Françesc Eiximenis y el homicidio de la mujer adúltera," *Estudios Franciscanos*, LXXIX (1978), 1–20.

Viforcas Marinas, María Isabel. "Los recogimientos, de centros de integración social a cárceles privadas: Santa María de Quito," *Anuario de Estudios Americanos*, L: 2 (1993), 59–92.

Villanueva, Margaret. "From Calpixqui to Corregidor: Appropriation of Women's Cotton Textile Production in Early Colonial Mexico," *Latin American Perspectives*, XII: 1 (winter 1985), 17–40.

Vinall, Shirley W., and Peter S. Noble. "Shrewd and Wanton Women: Adultery in the *ecameron* and *Heptameron*," in Zygmunt G. Baranski and Shirley W. Vinall, *Women and Italy: Essays on Gender, Culture and History*. New York: St. Martin's Press, 1991, 141–72.

Walby, Sylvia. "Theorizing Patriarchy," *Sociology*, XXIII: 2 (May 1989), 213–34.

Waters, Malcolm. "Patriarchy and Viriarchy: An Exploration and Reconstruction of Concepts of Masculine Domination," *Sociology*, XXIII: 2 (May 1989), 193–211.

Weber, Alison. "Between Ecstasy and Exorcism: Religious Negotiation in Sixteenth-Century Spain," *Journal of Medieval and Renaissance Studies*, XXIII: 2 (spring 1993), 221–34.

Whinnom, Keith. "The Problem of the 'Best Seller' in Spanish Golden Age Literature," *Bulletin of Hispanic Studies*, XVII (1980), 189–98.

Zamora, Hermenegildo. "Contenido franciscano de los libros del registro del Archivo de Indias de Sevilla hasta 1550," in *Actas del II Congreso Internacional sobre Franciscanos en el Nuevo Mundo (siglo XVI)*. Madrid: Editorial Deimos, 1988, 1–83.

Zulawski, Ann. "Social Differentiation, Gender and Ethnicity: Urban Indian Women in Colonial Bolivia, 1640–1725," *Latin American Research Review*, XXV: 2 (1990), 93–113.

Unpublished Works

Baernstein, P. Renee. "The Counter-Reformation Convent: The Angelics of San Paolo in Milan, 1535–1635 (Women Religious, Italy)." Ph.D. Diss., Harvard University, 1993.

Cussen, Celia. "Fray Martín de Porres and the Religious Imagination of Creole Lima." Ph.D. Diss., University of Pennsylvania, 1996.

Lavallé, Bernard. "Recherches sur l'apparition de la conscience créole dans la Vice-Royauté du Perou: L'Antagonisme hispano-créole dans les ordres religieux (XVIeme–XVIIeme siècles)." These, L'Université de Bordeaux, 1978. 2 vols.

Lehfeldt, Elizabeth A. "Sacred and Secular Spaces: The Role of Religious Women in Golden-Age Valladolid." Ph.D. Diss., Indiana University, 1996.

Lowry, Lynn Brandon. "Forging an Indian Nation: Urban Indians under Spanish Control (Lima, Peru, 1535–1765)." Ph.D. Diss., University of California at Berkeley, 1991.

Powers, Karen Vieira. "Gender and the Crucible of 'Conquest': Some Thoughts on Women, Language, and Mestizaje." Paper presented at the American Society for Ethnohistory Meeting, Mexico City, November 1997.

Suárez, Margarita. "Merchants, Bankers and the State in Seventeenth-Century Peru." Ph.D. Diss., University of London, 1997.

Wood, Alice. "Chains of Virtue: Seventeenth-Century Saints in Spanish Colonial Lima." Ph.D. Diss., Rice University, 1997.

Index

In this index an "f" after a number indicates a separate reference on the next page, and an "ff" indicates separate references on the next two pages. A continuous discussion over two or more pages is indicated by a span of page numbers, e.g., "57–59." *Passim* is used for a cluster of references in close but not consecutive sequence.

Abandoned children, 38–54 *passim*, 108f, 133, 213, 215, 238

Abandonment of household, 60–73 *passim*, 83ff, 90ff, 99, 132, 146, 225, 253. *See also* Conjugal contract; Conjugal relations; Divorce; Marriage; *Recogimiento*; Women, employment and support of household; Women, poor

Acapulco, 104

Acculturation, 12

Acllahuasi, 32f, 206, 267

Acllas, 33, 267

Acosta Africano, Cristóbal, xii, 5

Adultery, 7, 60, 65, 69, 78–86 *passim*, 92, 229

Aguilar, Antonia del, 84

Alberti, Leon Battista, 21

Alcántara, Pedro de, 142

Allioza, Gerónima de, 76

Almagro, Diego de, 32

Alumbrados, 19, 28, 267; in Lima, 117, 251, 258; in Mexico, 28, 117, 251; in Spain, 19, 117, 198. *See also Beatas*; Mystics

Alumbrismo, 19, 28, 117, 195, 199, 247

Alvarado, Alonso de, 49

Alvarado, Inés and Isabel, 49, 57, 218

Amancebamiento, *see* Concubinage

Amas de leche, 267

Amigas, 107

Andrade, Jorge de, 110, 171, 243

Andrés Martín, Melquiades, 194, 197, 250

Andrien, Kenneth, 238

Annulments, xiii, xv, xvi, 68, 71, 76, 80, 83, 87–92 *passim*, 98–100, 131f, 161f, 230ff; statistics, 132. *See also* Conjugal relations; Divorce; Marriage

Aragon, Catherine of, 23

Arbildo y Berriz, Ambrosio de, 107

Arequipa, *recogimiento* in, 164

Argüelles, Catalina de, 52

Arias de Ugarte, Archbishop Hernando, 110, 247

Aristotle, 21

Arrepentidas, 37, 59–62 *passim*, 69, 77, 145, 157, 220, 222, 232. *See also Casas de arrepentidas*; Concubinage; Prostitutes; *Distraídas*; *Recogimiento*; *Recogimientos*; Sexual transgressions; Sin

Astete, Isabel de, 121

Augustine, Saint, 21

Avila, Juan of, 206

Avila, Saint Teresa of, xi, 35, 103, 116–20

Gutiérrez, Ramón, 190
Gutiérrez de la Torre y Rocas, General Andrés, 136

Hall, Stuart, 40, 192
Heretics, 103, 153
Hernández, Catalina, 28f
Hernández, Domingo, 94
Hernández, Francisca, 28f
Hernández, Martha, 73
Hernández de Pereda, Marí, 169
Honor, 1, 4–5, 35, 43; among elites, 82, 105, 115ff; among slaves, 72ff, 132, 136; family, 30, 43, 49, 76, 115f, 211, 229f; female interpretations of, 1, 75, 81–92 *passim*, 96, 99, 132, 159–66 *passim*, 190f, 226, 233; and institutional practices, 24, 42, 52, 71ff, 90–92, 108f, 145, 157; male interpretations of, 40, 43, 72–78 *passim*, 94ff, 147; studies on, 3–5, 189f, 229f, 239, 264. *See also* Education; Identity; Institutional practices; *Recogimiento*
Horosco, Jacinta, 75
Hospicio de San Pedro de Alcántara, 171
Hospital de la Caridad (Lima), 7, 231f; *divorciadas* in, 66, 73–78 *passim*, 81, 92, 94–98 *passim*, 142, 185, 215, 225, 234, 237, 261, 265; discrimination in, 98, 234; *Hermandad de la Caridad y Misericordia*, 51, 215, 240. *See also Divorciadas*; Porras Marmolejo, Isabel; *Recogidas*; *Recogimiento*
Hospital de San Bartolomé, 149, 253
Hospital de San Diego, 69, 170
Hospital de Santa Ana, 66, 149, 169, 185
Hospitals, 31, 66, 104, 111, 126, 131, 133, 205. *See also specific hospitals*
Huánuco, 50, 66, 221
Humanism and female education, 23f, 30f
Hurtado de Mendoza, Andrés, Marqués de Cañete, Viceroy, 51, 53, 211
Hurtado de Mendoza, Viceroy García, 67

Ica, 141
Ichpochtlayacanqui, 35

Identity, 192; female forms of, 6, 21, 73, 82f, 159, 161, 229–30; internalized, 4, 6, 11, 73, 82f, 89, 99f, 153, 159; sexual, 5, 84, 132, 158, 190. *See also* Casa; Institutional practices; *Recogimiento*; Spirituality
Illegitimacy: in Peru, 39f, 43f, 51f, 65, 72, 79; in Spain, 39f, 49, 133–37 *passim*, 207f, 210f
Immigration, 45, 104, 219
Imprisonment, 62, 73–77 *passim*, 228; *recogimiento* and, 69–75 *passim*, 220. *See also* Jails; *Recogimientos*
Incas, 32f
Inquisition: in Lima, 258, 264f; in Mexico, 29, 31, 251; in Spain, 25, 35, 199, 203f, 256
Institutional practices, 1f, 6–9, 49ff, 56, 78–80, 126–33 *passim*, 140ff, 151ff, 156f, 161ff; and hierarchies of difference, 7, 38, 43, 59–62, 83f, 91f, 127, 142, 147, 156, 160; relation to female identity, 152, 99f, 234
Institutions, studies on, 6–10, 192, 220
Isabel, Empress of Spain, 28f, 202f
Isabel, Saint, 61
Italy, *recogimientos* in, 59f, 65; other institutions in, xvii, 8, 38, 61, 78f, 167, 192, 219, 231, 240, 253. *See also* Convents; *Conservatorios*; Education

Jaffary, Nora, 251
Jails, 185, 235. *See also* Imprisonment; *Recogimientos*
Jesuits; in Lima, 125, 235, 239; in Spain, 62, 68
Jesús, Inés María de, 145, 250
Jesús, Manuela de, 171
Jesús, María Josefa de, 138
Jesús, Teresa de, 137
Jesús, Ursula de, 129
Jiménez de Cisneros, Cardinal Francisco de, 19, 23ff, 34, 195, 200
Juana Josepha, 138

Kinship networks, 32–33, 101–4 *passim*, 112

Oaxaca, *recogimiento* in, 164
Obrajes, as place of deposit, 78
Observant convents: Latin America, 112; Lima, 10, 102–27 *passim*, 134, 138, 139, 152, 166, 169–74 *passim*, 244, 256, 268; in Spain, 26, 195, 247. *See also specific convents*
Ocampo, Martín de, 81
Ometochtzin, Don Carlos, 31
Ondegardo y Campuzano, María Antonia de, 121
Ormaza, Isabel de, 117
Orphans, 40, 46: charity toward, 46, 213, 240; in convents, 135, 244f; institutions for, 241; mestizas, 40, 46; in Spain, 39, 46, 210. *See also* Abandoned children, *Casa de los Huérfanos*; Poverty
Ortíz, Fernando, 12
Osorio, Alejandra, 194
Osuna, Francisco de, xi, 18–22, 25, 31, 35f, 59, 194–96, 246–51 *passim*
Ovando, Diego de, 48, 214
Ovando, Nicolás de, Governor of Hispaniola, 26
Oyague, Francisco de, 150, 263

Pachacamac, 32
Palencía, Juan de la, 53
Panaderías, 225, 269; as place of deposit, 75, 78
Pastor de Velasco, Mateo, 109, 170
Patria potestas, 5, 43f
Pecadoras públicas, see Prostitutes
Pecados públicos, 41, 46, 212. *See also* Sexual transgressions; Sin
Penitenciadas, xiv, 270
Pereyra, Benito, 74
Pérez, Ana María, 117
Pérez, Marí, 240
Pérez de Herrera, Cristóbal, 62, 69f
Perry, Mary Elizabeth, 220
Pescador, Luis, 170, 241
Philip II (1556–98), 34, 62, 66f
Philip III (1598–1621), 105, 242
Philip IV (1621–65), 105, 239, 245
Physical abuse of women, 5, 11, 43, 73, 75, 81, 85f, 98, 131, 210, 230, 235, 254

Piety, expressions of, 5–10 *passim*, 24–26, 87, 110–16 *passim*, 123–33 *passim*, 138, 141, 147, 151–58 *passim*, 251. *See also* Spirituality, female
Pilcosisa Palla, María, 39, 211
Pimentel, Valeriana, 132
Pipiltin, 31
Pizarro, Francisco, 32, 208
Pizarro, Gonzalo, 33
Pizarro, Hernando, 33, 206
Poblete, Antonio, 119
Poblete, María, 119
Polanco, Mathias, 135
Porras, Martin de, 10, 103, 128, 250
Porras Marmolejo, Isabel, 87, 116, 170, 188, 222, 231f, 242
Portocarrero, Josefa, 263
Portocarrero, Leonor, 169
Portocarrero Lazo de la Vega, Melchor, Count of Monclova, Viceroy, 130, 145, 263
Potosí, 74, 104, 237, 248
Poverty, 37–54 *passim*, 65, 207, 211, 252; and public welfare, 42ff, 45, 240; in Spain, 40–43, 47, 62, 108, 209, 211. *See also* Abandoned children; *Casas de misericordia*; Marginalized individuals; Orphans; *Recogimientos*, as centers of moral redemption; Women, poor
Practices, residual, dominant, or emergent, 2, 13, 23, 38, 57–60 *passim*, 78, 108, 122–27 *passim*, 152f, 157, 166. *See also* Transculturation; Williams, Raymond
Pratt, Mary Louise, 194
Prayer, 1, 10, 19, 20, 24, 62, 77, 87, 105, 114–22 *passim*, 128, 130, 138, 142–46 *passim*, 195, 248
Prisons, *see* Imprisonment; Jails
Private homes, deposit (*recogimiento*) in, 66, 72–100 *passim*, 147, 221, 234f, 254, 261
Prostitutes, 157; in Italy, 219; in Lima, 9, 59, 63, 65, 70, 79, 144; in Mexico, 63, 69, 144, 220, 259, 264; *Mujeres de mal vivir*, 269; in Spain, 60f, 69f, 84, 220, 263. *See also* Lost women; Sexual transgressions; Wayward women